Folk-Songs of the South

COLLECTED UNDER THE
AUSPICES OF THE WEST VIRGINIA
FOLK–LORE SOCIETY

AND EDITED BY

JOHN HARRINGTON COX, Ph.D., Litt.D.

FOREWORD BY
ARTHUR KYLE DAVIS, JR.

FOLKLORE ASSOCIATES, INC.
HATBORO, PENNSYLVANIA

1963

ML
3561
.F6
.C7
1963

FOREWORD

JOHN HARRINGTON COX
1863–1945

I

Just over a hundred years ago, John Harrington Cox was born in Madison County, Illinois, on May 27, 1863, son of Isaac Cox, farmer, and Mary Ann (Harrington) Cox. He was barely eighteen years old when he was graduated from the Illinois State Normal University in 1891. Six years were to intervene before he received his Ph.B. degree from Brown University in 1897, and three more before Harvard awarded him the A. M. in 1900, then a long jump of twenty-three years before his Harvard Ph. D. in 1923, with (essentially) the present book as his dissertation.

The earlier intervals were filled with a variety of educational positions. He was a country school teacher in his native Madison County for about seven years; Principal of schools in Western Springs, Illinois, for two years; a teacher in the Providence (R. I.) Evening High School for two years. In 1897–99 he served as Educational Director in the Twenty-Third Street Branch of the Young Men's Christian Association in New York City and, with his Harvard A. M. in hand he became Professor of English Language and Literature in the University of North Dakota for one year, 1902–3. In 1903 he came to West Virginia University as Instructor in English Philology, was advanced to Associate Professor in 1903 and to full Professor in 1904. He was to remain at West Virginia as a highly respected teacher and scholar until his retirement to Emeritus status just thirty years later in 1932. Indeed, after his retirement he and his wife, the former Mrs. Anna (Bush) Long, of Erie, Pennsylvania, whom he had married June 28, 1904, continued to make their home on Campus Drive in Morgantown until her death, which preceded his by several years. A devoted sister then came to live with him. He died in Morgantown, November 21, 1945, at the age of eighty-two.

II

There can be no doubt that Professor Cox left his impress as teacher, as scholar, and as personality very markedly upon the University and the State of West Virginia and beyond. He was highly successful in cultivating among his students an interest in Old and Middle English and in the study of Mediaeval narrative literature. In 1908 he founded Seo Beowulf Gedryht (The Beowulf Club), which continued its activities for more than twenty years. Photographs of all members of the club, grouped by years of graduation, long hung upon the walls of Professor Cox's old recitation room in Woodburn Hall. It would be pleasant to think that they still hang there, a tribute to the old philologist and humanist.

Not a few of Professor Cox's earlier publications have a certain textbook character, perhaps reflecting the economic necessities of that older academic world, but they also reveal his genuine interest in translating or adapting for the use of children or non-specialist readers heroic tales and tales of chivalry from Old English, Old French, and Middle High German sources. Among these publications of his, by no means to be scorned, are: *Knighthood in Germ and Flower*, 1910; *A Chevalier of Old France*, 1911; *Folk Tales of East and West*, 1912; and *Siegfried*, 1915. His school text editions include *Beowulf*, 1910; *A Knight of Arthur's Court*, 1910; *Sir Gawain and the Green Knight*, (London) 1911; *The Song of Roland*, 1912; *A Hero of Old France*, (London) 1913.

Among the learned societies of which he was a member are the Modern Language Association of America, the American Association of University Professors, the American Dialect Society, the American Folk-Lore Society, the Poetry Society of America, the Shakespeare Society of America, and Phi Beta Kappa, of which last he was a charter member of Alpha of West Virginia. Scholarly journals to which he contributed included especially the *Journal of American Folk-Lore* and *American Speech*.

The inadequate preparation of teachers, a problem still and perhaps always with us, must have been appalling at the start of the century, and not least among teachers of literature. Here too Cox made a genuine contribution. His name was often to be found among the instructors in the old "teachers' institutes," not only in West Virginia but also in Pennsylvania, Indiana, and Illinois. In this connection he published a little book called *Literature in the Common Schools*, 1908, reissued in 1912. His summer school teaching in the University of Chicago (1914), the University of Missouri (1922), and the University of Southern California (1927 and again in 1929) was not unrelated to this interest and this concern, though the latter appointments were more likely a product of his growing folk-song interest.

For, in the final analysis, Cox's still surviving fame rests more than anywhere else upon his labors as a collector and publisher of West Virginia's ballads and folk-songs—in other words, upon this book and its attendant activities.

III

It will be remembered that even before the start of the twentieth century there had been quite a stir of interest in America as well as in Britain in the whole field of folklore, and especially in the recovery of old ballads and folk-songs still surviving in oral tradition. The Folk-Lore Society had been founded in London in the eighteen seventies and in 1878 began to publish its Journal. Its American equivalent, the American Folk-Lore Society, was only ten years behind it, and also in 1888 began the publication of the *Journal of American Folk-Lore*. At almost the same time, the (English) Folk Song Society was formed, and in 1889 began the publication of its Journal, with a distinguished list of collectors and contributors, including Cecil Sharp, Lucy Broadwood, Vaughan Williams, and others. A great impetus was of course given by the completion and publication between 1882 and 1898 of Child's great collection of *The English and Scottish Popular Ballads* and by the gradually spreading knowledge that many of these glorious antiques were still known and sung not only in the English and Scottish countrysides, but almost all over rural America, especially in the more out-of-the way places, whither the songs had been brought by earlier and later settlers and preserved often with great fidelity. Since Child had largely ignored the tunes, a great effort was made—not always with dependable results—to take down the tunes as well as the words from the lips of the singers.

The time was ripe for the formation of state and regional folklore societies, and wherever proper leadership was supplied such societies sprang up. Phillips Barry had begun his collection of ancient British ballads in New England, but had not yet formed the Folk-Song Society of the Northeast. H. M. Belden and others seem to have founded the Missouri Folk-Lore Society as early as 1906. John A. Lomax and others were active in Texas, specializing in cowboy and other frontier songs. Professors Hubert J. Shearin and Josiah H. Combs headed the movement in Kentucky, soon to be joined by Josephine McGill, Loraine Wyman, and others. The three neighboring states of Virginia, North Carolina, and West Virginia, if not full-fledged pioneers, were very close to the vanguard.

C. Alphonso Smith, then Edgar Allan Poe Professor of English in the University of Virginia, founded the Virginia Folk-Lore Society on his own initiative in April, 1913, and was its presiding genius for a dozen years. At very near the same time, Frank C. Brown began his North Carolina collecting and made an appeal in an address delivered before the fifteenth annual session of the Literary and Historical Association of North Carolina, December 1–2, 1914, on "Ballad-Literature in North Carolina." The West Virginia Folk-Lore Society was organized in Morgantown, July 15, 1915, with John Harrington Cox as President, Archivist, and Editor, and just ten years later *Folk-Songs of the South*, product of the West Virginia collecting and edited by Cox, was published by the Harvard University Press.

Cox's own Introduction, here reprinted, tells much about the West Virginia collecting, with sketches of many personalities involved. It is of interest to note that though his first ballad was collected and sent on to Professor Kittredge early in 1913, little progress was made until the summer of 1915, when the magnetic speaker, C. Alphonso Smith, gave a series of lectures in the Summer School of West Virginia University. "One of these," says Cox, "was on the survival of popular English and Scottish ballads in the South. It was received with great enthusiasm by a large audience made up mostly of school teachers from various parts of the state. In answer to queries by Dr. Smith, it was discovered that several persons present either knew or had heard some of the ballads mentioned. Before he left the platform, he urged that an organized effort be made to collect and preserve whatever of this material might be recovered. Out of this suggestion grew the West Virginia Folk-Lore Society." It seems that Alphonso Smith is the father of both the Virginia and the West Virginia Folk-Lore Societies.

This is not, however, to withdraw any credit from Cox and his energetic leadership. Indeed, not only between the lines but overtly does he tell us how largely, if not completely, John Harrington Cox *was* the West Virginia Folk-Lore Society. Of course he had the help of a number of teachers and other collectors, but much of the speaking, traveling, visiting of singers, was done by himself. After describing the second annual meeting of the Society, he continues: "As it turned out, the second annual meeting was the last. The methods for collecting material were proving so successful that it was not worth while to hold annual meetings. From the beginning, the organization was of a very loose nature, and it soon became little more than a name under which we worked. The interest, though widespread, was chiefly individual, and gradually the activities of the Society centered in its President." The experience of a neighboring state has been roughly parallel.

It is hard to realize today how genuinely pioneering a publication *Folk-Songs of the South* was in 1925. A glance at Cox's meager bibliography of less than a page serves to emphasize this fact. Not a single major publication from American sources had at that time appeared, except perhaps Campbell and Sharp's slight one-volume edition of *English Folk Songs from the Southern Appalachians*. Of the Harvard Press series only Roland P. Gray's not very impressive *Songs and Ballads of the Maine Lumberjacks with Other Songs from Maine* had appeared, and that only the year before. Many regions were busy pushing their collecting and preparing for publication, but the great publications from Maine, Virginia, Missouri, the Ozarks, and North Carolina, and a number of lesser publications were all in the future. The West Virginia volume may claim priority as a large and varied publication of folk-song material from American sources edited by an American.

No doubt Professor Kittredge's friendly pressure and helpfulness and the fact that Cox was at work on a long-deferred Harvard dissertation as well as on a book account in part for the expedition. The doctorate was awarded in 1923 on a dissertation entitled "Folk-Songs from West Virginia." The title of the book published two years later was *Folk-Songs of the South*. While the change of title may not have pleased other state and regional collectors, it is accurate in that the songs included, though actually collected almost exclusively in West Virginia, are really the heritage of similar regions throughout the South and, to a lesser extent, the whole country. It is doubtful if Professor Kittredge had anything to do with the change of title, but on other counts the book is properly dedicated to him as "My Master and Friend."

Having as I do a great respect for the book and a deep conviction of the desirability of its reprinting at this time, I may perhaps be permitted to touch lightly upon one or two points which seem to be shortcomings. Professor Cox's Introduction has never seemed to be quite adequate or worthy of the book, either in content or in style. He tells of collecting and characterizes singers, but omits all general questions of definition, ordering or grouping, evaluation, and other problems implicit in his task. The tunes, given in an Appendix, are disappointingly few in number; no variants are recorded for successive stanzas; and some tunes fail to inspire confidence in the accuracy of their notation. But of course Cox, like many other literary collectors, had to depend upon others, notably Lydia I. Hinkle, of his University, for the melodies, and it is certainly better to have these, the best notations obtainable, than to have none. It is a pity, too, especially in view of the careful historical research evident in his elaborate headnote to "John Hardy," that he failed to distinguish the two familiar Negro songs, "John Henry" and "John Hardy," but prints both as versions or variants of the same song. Part justification for this is that so many of the West Virginia texts are contaminations of the two songs. But the two in their normal or purer forms are distinct: John Henry is the powerful steel-driving Negro who beats the steam drill down and dies heroically in the attempt; John Hardy is the bad man who kills another Negro in a card game and is hanged for the murder. It seems strange that Cox did not encounter a singer who knew both songs. His H version, printed as a version of "John Hardy," is a pure version of "John Henry." But it is hardly the duty of a Foreword writer to point out all the minor weaknesses in an essentially excellent book.

In the main the reviewers of 1925 gave the book a very favorable, if sometimes perfunctory-favorable, reception, and subsequent scholarly-specialist opinion has consolidated the esteem in which the book is held. The present writer, then a recent venturer into the folk-song field, reviewed the book for the first number of the Virginia Quarterly Review, April 1925, and he is pleased to record that what he there said of the book is very close indeed to what he now says almost forty years later, except that now he would be more tolerant than he then was of Cox's inclusion of some borderline material not fully vouched for as folk-song. It is a tribute to Cox's courage and foresight that, in a day when strict construction was an entrenched position in many quarters, he put into practice the more liberal view.

One of the great merits of his book, one can now see, is its comprehensive and miscellaneous character, including all types of old ballads and songs available in his region. His impressive total is 185 songs in 398 versions or variants, with 29 tunes for 26 different songs. The place of honor he properly gives to his 34 Child ballads, in 115 versions or variants, with 40 more texts briefly described but not printed. From this point on it is as difficult to follow his order as it is to follow Child's, though, as in Child, certain groupings are recognizable: there are local or near-local tragedies such as "John Hardy" and "The Wreck on the C. & O."; there are American historical and patriotic songs such as "Immortal Washington" and "The Rebel Soldier"; songs of early New England origin such as "Springfield Mountain" and "Fair Charlotte"; British broadside ballads, some of them reprinted in America, some not, such as "The Sheffield Apprentice" and "The Rich Merchant"; more lyrical pieces of English origin, such as "Charming Beauty Bright" and "Sweet William"; temperance songs and religio-moralistic songs such as "The Drunkard's Dream" and "The Little Family"; American frontier songs such as "The Dying Cowboy" and "The Lone Prairie"; American minstrel songs such as "Kitty Wells" and "The Yellow Rose of Texas"; comic and nonsense songs galore, such as "Old Joe Clog" and "The Arkansas Traveller"; and so on. Interspersed between, or even among, these is a rich profusion of songs of many sorts, traceable often to British or American broadsides or to early American songsters but all, presumably, obtained from "traditional" sources in West Virginia or nearby. My several efforts at working out a table of organization have been baffled. Since Cox neither presents nor claims such organization, we may as well admit, I think, that his order, despite some groupings, is somewhat haphazard. But for variety and comprehensiveness his book is hard to beat.

His headnotes to individual songs, too, though often quite brief, inspire confidence in his scholarship. They either give the available information or tell the reader where to find it. Cox had searched diligently through the publications of the Folk Song Society in England and through the files of the *Journal of American Folk-Lore* and other relevant learned journals. In addition, he had had access to Harvard's magnificent collections of broadsides, British and American, of manuscripts of ballads and folk-songs, and of rare American songbooks or songsters in which versions of so many of his songs were printed. No doubt he also profited occasionally—as what American ballad scholar of the period had not?—from the friendly guidance of one George Lyman Kittredge. With such redoubtable backing, what wonder that *Folk-Songs of the South* is a sound and substantial book?

Two subsequent publications in impermanent form made available additional ballads and songs from the West Virginia collection and have consolidated the position of Cox as collector and editor. Both are mimeographed paperback volumes issued during the "lean thirties" by the National Service Bureau in New York, a subsidiary of the Federal Theatre Project of the Works Progress Administration. They were *Traditional Ballads Mainly from West Virginia by*

John Harrington Cox (March, 1939) and *Folk-Songs Mainly from West Virginia by John Harrington Cox* (June, 1939). Both volumes were edited by Dr. George Herzog and Herbert Halpert. Halpert contributed to each an introductory essay and some supplementary notes. Herzog was responsible for the editing of the melodies, which are numerous and, in view of their editorship, very likely more dependable than their predecessors of 1925. It is a pleasure to know that this later material will shortly be reissued in more permanent form by the American Folklore Society. With these two valuable supplements, *Folk-Songs of the South* continues to be the basic West Virginia text.

IV

What sort of man was John Harrington Cox? It was my privilege to know him slightly some thirty-five years ago—more slightly, I regret to say, than I knew many of the "old guard" of American balladry of that day: Kittredge, Gordon Hall Gerould, Louise Pound, Phillips Barry, W. Roy Mackenzie, Robert Winslow Gordon, John A. Lomax, Alphonso Smith, and others. My most vivid recollection is of him as Chairman of the Comparative Literature II (Popular Literature) group of the Modern Language Association of America when I was to read my first paper before that, to me, august assemblage. He seemed a man of medium or lower-medium height, rather sturdily built, of somewhat swarthy complexion, graying hair, a small moustache, and a countenance which bespoke sturdy independence and an unpretentious good sense rather than literary flair or brilliance. His speech, though not uncultivated, was strongly marked with the idiom of his own locality. He gave the impression of having lived closer to the soil and to the folk than most professors, as indeed he had, for I learned later that gardening was one of his greatest passions, and he himself has told us (in his Introduction) of his adventures among the folk. In introducing me —it was a day when brief introductions were usual at MLA—he welcomed me to the field as "a fresh and vigorous young scholar" and added another kind word or two. In our subsequent conversations he was always friendly and willing to be helpful in the task which he knew lay ahead of me, but I do not remember that he came often to MLA meetings after that one. I must depend upon the testimony of those who knew him better than I.

One of these remarks, "No one who knew Professor Cox well had any doubt that his chief interests were art and literature, his chief recreation gardening, his religious faith Baptist, and his political convictions Republican." In spite of this formidable combination, all agree that he had a sense of humor and loved to laugh. Shortly before his death, having spent many years trying to terrace a garden on a steep West Virginia hillside, he expressed the hope that where he was going there would be a garden for him to work in and that it would be on level ground. He was deeply devoted to his wife, and they were fond of entertaining students and colleagues in their hospitable home. They had no children, but he was always devoted to children, and children listened with rapt attention to his gifted story-telling which for some years was a feature of the Sunday morning prefatory services of the Morgantown Baptist Church. Lighter moments and interests though he had, he took a rather serious view of life and lived up to a very high standard of business and personal integrity. His standards in the classroom and his requirements of students were also high. Some thought him too severe and found his classroom personality a bit forbidding. They called him "Grendel." But these were apt to be his less able and studious students. Good students had nothing to fear from him. In his social relations he was always genial and pleasant. All seem to agree that he was an outstanding, perhaps *the* outstanding professor in the English Department of West Virginia University for many years. His undergraduate classes in Anglo-Saxon, in Beowulf, and in Middle English were not only competent but interesting; his graduate courses in Chaucer and in folklore were thorough and stimulating, according to one who studied under him. Another finds appropriate comment in Oliver Goldsmith's couplet:

> Yet he was kind; or if severe in aught,
> The love he bore to learning was in fault.

Folk-Songs of the South clinched and climaxed his reputation as a scholar.

ARTHUR KYLE DAVIS, JR.

University of Virginia
July, 1963

TO

GEORGE LYMAN KITTREDGE

MY MASTER AND FRIEND

PREFACE

IT is a great satisfaction to be able to discharge a part of the trust confided in me as Archivist and General Editor of the West Virginia Folk-Lore Society by presenting in permanent form that portion of our collection of the most intrinsic worth. There still remains a large amount of interesting and valuable material to be arranged and prepared for the press. It is hoped that this work may be prosecuted without undue delay, so that the industry, enthusiasm, and loyalty of the members of the Society may be fully consummated.

I am profoundly indebted to Professor George Lyman Kittredge of Harvard University, not only for his inspiring tuition in the popular ballad, but for his keen interest in the progress of this work from its inception, and for his wise guidance and direct contributions as it developed, first, into a doctor's dissertation, and later, into a book. My obligations to him appear on almost every page.

For courtesies and helps not recorded elsewhere, I am indebted to Dr. Louise Pound, Dr. C. Alphonso Smith, Dr. H. M. Belden, Mr. Phillips Barry, Honorable George M. Ford, and, finally, to my wife, Annie Bush Cox, whose unwearied and efficient assistance of every sort has made this book possible.

The map at the end of the volume is reproduced by permission of the U. S. Geological Survey, Department of the Interior, Washington, D. C.

JOHN HARRINGTON COX.

WEST VIRGINIA UNIVERSITY.
January 16, 1924.

CONTENTS

CONTENTS

FOLK TUNES

INTRODUCTION

IN the early part of 1913, Mr. E. C. Smith, a student in West Virginia University from Weston, Lewis County, procured for me a copy of the popular song, "John Hardy." It was promptly forwarded to Professor Kittredge, and was printed in *The Journal of American Folk-Lore*, April–June, 1913, pp. 180–182. That was the beginning of the West Virginia Folk-Lore Collection. Throughout the campaign Mr. Smith continued to be one of our most ardent collectors, and at least seventeen songs are placed to his credit.

Little progress was made for a period of two years. In the summer of 1915, Dr. C. Alphonso Smith gave a series of lectures in the Summer School of West Virginia University. One of these was on the survival of popular English and Scottish ballads in the South. It was received with great enthusiasm by a large audience made up mostly of school teachers from various parts of the state. In answer to queries by Dr. Smith, it was discovered that several persons present either knew or had heard some of the ballads mentioned. Before he left the platform, he urged that an organized effort be made to collect and preserve whatever of this material might be recovered. Out of this suggestion grew the West Virginia Folk-Lore Society, which was organized July 15, 1915. The following officers were elected: President, Archivist, and General Editor, Professor John Harrington Cox, West Virginia University, Morgantown; Vice-President, Dr. Robert Allen Armstrong, West Virginia University; Secretary-Treasurer, Professor Walter Barnes, Fairmont Normal School, Fairmont.

Our first annual meeting was held at Morgantown in connection with the Summer School. There was a large audience present to hear the programme, which consisted of a reading and discussion, by the President, of the following songs and tale: "Fair Annie and Gregory," "Dandoo," "John Hardy," "The Dying Cowboy," "Father Grumble," "De Blue-Tail Fly," "De Hebbenly Road," "A Burial Song," and "The Witch Bridle." Professor Barnes sang several of the old ballads, among them "Barbara Allen." The officers for the first year were reëlected for three years. No other election of officers has ever been held.

In his first annual report the President acknowledged the obligation of the Society to the President of West Virginia University, Dr.

Frank Butler Trotter, whose sympathy with the movement had enabled the Editor to make numerous addresses in different parts of the state, and to the managing editor of the *West Virginia School Journal and Educator*, Dr. Waitman Barbe, who had afforded space for monthly articles. Much valuable material of all sorts had been collected, including twenty-five old ballads, one hundred and seventy-seven songs, thirteen ghost stories and witch tales, and a large number of counting-out rhymes, riddles, singing games, negro melodies, and so forth.

On the evening of June 28, 1917, at West Virginia University, the Folk-Lore Society held its second annual meeting. The programme consisted of a brief report of progress, a reading of specimens of West Virginia popular ballads, old songs, witch tales, local legends, negro melodies and spirituals by the President, and a singing of three of the old popular ballads by Professor Barnes. Sixty-five persons sent in material during the year, fifty-four of these being new contributors, thus making a total membership of one hundred and eighty. Five more of the popular English and Scottish ballads were found, bringing the number up to thirty. A large mass of other material was also sent in, making the total number of individaul communications approximately two hundred and forty.

As it turned out, the second annual meeting was the last. The methods for collecting material were proving so successful that it was not worth while to hold annual meetings. From the beginning, the organization was of a very loose nature, and it soon became little more than a name under which we worked. The interest, though widespread, was chiefly individual, and gradually the activities of the Society centered in its President.

The state of West Virginia holds its County Teachers' Institutes during the months of July, August, and September, and our first objective was to get the movement presented at each of these institutes. Dr. C. Alphonso Smith had left with the Editor a bulletin issued by the United States Bureau of Education, which he had been instrumental in getting out, in which was printed an article by him entitled, "A Great Movement in which Every One can Help." This article gave information about the English and Scottish Popular Ballads and suggestions as to how one might help in collecting them. It was followed by a complete list of the three hundred and five titles with their variants. A mimeograph copy was made of them and sent to one of the instructors in each of the County Institutes. The Editor knew many of these instructors personally, and the request to have the plans and purposes of the Society presented at the institutes received prompt and courteous attention. Almost immediately contributions began to come in. The enthusiasm of Professor Barnes did much to insure the early success of the movement. Including variants, twenty-nine ballads and songs are placed to his credit.

Without doubt the greatest single factor in our success was the *West Virginia School Journal and Educator,* then owned by Drs. Robert Allen Armstrong and Waitman Barbe of West Virginia University, and the Hon. M. P. Shawkey, State Superintendent of Schools. These men were all interested in the success of the Society. Dr. Barbe was the Managing Editor, and his unfailing courtesy in providing space whenever it was wanted deserves our profound gratitude. Since this periodical reached a large proportion of the teachers of the state, the Society was able to get its appeal voiced in practically every community.

The campaign through the state educational paper opened with the September number, 1915, and the last of the folk-lore articles appeared in the July issue, 1919, having run through a period of four years and numbering altogether thirty-seven.

From the inception of the movement, the President of the Society by personal letters and interviews sought the assistance of students and others throughout the state. The immediate response in enthusiasm and help was one of the greatest factors in our success. The diligence and methods of some of these persons were so notable that they deserve special mention.

Mr. Fred M. Smith of the Glenville Normal School by continuous assignments of such topics as folk-songs, superstitions, and local legends to his various composition classes throughout a year, secured a great mass of excellent material. He found also that the eagerness of the students to discover such things and to put them into good form furnished a motive not easily secured for composition work. Moreover, these exercises developed a keenness and an originality in getting material and organizing it which are seldom obtained. Thirty-eight contributions are accredited to Mr. Smith. Miss Sallie Evans of the Elkins High School pursued the same methods with equally good results. Her contributions number thirty-one. In addition, she enlisted especially the interest of the Sophomore Class, which, in order to secure a lecture on West Virginia folk-lore, dramatized the story of *Silas Marner.* With the proceeds of their performance, they obtained their lecturer, paid the expenses of him and his wife to Elkins, entertained them royally, and had some money left over with which they bought books for the library.

Miss Maud I. Jefferson, the teacher of English in the West Liberty Normal School, by talks on West Virginia folk-lore aroused the interest of thirteen girls. These girls, by searching the community and by writing home to their parents and friends, found a large number of valuable songs. They then prepared an original entertainment, made up in large part of songs, superstitions, and so forth, which they presented before the school and the people of the community. At this entertainment, the President of the Folk-Lore Society gave an address.

In response to a personal request, Mrs. W. M. Parker, Hinton, Summers County, with laborious and painstaking care hunted up people, interviewed railroad men, ferreted out data, wrote letters, and made it possible to secure complete information as to names, dates, and places concerning the wreck that occurred near that place on October 23, 1890, out of which grew the ballad, "The Wreck on the C. & O." She also secured other valuable material in the way of old songs and negro spirituals.

Mr. E. I. Kyle, a student in West Virginia University from Welch, McDowell County, performed like valuable service in the case of "John Hardy." He not only secured accurate information as to names, dates, places, and incidents, but by searching the court records he discovered the sentence pronounced upon the man by the Judge. Without his aid, the case would probably never have been entirely cleared up.

Mrs. Hilary G. Richardson, Clarksburg, Harrison County, who had long been an ardent folk-lorist, made a unique contribution of some thirty ballads and songs, practically all of which were procured from two genuine old ballad-singers, Mrs. Rachel Fogg and Mrs. Nancy McAtee, of whom full account is given below. She arranged also for a lecture by the President of the Society before the Woman's Club of Clarksburg, and later made it possible for him to become acquainted with the old ballad-singers, to hear them sing, and to secure pictures of them.

One of the most persistent and successful of our co-laborers was Miss Lily Hagans, Morgantown, Monongalia County. She not only inspired others with her enthusiasm but made directly nineteen contributions.

The first genuine ballad-singer discovered was Mr. George W. Cunningham, Elkins, Randolph County. He was attending the Summer School in the session of 1915 when the Society was organized. He not only knew some of the traditional ballads but he sang them to Professor Barnes, who communicated both words and music. These songs were, "The House Carpenter" (Child, 243), "The

Greenwood Siding" (Child, 20), "Six Kings' Daughters" (Child, 4), and "Barbara Allen" (Child, 84). Five other songs were reported by Professor Barnes as having come from him. His interest in the movement prompted his appointment as an Official Correspondent. Eight songs secured from other persons were communicated by him, making a total of seventeen contributions. I heard him sing some of the old songs on one occasion only. He sang in a loud, strong voice that had good carrying qualities. His personality and character can best be gathered from his photograph and his autobiography, which is as follows:

[Dated at Elkins, Randolph County, January 8, 1922.] I was born February 8, 1858, close to the Upper Fork of Cheat River, in Randolph County, West Virginia, then Virginia. My father was Jackson Cunningham, a poor man of unsettled, roving disposition. He removed eight or ten times during the nineteen years of his married life, my mother dying when I was sixteen years of age.

I was about ten years old when I started to school, but I had learned at home so that I could go with about the most advanced classes, and when school closed in about seven weeks, I " stood head " in an advanced spelling class many of whom were nearly twice as tall as I. I soon knew the multiplication table on "Hagerstown Almanac" to 25 times 25, and could do any common problem in fundamental rules or fractions, much more quickly mentally than I can now by figures. The morning I was eight years old I tried to calculate how many seconds old I was, but could not well remember the result.

During my narrow life between ten and twenty years, I managed to attend the crude country schools for about fifteen months, mostly under poorly prepared teachers; but I attended county Normals in Barbour County for four months in 1878, making a first grade certificate that fall in a text book test fully as exacting as I've ever seen under the uniform system.

This is my fortieth year as teacher and grade school principal, and my sixty-fifth term of school, three of which were subscription terms; my first three terms were taught in Barbour County, all the rest in Randolph County.

I have lived in Randolph County all my life, practically, except four years I lived in Barbour County. Living upon small farms owned by me in Dry Fork and Leadville districts successively, I made an honest though frugal and restricted living by teaching and farming in combination, as circumstances allowed.

When nearly twenty-six years old, I married Miss Mollie Hamrick of Barbour County, whose father, Graham Hamrick, emigrated in the late fifties from Rockingham County, Virginia, to Barbour County, rearing there a family of eight children by teaching singing schools, and by other strenuous employments. In his old age he discovered a wonderful process of embalming, but was too handicapped and feeble to handle it successfully.

My wife and I reared eight children, five girls and three boys, to mature age, the girls all being successful and popular teachers for some years. The mother passed to her reward on October 4, 1921.

My grandfather, Stephen Cunningham, was a native of Highland County, Virginia, and was of Irish descent. His father, William Cunningham, came across from either Ireland or Scotland, and had many awful adventures with the

Indians. My mother was Eleanor Wimer, a native of Pendleton County, West Virginia. Her father and mother were of Dutch or German descent. Her father, George Wimer, reared a steady, industrious family of twelve children, and her grandfather, Henry Wimer, was one of four brothers who came to Virginia from either Holland or Germany.

I am near sixty-four years old, five feet ten inches tall, weigh now one hundred eighty-five pounds; complexion dark, blue eyes, fair skin, hair fast turning gray. I was really never under the care of a physician, never had a fever, never had a dentist in my mouth except to extract a few teeth, never danced, never drank spiritous liquors of consequence. I pay my debts, try to attend to my own business, and am vitally concerned in the welfare of my posterity and of our country.

My father was a charming singer, though he knew nothing of the science of music. He sang many thrilling folk-songs and ballads. My mother could carry but few tunes. I was deeply interested in music from early childhood, learning all the songs and hymns that I could find. My people and acquaintances were mostly singers of songs. One of father's sisters, who never married, lived with us and taught me sketches of several rich old English ballads. Laban White, of Dry Fork District, taught me a few, but Ellen Howell, a noted woman who " worked round " and mingled freely in social pastimes, often lived with us, and freely taught me many folk-songs, ballads, and *ghost stories*. She, late in life, married an old widower named John Eye.

The social gatherings and entertainments of my early days were rather restricted and crude, and rough, yet they were generally real and impressive, and though my chance of mingling in them was narrow until I was about seventeen, yet I got a peep sometimes as most people do, ofttimes to their regret. House-raisings, log-rollings, corn-huskings, apple and pumpkin-cuttings, bean-stringings, kissing-plays, and last, but not least, drunken frolics were the order of the times among most of the people. Very generally the gatherings ended with a dance or play-party. Of course there was often some rough and lewd conduct, though I doubt whether there was really as much vicious conduct then as now, except in the line of drinking, which was almost universal then.

Mrs. Nancy McAtee, whom I visited December 10, 1921, is a genuine old ballad-singer living in Clarksburg, Harrison County. Her little house stands on the bank of the West Fork of the Monongahela River. A railroad passes in front of it, some ten or a dozen feet away. In several houses of the same style, stretched along a cinder path, live children and grandchildren. The place is known as "McAtee Row."

In answer to my knock, Mrs. McAtee appeared at the door. She had evidently just arisen from her morning meal and was still munching part of it. To my query as to whether I could get some breakfast she replied, "No, I hain't got nothin' in the house to feed a stranger." As she stood in the doorway, I beheld a woman about sixty-five or seventy years old, slightly above the medium height, lean, and with small, grayish-blue eyes. She was poorly clad, her shoulders a little stooped, and her cheek bones a trifle prominent.

She showed some hesitancy in inviting me into the house, volunteering the information that her husband was sick in bed. When I mentioned the name of Mrs. Richardson, her attitude became immediately one of friendliness, and she appeared greatly pleased at my saying I had come a long way to see her and to hear her sing. She began at once to say that she could not remember "them old things," and to talk of her husband and her family, a considerable number of whom had crowded into the room, from a stalwart son-in-law to a tousled baby in arms. Without delay the son-in-law took the lead in the conversation and told me a regular hard-luck story about unemployment. It took no little tact and patience to manage it so as to be alone with Mrs. McAtee and to get her to talk of things I wished to know about. Having seen the stranger and found in him nothing of great interest, the relatives gradually retired and gave me the opportunity sought.

Our common acquaintance with Mrs. Richardson was an open, sesame, and soon Mrs. McAtee was talking freely and with ease. Of average natural intelligence, she was innocent of all knowledge outside of her little world. Her father was Morris McDonald, born in Ireland and brought to this country while still a baby. The family eventually made its way to Randolph County, West Virginia, where her father located on a farm. Her mother's name was Emsey Barnett. There were nine children in the family, of whom she was the seventh. She had evidently led a hard life, as was indicated by the lines in her face. While I was getting all the information I could, I felt that she was calculating whether she could not get something out of me. This judgment turned out to be correct, for when the subject of pictures was broached she asked, "You 're goin' to give me Christmas gift, ain't ye?" A prompt reply in the affirmative removed all barriers of reluctancy. She told me about her own family, six children, two dead, the others "married and living right here in the Row." She mentioned Lucy, Maude, and Mamie, and their husbands, Eli Murphy, Sylvester Ashcraft, and John Hoop. There had been twenty-six grandchildren, now only thirteen. One of them was called in and exhibited by the proud father as a prodigy seven years old that had never had any front teeth. She and her family had been "right here over fifty years" where her "old man" had worked on the streets until he was too old and feeble to get about. She jerked her head toward a mound of bedclothes on one of the beds, saying, "That 's him," who, during all the time I was there, made not the least movement nor manifested the slightest sign of life.

I did not try to secure any songs from her because Mrs. Richardson had previously communicated to me what she knew. I was interested in seeing her, hearing her sing, and in getting her picture. Upon request she sang for me what she called "McAtee" ("McAfee's Confession") in a low, monotonous tone, with little modulation, in a voice not unpleasant, but with an inclination to be a little whiny, an approximation to a chant. The one song was all that she could remember at the moment, but Mrs. Richardson reports that she knows in whole, or in part, twenty-four ballads and songs. The ballads sent to me from her are "Barby Ellen" (Child, 84), "Lord Leven" (Child, 75), "Lady Margaret" (Child, 74), "Fair Ellender" (Child, 73), and "Geordie" (Child, 209). All these old things she said she had learned from the "kids" back in Randolph County.

It is evidently the custom of Mrs. McAtee to comment on the story as she sings or narrates, as is evidenced by the manuscripts sent me by Mrs. Richardson, in which Mrs. McAtee's remarks are enclosed in parentheses. Many like the following are to be found:

McAtee's Confession

All this day for you I 've sought.
    (Lettin' on he 's been thinkin' about her.)
All on her throat my hands I laid.
    (He 'lowed to give her a good chokin'.)

The Sheffield Apprentice

About half way through the ballad:
    (That 's a dog-gone long ballet.)
A gold ring on my finger,
    Just as I passed by,
She slipped into my pocket,
    And fur this I must die.
        (You see they hung 'em then fur that.)

A Pretty Fair Maid in a Garden

And if he stays for seven years longer,
    No man on earth shall marry me.
        (It was him a-talking to her but she did n't know it.)
You 'll never see his face again
    (He was jus' foolin' her.)

Davy Crockett

I 'll tell you where I come from,
    And where I got my learning.
        (This *is* a funny one!)

And he 'll pretty quick show you,
    How to grin a coon crazy.
        (This is jus' fun!)

In a letter dated February 7, 1918, Mrs. Richardson writes: "Poor old Mrs. McAtee! the one whose son was ' not redimpted ' came up yesterday to tell me she had had a telegram saying he was down by the ' water front,' and it was ' sure some big water,' and if they did n't send him soon ' he'd swim across an' git that Kaiser.' When he left he did not even know why, but told some one they were ' goin' to git that feller they 're sendin' us after.' So, you see, maybe in some ways he is being ' redimpted ' after all."

Leaving "McAtee Row," I hastened across the city to South Water Street to see Mrs. Rachel Fogg, the other old ballad-singer whose songs had been sent to me by Mrs. Richardson. Turning off the street and going up a little alley about five feet wide for a short distance, I found her house crowded in among others of its kind. In answer to my knock, the door was opened by a short, very stout, elderly woman, clad in a checked flannel dress of one piece, wearing on her head a sort of wool cap. She looked the picture of woe, and to my inquiry as to whether I could come in and visit with her a little while, she replied in a slow voice that drawled just a trifle that it was a mighty bad time for her to see me. Her son's wife, who lived at Akron, Ohio, had died just a few days before, and she was sorely troubled because none of the family living in and around Clarksburg had gone to the funeral. Her son was a cripple, and she was in great distress as to how he managed without any of his relatives at hand. Two of her daughters came in while I was there, and the matter was discussed in detail, while from time to time tears poured down the cheeks of the old ballad-singer when she thought of her best-beloved son among strangers in his hour of grief. Truly, it was a bad time for one to call on such a mission as mine.

But in the midst of all her perturbations, this old ballad-singer showed a remarkable composure, and again the mention of the name of Mrs. Richardson gained me entrance to a confidence that I fear would otherwise have been closed. Mrs. Richardson was her good angel, and from listening to her praises for a time it was easy to lead off into the story that I wanted.

She was "born and raised," she said, in Upshur County, between Flatwoods and the Little Kanawha, just a little way from Centersville, and had attended the public schools. At the age of sixteen, she was married to a whiskey-drinking, card-playing man named Erastus Fogg. He spent most of his time when they lived in the country in hunting and got a little money by shipping furs and turtles. Not long after their marriage they moved into Harrison County, where she had been for over forty years. Her husband was a blacksmith by trade, but did not work much. Her family had consisted of six sons and three daughters, one son and one daughter now dead. Of grandchildren she had seven living and six dead. Her father was Sam Eakles, "born and raised" in Bath County, Virginia, who had been in the war between the North and the South. Her mother was Elizabeth Ann Poling, born in Barbour County, West Virginia. She told me that her great-great-grandmother, Anna Easter, "came over the ocean in the time of the Indian wars. I think it was from Germany. She was German-Dutch. Her husband had come from Green County, Pennsylvania. He was Dutch-English." An incident of her childhood had left a strong impression on her memory. Once when she had been sent for the cows, she got lost while hunting for flowers. "It was on Sunday, and I got scairt and run on and on and could not get back home. When they found me and got me back, I could n't sleep none that night. I was crazy in my head."

When I visited this old ballad-singer, December 10, 1921, she was sixty-three years old. Her large dark eyes, still fine, must have been beautiful in her youth, eyes which readily lit up with the trace of a twinkle at the suggestion of humor. She made her living, she told me, by washing, begging, and selling off things that she could get along without. Times were hard, men were out of work, and women were doing their own washing instead of sending it out. She readily sang at my request, two songs, "Jesse James" and "Johnny Collins," in a low contralto voice, heavy and mournful. She carried the tunes well. She had had an excellent voice once, she said, but it had been ruined by sickness, "measles, broncheetis, and tonsileetis." Diphtheria had visited her twice also. Formerly she had been an ardent member of the Salvation Army, but latterly she seldom attended.

A small Christmas gift voluntarily bestowed caused her to hasten into another room and bring out some pictures of her family and one of herself, taken when she was "dressed up" and using crutches on account of a serious accident. She impressed me as having a strong personality that in some way would weather all the storms of adversity.

Another West Virginia ballad-singer is John B. Adkins, whose post-office is Branchland, Lincoln County, in the far southern part of the state, and so I have never had the good pleasure of seeing him or hearing him sing. Thirteen contributions are placed to his credit, among them three of the traditional ballads, namely, "Little Willie" (Child, 49), "Lady Gay" (Child, 79), and "Lord Batesman" (Child, 53). At my request he wrote the following sketch and sent me his picture and a picture of his house.

I am thirty-three years old, born October 14th, 1888, in Cabell County, West Virginia, on the farm where I now live. My situation is in the extreme southeast corner of Cabell County, near the Wayne and Lincoln County lines, about twenty-five miles southeast of Huntington. Have never lived anywhere else. I weigh a hundred seventy-five pounds, six feet tall, medium light complexion, black hair and brown eyes. Education limited, as I was forced to leave school at an early age (at sixteen) and have been an invalid and semi-shut-in ever since. For a livelihood I have a small hand printing plant on which I do very creditable work, such as printing letter-heads, envelopes, cards, tags, etc., and my trade comes mostly by the mail-order route. I also do photograph work on a small scale and have a magazine subscription agency with my shop, and also do repair work on watches, clocks, guns, telephones, phonographs, and other portable machinery that is brought to me, so you see I have quite a variety of things going on at times, and my place is known as "Sundry Service Station," but after all, my earning capacity is small, owing to isolated conditions and ill health.

My parents were both born and raised in Cabell County; Mother is Irish and Father is of English descent. His fore-parents came here from Giles County, Virginia, many years ago. Mother's maiden name was Keenan. She is the granddaughter of Patrick Keenan, an Irish emigrant who came to this country over one hundred years ago and settled at Kanawha Falls, Virginia (now West Virginia).

The old songs which I sent you I learned when a boy, by hearing them sung by different people, some at log-rollings, others at house-raisings, parties, dances, etc., which was the most popular place for some singer to be called upon to render some one or more selections of these old-time songs. Like all boys the "doings" of these older people naturally interested me and I learned some of the old songs by trying to imitate them.

In addition to the activities already mentioned, the President of the Society performed important duties in various other directions. Scores of lectures were delivered throughout the campaign to colleges, normal schools, high schools, grade schools, colored schools, teachers' institutes, round table meetings, women's clubs, commencements, entertainments, and social functions of different kinds. The large Summer School at the University gave him an admirable opportunity to speak to many students and teachers from every corner of the state. At some time during the first semester of each college year, he delivered a lecture on folk-lore to all the numerous sections of freshmen in the University. This personal touch had much to do with keeping the interest alive.

At the annual meeting of the Ohio Valley Historical Association in Pittsburgh during the Christmas holidays in 1917, it was decided that at the next meeting to be held at Berea, Kentucky, in the autumn of 1919, there should be a session devoted to folk-lore. Through the suggestions of Dean J. M. Callahan of West Virginia University, and the Hon. Wilson M. Foulk, State Historian and Archivist of West Virginia, the President of the West Virginia Folk-

Lore Society was invited to read a paper at that meeting. In order that he might secure certain material in the extreme southern part of the state, the Department of History and Archives appropriated seventy-five dollars toward the expenses of such a trip and the State Department of Free Schools arranged for him to help conduct several institutes in that section. The venture turned out well. The material was secured and the paper read at Berea as planned.

Some of the incidents of this tour are worth recording and some of the personages worth describing as an essential part in the history of this movement. The last two weeks of July and the first two weeks of August were devoted to the work. The field, only partially covered, was the counties of Mingo, Welch, Boone, and Clay. In the last two of the counties named the work was all done at the county institutes. In the other two it was more important and needs to be told in detail.

Leaving Huntington, Cabell County, on Sunday morning, I made my first stop at Richards, a small station on the Norfolk and Western Railroad, on the West Virginia side of the Big Sandy River. I had previously been informed by Mr. A. C. Davis, Superintendent of Schools at Williamson, Mingo County, that on the opposite side of the river from Richards lived a Mr. Sam Turman, who knew many old ballads and songs.

I arrived at his house about noon and met with a most cordial reception. A good portion of the afternoon was spent in walking about, looking at the place, and in getting acquainted. During the late afternoon and all the evening, I wrote down the words of old songs as he sang or recited them. Country people go to bed early, and we planned to finish the work in the morning. But alas! "The best laid schemes o' mice an' men Gang aft a-gley," and so did ours. While we were at breakfast the next morning, we heard a crash and loud shrieks. A freight train had struck a gasoline hand-car right in front of his house. We all rushed to the door where a most horrible sight greeted us. Men scattered in all directions, some of them literally masses of flame, burning alive. It is not necessary to give details. In spite of all our efforts, four of the men were dead in a short time and others terribly mangled. It was almost noon before they were all transported to a hospital at some place several miles up the river. Dinner was a solemn affair. No more ballad-collecting that day, and in the afternoon I continued my journey up the river, crossing back into West Virginia.

In a letter dated December 1, 1921, Buchanan, Kentucky, Mr. Turman furnishes the following data concerning himself:

I was born and raised here at what has always been known as Turman's Ferry, on the Big Sandy, twelve miles east of Cattletsburg, Ky., and thirteen miles west of Louise, Ky. My father owned the first farm in Boyd County, adjoining Lawrence County, Ky., which farm I now own. We had a three months school each year when I was a boy, a log school house with hewed logs for seats. I attended those schools until I was sixteen years old. I never got farther than long division in arithmetic. Reading and writing was about all that was taught at that day.

Our country back of the river was almost a virgin forest, so old settlers would have a log-rolling and a quilting and a play or dance at night. So the folks would all gather in and play and sing and dance all night. We just went from one neighbor's house to another's in winter. My grandfather, John Turman, came from old Virginia. My grandmother's maiden name was Jones. My grandfather on my mother's side was German and English. Grandfather Turman was English.

In 1880 I began to assist the old soldiers in getting their pensions. I gave that a study and I don't guess there ever was or ever will be another man that has done for those old widows and orphans as I have done. I have always taken their claims, furnished the money and time to work up their claims, and few there are that were not placed on the roll. I have been for the last fifteen years connected with two law firms, who call me into some big cases for my advice and opinion. Although I never had a licence to practice law there are but few lawyers who know more than I do. The man that you and I cut and tore the clothes off that was burning, died before they got him to the hospital. His wife employed me to look after her interest, and two other of the men who were injured employed me, so I furnished the money and fought it all through the courts; came out with $23,000 damages. The man that was burning down under the railroad in the field died. His wife and the four got only $4000 each.

Mr. A. C. Davis, mentioned above, furnishes additional information:

Mr. Turman is seventy years old. He is a very shrewd man in his work as Pension attorney. Some people have accused him of overdoing his shrewdness. I do not know whether this is true or not, but even if he has, I think he makes up when he finds some one in trouble or needing help. I have never known any one more willing to help in trouble than Mr. Turman.

He is always jolly and in a good humor, has reared a family of boys who are also jolly and are doing well in their professions.

You remember that the railroad runs near his house and through his farm. Ever since I have known him he has been in some suit with the railroad company for some sort of damage and I have never known him fail in winning a verdict. He helped some of the widows and other defendents in their suit against the railroad which came as a result of the wreck while you were at his home, winning some pretty big damage suits.

A joke which is told of him I know you will enjoy. He was assisting a certain soldier in getting a pension and the fellow was supposed to be deaf or nearly so. The time for the medical examination came and one of the examiners suspicioned that there might be some fixing up, so some time during the procedure this examiner began talking to this fellow and telling him jokes. At last he said he wanted to tell him one concerning Mr. Turman, so he whispered it. When he was through with the joke the applicant gave a very hearty laugh. As a result, the applicant did not get as high a rate of pension as he had planned.

Mr. Turman weighs one hundred and sixty-five pounds, is about five feet seven inches high, and has very bright, keen blue eyes. He sings the old songs in a loud, stentorious voice, with much gusto, and in a style approaching what is characterized in Mr. McKenzie's "Quest of the Ballad" as *roaring*.

On a previous trip to the southern part of the state I had made the acquaintance of Mr. Charles H. Ellis, County Superintendent of Schools of Mingo County. He belongs to the famous Hatfield family of West Virginia, the one that carried on the feud for so many years with the McCoys. His mother was Nancy Hatfield, daughter of Ali, who married Ballard Ellis. She died when her son Charles was three months old, and he was taken and brought up by his uncle, Joseph Hatfield. It was a great privilege to hear from Mr. Ellis the history of the feud as the Hatfields knew it. The notes taken, however, are confidential and at this time of writing may not be made public. Mr. Ellis contributed the Tolliver-Martin Feud Song contained in this volume and gave valuable aid toward furthering the search. He planned to make a trip with me over the mountains to visit "Devil Anse" Hatfield, the famous leader of the Hatfield feudists, but on account of its being war times we found it impossible to secure horses for the trip. Since then "Devil Anse" has died, and I feel that fate has cheated me out of a bit of experience really worth while.

One man only was found in Williamson who could sing any of the old songs. He knew "Logan County Court House," in this volume, and several fragments. Not much was learned about him. He was a store-keeper, a man about sixty years old, strong and vigorous. He had a good voice and sang in a loud tone. His name was J. D. James.

Mr. W. C. Cook, County Superintendent of McDowell County, was also very courteous and helpful. Through him introductions were secured to various county officers, and men previously in office, some of whom had known John Hardy and had been present at his trial and hanging. Some important data were secured from these men about the famous negro criminal. He also introduced me to a prominent negro, Mr. James Knox Smith, of Keystone, from whom I got some of the most valuable information concerning John Hardy and a version of "The Vance Song," all of which is recorded in the proper place in this volume.

Mr. Smith was a practising lawyer. He was born in Tazewell County, Virginia, near the courthouse. His parents were slaves. His early legal knowledge was acquired by studying in the law office of Judge Christian. When he applied to the circuit judges for an examination for admission to the bar, he was refused on the ground that he was a negro. He then read law some further under Major Cecil, who advised him to apply to the supreme court of West Virginia for admission to practice. He did so in 1894 and was admitted. The judges who admitted him were Brandon, Holt, and English. Ever since, he has practised in the circuit and federal courts of West Virginia, Virginia, North Carolina, and Kentucky. These statements are given on the authority of Mr. Smith himself.

Mr. Smith is a good-looking negro, about sixty years old, of average height, stockily built, and very black. He has an easy manner, plenty of self-confidence, and is a fluent speaker. I called on him one afternoon in his office in Keystone and found hanging on one of his walls a photograph of John Hardy on the gallows. It had formerly hung for many years in the City Hall in Keystone, but when that building burned Mr. Smith rescued it. It seemed to give him much pleasure to present it to the Folk-Lore Society.

On a Sunday morning Mr. Cook drove me over from Welch to English, where I took the train for Barclay, at which place I was to see a Mr. A. C. Payne. He was sixty-seven years old when I saw him, a big, raw-boned man, over six feet tall. In his younger days he had been handsome, with strong, fine features, and raven-black hair, now streaked with gray. He had been born near English and had always lived in McDowell County. He was one of the jurymen that convicted John Hardy.

Mr. Payne was an old-time fiddler, whose fame is ever green in that part of our state and no doubt will be so for a long while to come. Although he bore traces of his sixty-seven years and the ravages of rheumatism, he had about him something of the air of everlasting youth. I spent the whole Sunday with him, listening to him play the fiddle, sing snatches of old songs, and get off some of the "lingo" that he used to give at dances, song or fiddle tune interspersed with comments. His voice was still fairly good and he sang with appreciation and in a manner not out of the ordinary. He was living with his daughter, who kept a sort of boarding-place.

The last place at which a genuine singer was found on this trip was Matewan, Mingo County, a place since made notorious on account of the battle between Sid Hatfield and his followers on one side and the Baldwin-Felts detectives on the other. This man was W. E. Boggs, a short, somewhat fleshy man with a round, smooth face, jolly and good-natured as the day is long. I discovered him as I walked along the railroad. He was driving a mule-team hitched to a wagon-load of coal. He sang because he could not help it, I judge, in a high tenor voice, very penetrating and far-reaching. He was just a hired man of the old-time sort, never expected to be anything different, nor cared for anything different. He was happy at his work, enjoyed a song and a jest, or a glass of "moonshine," which might be readily had from Kentucky just across the river. He told me that he learned the songs he sang from his brother, thirty-five years ago, who was afterward killed in Ashland, Kansas, by cowboys. His memory was not very good and he knew nothing perfectly. When he lost the exact words he gave the thought in prose and did not seem to be able to extemporize in the least.

Mr. Burwell Luther, another of the genuine ballad-singers whose contributions appear in this volume, lived at Shoals, Wayne County, West Virginia. His niece, Anna Copley, writes of him under date of March 4, 1922, as follows:

Mr. Burwell Luther was born in 1860 and died in 1920, just before his sixtieth birthday. Height, five feet, ten inches; weight, close to two hundred pounds when in health; complexion, dark; brown eyes, brown hair. Born in Wayne County, West Virginia. Lived here most of his life. Has been in the West but not for long periods. Was attendant and Supervisor at Spencer Hospital several years and at West Virginia Asylum at Huntington. Farming was the main occupation of his life. He was interested in politics and kept well up on current events. He was very fond of children. Was never married. His father was English. His mother was a Stephenson before marriage, and this family was supposed to have come from the Carolinas, and was Scotch, or half Scotch. His parents were both born in Wayne County. He was a great reader, mostly the Bible, religious books, history and fiction. He was interested in religion and always attended church and Sunday School. He seemed inclined to the Christian faith but late in life joined the M. E. Church. He was fond of social life, was a good dancer, and often "called" for the old-time square dances. These dances were often preceded by log-rollings, corn-huskings, house-raisings, etc. He often talked of these things but I do not remember anything of particular interest. He was fond of dogs and horses, but was what you might call an indifferent sportsman.

He learned the old songs when a child from his mother. He had a tenor voice, sang loud, and carried the tune well. This may have been only his way of singing, as he sang rather loudly any song.

Another old-time fiddler, whom I discovered at Fairmont, Monongalia County, was a blind man by the name of J. T. Doolittle. I think he must have been in the neighborhood of sixty years of age when I saw him in June, 1918 — a man of large frame, well built, and having a fine head. He had a genius for making musical instruments, and had made in his day, so he told me, ninety fiddles, fifty-four guitars, thirty mandolins, seven bass viols, five dulcimers, and one ukelele. He had no fiddle at the place where I met him, nor did he sing for me.

Official correspondents of the Society are as follows:

John B. Adkins, Branchland, Lincoln Co.
I. O. Ash, Middlebourne, Tyler Co.
Miss Sarah A. Barnes, Bruceton Mills, Preston Co.
Wallie Barnett, Leon, Mason Co.
Anna Copley, Shoals, Wayne Co.
G. W. Cunningham, Elkins, Randolph Co.
Miss Fannie Eagan, Hinton, Summers Co.
Miss Maude Groves, Deepwell, Nicholas Co.
Miss Lily Hagans, Morgantown, Monongalia Co.
Rex Hoke, Second Creek, Monroe Co.
Mrs. E. A. Hunt, Belington, Barbour Co.
Miss Sallie D. Jones, Hillsboro, Pocahontas Co.
Miss Lalah Lovett, Bulltown, Braxton Co.
J. Harrison Miller, Wardensville, Hardy Co.
Mrs. W. M. Parker, Hinton, Summers Co.
George Paugh, Thomas, Tucker Co.
Miss Mabel Richards, Fairmont, Marion Co.
Mrs. Hilary G. Richardson, Clarksburg, Harrison Co.
Miss Elizabeth Sarver, West Liberty, Ohio Co.
E. C. Smith, Weston, Lewis Co.
Fred M. Smith, Glenville, Gilmer Co.
W. H. S. White, Piedmont, Mineral Co.

J. H. C.

MR. GEORGE W. CUNNINGHAM
ELKINS, RANDOLPH COUNTY

MR. LUTHER BURWELL
SHOALS, WAYNE COUNTY

RESIDENCE OF MR. LUTHER BURWELL
SHOALS, WAYNE COUNTY

MRS. RACHEL FOGG
CLARKSBURG, HARRISON COUNTY

MRS. NANCY McDONALD McATEE
CLARKSBURG, HARRISON COUNTY

MR. AND MRS. SAM TURMAN
BOYD COUNTY, KENTUCKY

RESIDENCE OF MR. AND MRS. SAM TURMAN
BOYD COUNTY, KENTUCKY

MR. JOHN B. ADKINS
BRANCHLAND, LINCOLN COUNTY

Folk-Songs of the South

ABBREVIATIONS

BARRY: Phillips Barry, *Ancient British Ballads* [etc.]. [A privately printed list.]

BELDEN: H. M. Belden, *A Partial List of Song-Ballads and Other Popular Poetry known in Missouri.* Second Edition. [1910.]

BROWN: F. C. Brown, *Ballad-Literature in North Carolina. Reprinted from Proceedings and Addresses of the Fifteenth Annual Session of the Literary and Historical Association of North Carolina, December 1–2, 1914.*

BULLETIN: *The Virginia Folk-lore Society, Bulletin.*

CAMPBELL AND SHARP: Olive Dame Campbell and Cecil J. Sharp, *English Folk Songs from the Southern Appalachians.* New York, 1914.

CHILD: Francis James Child, *The English and Scottish Popular Ballads.* Boston, [1883 ff.].

COX: John Harrington Cox, contributions to *The West Virginia School Journal and Educator.* Morgantown.

GRAY: Roland Palmer Gray, *Songs and Ballads of the Maine Lumberjacks with Other Songs from Maine.* Cambridge, 1924.

JONES: Bertrand L. Jones, *Folk-Lore in Michigan. Reprint from Kalamazoo Normal Record, May, 1914, Western State Normal School, Kalamazoo, Michigan.*

JOURNAL: *The Journal of American Folk-Lore.*

LOMAX: John A. Lomax, *Cowboy Songs and Other Frontier Ballads.* New York, 1910, 1922.

McGILL: Josephine McGill, *Folk-Songs of the Kentucky Mountains.* New York, copyright 1917.

MACKENZIE: W. Roy Mackenzie, *The Quest of the Ballad*, Princeton, 1919.

POUND (with page reference only): Louise Pound, *Folk-Song of Nebraska and the Central West, A Syllabus.* Nebraska Academy of Sciences, *Publications*, Vol. IX, No. 3.

POUND (with number reference), or Pound, *Ballads*: Louise Pound, *American Ballads and Songs.* New York [1922].

SHEARIN AND COMBS: Hubert G. Shearin and Josiah H. Combs, *A Syllabus of Kentucky Folk-Songs.* (*Transylvania Studies in English*, II.) Lexington, Kentucky, 1911.

SHOEMAKER: Henry W. Shoemaker, *North Pennsylvania Minstrelsy.* Altoona, Pennsylvania, 1919.

SMITH: C. Alphonso Smith, *Ballads Surviving in the United States. Reprinted from the January, 1916, Musical Quarterly.*

WYMAN AND BROCKWAY: *Lonesome Tunes, Folk-Songs from the Kentucky Mountains.* The Words collected and edited by Loraine Wyman; the Pianoforte Accompaniment by Howard Brockway. New York [1916].

LADY ISABEL AND THE ELF KNIGHT

(CHILD, No. 4)

THIS ballad is known in West Virginia as "Pretty Polly," "Six Kings' Daughters," "The King's Daughter," "The False Lover," and "The Salt-Water Sea." Nine variants have been recovered.

For American variants see Child, III, 496 (Virginia; from Babcock, *Folk-Lore Journal*, VII, 28); *Journal*, XVIII, 132 (Barry; Massachusetts); XIX, 232 (Belden; Missouri); XXII, 65 (Beatty; Wisconsin), 76 (Barry; New Jersey, tune only), 374 (Barry; Massachusetts; from Ireland; also readings from other texts); XXIII, 374 (Mackenzie; Nova Scotia; cf. *Quest of the Ballad*, pp. 93, 174, 183); XXIV, 333, 344 (Barry; Massachusetts and Illinois; from Irish sources); XXVII, 90 (Gardner; Michigan); XXVIII, 148 (Perrow; North Carolina); XXXV, 338 (Tolman and Eddy; Ohio); Wyman and Brockway, p. 82 (Kentucky); Campbell and Sharp, No. 2 (Massachusetts, North Carolina, Kentucky, Georgia); Focus, IV, 161, 212 (Virginia); Child MSS., XXI, 4 (4, 6); Minish MS. (North Carolina). In *Charley Fox's Minstrel's Companion* (Philadelphia, Turner & Fisher), p. 52, may be found "Tell-Tale Polly. Comic Ballad. (As sung by Charley Fox.)"

For references to American versions, see *Journal*, XXIX, 156, note, 157; XXX, 286. Add Shearin and Combs, p. 7; *Bulletin*, Nos. 6-10. For recent British references see *Journal*, XXXV, 338; Campbell and Sharp, p. 323.

A

"Pretty Polly." Communicated by Mr. George Paugh, Thomas, Tucker County, August 28, 1915; dictated by Mrs. S. R. Paugh.

1   He followed me up, he followed me down,
       He followed me into my room;
    I had n't the heart to speak one word,
       Nor the tongue to say him nay, nay, nay,
       Nor the tongue to say him nay.

2   "Go gather up your father's gold,
       Likewise your mother's fee,
    Two of your father's best horses,
       That ride for thirty and three, three, three,
       That ride for thirty and three."

3　She mounted on the pony [1] brown,
　　　And him on the bible [2] bay;
　They rode along the salt-water sea
　　　This lonesome, long summer's day, day, day,
　　　This lonesome long summer's day.

4　At last he said, "Get you down,
　　　Get you down, my Pretty Polly; [3]
　For here I have drowned six kings' daughters,
　　　And you the seventh shall be, be, be,
　　　And you the seventh shall be."

5　"Take off, take off those costly robes
　　　And hang them on yonders tree,
　For they are too fine and costly
　　　To swim in the salt-water sea, sea, sea,
　　　To swim in the salt-water sea."

6　"O turn your body round and about,
　　　And your face to the leaves on the tree,
　For a naked woman is the awfullest sight
　　　For all sorts of men for to see, see, see,
　　　For all sorts of men for to see."

7　He turned his body around and about,
　　　His face to the leaves in the tree;
　She picked him up so manfully
　　　And dashed him to the bottom of the sea, sea, sea,
　　　And dashed him to the bottom of the sea.

8　"O help, O help, my Pretty Polly!
　　　O help!" said he;
　"For if ever I again recover.
　　　To you I'll faithful be, be, be,
　　　To you I'll faithful be."

9　"Lie there, lie there, you false-hearted man,
　　　Lie there instead of me!
　Here you have drowned six king's daughters,
　　　But I the seventh won't be, be, be,
　　　But I the seventh won't be."

1. Probably for *bonny*.　　　　2. Probably for *dapple*.
3. Variant line: "Get you down, get you down," said he.

10 She mounted upon the pony brown
  And led the bible bay,
 And arrived at home at her father's house
  Just three hours before 't was day, day, day,
  Just three hours before 't was day.

11 She placed back her father's gold,
  Likewise her mother's fee,
 And two of her father's best horses
  That ride to thirty and three, three, three,
  That ride to thirty and three.

12 Up rose the pretty little parrot
  Which in its cage did stay,
 Saying, "What are you doing, my Pretty Polly,
  So long before it is day, day, day,
  So long before it is day?"

13 "Get you down, get you down, my pretty parrot,
  And tell no tales on me,
 And your cage shall be made of the hard witten [1] gold,
  And your door of ivory-ry-ry,
  And your door of ivory."

14 Up rose this good old man
  Who in his chamber lay,
 Saying, "What are you doing, my pretty parrot,
  So long before it is day, day, day,
  So long before it is day?"

15 "There were three cats at my cage door,
  A-trying their vengeance on me;
 I was just a-calling Pretty Polly,
  To drive those cats away, 'way, 'way,
  To drive those cats away."

1. Probably for *beaten*.

ℬ

"Six Kings' Daughters." Communicated by Professor Walter Barnes, Fairmont, Marion County, July, 1915; obtained from Mr. G. W. Cunningham, Elkins, Randolph County, who learned it shortly after the Civil War from Laban White, Dry Fork. Printed by Cox, XLIV, 269.

1 He followed me up, he followed me down,
    And he followed me into the room;
  I had not the power to speak one word,
    Nor a tongue to answer nay.

2 "Go bring me some of your father's gold
    And some of your mother's fee,
  And I will take you to Scotland,
    And there I'll marry thee."

3 She brought him some of her father's gold
    And some of her mother's fee;
  She took him to her father's barnyard,
    Where the horses stood thirty and three.

4 "Mount on, mount on that pretty, pretty brown,
    And I on the dapple gray;
  And we will ride through some long, lonesome woods,
    Three long hours before it is day."

5 She mounted on the pretty, pretty brown,
    And he on the dapple gray;
  They rode on through some long, lonesome woods,
    Till they came to the salt-water sea.

6 "Mount off, mount off your pretty, pretty brown,
    And I off the dapple gray;
  For six kings' daughters have I drownèd here,
    And you the seventh shall be."

7 "O hush your tongue, you rag-villain!
    O hush your tongue!" said she;
  "You promised to take me to Scotland
    And there to marry me."

8 "Haul off, haul those fine clothing,
    Haul off, haul off," said he;
  "For they are too costly and too fine,
    To be rotted all in the sea."

9   "Well, turn your face toward the sea,
     Your back likewise to me,
  For it does not become a rag-villain
     A naked woman for to see."

10   He turned his face toward the sea,
     His back likewise to me;
  I picked him up all in my arms
     And plunged him into the sea.

11   "O help, come help, my little Aggie!
     Come help, I crave of thee,
  And all the vows I've made unto you,
     I will double them twice and three."

12   "Lie there, lie there, thou rag-villain,
     Lie there instead of me;
  For six kings' daughters have you drownèd here,
     And yourself the seventh shall be."

13   I mounted on the pretty brown
     And led the dapple gray;
  I rode home to my own father's barn,
     Two long hours before it was day.

14   "O what is the matter, my little Aggie,
     That you call so long before day?"
  "I've been to drown the false-hearted man
     That strove to drown poor me."

15   "O hold your tongue, my little parrot,
     And tell no tales on me,
  And your cage shall be made of the brightest bit of gold,
     And your wings of pure ivory."

16   "O what is the matter, my little parrot,
     That you call so long before day?"
  "A cat came to my cage door,
     And strove to weary off [1] me,
  And I called upon my little Aggie
     To come and drive it away."

1. For *worry of:* cf. Child, C, 17.

C

"Pretty Polly." Communicated by Mrs. Anna Copley, Shoals, Wayne County, December 19, 1915; dictated by her cousin Mr. Burwell Luther, who learned it from his mother about fifty years ago. Mrs. Luther's name was Julia Stephenson. She learned it from her mother, whose maiden name was Peyton. The Peytons were English and the Stephensons were Highland Scotch. The Luthers and Stephensons have lived in Wayne County for over a century, the latter having come from Georgia.

1 He followed me up and he followed me down,
        He followed me all the day;
    I had not the power to speak one word,
        Or a tongue to answer nay.

2 "Go bring me some of your father's gold
        And some of your mother's fee,
    And I will take you to fair Scotland,
        And there I'll marry thee."

3 She brought him some of her father's gold
        And some of her mother's fee;
    She took him to her father's barn,
        Where the horses stood thirty and three.

4 "Mount on, mount on that brownie, brownie bay,
        And I on the dapple gray,
    And we'll ride away through the lonesome woods
        Three long hours before it is day."

5 She mounted on the brownie, brownie bay,
        And he on the dapple gray,
    And they rode away through the lonesome woods
        Till they came to the deep blue sea.

6 "Dismount, dismount from your brownie, brownie bay,
        And I off the dapple gray;
    Six pretty fair maids I have drownèd here
        And the seventh one you shall be."

7 "O hold your tongue, you villain!" she said,
        "O hold your tongue!" said she;
    "You promised to take me to bonny Scotland
        And there to marry me."

8 "Take off, take off those fine clothing,
    Take off, take off," said he;
  "For they are too costly and too fine
    To be rotted in the sea."

9 "O turn your body round and about
    To view the leaves on the tree;
  'T is a pity such a villain as you
    A naked woman should see."

10 He turned his body round and about
    To view the leaves on the tree;
  She clasped him tight in her arms so white
    And plunged him into the sea.

11 "Lie there, lie there, you villain," she said,
    "Lie there instead of me!
  Six pretty fair maids you have drownèd here,
    And the seventh one has drownèd thee."

12 She jumped upon her brownie, brownie bay
    And led the dappled gray,
  And she returned home to her father's house,
    Two long hours before it was day.

13 "O where have you been, my pretty Collin,
    So long before it is day?"
  "I have been to drown that false-hearted man,
    That strove to drown poor me."

14 "O hold your tongue, my pretty Polly,
    Don't tell no tales on me,
  And your cage shall be made of glittering gold,
    Instead of the greenwood tree."

15 "The old cat came to my cage door,
    Intending to weary [1] me,
  And I had to call on pretty Collin,
    To drive the old cat away."

16 "Well turned, well turned, my pretty little bird,
    Well turned, well turned!" said she;
  "And your nest shall be made of leaves of gold,
    Instead of the green willow tree."

1. For *worry*.

D

"Pretty Polly." Communicated by Mrs. Elizabeth Tapp Peck, Morgantown, Monongalia County, March 31, 1916; obtained from her mother, Mrs. Elizabeth Wade Mack, who learned it in her youth while living near Bethel Church.

1 He followed her up, he followed her down,
    In the bedchamber where she lay,
And she had not the wings of a dove for to fly,
    Nor the tongue for to say nay, nay.

2 Said he, "Take all your father's beaten gold,
    And put on your mother's shoes,
And take two of the best horses in your father's stable,
    Wherein lie thirty and three."

3 She mounted on the bonny brown,
    And he on the dapple gray,
And they rode till they came to the green river's side,
    Three long hours before it was day.

4 "Take off, take off that silken gown
    And hand it unto me,
For it is too rich and costly
    To rotten in the salt, salt sea."

5 . . . .
    . . . .
"For six king's daughters have I drowned here,
    And the seventh one you shall be."

6 Then she mounted on the bonny brown
    And led the dapple gray,
And she rode till she came to her own father's door,
    One long hour before it was day.

7 Then up spoke the pretty parrot
    From the cage wherein she lay,
Saying, "What is the matter with my pretty Polly,
    That she's traveling so long before day?"

8 "Lie still, lie still, my pretty parrot,
    And tell no tales on me,
And your cage shall be lined with my father's beaten gold,
    And be hung in the green willow tree."

9   Then up spoke the old man himself
     From the bedchamber where he lay,
    Saying, "What is the matter with my pretty parrot,
     That she's chattering so long before day?"

10   "The old cat came to my cage door
     And said she would murder me,
    And I had to call to the Pretty Polly
     To drive the old cat away."

E

"Pretty Polly." Communicated by Mr. Rex Hoke, Second Creek, Monroe County, November 8, 1915; obtained from Mrs. L. F. Hoke, who learned it about forty years ago from Mr. Wise W. Lively. Printed by Cox, XLV, 240.

1   He followed her up and he followed her down,
     And he followed her into the room;
    He never give her time for her to turn herself around,
     Nor time for to say nay, nay, nay,
     Nor time for to say nay.

2   "Go take a part of your father's gold
     And a part of your mother's fee;
    Go take two of your father's best horses,
     In where there's thirty and three, three, three,
     In where there's thirty and three."

3   She took a part of her father's gold
     And a part of her mother's fee;
    She took two of her father's best horses,
     In where there's thirty and three, three, three,
     In where there's thirty and three.

4   She mounted herself on the barney [1] bright,
     And he on the iron gray;
    They rode till they came to the salt-water sea,
     At the end of the long summer day, day, day,
     At the end of the long summer day.

5   "Mount off, mount off, my Pretty Polly,
     Mount off, mount off, I tell thee;
    I've drowned six of the king's daughters here,
     O you the seventh shall be, be, be,
     O you the seventh shall be.

1. Probably for *bonny black:* cf. I, 1.

6 "Take off, take off that silk so fine
     And lay it down to me,
   For it was never intended silk so fine
        To rot in the salt-water sea, sea, sea,
        To rot in the salt-water sea."

7 "You turn your eyes all around and about
     And onto the leaves of the tree;
   For you are not a fitten man
        An undressed woman for to see, see, see,
        An undressed woman for to see."

8 He turned his eyes around and about
     And onto the leaves of the tree;
   She caught him around the waist so slim,
        And she tripped him in the salt-water sea, sea, sea,
        And she tripped him in the salt-water sea.

9 "Come help, come help, my Pretty Polly,
     Come help, come help, I beg thee!
   And I will take you to old Scotland,
        And there I will marry thee, thee, thee."

10 "Lie there, lie there, my false-hearted man,
      Lie there instead of me!
    You drowned six of the king's daughters there,
         O you the seventh shall be, be, be,
         O you the seventh shall be."

11 She mounted herself on the barney bright
      And led the iron gray;
    She rode till she came to her father's hall,
         Two long hours before it was day, day, day,
         Two long hours before it was day.

12 Up spoke, up spoke her little parrot bird:
      "Pretty Polly, Pretty Polly," said she,
    "Pretty Polly, Pretty Polly, what are you doing
         So long before it is day, day, day,
         So long before it is day?"

13 "Lie still, lie still, my pretty parrot bird,
      And keep this secret on me!
    I'll build you a cage and I'll line it with gold,
         And I'll hang it on a sweet willow tree, tree, tree,
         And I'll hang it on a sweet willow tree."

F

"The King's Daughter," or, "The False Lover." Communicated by Miss Mildred Joy Barker, Morgantown, Monongalia County, October 2, 1916; obtained from her mother, whose family came to Monongalia County before the Revolution. Its members have known the ballad for many years.

1 "O come with me, my fair, fair lad,
    And we'll sail over the sea;
  We'll sail to bonny Scotland,
    And there you will marry me, me, me,
    And there you will marry me.

2 "If you will steal your father's gold,
    Likewise your mother's fee,
  I'll take you over to old Scotland,
    And there'll I marry thee, thee, thee,
    And there I'll marry thee."

3 "O I have stole my father's gold,
    Likewise my mother's fee,
  And two of the best horses in my father's stable,
    Wherein stand thirty and three, three, three,
    Wherein stand thirty and three."

4 She mounted on the milk-white steed,
    And he upon the bay;
  And they rode till they came to the salt, salt sea,
    Three long hours before it was day, day, day,
    Three long hours before it was day.

5 "Light off, light off, my pretty fair maid,
    Light off, light off!" said he;
  "For six king's daughters have I drowned here,
    And you the seventh shall be, be, be,
    And you the seventh shall be."

6 "O, turn yourself three times around,
    And look to yonder tree." . . .

    .   .   .   .

    .   .   .   .

7 She gathered him up in her lily-white arms,
    And cast him into the sea, sea, sea,
    And cast him into the sea.

8   "Lie there, lie there, you false-hearted knight,
         Lie there, lie there instead of me!
     For you promised to take me to old Scotland,
         And there you'd marry me, me, me,
         And there you'd marry me."

9   She mounted on her milk-white steed
         And home she led the bay;
     She rode till she came to her own father's stable,
         One long hour before it was day, day, day,
         One long hour before it was day.

10   The king cried out from his silken couch,
         In the bower where he lay,
     "O what has disturbed my pretty parrot
         So long before it is day, day, day,
         So long before it is day?"

11   "Hush up, hush up, my pretty parrot,
         And tell no lies on me,
     And your cage shall be made of yellow beaten gold,
         And hung on yon willow tree, tree, tree,
         And hung on yon willow tree."

G

"The Salt-Water Sea." Communicated by Professor Walter Barnes, Fairmont, Marion County, December, 1916; obtained from Mr. George Gregg,
Durbin, Pocahontas County. He got it from his mother, who learned it when
a child.

12   She rode upon her bonny, bonny brown,
         And he on the dapple gray;
     They rode till they came to the salt-water sea.
             .   .   .   .

13   "It is here, it is here," said he,
         "It is here I have drowned six kings' daughters,
     And the seventh one you shall be, be, be,
         And the seventh one you shall be.

14   "Pull off that costly robe of yours,
         And hang it on yonder tree,
     For such a costly robe," said he,
         "Cannot be rot in the salt-water sea, sea, sea,
         Cannot be rot in the salt-water sea."

15 "Turn, turn your back to the salt-water sea,
    For to gaze on yonder throne;
  For such a villain as you never can see,
    A handsome lady for to see, see, see."

16 He turned his back to the salt-water sea,
    For to gaze on yonder throne;
  She picked him up in her arms so strong,
    And she threw him into the sea, sea, sea.

17 "Some help, some help, my pretty Polly,
    Some help, some help!" said he,
  "And if I get on shore again,
    I sure will marry thee."

18 "Lie there, lie there, you false-hearted lover,
    Lie there, lie there!" said she;
  "For it is here you have drowned six kings' daughters,
    And the seventh one you shall be, be, be,
    And the seventh one you shall be."

19 She mounted upon her bonny, bonny brown,
    And she led the dapple gray;
  She rode all along the most lonesome road,
    Three hours before it was day, day, day.

20 She rode till she came to her father's house,
    Which was in sight of town,
  And down she jumped and in she slipped
    And shut the gates all round, round, round,
    And shut the gates all round.

H

"Pretty Polly." Communicated by Miss Lucile V. Hays, Glenville, Gilmer County, November, 1916; obtained from her mother, who could recall it in part only.

(The lover comes and the elopement is planned.)

(They go to the stable where there are thirty-and-three horses and take two.)

1 She mounted on the bonnie, bonnie brown,
    And he on the dappled gray,
  And away they rode from her father's house,
    Before the break of day.

(They rode until they came to the sea.)

2 "Take off, take off those diamonds fair
     And give them unto me,
   For is n't it a shame such jewels as those,
     Should lie with you in the sea?"

3 "Take off, take off that pretty silk dress
     And hang it upon yon tree,
   For is n't it a shame such . . .
     Should lie with you in the sea?"

4 "Turn your face to the tree of the wood
     And your back to the bank of the sea,
   For it does not become any young man
     A naked woman's body for to see."

5 He turned his face to the tree of the wood
     And his back to the bank of the sea,
   And manfully she took him in her arms
     And tripped him into the sea,

6 Saying, "Lie there, lie there, you false-hearted man,
     Lie there instead of me!
   For you promised to take me to St. Mary's,
     And there you would marry me."

7 Then she mounted on the bonnie, bonnie brown
     And led the dappled gray,
   And away she rode to her father's house,
     Before the break of day.

8 "Hold your tongue, my pretty parrot bird,
     Don't tell any tales on me,
   And your cage shall be made of yellow beaten gold,
     And the doors of ivory."

I

"Six Kings' Daughters." Communicated by Miss Mabel Richards, Fairmont, Marion County, October, 1915; obtained from Mrs. P. J. Long, who learned it from Mrs. Katherine Zinn, Monongalia County.

1 He helped her on the bonny, bonny black
     And himself on the dappled gray,
   And away they went through the green fields and trees,
     Till they came to the brink of the sea, O sea,
     Till they came to the brink of the sea.

2 "Light off, light off, you fair lady,
        Pull off this shining gown,
    For 't is too fine and costly
        To rot in the waves of the sea, O sea."

3 "You 've drowned six king's daughters here,
        Yourself the seventh shall be;
    You 've drowned six king's daughters here,
        And your body shall lie in the sea, O sea,
        And your body shall lie in the sea."

4 She turned herself around and about
        To gaze on the leaves of the tree;
    She picked him up as many [1] as she could
        And plunged him into the sea, O sea,
        And plunged him into the sea.

5 "Lie there, lie there, you false-hearted knight;
        This ain't what you promised me:
    You promised me to fair Scotland we 'd go,
        And married we would be, O be,
        And married we would be."

6 She helped herself on the bonny, bonny black
        And led the dappled gray,
    And away she went from the green fields and trees,
        And she rode three hours before day, O day,
        And she rode three hours before day.

        1. For *manly* or *manfully:* Cf. H, 8, A, 7.

2

EARL BRAND

(CHILD, No. 7)

ONE version only of this ballad has been recovered in West Virginia, under the title of "The Seven Sleepers." A comparison with the Child versions shows that it follows most nearly B.

For American texts see Barry, *Modern Language Notes*, XXV, 104 (New Hampshire); Perrow, *Journal*, XXVIII, 152 (North Carolina); Campbell and Sharp, No. 3 (North Carolina, Georgia); Mackenzie, p. 60 (Nova Scotia); Minish MS. (North Carolina). Cf. F. C. Brown, p. 9; Shearin and Combs, p. 7; Reed Smith, *Journal*, XXVIII, 200; *Bulletin*, Nos. 2, 4–6, 10.

"The Seven Sleepers." Communicated by Mr. J. Harrison Miller, Wardensville, Hardy County, January 29, 1916; obtained from his mother, who learned it when a girl from Scotch Roach. Reported by Cox, XLV, 160 (*Journal*, XXIX, 400); printed, XLVI, 83.

1 Wake up, wake up, my seven sleepers,
    And do beware of me;
O do take care of your oldest daughter,
    For the youngest is going with me.

2 Wake up, wake up, my seven bold sons,
    Put your armor on so bright;
O it shall never be said that a daughter of mine
    Shall be with Sweet William all night.

3 He mounted a roan,[1] she a milk-white steed,
    Whilst himself upon a dapple gray;
He drew his buckles down by his side,
    And away he went riding away.

4 He rode, he rode, he better had 'a' rode,
    Along with his lady so gay,
Until he saw her seven brothers bold,
    And her father a-walking so nice.

5 "Get you down, get you down, Lady Margaret,"
    he said,
    "And hold my steed for a while;
While I fight your seven brothers bold,
    And your father a-walking so nice."

6 She held, she held, she better had 'a' held,
    And never shed a tear,

---

1. A corruption for "He mounted her on."

Until she saw her seven brothers fall,
And her father she loved so well.

7 "Hold your hand, hold your hand, Sweet William," she said,
"Hold your hand, hold your hand for a while;
O it's a many, a many a sweetheart I could have had,
But a father I'll never have no more."

8 "You can choose for to go," Sweet William he said,
"You can choose for to go or stay."
"I'll go, I'll go, Sweet William, you know,
For you've left me without any guard."

9 He mounted a roan, she a milk-white steed,
Whilst himself upon a dapple gray;
He drew his buckles down by his side,
And away he went bleeding away.

10 He rode, he rode, he better had 'a' rode,
Along with his lady so gay,
Until he came to his own mother's house,
And a mother she was to him.

11 "O mother, O mother, O make my bed,
Make it both long and wide,

.   .   .   .

And lay my lady down at my side."

12 Sweet William he died before midnight,
Lady Margaret before it was day;
And the old lady died for the loss of her son,
And there were eleven lives lost.

3

THE TWA SISTERS

(CHILD, No. 10)

THREE variants of this ballad have been found in West Virginia, two with the title, "The Miller's Two Daughters," and one with no title (cf. Cox, XLV, 159). A tells a complete story in which Johnny Ray loves the younger sister and buys her a gay gold ring and a beaver hat. The elder is jealous and pushes her sister into the stream, in which she floats down to her father's dam and is drowned. He drags her out and robs her. The father is hanged on the gallows and the sister is burned at the stake. B is fragmentary and the story is somewhat confused. There are three or four daughters of an "old lady," in which detail it agrees with C. The gift of the beaver hat is omitted. All three belong to the group represented by Child R, S, U, and Y, as is shown in particular by the refrain, the beaver hat, and the wicked miller. A freak of tradition in A makes him the father of the two sisters, and this relationship is involved in the title of B.

For American texts see Child, I, 137 (Long Island, New York); *Journal*, XVIII, 130 (Barry; Rhode Island and Maine); XIX, 233 (Belden; Missouri and Kentucky); XXX, 287 (Missouri, Nebraska); Campbell and Sharp, No. 4 (North Carolina, Virginia); Sharp, *Folk-Songs of English Origin Collected in the Appalachian Mountains*, 2d Series, p. 18 (same as Campbell and Sharp, No. 4 C, but with stanzas from other variants). For references see Campbell and Sharp, p. 323; Kittredge, *Journal*, XXX, 286. Add *Bulletin*, Nos. 6–8.

A

"The Miller's Two Daughters." Communicated by Miss Mabel Richards, Fairmont, Marion County, October, 1915; obtained from Mrs. John Hood, who learned it about forty-seven years ago. Printed by Cox, XLIV, 428, 441.

1   The miller's two daughters brisk and gay,
  Sing lie down, sing lie down;
 The miller's two daughters brisk and gay,
 The young one belonged to Johnny Ray,
  And I'll be kind to my true love,
  Because he's kind to me.

2   Johnny bought the young one a gay gold ring,
 The old one swore she had n't a thing.

3   Johnny bought the young one a beaver hat,
 The old one swore she did n't like that.

4   The miller's two daughters walking along the stream,
 The old one pushed the young one in.

5 "O dear sister, give me your hand,
And you shall have my house and land.

6 "O dear sister, give me your glove,
And you shall have my own true love."

7 Sometimes she sank and sometimes she swam,
And she was drowned in her father's dam.

8 The father drew her near the shore
And robbed her of her golden ore.

9 The father was hanged on the gallows so high,
And the sister was burned at the stake near by.

𝓑

"The Miller's Two Daughters." Contributed by Mr. Wallie Barnett, Leon,
Mason County, 1915. He learned it from his mother, who does not remember
where she got it.

1 There was an old woman who lived near the seashore,
        Bow down;
There was an old lady who lived near the seashore,
        Bow and bend to me;
There was an old lady who lived near the seashore,
She had some daughters three or four,
        I'll be true to my love,
        My love will be true to me.

2 "O sister, O sister, let us walk the seashore,
And watch the boats as they sail o'er."

3 The elder one pushed the younger one o'er,
As they were watching the boats sail o'er.

4 "O sister, O sister, please lend me your hand,
And I will bring you safe to dry land."

5 "I'll neither lend you my hand nor my glove,
For all that you want is my own true love."

6 . . . .
She drifted down to the miller's dam.

7 The miller threw out his drifting hook
And brought this lady from the brook.

C

No local title. Communicated by Mr. S. M. Kelley, Suter, Pennsylvania, 1919; collected in West Virginia.

1   There lived an old lady in the North Country,
        The bough has been to me;
     There lived an old lady, in the North Country,
     She had daughters one, two, three,
        True to my love,
        My love be true to me.

2   There came a young man a-courting there,
     And he made choice of the youngest there.

3   He made her a present of a beaver hat,
     The oldest thought a heap of that.

4   "O sister, O sister, give my hand,
     And I will give you my house and land."

5   "I will not give you my hand,
     But I will marry that young man."

6   The miller picked up his drop hook,
     And then he fished her out of the brook.

7   The miller got her ring,
     The miller pushed her back again.

8   The miller was hung at his mill gate
     For drowning my sister Kate.

4

LORD RANDAL

(CHILD, NO. 12)

TWELVE variants have been recovered in West Virginia, under the titles "Lord Randal," "Johnny Randolph," "Johnny Randal," "Johnny Ramsey," and "Johnny Reeler." A, B, C, D, and E, are all fine vigorous ballads, telling practically the same story, except in E, where the hero has been to visit his sister. In A the lover has been to the greenwood, spent the night with his true-love, and had for supper fried eels and fresh butter. In form and content, it is most like Child A, but verbal similarities and the refrain connect it with Child B, D, E, and F. B resembles most closely Child B, but shows other relations. The refrain is similar to that of Child H. The title is no doubt due to the fame of John Randolph of Virginia. C is so similar in arrangement and diction to B that further comment is unnecessary. D, while not so complete as B and C, belongs to the same group. E shows many variations from the preceding ballads. The name "Henry" suggests the "King Henry" of Child C. The red, black, and yellow poison may be an echo from Child B. "Ropes to hang her" suggests Child B and I. The statement that he had been to his sister's may be a corruption for grandmother's or stepmother's. Cf. Child I, J, K, L, M, N, and O. The remaining variants are more or less incomplete and need no special comment. C was printed by Cox, XLV, 266.

Scores of variants have been collected in this country, and new copies keep coming in from various states: see references in *Journal*, XXIX, 157; XXX, 289; XXXV, 339. Add Shoemaker, p. 123; Pound, No. 1; *Bulletin*, Nos. 7-10.

A

"Lord Randal." Contributed by Miss Polly McKinney, Sophia, Randolph County, February 2, 1916, who writes: "I am sending it to you as I learned it from my aunt. My grandmother says Lord Randal's name was William V and that the song is sometimes sung 'O William, my son,' instead of 'Lord Randal.'"

1 "O where have you been, Lord Randal, my son?
   O where have you been, my handsome young man?"
   "I ha' been to the greenwood; mother, make my bed soon,
   For I'm wearied wi' hunting, and would freely lie down."

2 "Where did you stay last night, Lord Randal, my son?
   Where did you stay last night, my handsome young man?"
   "I stayed wi' my true-love; mother, make my bed soon,
   For I'm wearied wi' hunting, and would freely lie down."

3 "What did you eat for your supper, Lord Randal, my son?
   What did you eat for your supper, my handsome young man?"
   "Fried eels and fresh butter; mother, make my bed soon,
   For I'm sick to my heart, and would freely lie down."

4 "What do you will to your father?"
"A dead son to bury."

5 "What do you will to your mother?"
"My trunk full of money."

6 "What do you will to your brother?"
"My land and my houses."

7 "What do you will to your sister?"
"My town in yon island."

8 "What do you will to your uncle?"
"My horses and saddle."

9 "What do you will to your sweetheart?"
"A rope for to hang her."

B

"Johnny Randolph." Communicated from Mr. Harrison Miller, Wardens-ville, Hardy County, January 24, 1916; obtained from his mother; learned from Susan Stewart; she, from her stepfather, John Jennings, who came from England.

1 "O where have **you** been, Johnny Randolph, my son?
O where have you been, my dear little one?"
"I've been courting my sweetheart; mother, make my bed soon,
I've a pain at my heart, and I want to lie down."

2 "Have you had your supper?"
"Yes, I've had my supper."

3 "What did you have for your supper?"
"Fried eels in fresh butter."

4 "What color was the eel?"
"Yellow and black spotted."

5 "What do you will to your father?"
"My farm and utensils."

6 "What do you will to your mother?"
"My house and my household."

7 "What do you will to your brother?"
"Horse, saddle, and bridle."

8 "What do you will to your sister?"
"The fairest in heaven."

9 "What do you will to your sweetheart?"
"Brimstone and hell-fire."

C

"Lord Randal." Contributed by Miss Ada Keith, Harrisville, Ritchie County, December 14, 1915; learned from Mrs. Olive Rexwood, who learned it from her brother, George W. Hardman; all of Ritchie County.

1 "O where ha' you been, Lord Randal, my son?
    O where ha' you been, my handsome young man?"
  "I ha' been out courting pretty Polly; mother, make my bed
      soon,
    For I ha' a pain in my heart, and I want to lie down."

2 "Ha' you had your supper?"
  "Yes, I've had my supper."

3 "What did you ha' for your supper?"
  "I had fresh eels fried in butter."

4 "Do you think you will die?"
  "Yes, I think I will die."

5 "What do you will to your father?"
  "I will him house and dwelling."

6 "What do you will to your brother?"
  "I will him horse, saddle, and bridle."

7 "What do you will to your sister?"
  "I will her sweet heaven."

8 "What do you will to your true-love, Lord Randal, my son?
    What do you will to your true-love, my handsome young
      man?"
  "I will her hell's fire and brimstone to scorch her so brown;
    She's the cause of this pain in my heart, and I want to lie
      down."

D

"Johnnie Randal." Communicated by Mr. George Paugh, Thomas, Tucker County, January 10, 1916; obtained from Mrs. S. R. Paugh, who learned it about forty years previous from Mike Hedrick, while living near Spruce Mountain in Pendleton County.

1 "Where have you been, Johnnie Randal, my son?
    . . . my dear little one?"
  "To see my sweetheart; mother, make my bed soon,
    I've a pain at my heart, and I want to lie down."

2 "What did you have for your supper?"
   "Fried eels and butter."

3 "What do you will to your mother?"
   "A home in bright heaven."

4 "What do you will to your father?"
   "My farm and my cattle."

5 "What do you will to your brothers?"
   "My horse and my saddle."

6 "What do you will to your sisters?"
   "My cottage."

7 "What do you will to your sweetheart, Johnnie Randal, my son?
        . . . my dear little one?"
   "Hell's fire and brimstone, dear mother, to scorch her bones
        brown;
        She's the cause of this pain at my heart, and I want to lie
        down."

ℰ

No local title. Communicated by Mr. W. H. S. White, Piedmont, Minera
County, January 28, 1916; obtained from Miss Gertrude Shapiro, who got it
from her mother.

1 "Where have you been all day, Henry, my son?
        Where have you been all day, my loving one?"
   "Up sister's, up sister's; make my bed soon,
        For there's a pain in my side, and I must lie down and die."

2 "What did she give you there?"
   "Poison, poison."

3 "What color was the poison?"
   "Red, black, yellow, red, black, yellow."

4 "What will you leave for father?"
   "Watch and chain, watch and chain."

5 "What will you leave for mother?"
   "Silk and satin, silk and satin."

6 "What will you leave for brother?"
   "Toys, toys."

7 "What will you leave for baby?"
"A kiss from Henry, a kiss from Henry."

8 "What will you leave for sister?"
"Ropes to hang her, ropes to hang her."

F

No local title. Contributed by Mrs. Anna Copley, Shoals, Wayne County, January 28, 1916, who has known it ever since she was a child.

1 "Where have you been, Willie, O Willie, my son?
Where have you been, my fair and pretty one?"
"I have been to see my true-love; mother, make my bed soon,
For I'm sick at my heart, and I want to lie down."

2 "Where have you been, Willie, O Willie, my son?
Where have you been, my fair and pretty one?"
"I have been to see my true-love; mother, make my bed soon,
For I believe I am dying, and I want to lie down."

3 "What'll you will to your father, O Willie, my son?
What'll you will to your father, my fair and pretty one?"
"My land and money; mother, make my bed soon,
For I'm sick at my heart, and I want to lie down."

4 "What'll you will to your mother?"
"My bed and my clothing."

5 "What'll you will to your brother?"
"My horse and my buggy."

G

"Johnny Randolph." Communicated by Miss Lily Hagans, Morgantown, Monongalia County, January 20, 1916; obtained from Mrs. Beulah Bay Richey, who learned it from her mother, a member of the Caldwell family of Wheeling, a family of Irish descent who came to Wheeling before the Revolution. A fragment of four stanzas.

H

"Johnny Ramsey." Communicated by Miss Margaret Richards, Fairmont, Marion County, April 26, 1916; obtained from Mrs. Lawrence Roby, Lowesville. A fragment in five stanzas in which Johnny Ramsey has been out with his dogs and had cold cakes and warm coffee for dinner.

I

"Lord Randal." Communicated by Mr. Harold Staats, Ripley, Jackson County, July, 1921, who writes: "This song is given in the diary of my great-great-grandfather, Abraham Staats, as sung by the early pioneers in Jackson County. I have heard it sung by different people, especially in the country. A fragment in five stanzas, in which the hero has had a cup of poison and wills to his sweetheart "Ten thousand weights of brimstone to burn her bones brown."

J

"Lord Randal." Communicated by Mr. S. M. Kelley, Suter, Pennsylvania, July, 1921, but collected in West Virginia. A fragment in five stanzas, almost exactly like variant I.

K

"Johnny Reeler." Communicated by Mr. C. R. Bishop, Green Bank, Pocahontas County, 1921; obtained from Miss Blanche Patterson, from Mrs. Dora Moomau, who learned it at school in Timberville, Virginia. A fragment in six stanzas, in which Johnny has for supper "Fresh seals fried in butter."

L

No local title. Contributed by Mrs. Hilary G. Richardson, Clarksburg, Harrison County, December 7, 1917, as sung by a colored servant forty years previous. One stanza, in which the hero is called "my little rambling son."

5

THE CRUEL MOTHER

(CHILD, No. 20)

THREE variants have been recovered in West Virginia under the titles, "Down by the Greenwood Side," and "The Greenwood Siding" (see Cox, XLV, 159). A is an excellent version, following Child E in most details. B is confused at the beginning and one verse of stanza 4 is missing. In the main it agrees clearly with Child C. The only thing in variant C that may be of help in determining its relationship is the last line: "You shall be keeper of hell's gates." Cf. Child, I, 15: "Seven years a porter in hell," and Child, K, 7: "And seven years a porter in hell."

For American texts see Mackenzie, *Journal*, XXV, 183 (Nova Scotia; also *Quest*, p. 104); McGill, p. 83 (Kentucky); Campbell and Sharp, No. 9 (North Carolina, Georgia, Tennessee, Virginia); Sharp, *Folk-Songs of English Origin Collected in the Appalachian Mountains*, 2d Series, p. 2 (Kentucky); Jones, p. 5 (South Carolina by way of Kentucky); *Journal of the Folk-Song Society*, II, 109 (Kentucky). For other references see *Journal*, XXX, 293.

A

"Down by the Greenwood Side." Communicated by Mrs. Hilary G. Richardson, Clarksburg, Harrison County, March 15, 1916; obtained from Mrs. Rachel Fogg, originally from Doddridge County, who learned it from her mother, and she from her mother. Printed by Mrs. Richardson, *Journal*, XXXII, 503, and by Cox, XLVI, 65.

1 There was a lady lived in York,
    Ha liley and loney;
  She fell in love with her father's clerk,
    Down by the greenwood side.

2 She loved him up and she loved him down,
  She loved him till she filled her arms.

3 She placed her foot against an oak,
  First it bent and then it broke.

4 Then she placed her foot against a thorn,
  There those two little babes were born.

5 She pulled a knife both keen and sharp
  And thrust those two little babes to the heart.

6 She buried those two little babes under a marble stone,
  Thinking this would never be known.

7 One day, sitting in her father's hall,
  She spied those two little babes playing ball.

8   "O babes, O babes, if you are mine,
 I'll dress you up in silks so fine."

9   "O mother, when we were thine,
 You never dressed us up in coarse nor fine.

10 "Now we are up in heaven to dwell,
 And you are doomed to hell."

$\mathcal{B}$

"Down by the Greenwood Side." Communicated by Mr. George Paugh, Thomas, Tucker County, January 10, 1916; obtained from Mrs. S. R. Paugh, who learned it about forty years previous from Mr. John Cox in Pendleton County.

1   She placed her foot against a rock,
 And there twin babes were born,
  Down by the greenwood side.

2   She drew her garter from her leg
 And tied them up both hand and foot.

3   She dug a grave both wide and deep,
 She placed them in, both hand and feet.

4   .   .   .   .
 She thought this murder would never be known.

5   One day she was sitting in her father's hall,
 She saw those twin babes play ball.

6   "O sweet little babes if you were mine,
 I'd dress you in the silks so fine."

7   "You false-hearted mother, when we were thine,
 You neither dressed us rough nor fine."

C

"The Greenwood Siding." Communicated by Professor Walter Barnes, Fairmont, Marion County, July, 1915; obtained from Mr. G. W. Cunningham, Elkins, Randolph County, who learned it from Ellen Howell of Dry Fork.

1   "O baby, O baby, if you were mine,
  All along and alone-y;
 I would dress you up in scarlet so fine,
  All along by the greenwood siding."

2   "O mother, O mother, when I was yours,
 You pierced me through my poor tender heart.

3   "O mother, O mother, thou hast cut stakes,
 You shall be keeper of hell's gates."

6

THE THREE RAVENS

(CHILD, No. 26)

Two variants have been found in West Virginia under the title of "The Three Crows" (cf. Cox, XLV, 160). Each is in four stanzas with a refrain. The close similarity of the stanzas and the refrain indicate that they have a common source. Stanzas 1 and 2 closely resemble 1 and 2 of Child; from this point on there is a wide variance. In the "Twa Corbies" of Child it is the knight that is slain and one corbie is to sit on his "hause-bane" and the other is to pick out his eyes. In the West Virginia variants it is the horse that is slain, whose eyes the crows are going to pluck out. These variations may be due to adaptation to environment. The references to the hawk, the hound, and the doe would naturally be the first to drop out.

"The Three Crows" is a more or less comic variety of "The Three Ravens" (Child, No. 26). It was once popular on the stage and has become a college song: see *Christy's New Songster and Black Joker* (cop. 1863), p. 58; *Singer's Journal*, I, 239; Waite, *Carmina Collegensia* (Boston, cop. 1868), p. 26; *The McGill University Song Book* (Montreal [1921]), p. 94; *The Scottish Students' Song Book*, p. 268; *Songs that Never Grow Old* (cop. 1909), p. 74. A further variation, "The Four Vultures. A Burlesque Quartette," may be found in *Frank Brower's Black Diamond Songster* (cop. 1863), p. 30, and *Frank Converse's "Old Cremona" Songster* (cop. 1863), p. 56 (included in *The Encyclopædia of Popular Songs*, N. Y., cop. 1864).

For American texts from oral sources see Tatlock, *Journal*, XXXI, 273 (Ohio); *Focus*, V, 281 (Virginia); Campbell and Sharp, No. 10 (Virginia); Sharp, *Folk-Songs of English Origin*, 2d Series, p. 22 (Virginia); Belden's Missouri collection. Cf. Barry, No. 27; Jones, p. 4 (Michigan); F. C. Brown, p. 9 (North Carolina); Reed Smith, *Journal*, XXVII, 63, and XXVIII, 201 (South Carolina and Tennessee); *Bulletin*, Nos. 4, 5, 7–10. The Scottish text printed by Beatty (*Journal*, XX, 154) is an interesting adaptation of the tragic English ballad to the pious uses of children.

A

"The Three Crows." Contributed by the General Editor, Morgantown, Monongalia County, 1915; learned from his father in Illinois.

1 There were three crows sat on a tree,
   And they were black as black could be.
      Philly McGee McGaw!

2 One of them said unto his mate,
   "What shall we do for meat to ate?"
      Philly McGee McGaw!

3 "There lies a steed on yonder plain
   That by his master has been slain."
      Philly McGee McGaw!

4   "We'll perch ourselves on his backbone
    And pluck his eyes out one by one."
        Philly McGee McGaw!

B

"The Three Crows." Contributed by Messrs. Guy Dowdy and Floyd M.
Sayre, students in West Virginia University; learned from fellow students at
Marshall College, Huntington, Cabell County.

1   There were three crows sat on a limb,
        O Billy McGee McGar!
    There were three crows sat on a limb,
        O Billy McGee McGar!
    There were three crows sat on a limb,
    And they were black as crows could be,
        And they all flapped their wings and cried,
            "Caw! Caw! Caw!"
        And they all flapped their wings and cried,
            "O Billy McGee McGar!"

2   Said one old crow unto his mate,
    "What shall we do for grub to ate?"

3   "There lies a horse on yonder plain,
    'T was by some cruel butcher slain.

4   "We'll perch ourselves on his backbone,
    And pick his eyes out one by one."

7

THE TWA BROTHERS

(CHILD, No. 49)

Two variants have been found in West Virginia under the titles: "The Two Brothers" and "Little Willie" (reported by Cox, XLV, 160). A, although more or less fragmentary and confused, is pretty clearly related to Child B. No proper names are given. In B there are the names John and Willie, days of the week mentioned, the references to stone-throwing and ball-playing, and the deliberate use of the knife. In all these there is a strong similarity to Child G. Some striking likenesses in language are also to be noticed.

For American texts see Child, I, 443 (Massachusetts, New York); *Journal*, XXVI, 361 (Pound; Nebraska by way of Missouri); XXIX, 158 (Tolman; Indiana); XXX, 294 (Kittredge from Belden; Missouri); McGill, p. 54 (Kentucky); Campbell and Sharp, No. 11 (North Carolina, Virginia); Sharp, *American English Folk-Songs*, 1st Series, p. 8 (Kentucky); Pound, No. 18 (Missouri by way of Washington); *Journal of the Folk-Song Society*, VI, 87; Belden's Missouri collection. For references see *Journal*, XXX, 293. Add *Bulletin*, Nos. 7, 9, 10.

A

"The Two Brothers." Communicated by Professor Walter Barnes, Fairmont, Marion County, April, 1915; obtained from Mrs. Charles Snider, Spencer, Roane County.

1 There were two brothers in a foreign land,
  Their lessons for to learn;
 Said the elder brother to the younger brother,
  "Dear brother, let us play ball."

2 . . . .

  . . . .

 "I am too little, I am too young,
  Dear brother, please leave me alone."

3 He had a knife all by his side,
  Which was both keen and sharp;
 He ran it through his brother's breast,
  Which bled him to the heart.

4 "Now take my shirt all off my back,
  And rip it from gore to gore,
 And bind it round my bleeding side."
  But still it bled the more.

5   "Now take me all upon your back
          And carry me to yon churchyard,
      And there dig me a fine big grave,
          Which is both deep and wide.

6   "And if my father should ask for me,
          Dear brother, when you go home,
      Tell him I'm at school with my playmates,
          And early I'll be home.

7   "And if my mother should ask for me,
          Dear brother, when you go home,
      Tell her I'm at school in a foreign land,
          And early I'll come home.

8   "And if my schoolmates should ask for me,
          Dear brother, when you go home,
      Tell them I'm dead and in my grave,
          As cold as any stone."

B

"Little Willie."   Contributed by Mr. John B. Adkin, Branchland, Lincoln
County, April 1, 1916.

1   Two little boys a-going to school,
          Two little boys were they;
      I've often wished myself with them,
          Their playmates for to be,
          Their playmates for to be.

2   On Monday morning they started to school,
          On Saturday they returned,
      A-combing back their olivewood locks,
          To see their parents at home,
          To see their parents at home.

3   "O Willie, can you toss the ball,
          Or can you throw a stone?"
      "I am too little, I am too young,
          Pray, brother, O leave me alone."

4   John pulled out his long, keen knife,
          It being both keen and sharp;
      Between the long ribs and the short
          He pierced it to his heart,
          He pierced it to his heart.

5 He then pulled off his olivewood shirt
    And tore it from gore to gore;
Although to wrap the bleeding wound,
    But still it bled the more,
    But still it bled the more.

6 "Pick me up, dear brother," said he,
    "And lay me out so straight;
O pick me up, dear brother," said he,
    "And lay me at the gate,
    And lay me at the gate.

7 "If you meet mother on the way
    And she seems uncearned,[1]
Just tell her I'm going to the old campground,
    My prayer book there to learn,
    My prayer book there to learn."

[1] For *concerned*.

8

YOUNG BEICHAN

(Child, No. 53)

THREE variants have been found in West Virginia under the titles: "Lord Bateman" and "Lord Batesman" (cf. Cox, XLV, 160). These three are so similar in language and story that they must needs have a common source. Lord Bateman, an Englishman of high degree, grows discontented and takes a sea journey. He is captured by the Turks, put into prison, has a hole bored through his left shoulder, and is set at hard labor. The King's daughter steals the keys to the prison, takes him to her father's hall, and regales him with the finest wine. He promises to bestow upon her house and lands if she will set him free. Thereupon they mutually vow that for seven years he is to marry no other lady and she is to marry no other man. After seven years and almost three, she crosses the ocean to find him and comes to his hall upon his wedding day. When the porter announces her arrival, Lord Bateman leaps from his chair, vows he will have the Turkish lady, and peremptorily sends the bride home.

The similarities of this version to Child L are so striking that there must be some connection between them. There is also a notable differentiation. Stanza A 3, substantially the same in B and C, does not appear in Child L, while Child L 3, a striking stanza telling of the tree which grew in the prison, to which Lord Bateman was chained, is not found in the West Virginia version. It would seem that Child L and the West Virginia version have a common source, in which occurred the boring of the hole in his shoulder and the growing of the tree in the prison.

For a list of American texts, with English and American references and discussion, see Kittredge, *Journal*, XXX, 294. Add Campbell and Sharp, No. 12 (North Carolina, Kentucky); Mackenzie, p. 115 (Nova Scotia); Pound, No. 14 (Indiana); cf. *Journal*, XXXV, 340; *Bulletin*, Nos. 6–9.

A

"Lord Bateman." Communicated by Anna Copley, Shoals, Wayne County, December 26, 1915; learned by her brothers and Mr. Luther Burwell about thirty-five years previously from Mr. James Forbes.

1 Lord Bateman was in England born,
    And he was of a high degree;
  He grew uneasy and discontented
    And made a vow he would go to sea.

2 He sailed east and he sailed west,
    Until he came to the Turkish shore,
  And there was taken and put in prison,

   . . . .

3   Through his left shoulder a hole they bore,
      And through the same a rope was tied,
    And he was made to drag cold iron,
      Till he was sick and like to died.

4   The Turkish king had a daughter fair,
      And she was of a high degree;
    She stole the keys of her father's prison
      And vowed Lord Bateman she would set free.

5   She took him into her father's hall,
      And drew for him the best of wine;
    And every health she drank unto him,
      She said, "Lord Bateman, I wish you were mine.

6   "O have you lands and have you living,
      And have you houses of high degree?
    And would you give to a Turkish lady,
      Who out of prison set you free?"

7   "O I have lands and I have living,
      And I have houses of high degree;
    And I would give to a fair lady,
      Who out of prison set me free."

8   "Let's make a vow, let's make a strong one,
      Let's make a vow seven years to stand:
    If you never will marry no other woman,
      I never will wed no other man."

9   . . . .
      Seven years had gone and almost three,
    She gathered up her gay clothing,
      And vowed Lord Bateman she would go see.

10   She rode till she came to Lord Bateman's hall
      And there did knock and loud did call.
    "Who's there?   Who's there?" cried the proud porter,
      "Who knocks so loud and don't come in?"

11   "Is this Lord Bateman's hall?" she said,
      "Or is he here himself within?"
    "O yes, O yes," cried the proud porter,
      "He has this day his bride brought in."

12   "Go bid him mind of the wine so strong;
    Go bid him mind of the roaring sea;
    Go bid him mind of the Turkish lady
      Who out of prison set him free."

13   "There is a lady at yonders hall,
    And she is of a high degree;
    She wears a gold ring on her fourth finger
    And round her waist has diamonds three.

14   "She bids you mind the wine so strong;
    She bids you mind the roaring sea;
    She bids you mind of a Turkish lady
      Who out of prison set you free."

15   He rose from the chair wherein he sat
    And bursted the table in pieces three,
    Saying, "I'll lose my life for the Turkish lady
      Who out of prison set me free.

16   "Take away, take away this bride of mine,
    For she is none the worse for me;
    She came to me on a horse and saddle,
      I'll send her away in coaches three."

B

"Lord Batesman." Communicated by Mr. John B. Adkins, Branchland, Lincoln County, April 1, 1916; dictated by Mr. Marvel Adkins, who learned it several years before from Mandy Conley. Printed by Cox, XLVI, 20.

1   In England lived an English lord,
    And he was of some high degree;
    He grew, he grew so discontented,
      He vowed some girl he'd go and see.

2   So he sailed east and he sailed west,
    He sailed till he came to the Turkish shore,
    And there he was caught and put in prison,
      His freedom never to enjoy no more.

3   They bored a hole through his left shoulder,
    And through the same a rope did tie;
    They made him load cold calks [1] of iron,
      Till he took sick and like to 'a' died.

[1] Cf. the word *cards* of C 3; mistakes, possibly for the word *carts*.

4   The Turkish king had a fair young lady,
        And she was of some high degree;
    She stoled the keys from her father's dwelling
        And out of prison set him free.

5   She taken him through her father's hall,
        And there was drinking of strong wine,
    And every health she drank unto him,
        She devowed, "Lord Bateman, if you was mine!

6   "Let's make a vow and make it strong,
        Let's make it seven years to stand:
    If you won't marry no other woman,
        I won't marry no other man."

7   Seven years had passed and almost three,
        Then she vowed her mate she would go and see;
    She sailed till she came to Lord Bateman's hall,
        She first did knock and then did call.

8   She says, "Is this Lord Bateman's hall,
        And is he in there all alone?"
    "O no, O no," cried the proud porter,
        "To-day a bride he's just brought home."

9   "Go remind him of the wine so strong,
        And remind him of the roaring sea;
    Go remind him of the Turkish lady,
        Who out of prison set him free."

10 "Here is a lady at your gate,
        And she is of some high degree;
    She wears a ring on her left forefinger
        And on the rest of them wears three."

11 He arose from where he sat
        And burst his table in pieces three,
    Saying, "I'll bet my land and all my living
        That Susie Pines has crossed the sea."

C

"Lord Bateman." Contributed by Mr. F. E. Smith, Dothan, Fayette County, January, 1917; learned from an older brother several years before in Roane County.

1 Lord Bateman was of England born,
    And he was of some high degree;
  He grew uneasy and discontented,
    Until one voyage he took to sea.

2 He sailed east, he sailed west,
    He sailed to the Turkish shore,
  And there they caught him and put him in prison,
    And he lived in hopes of freedom no more.

3 Through his left shoulder they bored a hole,
    And through that hole they tied a string;
  They made him pull cold cards of iron,
    Till he was tired, sick, and sore.

4 The Turkish king had a lady fair,
    And she was of some high degree;
  She stoled the keys of her father's prison,
    Saying, "Lord Bateman I'll set free."

5 She took him down into the cellar
    And drew unto him the strong wine,
  And every health she drank unto him,
    Saying, "Lord Bateman, if you will be mine,

6 "I'll make a vow, I'll make it strong,
    For seven long years or more to stand,
  If you won't marry no other woman,
    I won't marry no other man."

7 Seven long years had passed and gone,
    Seven long years and almost three;
  She gathered up her rich clothing,
    Saying, "Lord Bateman I'll go to see."

8 She sailed east, she sailed west,
    She sailed to Lord Bateman's home

   .   .   .   .

     .   .   .   .

9 . . . .
    She knocked and jingled at the rings,
      When none was so ready as the proud porter
        To rise and let this lady in.

10   "There is a lady at your gate,
      The finest lady you ever did see;
    She has enough gold around her neck, sir,
      To buy your bride and company."

11   Young Bateman rose up from his table
      And split it into splinters three,
    Saying, "Since I've met this Irish lady,
      You are none the worst by me."

𝒟

"Lord Thomas." Contributed by Mr. Sam Turman, Buchanan, Boyd County, Kentucky, July, 1918. Nineteen stanzas.

9

YOUNG HUNTING

(Child, No. 68)

Two copies of this ballad have come to hand under the titles: "Lord Henry" and "Love Henry," the latter an abbreviated variant of no special significance. The former is an excellent ballad most like F of the Child versions, as indicated by the throwing of the body into the deep well (stanza 9) and the wishing for a bow and arrow (stanza 14). Cf. Child F 8 and 12.

For American texts see *Journal*, XX, 252 (Pettit; Kentucky); XXX, 297 (Kittredge; Kentucky, Missouri, Indiana), where references will be found; Campbell and Sharp, No. 15 (North Carolina, Virginia, Georgia). *The William and Mary Literary Magazine*, May, 1922, XXIX, 664 (Virginia). Cf. *Bulletin*, Nos. 6, 7, 10.

A

"Lord Henry." Contributed by Mr. John Hill, Hughey, Logan County, January 7, 1916; learned many years ago from his mother. Reported by Cox, XLV, 160.

1   It happened on one evening late,
        As the maid was going to bed,
    She heard a sound, a beautiful sound,
        That made her heart feel glad.

2   She thought it was her brother John,
        Returning from the cane;
    But who should it be but Lord Henry,
        Just from his wild hunting?

3   "Get down, get down, Lord Henry,
        And stay all night with me;
    For the very best lodging in Mulvering Town,
        The best I'll give to thee."

4   "I won't get down, I shan't get down,
        To stay all night with you;
    For there's a prettier girl in the merry green lands,
        That I love much better than you."

5   As he leaned o'er his milk-white steed
        And kisses gave her three,
    She held up a knife in her right hand
        And pierced him heartily.

6   "O live, O live, Lord Henry,
      Half an hour or more;
  For the very best doctors in Mulveren Town,
      You'll soon be in their care."

7   "O live, O live! how can I live,
      How can I live you see,
  When I can feel my own heart's blood,
      Come trinkling o'er my knee?"

8   She called her waiting maids unto her
      To view his body so fair,
  Saying, "Of all this finery you see around here,
      The finest you shall wear."

9   Some took him by his curly locks,
      Some by his hands and feet,
  And threw him in the cold, dark well,
      Which was both cold and deep.

10   "Lie there, lie there, Lord Henry,
      Till the flesh rots off your bones!
  That prettier girl in the merry green lands,
      Shall mourn for your return."

11   There was a pretty parrot bird,
      Sitting high upon a limb,
  Saying, "You murdered Lord Henry,
      And in the well threw him."

12   "Come down, come down, my pretty parrot bird,
      And sit on my right knee;
  Your cage shall be the finest gold,
      And the door of ivory."

13   "I won't come down, I shan't come down,
      To sit on your right knee;
  For you have murdered Lord Henry,
      And soon you'd murder me."

14   "I wish I had my bended bow,
      My arrow and my string;
  I'd pierce a dart so close your heart,
      Those notes no more you'd sing."

15 "O if you had your bended bow,
     Your arrow and your string,
   I'd take my flight to the merry green lands
     And tell what I'd seen."

𝓑

"Love Henry." Contributed by Miss Polly McKinney, Sophia, Raleigh
County, 1919.

1 "Come in, come in, Love Henry," she said,
     "And sit on my right knee;
   I'll give you a chair of yellow green gold,
     And all the best is for thee."

2 "I can't come in, nor I shall not come in,
     To sit on your right knee;
   For the girl I left in the India land
     Will think long of my coming home."

3 She leant herself all over the fence,
     The kisses she gave were three;
   A little penknife all in her hand,
     She would it in fully.[1]

4 "O live, O live, Love Henry," she said,
     "A half an hour or more,
   And all the doctors in the town
     Shall be here at your cure."

5 "O how can I live, O how can I live,
     O how can I live?" said he;
   "For don't you see my own heart's blood,
     Come trinkling to my knee?"

6 "Come down, come down, Polly Parrot," she said,
     "And sit on my right knee;
   I'll give you a cage of yellow green gold,
     And all the best is for thee."

7 "I can't come down, nor I shall not come down,
     To sit on your right knee;
   For it haven't been long since you killed Love Henry —
     How soon you might kill me!"

---

[1] She wished to thrust it completely into his bosom.

10

LORD THOMAS AND FAIR ANNET

(CHILD, No. 73)

ELEVEN variants have been recovered under the following titles: "The Brown Girl," "Fair Ellender and the Brown Girl," "Fair Ellender," "Fair Ellenger," "Lord Thomas," "Lord Thomas and Fair Eleanor," and "Lord Thomas and Fair Ellender" (cf. Cox, XLV, 120). All of these variants belong to the same version, and nine of them tell a complete story. D and H begin with a description of Lord Thomas. In the other variants the story begins by the hero's asking his mother to solve the riddle as to whether he shall marry Fair Eleanor or bring the brown girl home. Since the brown girl has house and lot (land) and Fair Eleanor has none, she advises him to marry the brown girl. Thereupon he dresses himself up in state, takes his merry men with him, rides to Fair Eleanor's hall, and invites her to his wedding on the morrow. She says that is very bad news to her for she expected to be his bride. Later she asks her mother to solve the riddle as to whether she shall go to Lord Thomas's wedding or stay at home. Her mother advises her to stay at home since she will have few friends at the wedding and many enemies, but she is determined to go. Thereupon she arrays herself in her finery, takes her merry maids with her, and rides to Lord Thomas's hall. In answer to her knocking, Lord Thomas himself lets her in, leads her into the hall, and chooses for her the highest seat. Fair Eleanor twits him with having married such a brown wife, whereupon the brown girl stabs her with a penknife between the short ribs and the long. Lord Thomas asks why she looks so pale and she suggests that he must be blind not to observe her heart's blood trickling down to her knee. With a little hand-sword Lord Thomas cuts off the head of the brown girl, kicks it against the wall, and then slays himself with the same sword. Before he dies, he requests that Fair Eleanor be buried in his arms and the brown girl at his feet.

The West Virginia variants are closely related to group D of Child, as is shown by many striking incidents in common, such as the meeting and quick parting of the lovers; Lord Henry loves the little finger of Fair Eleanor better than he does the whole body of the brown girl; Lord Thomas dressed in green and taken for a king; Lord Thomas dressed in black (the rhyme requires the word white) and taken for a knight; Fair Eleanor taken for a queen; Fair Eleanor seated in the noblest chair, or chair of gold, or given the highest seat; the well in the yard of Fair Ellen's father.

For American texts see Child, III, 509 (Virginia; from Babcock, *Folk-Lore Journal*, VII, 33); *Journal*, XVIII, 128 (Barry; Vermont, Massachusetts by way of New Jersey); XIX, 235 (Belden; Missouri, Arkansas); XX, 254 (Pettit; Kentucky); XXVII, 71 (Barry; tune only); XXVIII, 152 (Perrow; North Carolina); XXIX, 159 (Tolman; Pennsylvania by way of Kansas; texts reported from Virginia and Indiana); McGill, p. 26 (Kentucky); Focus, III, 204, and IV, 162 (Virginia); Shoemaker, p. 138 (Pennsylvania); Campbell and Sharp, No. 16 (North Carolina, Georgia, Tennessee, Virginia, Massachusetts); Pound, No. 12 (Maryland by way of Nebraska); Mackenzie, p. 97 (Nova Scotia); Means, *Outlook*, September 9, 1899, LXIII, 120; *Berea Quarterly*, April, 1905, IX, No. 3,

p. 10; October, 1910, XIV, No. 3, p. 27; October, 1915, XVIII, No. 4, p. 14; Child MSS., XXIII, article 73; Wyman MS., No. 9 (Kentucky); Minish MS. (North Carolina); *The Forget-Me-Not Songster* (New York, Nafis & Cornish), p. 236. See also Belden, No. 4; Shearin and Combs, p. 8; Pound, p. 11; F. C. Brown, p. 9; *Bulletin*, Nos. 2, 3, 5–10; Campbell, *The Survey*, New York, January 2, 1915, XXXIII, 374; Reed Smith, *Journal*, XXVII, 62; XXVIII, 200.

A

"The Brown Girl." Communicated by Mrs. W. M. Parker, Keyser, Mineral County, July 17, 1916; obtained from Mrs. Bertha Urice, who got it from her father, Joseph Rogers, who learned it from Zimri Rush more than fifty years ago. Printed by Cox, XLV, 186.

1   "Come riddle, come riddle to me, dear mother,
       Come riddle to me this one:
   Whether I shall marry Fair Eleanor,
       Or bring the brown girl home."

2   "The brown girl she has house and lot,
       Fair Eleanor she has none;
   Therefore I bid you, 'out ado,
       To bring me the brown girl home."

3   He dressed himself in his silk so fine,
       And his married men in green;
   And every town that he passed through,
       He was taken to be some king.

4   He rode up to Fair Eleanor's hall,
       And he knuckled at the ring;
   There was none so ready as Fair Eleanor herself
       To arise and let him in.

5   "O what's the matter, Lord Thomas?" she said,
       "O what's the news for me?"
   "I came to bid you to my wedding to-morrow."
       "That's very bad news to me."

6   "Come riddle, come riddle to me, dear mother,
       Come riddle to me this one:
   Whether I shall go to Lord Thomas's wedding,
       Or shall I stay at home?"

7   "There are hundreds there that will be your friends,
       And thousands that are your foes."
   "Therefore to Lord Thomas's wedding
       At the risk of my life I'll go."

8 She dressed herself in her silk so fine,
   And her married maids in green;
And every town that she passed through,
   She was taken to be some queen.

9 She rode up to Lord Thomas's hall
   And knuckled at the ring;
There was none so ready as Lord Thomas
   To arise and let her in.

10 He took her by her lily-white hand,
   And he led her through the hall;
And out of four and twenty gay ladies
   She was the fairest of them all.

11 "Is this your wife, Lord Thomas?" she said,
   "I think she's tremendous brown;
When you could have had as fair a lady
   As ever the sun shone on."

12 The brown girl had a little penknife,
   The blades were keen and sharp;
Between the long ribs and the short
   She pierced Fair Eleanor's heart.

13 "O what's the matter, Fair Eleanor?" he said,
   "What makes you look so pale?
You used to have such red rose cheeks,
   But now you have turned quite pale."

14 "O are you blind, Lord Thomas?" she said,
   "Or cannot you well see?
Don't you see my very heart's blood
   A-trickling down my knee?"

15 Lord Thomas had a little hand-sword,
   As he passed through the hall,
And as he cut off the brown girl's head,
   He cast it against the wall.

16 "Go dig my grave in yonder churchyard,
   Go dig it wide and deep,
And bury Fair Eleanor in my arms,
   And the brown girl at my feet."

17 He placed the sword hilt in the ground,
    And the point ran at his heart,
Crying, "There were never three lovers met,
    As quick as we did part."

ℬ

"Fair Ellender and the Brown Girl." Communicated by Miss Mabel Myers, Summersville, Nicholas County, August 2, 1916; obtained from Miss Pearl Bronley, White's Creek, Wayne County, who received it from her uncle, William Bronley, Huntington, Cabell County.

1 "O mother, O mother, come riddle us all,
    Come riddle us all in one:
And say shall I marry Fair Ellender,
    Or bring the brown girl home."

2 "The brown girl has a house and lot,
    Fair Ellender has none;
I think it would be the wisest choice
    To bring the brown girl home."

3 He called together his merry men all
    And dressed himself in black;
And every town that he rode through,
    They took him to be some knight.

4 He rode till he came to Fair Ellender's house,
    He knocked so loud on the door;
And none was so ready as Fair Ellender herself
    To rise and let him in.

5 "What news, what news, Lord Thomas?" she said,
    "What news have you brought unto me?"
"I have come to invite you to my wedding,
    And that is sad news to thee."

6 "Sad news, sad news, Lord Thomas," she said,
    "Sad news have you brought unto me;
For I was expecting to be the bride,
    And you the bridegroom to be."

7 "O mother, O mother, come riddle us all,
    Come riddle us all as one:
And say shall I go to Lord Thomas's wedding,
    Or whether I tarry at home."

8 "O tarry at home, my daughter," cried she,
      "Yes tarry at home with me."
   "I'll go to Lord Thomas's wedding," said she,
      "If death waits me at the door."

9 She called together her merry maids all
      And dressed herself in green;
   And every town that she rode through,
      They took her to be some queen.

10 She rode till she came to Lord Thomas's home,
      She knocked so loud on the door;
   And none was so ready as Lord Thomas himself
      To arise and let her in.

11 He took her by the lily-white hand
      And led her across the hall;
   And chose for her the highest seat
      Among the merry maids all.

12 "Is that your bride, Lord Thomas?" she cried,
      "I think she is mighty brown;
   When you could have married the fairest girl
      That e'er the sun shone on."

13 The brown girl having a pocket knife,
      It being both long and sharp,
   Between the long rib and the short
      She pierced Fair Ellender's heart.

14 Lord Thomas having a sword by his side,
      It being both keen and tall,
   He cut the brown girl's head off
      And kicked it against the wall.

15 He placed the handle against the wall,
      The point against his heart:
   Sing, "Ever when was it three lovers did meet,[1]
      And ever so soon did part?"

[1] Line should read, *Saying,* "*Ever when,*" *etc.*

C

"Fair Elendar and the Brown Girl." Contributed by Miss Snoah McCourt, Orndoff, Webster County, May 16, 1916; learned from her mother.

1   "Come riddle, come riddle us both, dear mother,
         Come riddle us both as one:
     Shall I marry Fair Elendar,
         Or bringeth the brown girl home?"

2   "The brown girl she has house and land,
         Fair Elendar she has none;
     I charge you once with my blessing,
         Go bringeth the brown girl home."

3   He rode up to Fair Elendar's bower,
         So clearly he knocked at the ring;
     There's none so ready as Fair Elendar
         To rise and let him in.

4   "What news, what news, Lord Thomas?" she said,
         "What news have you brought unto me?"
     "I've come to invite you to my wedding,
         So sorrowful news unto me."

5   .   .   .   .
         "So sorrowful news unto me,
     For I was in hopes to have been the bride,
         And you the bridegroom to be."

6   "Come riddle, come riddle us both, dear mother,
         Come riddle us both as one:
     Shall I attend Lord Thomas's wedding,
         Or tarry with thee at home?"

7   "O some may be your friends, dear daughter,
         Whilst thousands may be your foes;
     I charge you once with my blessing
         To tarry with me at home."

8   "O some may be our friends, dear mother,
         Whilst others may be our foes;
     If it be the cause of my death,
         To Lord Thomas's wedding I'll go."

9   She dressed herself in silks so fine,
        All trimmed off in green;
    And every bower that she passed through,
        They took her to be a queen.

10   She rode up to Lord Thomas's bower,
        So clearly she knocked at the ring;
    There was none so ready as Lord Thomas himself
        To arise and let her in.

11   He took her little white hand
        And led her through the hall;
    He led her through the brown girl's chamber
        And sat her above them all.

12   "Is this your wife, Lord Thomas?" she said,
        "I'm sure she's very brown;
    When once you could have married as fair a lady,
        As ever the sun shone on."

13   "Despise her not," Lord Thomas said,
        "Despise her not unto me;
    For I do love your little finger,
        More than her whole body."

14   The brown girl had a knife in her hand,
        The point being keen and sharp;
    Between the long rib and the short
        She pierced Fair Elendar's heart.

15   "O are you sick?" Lord Thomas said,
        "What makes you look so pale?
    When once you had as cherry-red cheeks,
        As ever my eyes beheld?"

16   "O are you blind, Lord Thomas?" she said,
        "Or can you very well see;
    Or can you see my own heart's blood
        Come trickling down to my feet?"

17   Lord Thomas had a sword in his hand,
        He walked up through the hall,
    And cut the brown girl's head off
        And dashed it against the wall.

18　Lord Thomas had a knife in his hand,
　　　The point being keen and sharp;
　　Between the long rib and the short
　　　He pierced it through his heart,
　　Saying, "Here's three lovers so merry did meet,
　　　So sorrowful they must part!

19　"Go bury Fair Elendar at my right side,
　　　The brown girl at my feet;
　　Go place a new Bible under my head:
　　　So solemnly we may sleep!"

D

"Fair Ellender." Communicated by Mr. I. B. Boggs, Wallback, Roane County, February, 1917; obtained from his wife, who learned it when a little girl from her associates.

1　Lord Thomas he was a gay gentleman,
　　　He was lord of many a town;
　　He fell in love with pretty Fair Ellen,
　　　The fairest of all around.

2　"Come father, come mother, come tell me now,
　　　I'll ask you both at one:
　　Whether I must marry pretty Fair Ellen,
　　　Or bring the brown girl home."

3　"The brown girl she has house and lands,
　　　Fair Ellen she has none;
　　So I'll advise you as a great blessing
　　　To bring the brown girl home."

4　He rode up to Fair Ellender's gate,
　　　So loudly he tingled and called;
　　Who more ready to bid him walk in
　　　Than pretty Fair Ellen herself!

5　"What's your news, Lord Thomas?" she said,
　　　"The news you bring to me?"
　　"I've come to ask you to my wedding."
　　　"It's very sad news to me."

6　"Lord Thomas, it's very sad news," she said,
　　　"And it's very sad news to me;
　　For I intended your bride to be,
　　　And you bridegroom to me."

7   "Come father, come mother, come tell me now,
      I'll ask you both as one:
  Whether I must go to Lord Thomas's wedding,
      Or tarry with thee at home."

8   "There may be many and many your friends,
      While there may be many your foes;
  And I'll advise you as a grand blessing
      To tarry with me at home."

9   "Little do I care for friends who'll be there,
      Still less do I care for foes;
  For I must go to Lord Thomas's wedding,
      To Lord Thomas's wedding I'll go."

10   She dressed herself in scarlet red,
      All trimmed in an immense of green;
  And every city that she rode through,
      She was taken to be some queen.

11   She rode up to Lord Thomas's gate,
      So loudly she tingled and called;
  Who more ready to bid her walk in
      Than Lord Thomas, Lord Thomas of all!

12   He took her by the lily-white hand
      And led her through the hall,
  And sat her down at the head of the table
      Among the ladies all.

13   "Throw none of your slurs, Fair Ellen," he said,
      "Throw none of your slurs at me;
  For I love the end of your little finger,
      More than her whole body."

14   The brown girl she had a little penknife,
      Both blades were keen and sharp;
  And between the long rib and the short one
      She pierced Fair Ellen's heart.

15   "O what's the matter, Fair Ellen?" he said,
      "I think you are wonderful pale;
  For once you were as fair a young color
      As any one in the dale."

16 "O what's the matter, Lord Thomas?" she said,
　　"Why can't you plainly see?
　I can feel my own heart's blood
　　Go trickling down my knee."

17 He took the brown girl by the hand,
　　He led her through the hall,
　And with a sword cut off her head,
　　And threw it against the wall.

18 He put the sword against the wall,
　　The blade against his breast,
　Saying, "Here goes the life of three young lovers;
　　God send their souls to rest!"

$\mathcal{E}$

"Loyd Thomas." Contributed by Mrs. E. A. Hunt, Belington, Barbour County, February 21, 1916; learned when a child from her mother, Mrs. C. E. Bennett.

1 "O mother, O mother, come riddle us two,
　　Come riddle us two in one:
　Must I go marry Fair Ellen, my dear,
　　Or bring the brown girl home?"

2 "The brown girl she has house and money,
　　Fair Ellen she has none;
　Be tired of your life, beware of your death;
　　Go bring the brown girl home."

3 He dressed himself in a suit of red,
　　His fair men all in green;
　And every town that he passed through,
　　They took him to be a king.

4 He rode up to Fair Ellen's door,
　　All jingling in the rings,
　And none was so willing to let him in
　　As Fair Ellen, his own dear.

5 "Sad news, sad news to you I bring,
　　Sad news to you I declare:
　I come to invite you to my wedding,
　　Sad news, sad news I declare."

6 "I God forbid that ever such news,
       That ever such news I should hear;
   For I the bride had took it to be,
       And you the groom would be."

7 "O mother, dear mother, come riddle us two,
       Come riddle us two in one;
   Must I stay here and tarry all night,
       Or to Loyd Thomas' wedding go."

8 "Be tired of your life, beware of your death:
       To Loyd Thomas' wedding don't go."
   "I'll be tired of my life, beware of my death:
       To Loyd Thomas' wedding I'll go."

9 She dressed herself in a suit of red,
       Her fair maids all in green;
   And every town that they passed through,
       They took her to be a queen.

10 They rode up to the brown girl's door,
       All jingling in the rings;
   And none was so willing to let her in
       As Loyd Thomas, her own dear.

11 He took her by the lily-white hand,
       He led her through the hall;
   He placed her at the head of the table
       Among the merry maids all.

12 The brown girl spoke up and said,
       Spoke up as if for spite,
   Saying, "Where did you get the water, my pretty fair lady,
       That washes your hands so white?"

13 "In father's garden there is a well,
       Which flows both wide and deep;
   And you may search there till you go blind,
       That well you never could find."

14 The brown girl she had a penknife
       That was both keen and sharp;
   She pierced it through the long ribs short,
       She pierced fair Ellen's heart.

15 "O what is the matter, Fair Ellen, my dear?
        What makes you look so pale?
    You used to be as fair a lady
        That ever the sun shone on."

16 "O don't you see, Loyd Thomas," said she,
        "What is the matter with me?
    My own heart's blood came trinkling down,
        Came trinkling down, you see."

17 Loyd Thomas he had a sword in his hand
        Which was both keen and sharp;
    He cut off the head of his own brown girl
        And kicked it against the wall.

18 He bent his sword all to the floor,
        He pierced it through his heart;
    Well met, well met, three lovers well met,
        But sadly they did part.

19 "Go dig my grave both wide and deep,
        Through thunders may I sleep;
    Go bury Fair Ellen at my side,
        The brown girl at my feet."

F

"Lord Thomas." Communicated by Mr. J. Harrison Miller, Wardensville, Hardy County, June 24, 1916; obtained from his mother, who learned it from her mother, Mrs. Lucinda Ellis, who learned it from her grandmother, Mrs. Strawnsnider. Mr. Miller thinks the ballad has been known in the family for about two hundred years.

1 "O mother, O mother, come tell unto me,
        And tell the story true:
    Whether I shall bring Fair Ellen dear home,
        Or bring the brown girl home, home, home,
        Or bring the brown girl home."

2 .   .   .   .
        .   .   .   .
    "I charge you with all my heart, my dear,
        To bring the brown girl home, home, home,
        To bring the brown girl home.

3   "The brown girl she has houses and land,
      Fair Ellen dear has none;
  I'll charge you with all my heart, my dear,
      To bring the brown girl home, home, home,
      To bring the brown girl home."

4   Lord Thomas he mounted his milk-white steed
      And went to invite Fair Ellen dear home,
  Home on his wedding day, day, day,
      Home on his wedding day.

5   He rode till he came to Fair Ellen's hall,
      And then he rang the bell;
  There were none so ready to let him in
      As Fair Ellen dear was, was, was,
      As Fair Ellen dear was.

6   "O what is the matter, my dear?"
      "I've come to invite you home this day,
  Home on my wedding day, day, day,
      Home on my wedding day."

7   "O mother, O mother, come tell unto me,
      And tell me the story true:
  Whether I shall go to Lord Thomas's wedding,
      Or stay at home with you, you, you,
      Or stay at home with you."

8   . . . .

      . . . .

  "I'll charge you with all my heart, my dear,
      To Lord Thomas's wedding don't go, don't go,
      To Lord Thomas's wedding don't go."

9   She dressed herself in scarlet red,
      Her maidens all in green;
  And every city that she passed through,
      They took her to be some queen, queen, queen,
      They took her to be some queen.

10   She rode till she came to Lord Thomas's hall,
      And then she rang the bell,
  There was none so ready to let her in
      As Lord Thomas dear was, was, was,
      As Lord Thomas dear was.

11   He took her by the lily-white hand
       And led her through the hall,
   And set her down at the head of the table
       Among his nobles all, all, all,
       Among his nobles all.

12   "Is this your bride, Lord Thomas?" she replied,
       "I am sure she is wondrous brown;
   You could once have married as fair a young lady
       As ever the sun shone on, on, on,
       As ever the sun shone on."

13   "O don't despise her for me,
       For I think more of your little finger
   Than I do of her whole bodie-ie-ie,
       Than I do of her whole bodie."

14   The brown girl had a little penknife in her pocket,
       It was both keen and sharp;
   Between the short ribs and the lungs
       She wounded Fair Ellen's dear heart, heart, heart,
       She wounded Fair Ellen's dear heart.

15   "O what is the matter, my dear?"
       "O don't you see my very heart's blood
   Come trickling over my knee, knee, knee,
       Come trickling over my knee?"

16   Lord Thomas he drew his two-edged sword
       And cut off the brown girl's head,
   And kicked it against the wall, wall, wall,
       And kicked it against the wall,

17   Saying, "O bury Fair Ellen at my side,
       And the brown girl at my feet, feet, feet,
       And the brown girl at my feet."

G

"Fair Ellenger." Communicated by Mrs. Hilary G. Richardson, Clarksburg, Harrison County, 1917; obtained from Mrs. Nancy McDonald McAtee (cf. *Journal*, XXXII, 499, 504).

1   "O mother, dear mother, come tell to me,
       Come tell to me in one:
   Whether I shall marry Fair Ellenger,
       Or the brown girl go bring home."

2 "The brown girl she has house and land,
　　Fair Ellenger she has none;
　And before I charge you with my bless-on
　　The brown girl go bring home."

3 He put his foot in his right stir-rup,
　　So merrily rode away;
　He rode till he come to Fair Ellenger's hall,
　　And tingered low down at the ring.

4 There was none so ready as Fair Ellenger
　　To git up and let him in.
　"What news have you brought to me,
　　Lord Thomas?" she said.

5 "I've come to ask you to my wed-ding;
　　May the Lord have mercy on me."

6 "Now mother, now mother," she says to me,
　　"Come tell to me in one:
　Whether I shall go to Lord Thomas' wedding,
　　Or shall I tarry at home?"

7 "Perhaps a great many of your friends will be there,
　　And perhaps a great many of your foes;
　Before I charge you with my bless-on,
　　To Lord Thomas' wedding don't go."

8 She turned herself around about
　　And gazed up agin the wall:
　"Now mother," she says,
　　"To Lord Thomas' wedding I'll go."

9 Lord Thomas dressed himself in white,
　　Fair Ellenger dressed in green,
　And every town that they rid through,
　　They took her to be some queen.

10 They rid till they came to the brown girl's hall,
　　　He took Fair Ellenger by the hand,
　And led her through where the beds were made,
　　　And the tables were spread and the ladies were dancing
　　　　thereby.

11 He took her by the lily-white hand
　　And led her through the hall,
　And set her down in a golden cheer
　　Before the quality all.

12　"Is this your bride, Lord Thomas?" she said,
　　　"I'm sure she's wonderful brown;
　　You mought 'a' had me, as fair a ladee
　　　As ere the sun shone on."

13　The brown girl had a little penknife,
　　　The blade was keen and sharp;
　　She pierced it through Fair Ellenger's breast
　　　And pierced it to her heart.

14　Lord Thomas rode up in the hall
　　　Before the quality all,
　　And cut the brown girl's head off
　　　And kicked it agin the wall.

15　Lord Thomas he had a sword,
　　　The blade was keen and sharp;
　　He placed the handle agin the wall,
　　　The point toward his heart.

16　"Go dig my grave both wide and long,
　　　Go dig it wide and deep;
　　Place Fair Ellenger in my arms,
　　　The brown girl at my feet."

H

"The Brown Girl." Communicated by Miss Lalah Lovett, Bulltown, Braxton County, May, 1917; obtained from Caroline Flemming of Napier, West Virginia, who learned it from Lulu Bosely of Bulltown.

1　Lord Thomas, Lord Thomas was a fine young man,
　　　He was lord of three great towns;
　　He courted Fair Ellen to make her his bride,
　　　And to make a bridegroom for her.

2　"Come, father, come, mother, I'd ask your advice,
　　　I'd ask you both at once:
　　Whether to marry Fair Ellen, my dear,
　　　Or bring the brown girl home."

3　"The brown girl has both house and land,
　　　Fair Ellen she has none;
　　As my advice, 't would be a God's blessing,
　　　To bring the brown girl home."

4 He saddled up his milk-white horse,
    Rode down to Fair Ellen's home;
And none was so ready as Fair Ellen herself
    To arise and bid him walk in.

5 "What news, what news, Lord Thomas," she said,
    "What news have you brought to me now?"
"I've come to ask you to my wedding."
    "That's very sad news," said she.

6 She dressed herself in scarlet red,
    Her seven maids in green;
And every town that they rode through,
    They took her to be some queen.

7 They rode till they came to Lord Thomas' gate,
    They rang their bells and dingled their rings;
And none was so ready as Lord Thomas himself
    To arise and bid her walk in.

8 He took her by the lily-white hand,
    And led her in at the hall,
And set her down at the head of the table
    Among the ladies all.

9 "Is that your wife, Lord Thomas?" she said,
    "Indeed she looks quite brown;
You once could have married as fair a young lady
    As ever came into this town."

10 "Don't throw on slurs, Fair Ellen," he said,
    "Don't throw on slurs at me;
For I'd much better love the brown girl's home
    Than to love your hope by day."

11 The brown girl having a knife in her bosom,
    It being both sharp and keen,
She plunged it through Fair Ellen's ribs
    Between the short and the long.

12 "O what is the matter, Fair Ellen?" he said,
    "What makes you look so pale?
You once had two as red rosy cheeks
    As ever two eyes did see."

13   "O what is the matter, Lord Thomas?" she said,
         "O can't you plainly see?
     O can't you see my own heart's blood
         A-flowing away from me?"

14   He took the brown girl by the hand
         And led her out into the hall,
     And with the sword cut off her head,
         And kicked it against the wall.

15   Then placing the sword against the wall,
         The spear next to his heart,
     Saying, "Here lies three persons all bound to die —
         Lord send their souls to rest!"

16   "Go dig our grave in the roses red,
         Go dig it wide and deep,
     And bury Fair Ellen all in my arms,
         And the brown girl at my feet."

I

"Lord Thomas."   Communicated by Miss Maude Groves, Deepwell,
Nicholas County, July, 1917; obtained from Minnie Taylor, Fenwick, West
Virginia, who learned it from Mrs. Rhode Ramenes, Yadkin, Arkansas, 1914.

1   "O mother, come and riddle to me,
        The things I dreamed last night:
    Which to bring the brown girl home,
        Or make Fair Elender my bride."

2   "The brown girl having house and land,
        Fair Elender she has none;
    O go and please your dear mother,
        And bring the brown girl home."

3   Lord Thomas he rode and he rode,
        Till he came to Fair Elender's hall,
    And none was half so willing as Fair Elender herself
        To rise and let him in.

4   "Lord Thomas . . .
        What news have you brought to me?"
    "I have come to ask you to my wedding,
        To-morrow it shall be."

5   "Bad news, bad news, Lord Thomas," she said,
      "Bad news to me," . . .

   .   .   .   .

    .   .   .   .

6   Next day she dressed in her scarlet bright,
      Her maids all dressed in green;
  Every city they'd pass through,
      They were taken to be some queen.

7   She rode, she rode till she came to Lord Thomas' hall,
      She jingled at the ring;
  None was half so willing as Lord Thomas himself
      To rise and let her in.

8   He took her by the lily-white hand,
      And led her through the marble hall;
  He took her in the parlor,
      And set her among those ladies all.

9   "Lord Thomas, is this your bride?
      Why, she is scornfully brown;
  When you could have chosen a fairer lady
      As ever the sun shone on."

10   The brown girl having a little penknife,
      Though very keen and sharp,
  Between the long ribs and the short
      She pierced Fair Elender's heart.

11   Lord Thomas having a little sword,
      Very keen and sharp,
  He cut off the brown girl's head
      And kicked it against the wall.

12   Placing the handle to the floor,
      The point toward the heart:
  "Did you ever see three lovers meet,
      As soon as these three part?

13   "So take us to the graveyard,
      So wonderfully complete;
  Bury Fair Elender in my arms,
      The brown girl at my feet."

J

"Lord Thomas and Fair Eleanor."   Communicated by Mrs. Elizabeth Tapp Peck, Morgantown, Monongalia County, March 31, 1916; obtained from her mother, Mrs. Thomas H. Tapp, who learned it from her mother, Mrs. Elizabeth Wade Mack, who lived near Bethel church.   An abbreviated variant in nine stanzas.

K

"Lord Thomas and Fair Ellender." Communicated by Miss Mabel Richards, Fairmont, Marion County, October, 1915; obtained from Mrs. J. P. Lang, who learned it from Mrs. Katherine Zinn of Monongalia County.   A fragment of two stanzas.

I I

FAIR MARGARET AND SWEET WILLIAM

(CHILD, No. 74)

SEVEN variants have been recovered in West Virginia under the titles: "Sweet William," "Lady Margaret," and "Lady Margaret's Ghost." A glance at these ballads shows that they are largely identical; a comparison with the Child versions indicates that they are to be classed with group A, B, as witnessed by the blue suit, the dream of white swine, and the seven brethren.

For American texts see Child, v, 293 (Massachusetts); *Journal*, XIX, 281 (Belden; Missouri); XXIII, 381 (Combs; Kentucky); XXVIII, 154 (Perrow; North Carolina); XXX, 303 (Kittredge; Missouri); XXXI, 74 (Waugh; Ontario); XXXV, 340 (Tolman and Eddy; Ohio); Wyman and Brockway, p. 94 (Kentucky); McGill, p. 69 (Kentucky; reprinted by Pound, No. 16); Campbell and Sharp, No. 17 (Tennessee, Kentucky, North Carolina, Virginia); *Focus*, IV, 426 (Virginia); Ralph, *Harper's Monthly Magazine*, July, 1903, CVII, 272 (Kentucky); Mackenzie, p. 124 (Nova Scotia); Smith, p. 18 (two tunes); Minish MS. (North Carolina). Cf. Shearin and Combs, p. 8; Belden, No. 5; F. C. Brown, p. 9; *Bulletin*, Nos. 2–6, 8–10; Cox, XLV, 159; Reed Smith, *Journal*, XXVIII, 200.

A

"Sweet William." Communicated by Mr. G. T. Federer, Morgantown, Monongalia County, January, 1917; taken from a manuscript song book belonging to Lizzie Kelley, Independence, Preston County, who obtained it from Mintie Herskille.

1 Sweet William arose one merry May morning
    And dressed himself in blue:
 "Come and tell of the long, long love
    Between Lady Margaret and you."

2 "I know nothing of Lady Margaret,
    Lady Margaret knows nothing of me;
 And before eight o'clock on to-morrow, morrow morn
    Lady Margaret my bride shall be."

3 As Lady Margaret was sitting in her bedroom door,
    A-combing her long yellow hair;
 And who should she spy but Sweet William and his bride,
    As the churchyard they passed by?

4 'T was down she threw her ivory comb
    And back she threw her hair;
 There was a fair maid went out of the room
    That was nevermore seen there.

5   When the day was gone and the night come on,
        When most of the men were asleep,
    Sweet William he dreamed he saw Lady Margaret,
        Standing at his bed's feet.

6   When the night was gone and the day come on,
        And most of the men were awake,
    Sweet William he told of a dream
        That made his heart to ache.

7   Sweet William he called the merry maids all,
        They came by one, two, three;
    He asked liberty of his newly-married bride
        Lady Margaret to go and see.

8   He rode until he came to Margaret's gate,
        He rattled on the ring;
    Then was none so ready as Lady Margaret's brother
        To arise and let him in.

9   "Is Lady Margaret in the dining room?
        Or is she in the hall?
    Or is she in her high chamber,
        Among the merry maids all?"

10 "She is not in the dining room,
        Nor is she in the hall;
    She is in her lead coffee,[1]
        With her pale face turned to the wall."

11 "Roll down, roll down those snow-white sheets
        That are of Holland so fine;
    Let me kiss those pale cold lips
        That so ofttimes have kissed mine."

12 'T was once he kissed her snow-white brow,
        And twice he kissed her chin;
    Three times he kissed her pale cold lips:
        That pierced his heart within,

13 Lady Margaret was buried on Wismer day,[2]
        Sweet William was buried to-morrow;
    Lady Margaret was buried under a weeping willow,
        Sweet William was buried under another.

---

1. For *coffin*.   2. A mistake for *as it were to-day*.

14 And out of her grave there sprang a red rose,
    And out of his a brier;
  They grew and they tied in a true lover's knot,
    The red rose around the brier.

15 They grew and they tied in a true lover's knot,
    And they lived and died together;
  Lady Margaret she died of pure, pure love,
    Sweet William died of sorrow.

ℬ

"Lady Margaret." Communicated by Mr. J. R. Waters, Morgantown, Monongalia County; obtained from Mrs. W. F. Brown, Belington, Barbour County, who learned it more than fifty years ago in Delaware County, Ohio. Printed by Cox, XLV, 378, 388.

1 Sweet William rose one morning bright,
    And dressed himself in blue:
  "Come tell to me the long lost love,
    Between Lady Margaret and you."

2 "I know no harm of Lady Margaret," said he,
    "And I hope she knows none of me;
  But to-morrow morning before eight o'clock,
    Lady Margaret my bride shall be."

3 As Lady Margaret was in her chamber high,
    A-combing up her hair,
  She spied Sweet William and his bride,
    As they to the church drew near.

4 She threw down her ivory comb
    And tossed back her hair;
  And from the room a fair lady came
    That was seen in there no more.

5 The day being gone and the night being come,
    When most men were asleep,
  Sweet William spied Lady Margaret's ghost,
    A-standing at his bed feet.

6 "How do you like your bed?" said she,
    "And how do you like your sheet?
  And how do you like the fair lady,
    That lies in your arms asleep?"

7 "Very well do I like my bed," said he,
    "Very well do I like my sheet;
But better do I like the fair lady,
    That is standing at my bed feet."

8 The night being gone and the day being come,
    When most men were awake,
Sweet William said he was troubled in his head
    From a dream he had last night.

9 He called his weary waiting maids,
    By one, by two, by three;
And last of all, with his bride's consent,
    Lady Margaret he went to see.

10 He went unto the parlor door,
    He knocked until he made things ring;
But none was so ready as her own dear brother
    To arise and let him in.

11 "Is Lady Margaret in the parlor?" said he,
    "Or is she in the hall?
Or is she in her chamber high
    Among the gay ladies all?"

12 "Lady Margaret is not in the parlor," said he,
    "She is neither in the hall;
But she is in her coffin
    And a-lying by the wall."

13 "Tear down, tear down those milk-white sheets,
    They are made of silk so fine;
That I may kiss Lady Margaret's cheek,
    For ofttimes she has kissed mine."

14 The first that he kissed was her rosy cheek,
    The next was her dimpled chin;
The last of all was her clay-cold lips:
    That pierced his heart within.

15 "Tear down, tear down those milk-white sheets,
    They are made of silk so fine;
To-day they hang around Lady Margaret's corpse,
    And to-morrow they will hang around mine."

16 Lady Margaret died of pure, pure love,
    Sweet William died of sorrow;
  They are buried in one burying ground,
    Both side and side together.

17 Out of her grave grew a red rose,
    And out of his a briar;
  They grew in a twining true-lover's knot,
    The rose and the green briar.

C

"Sweet William." Contributed by Miss Sallie D. Jones, Hillsboro, Pocahontas County, January, 1917; learned about forty-six years ago from Miss
M. E. Harper, Pendleton County; assisted in remembering by Mrs. Dickenson
and Mrs. Forest Hammer, Franklin, Pendleton County.

1 Sweet William arose one May misty morning,
    And dressed himself in blue:
  "Come tell unto me the long, long love
    Between Lady Margaret and you."

2 "I know nothing about Lady Margaret," he said,
    "Lady Margaret knows nothing about me;
  But to-morrow morning about eight o'clock,
    Lady Margaret my bride shall be."

3 Lady Margaret was sitting in her high dawning window,
    Combing her long, yellow hair;
  When whom should she spy but Sweet William and his
      bride,
    As they drew nigh to the church.

4 She dashed down her ivory comb
    And tossed back her long, yellow hair,
  And departed from the high dawning window,
    And was never more seen there.

5 The day being past and night coming on,
    When most of the men were asleep,
  Lady Margaret's ghost it did appear
    At Sweet William's own bed feet.

6 "How do you like your bed?" said she,
    And how do you like your sheet?
  And how do you like your newly-wedded bride,
    Who lies in your arms asleep?"

7 "Very well do I like my bed," said he,
    "Very well do I like my sheet;
But the dearest of all is the dear little girl,
    Who stands at my bed feet."

8 The night being past and the day coming on,
    When most of the men were awake,
Sweet William he said, "I am troubled in my mind,
    By the dream that I dreamed last night."

9 . . . .
      . . . .

"I dreamed that my hall was haunted by white swine,
    And my bed was floating away."

10 He called up his merry maids all
    And dressed six of them in green,
Saying, "Take up my newly wedded bride,
    For Lady Margaret I'll go see."

11 . . . .
      . . . .

He rode all day and he rode all night,
    He rode till he came to her hall.

12 Sweet William tingled at the bell,
    As there was no other;
Who was so ready as to rise and let him in
    As Lady Margaret's own brother?

13 "O is she in her chamber high?
    Or is she in the hall?
Or is she in her kitchen room,
    Among her maidens all?"

14 "She is neither in her chamber high,
    She is neither in her hall;
But yonder she lies on her cold coffin lid,
    With her pale face turned to the wall."

15 "Fall down, fall down, ye milk-white sheets,
    White hollands ye are so fine,
That I may kiss the clay-cold lips
    That ofttimes have kissed mine."

16   Three times he kissed her on the cheek,
            Three times he kissed her chin;
        Three times he kissed her clay-cold lips,
            And it pierced his heart within.

D

"Lady Margaret's Ghost."   Communicated by Mr. George Paugh, Thomas,
Tucker County, April 15, 1916; obtained from Mrs. Martha Johnson, Hen-
dricks, Tucker County, who learned it when a girl.

1   Sweet William arose one May morning,
            And dressed himself in blue:
        "Come tell unto me this long, long love
            That's between Lady Margaret and you."

2   "I know nothing of Lady Margaret,
            And Lady Margaret knows nothing of me;
        But to-morrow morning at eight o'clock
            Lady Margaret my bride shall be."

3   Lady Margaret was sitting in her bow [1] door
            Combing her yellow hair,
        And who should she spy but Sweet William and his bride,
            In the church yard they passed by.

4   Down she threw her ivory comb,
            Back she flung her hair,
        Down she fell from her bowing [1] door,
            And never again seen there.

5   As the day being done and the night drawing on,
            And most of the men were asleep;
        Who should appear at Sweet William's bed,
            But gay Lady Margaret's ghost?

6   "How do you like your bed?" said she,
            "And how do you like your sheet?
        And how do you like this new wedded wife
            That lies in your arms asleep?"

7   "Very well, very well do I like my bed,
            Better do I like my sheet;
        And best of all is that gay lady
            That stands at my bed feet."

1. Mistake for *bower*.

8   As the night being gone and the day drawing on,
     And most of the men were awake,
   Sweet William said he was troubled in his head
     Of the dream he had last night.

9   "O is she in her dining room?
     Or is she in the hall?
   Or is she in her bed chamber
     Among her maidens all?"

10   "She is not in her dining room,
     Or is she in her hall;
   But she is laying in her lead coffin,
     With her pale face turned to the wall."

11   "Turn down, turn down those lily-white sheets,
     Lay back those laces fine;
   And let me kiss those cold, cold lips
     That ofttimes have kissed mine."

12   Up spoke her brothers, all but one,
     "Go home, go home, go home!
   Go home to your wedded wife,
     And let our dead sister alone."

13   Sweet William he died of pure love,
     Lady Margaret died of sorrow;
   Lady Margaret was buried in the church yard,
     And Sweet William buried by her.

14   Out of her grave grew a red, red rose,
     And out of his grew a brier;
   They grew up to the church steeple top,
     Till they could grow no higher;
   And there they tied in a true lover's knot,
     The red rose and the brier.

ℰ

"Lady Margaret." Communicated by Mrs. Hilary G. Richardson, Clarksburg, Harrison County, 1917; obtained from Mrs. Nancy McDonald McAtee.

1   Her father says to Sweet William:
     "Come tell to me this long, long love
     Betwixt Lady Margaret and thee."

2 "I know nothing of Lady Margaret,
       Nor Lady Margaret knows nothing of me;
   But to-morrow, agin eight o'clock,
       Lady Margaret my bride shall be."

3 Lady Margaret up in her high story,
       A-combin' her long yellow hair;
   And who should she see but Love William with his bride,
       As they went ridin' by?

4 Down she throwed her ivory comb,
       And tore down her long yellow hair,
   And throwed herself from the top of the high hall,
       Where she never was no more seen.

5 The very next morning Love William arose,
       And he dressed in the best of his clothes,
   And he said, "I am troubled in my mind
       With a dream I dremp last night.

6 "For I dremp that my household
       Was all covered with a white shroud,
   And my merry maids all in tears."

7 And he never rested till he got relief,
       From his nuby [1] wedded wife,

   .   .   .   .

       Lady Margaret he might see.

8 He put his foot in his right stirrup
       And merrily rode away;
   He rode till he came to Lady Molly's hall,
       And tingered low at the ring.[2]

9 There was none so ready as the seventh brother
       To git up and let him in:
   "Where is Lady Molly?   Is she in her chamber hall,
       Or is she in her chamber so high?"

10 "Lady Molly she's not in her chamber hall,
        Lady Molly's in her lead coffin,
    And her face cold against the wall."

1. Mistake for *newly*.
2. With this stanza compare G 3 of "Lord Thomas and Fair Annet," p. 59.

11   "Tear down those milk-white sheets,
          And let me git a kiss from her cold dyin' lips,
      For ofttimes she's kissed mine."

12   Three times he kissed her cold dyin' lips,
          Three times he kissed her chin;
      And when he kissed her cold dyin' lips,
          He pierced his heart with tears.

13   Lady Molly died this one glad day,
          Sweet William died to-morrow;
      Lady Molly died for the loss of her dear,
          Sweet William died for sorrow.

14   Lady Molly was buried in the green churchyard,
          Sweet William was buried close by her;
      And out of her breast grew a red rose bush,
          And from his'n there grew a brier.
      And there they tied in a true-lover's knot,
          The red rose and the brier.

F

"Lady Margaret." Contributed by Miss Polly McKinney, Sophia, Raleigh
County, 1919.

1   Sweet William arose one May, May morning,
          He dressed himself in blue:
      "Pray tell to me a long, long life
          Between Lady Margaret and you."

2   "I know no harm of sweet Lady Margaret,
          And she knows none of me;
      By eight o'clock to-morrow morning
          Lady Margaret my bride shall be."

3   Lady Margaret was sitting in her own dining room,
          Combing back her yellow hair,
      When who should she see but Sweet William and his bride,
          Both down to the church did go?

4   "Is Lady Margaret in her dining room?
          Or among those ladies all?
      Or is she dead and in her coffin,
          A-leaning against the wall?"

5　"Lady Margaret is neither in her own dining room,
　　　Nor among those ladies all;
　　But she is dead and in her coffin,
　　　A-leaning against the wall."

6　"Raise up, raise up those winding sheets
　　　That look so neat and fine,
　　And let me kiss Lady Margaret's lips,
　　　As often as she's kissed mine."

7　The first he kissed was on her cheek,
　　　The next was on her chin;
　　The next he kissed was her cold clay lips,
　　　And he wished that life was in.

8　Lady Margaret was buried in the old churchyard,
　　　Sweet William by her side;
　　Out of her grave there sprang a red rose,
　　　And out of his grave a green brier.

9　They grew to the top of the old church wall,
　　　They could not grow any higher;
　　They twittered and they twined in a true lovers' knot,
　　　The red rose and the green brier.

G

"Sweet William." Communicated by Mr. C. Woofter, Glenville, Gilmer County, December 1923; obtained from Mr. Charles L. Ayers, Revere, who was killed in France, 1918. He got it on Standing Stone, Wirt County.

1　Sweet William rode one morning bright,
　　　And dressed himself in blue:
　　"Come tell me the long lost love
　　　Between Lady Margaret and you."

2　"I know no harm of Lady Margaret," said he,
　　　"And I hope she knows none of me,
　　But to-morrow morning before eight o'clock
　　　Lady Margaret my bride shall be."

3　As Lady Margaret was in her chamber high,
　　　A-combing up her hair,
　　She spied Sweet William and his bride,
　　　As they to the church drew near.

4   She threw down her ivory comb
    And tossed back her hair;
And from the room a fair lady came,
    That was seen in there no more.

5   The day being gone and the night being come,
    When most men are asleep,
Sweet William spied Lady Margaret's ghost,
    A-standing at his bed feet.

6   "How do you like your bed?" said she,
    "And how do you like your sheet?
And how do you like the fair lady
    That lies in your arms asleep?"

7   "Very well I like my bed," said he,
    "Very well I like my sheet,
But better do I like the fair lady
    That is standing at my bed feet."

8   The night being gone and the day being come,
    When most men are awake,
Sweet William said he was troubled in his head
    From a dream he had last night.

9   He called his weary waiting maids,
    By one, by two, by three;
And the last of all, with his bride's consent,
    Lady Margaret he went to see.

10 He went unto the parlor door,
    He knocked till he made things ring:
But none was so ready as his own dear brother
    To rise and let him in.

11 "Is Lady Margaret in the parlor?" said he,
    "Or is she in the hall?
Or is she in her chamber high
    Among the gay ladies all?"

12 "Lady Margaret is not in the parlor," said he,
    "She is neither in the hall;
But she is in her coffin,
    A-lying by the wall."

13 "Tear down, tear down those milk-white sheets,
    They are made of silk so fine,
That I may kiss Lady Margaret's cheek,
    For ofttimes she has kissed mine."

14 The first that he kissed was her rosy cheek,
    The next was her dimpled chin;
The last of all was her clay-cold lips:
    That pierced his heart within.

15 "Tear down, tear down those milk-white sheets,
    They are made of silk so fine;
To-day they hang around Lady Margaret's corpse,
    And to-morrow they will hang around mine."

16 Lady Margaret died of pure, pure love,
    Sweet William died of sorrow;
They are buried in one burying ground,
    Both side and side together.

17 Out of her grave grew a red, red rose,
    And out of his a green briar;
They grew and they grew to the church-steeple top,
    And they could not grow any higher.

18 They grew into a twining true-lover's knot,
    The rose and the green briar;
They grew into a twining true-lover's knot,
    For all true lovers to admire.

I 2

LORD LOVEL

(CHILD, NO. 75)

FIVE variants have been recovered, under the titles: "Lord Lovel," "Lord Lover," and "Lord Leven." They are all to be classed with Child H. A is practically identical with Child H to the end of the seventh stanza. Stanza 8 is made up of verses 1 and 2 of Child 8, and 3 and 4 of Child H 9. Stanza 9 is the same as Child H 10. In additions and corrections to "Lord Lovel" Mr. Child has the following: "211 H. I have received a copy recited by a lady in Cambridge, Massachusetts, which was evidently derived from print, and differs but slightly from a, omitting 8 $^{3, 4}$, 9 $^{1, 2}$." It would seem that the Massachusetts version and West Virginia A are identical.

B is the same as Child H stanza for stanza, but the phraseology is not quite so close as is that of West Virginia A. C, more or less fragmentary, does not differ materially from A and B. Stanza D 4 is not found in Child H. Cf. Child C 4. E shows some likenesses to Child D. The name "Lady Ouncebell" is found in this form in Child A 1.

For American texts see *Journal*, XVIII, 291 (Barry; Massachusetts, Connecticut, Rhode Island); XIX, 283 (Belden; Kentucky, Missouri); Shoemaker, p. 124 (Pennsylvania); McGill, p. 9 (Kentucky); Focus, IV, 215 (Virginia); Campbell and Sharp, No. 18 (North Carolina); Clifton Johnson, *What They Say in New England*, p. 225; Pound, No. 2 (Illinois, Wyoming); Ralph, *Harper's Monthly Magazine*, July, 1903, CVII, 272; Minish MS. (North Carolina). Cf. Barry, No. 14; Belden, No. 6; Shearin and Combs, p. 8; Pound, p. 9; *Bulletin*, Nos. 2–10; Reed Smith, *Journal*, XXVIII, 199.

No old ballad has oftener been printed in American song-books and broadsides. See references, which could be indefinitely extended, in *Journal*, XXIX, 160, note 1. It has sometimes been sung as a comic ditty: see, for example, *Bob Smith's Clown Song Book*, p. 51 ("as sung by Bob Smith"). A satirical parody beginning "Lord Lovell he sat in St. Charles's Hotel," was popular in the sixties and has often been printed (for example, in *Tony Pastor's New Union Song Book*, cop. 1862, p. 66, "The New Ballad of Lord Lovell" in *Frank Moore's Songs of the Soldiers* [New York, 1864], p. 174; and in R. G. White's *Poetry, Lyrical, Narrative, and Satirical of the Civil War* [New York, 1866], p. 115); Belden has found it in Missouri (No. 128). Another, called "Ye Ballade of Mans. Lovell," is in Frank Moore's *Personal and Political Ballads* (New York, 1864), p. 321. A Confederate parody, "Where are you going, Abe Lincoln?" is printed in *Allan's Lone Star Ballads* (Galveston, 1874), p. 31. For a recent parody see Carolyn Wells, *A Parody Anthology*, p. 326.

A

"Lord Lovel." Contributed by Miss Blanche Satterfield, Fairmont, Marion County, 1915; learned from her mother, who learned it from her mother, a lady of English descent, who came from Washington County, Pennsylvania. Printed by Cox, XLIV, 350.

1   Lord Lovel he stood at his castle gate,
        A-combing his milk-white steed;
    When along came Lady Nancy Bell,
        A-wishing her lover good speed,
        A-wishing her lover good speed.

2   "O where are you going, Lord Lovel?" she said,
        "O where are you going?" said she;
    "I'm going, my dear Nancy Bell,
        Strange countries for to see."

3   "O when will you be back, Lord Lovel?" she said,
        "O when will you be back?" said she.
    "In a year or two or three at the least
        I'll return to my Lady Nancy."

4   He had n't been gone but a year and a day,
        Strange countries for to see,
    When a languishing thought came into his mind,
        Lady Nancy Bell he must see.

5   He rode and he rode upon his white steed,
        Till he came to London Town;
    And there he heard St. Varner's bell,
        And the people all mourning round.

6   "Is anybody dead?" Lord Lovel he said,
        "Is anybody dead?" said he.
    "A lord's daughter 's dead," a lady replied,
        "And some call her Lady Nancy."

7   He ordered the grave to be opened forthwith
        And the shroud to be folded down;
    And there he kissed the clay-cold lips,
        Till the tears came trinkling down.

8   Lady Nancy she died as it might be to-day,
        Lord Lovel he died to-morrow;
    And out of her bosom there grew a red rose,
        And out of Lord Lovel's a briar.

9 They grew and they grew till they reached the church top,
   And there they could n't grow any higher;
And there they entwined in a true lover's knot,
   Which true lovers always admire.

B

"Lord Leven." Communicated by Mrs. Hilary G. Richardson, Clarksburg, Harrison County, who obtained it from Mrs. Nancy McDonald McAtee.

1 Lady Nancy Belle was standing in her door,
   And who should she spy
But Lord Leven,
   A-dressing up his milk-white steed.

2 "Where are you going, Lord Leven?" she said,
   "O where are you going from me?"
"I am a-going, Lady Nancy Belle,
   Strange countries for to see."

3 "How long will you be gone, Lord Leven?" she said,
   "How long will you be gone from me?"
"Twelve months and a day, Lady Nancy Belle,
   And then I'll return to thee."

4 "That's too long, Lord Leven," she said,
   "Too long to be gone from me;
You'll soon forget Lady Nancy Belle
   And take up with some other ladie."

5 . . . .
     . . . .
He put his foot in his right stirrup,
   And merrily rode away.

6 He had not rode not many miles,
   Not over two or three,
Till a ring busted off his little finger,
   And his nose began to bleed.

7 . . . .
     . . . .
"I'll turn myself back home again,
   Lady Nancy Belle I'll see."

8 He had not rode not half way home again,

   . . . .

 Till he heard the noise of the church-bell ring,
  And the ladies come mourning thereby.

9 "O who is sick, or who is dead,
  I pray you will me tell."
 "It's a fine young lady," some answered and said,
  "And her name it is Nancy Belle."

10 Nancy Belle died this one glad day,
  Lord Leven died to-morrow;
 Nancy Belle died for the loss of her dear,
  Lord Leven died for sorrow.

11 Lady Nancy was buried in the green church yard,
  Lord Leven was buried close by;
 From her breast grew a red, red rose,
  From his'n grew a brier.
 They grew till they come to the top of the church,
  And they could not grow no higher.

C

"Lord Lovel." Contributed by Miss Maud Groves, Deepwell, Nicholas County, 1915, who learned it about twenty years ago from Mrs. Margaret McClung. Reported by Cox, XLV, 159.

1 Lord Lovel was standing at his own castle gate,
  Saddling his own white steed;
 When who should come along but Lady Ouncebell,
  A-wishing her lover God speed?

2 "O where are you going, Lord Lovel?" she said,
  "O where are you going to-day?"
 "I am going away to some far, far land,
  I am going away to sea."

3 "When will you return, Lord Lovel?" she said,
  "When will you return to me?"
 "In the space of three years I'll return, my love,
  To the face of a fair lady."

4 He had not been gone not more than two weeks,
  I'm sure it was not three,
 Till something came over his mind,
  Lady Ouncebell he must see.

5   He rode, he rode along the way,
        Till he came to London Town;
    And there he heard St. Mary's church bell;
        The ladies were weeping around.

6   "O who is dead?" Lord Lovel he said,
        "O who's to be buried to-day?"
    "Lady Ouncebell died for a false young man;
        Lord Lovel she called his name."

7   He ordered the coffin be opened,
        The snow white sheets let down;
    And as he kissed the clay-cold lips,
        The tears came trinkling down.

8   "These are your clay-cold lips I kiss,
        But you will never kiss mine;
    I vow, I vow, and I'll vow to thee,
        I'll never kiss lips but thine."

9   Lady Ouncebell died as it were to-day,
        Lord Lovel he died to-morrow,
    Lady Ouncebell died of a pure, pure love,
        Lord Lovel he died of sorrow.

10 Lady Ouncebell was buried in St. Mary's churchyard,
        Lord Lovel was buried close by her;
    And out of her grave, a rose grows,
        And out of Lord Lovel's, a brier.

11 They grew, they grew up the church wall,
        Till they could grow no higher;
    And there they entwined in a true-lover's knot
        And remain there forever.

D

"Lord Lovel." Communicated by Miss Lucille V. Hays, Glenville, Gilmer County, November 22, 1916; obtained from her mother, who learned it from her mother, and she from her mother, Mrs. Zackwell Morgan, a lady of Welsh descent. Very similar to A.

E

"Lord Lover." Communicated by Mrs. Mabel Richards, Fairmont, Marion County, December 14, 1915; obtained from Mrs. P. J. Lang, Lowesville, who learned it about thirty years ago from Mrs. Katherine Zinn, Monongalia County. Reported by Cox, XLV, 159. Very similar to A.

13

THE LASS OF ROCH ROYAL

(CHILD, No. 76)

ONE complete version (A) and a fragment (B) have been recovered in West Virginia.

A

"Fair Annie and Gregory." Contributed by Mrs. J. J. Haines, Parkersburg, Wood County, January 15, 1916, who writes: "I have heard these old ballads sung from my earliest recollection by my grandparents and others. Grandfather's name was Benjamin Franklin Roberts; grandmother's name was Mary Leatherman Roberts. Grandfather's mother was a descendant of the Franklins, but I do not know whether of Benjamin Franklin's father's family, or a brother. My ancestors on both sides came to America in the time of the colonization." Printed by Cox, XLV, 347.

This excellent version of "The Lass of Roch Royal," though derived by the contributor from an oral source, probably goes back to print. It seems to be formed from Jamieson's text (*Popular Ballads*, 1806, I, 37) and from Scott's (*Minstrelsy*, 1802, II, 49), chiefly from the former. Thus one may account for its close resemblance to Child's D and for the points which it has in common with Child's E, as well as for the name "Loch Royan" (Child's B). Cf. *Journal*, XXX, 304.

1 "O who will shoe my bonny feet,
       Or who will glove my hand,
   Or who will lace my middle waist
       With a new-made London band?

2 "And who will comb my yellow hair
       With a new-made silver comb?
   And who will be my bairn's father,
       Till love Gregory comes home?"

3 "Your father will shoe your bonny feet,
       Your mother will glove your hand,
   Your sister will lace your middle waist
       With a new-made London band.

4 "Myself will comb your yellow hair
       With a new-made silver comb,
   And the Lord will be the bairn's father,
       Till Gregory comes home."

5 "O if I had a bonny ship,
       And men to sail with me,
   I would go to my true love,
       Since he will not come to me."

6 Her father gave her a fair ship
    And sent her to the strand;
  She has taken her young son in her arms
    And turned her back to land.

7 She had been sailing on the sea
    About a month or more,
  When she landed her bonny ship
    Near to her true love's door.

8 The night was dark and the wind was cold,
    And her love was fast asleep;
  And the bairn that was in her arms,
    Full sore began to weep.

9 Long stood she at her lover's door
    And long twirled at the pin;
  At length up got his false mother,
    Saying, "Who's that, that would be in?"

10 "O it is Annie of Loch Royan,
    Your love, come over the sea;
  Also your young son in her arms,
    So open the door to me."

11 "Away, away, you ill woman,
    You're not come here for good;
  You're but a witch or a vile warlock,
    Or a mermaid of the flood."

12 "I'm not a witch or a vile warlock,
    Nor a mermaiden," said she;
  "But I am Annie of Loch Royan;
    Please open the door to me."

13 "O if you be Annie of Loch Royan,
    As I believe you not to be,
  Now tell me some of the love tokens
    That have passed between thee and me."

14 "O do you mind, love Gregory,
    When we sat at the wine,
  How we changed the napkins from our necks?
    It's not so long a time.

15 "And yours was good, and good enough,
        But not so good as mine;
    For yours was of the cambric clear,
        But mine of the silk so fine.

16 "And do you not mind, love Gregory,
        As we two sat to dine,
    How we changed the rings from our fingers?
        And I can show thee thine.

17 "So open the door, love Gregory,
        And open it with speed,
    Or our young son in my arms
        From cold will soon be dead."

18 "Away, away, you false woman,
        Go from your door for shame;
    For I have gotten another fair love,
        So you may hie you home."

19 "O have you gotten another fair love,
        For all the oaths you sware?
    Then farewell, false Gregory,
        You will never see me more."

20 O early, early went she back,
        As the day began to peep;
    She set her foot on her good ship,
        And sorely she did weep.

21 Love Gregory started from his sleep
        And to his mother did say:
    "I dreamed a dream this night, mother,
        That fills my heart with woe.

22 "I dreamed that Annie of Loch Royan,
        The flower of all her kind,
    Was standing mourning at my door,
        And none would let her in."

23 "If it be Annie of Loch Royan,
        That you make all this din,
    She stood all last night at your door,
        But I'm sure she was not in."

24 "O woe betide you, false woman,
    An ill death may you die,
That would not open the door to her,
    Nor yet would waken me!"

25 O quickly, quickly raised he up
    And fast run to the strand;
And then he saw his fair Annie,
    Was sailing far from land.

26 "O Annie, and it's O Annie,
    O Annie, where do you abide?"
But all the more he cried "Annie,"
    The faster ran the tide.

27 The wind grew loud and the sea grew rough,
    And the ship was rent in twain;
And soon he saw his fair Annie
    Come floating through the foam.

28 He saw his young son in her arms,
    Both tossed about the tide;
He wrung his hands and fast he ran,
    And plunged into the sea so wide.

29 He caught her by the yellow hair,
    He drew her to the strand;
But cold and stiff was every limb,
    Before he reached the land.

30 O first he kissed her pale cheeks,
    And then he kissed her chin;
And then he kissed her bonny lips,
    But there was no breath within.

31 And he mourned over his fair Annie,
    Till the sun was going down;
Then with a sigh his heart did break,
    And his soul to heaven has flown.

B

"My Lady's Slipper." Communicated by Mr. R. S. Ridenour, Farmington, Marion County, January 1916; obtained from the Rev. W. J. Sharpes, who learned it about seventy years ago.

These two stanzas sometimes occur by themselves; so Child, III, 512 (from "the Carolina mountains"); Cox C; *Focus*, IV, 49. But they easily become associated with any song on the theme of lovers' parting. They turn up, accordingly, (1) in "The New-Slain Knight" (Child, No. 263); (2) in some forms of "The True Lover's Farewell" (as Cox, No. 137, and Campbell and Sharp, No. 61 A; Belden's collection); (3) in one version of "The Rejected Lover" (Campbell and Sharp, No. 56 A); (4) in "Cold Winter's Night" (Shearin, *Modern Language Review*, VI, 514; cf. Shearin and Combs, p. 8), which is a cross between (2) and (3); (5) in some forms of "Careless Love" (Perrow, *Journal*, XXVIII, 147, mixed with "The True Lover's Farewell"; *Focus*, III, 275); (6) in some versions of "The False Young Man" (Campbell and Sharp, No. 94 C; Babcock, *Folk-Lore Journal*, VII, 31, reprinted by Child, III, 511); (7) in "Kitty Kline" (Bascom, *Journal*, XXII, 240; cf. F. C. Brown, p. 9); (8) in "Blue-eyed Boy" (Belden's Missouri collection); in (9) in a comic ditty (Lomax, *The North Carolina Booklet*, July, 1911, XI, 29). The same stanzas, alone or in combination, are recorded in *Bulletin*, Nos. 2–10. They occur also in a West Virginia text of "The House Carpenter" (No. 25 C), in "John Hardy" (No. 35 E), and apparently in a North Carolina version of "Lord Randal," Child, No. 12 (F. C. Brown, p. 9). Cf. Reed Smith, *Journal*, XXVIII, 201, 202.

1   "Who will shoe your pretty little feet?
        Who will glove your hand?
    Who will kiss your sweet rosy lips,
        When I'm in a foreign land?"

2   "My father will shoe my pretty little feet,
        My mother will glove my hand,
    And you may kiss my sweet rosy lips,
        When you come from the foreign land."

14

THE WIFE OF USHER'S WELL

(CHILD, No. 79)

SEVEN variants have been recovered in West Virginia, under the titles: "A Moravian Song," "Lady Gay," "The Three Little Babes," and "A Lady Gay" (cf. Cox, XLV, 160). They all belong to the same version, and of the three versions printed by Child, they resemble most A. The best of the West Virginia copies are practically identical with the American text printed in Child V, 294. The main lines of the story are these: A lady who had three fair children sent them away to the North country to school, where, in short time, they died. She prays to the King in heaven to send them down to her, and about Christmas time they appear. She spreads a bountiful table for them, but they refuse to eat because they have food divine. She makes up a downy bed for them, with clean sheets and a golden spread, but they command her to take it off because it is vanity and sin. At the break of day they depart.

The prayer of the mother to have the children come back is not found in Child A. Cf. Child C 1. West Virginia texts A 9 and D 8 indicate the children come back to forbid obstinate grief, as the dead often do. This motive is not found in the Child versions. An ancient law compelled ghosts to return to their graves at the crowing of the cock. This law is observed in the Child versions, but in the West Virginia variants they act in obedience to the will of their Savior. A curious combination of the two compelling forces is found in West Virginia B 8.

For references to English and American versions see *Journal*, XXX, 305. Add Campbell and Sharp, No. 19; Pound, No. 7; Wyman MS., No. 16 (Kentucky); Minish MS. (North Carolina); *Bulletin*, No. 3, p. 5; No. 9, p. 6.

A

"A Moravian Song." Contributed by Miss Bettie R. Loy, Glebe, Hampshire County, February 17, 1916. She writes: "I am sending you a song that my mother learned of her mother, who was of Dutch descent, but either she or her parents learned it of a Moravian preacher and she called it a Moravian song."

1   There was a lady, a fair lady,
    And she had fair children three;
  She sent them away to the North country,
    To be taught their grammaree.

2   They'd been gone but a short time,
    About three weeks and a day,
  When death, swift death, came hastening along,
    And took those pretty ones away.

3 "There's a king in heaven, I know,
        A king that wears a crown;
   Pray send me down my children dear,
        To-night or in the morning soon."

4 It was about the New Year's time,
        The nights being long and cold,
   When lo! she saw her three little ones,
        Coming down to their mother's home.

5 She spread a table bounteously,
        And on it spread bread and wine,
   Saying, "Come eat and drink, children dear,
        Come eat and drink of mine."

6 "We want none of your bread, mother,
        And we want none of your wine;
   For we are children of the King,
        We have food and drink divine."

7 She spread a downy bed for them,
        And on it spread clean sheets;
   And on it she spread a golden spread,
        That they might for the better sleep.

8 "Take it off, take it off," the oldest said,
        "'T is vanity and sin;
   And woe, woe be to this wicked world,
        Since pride has so entered in!

9 "Place marble at our heads, mother,
        And cold clay at our feet;
   For all those tears that have been shed
        Shall but wet our winding sheet."

$\mathcal{B}$

"Lady Gay." Communicated by Anna Copley, Shoals, Wayne County,
January 28, 1916; written from the dictation of Mr. Burwell Luther.

1 Once there was a lady gay,
        And children she had three;
   She sent them away to the North country,
        To learn their grammaree.

2 They had n't been gone but a mighty little while,
        It was six weeks and a day,
   Till death came hastening all around,
        And killed those babes all three.

3   The Christmas times were coming on,
        And the nights were long and cold,
    When those three babes came running along,
        Down to their mother's hall.

4   She set a table before them,
        All covered with bread and wine;
    Saying, "Come my babes, my three little babes,
        Come and eat and drink of mine."

5   "We can't eat of your bread, mamma,
        Nor drink none of your wine;
    For woe be unto this wicked world,
        Since pride has first begun!"

6   She made a bed in the best room,
        All covered with white sheets;
    And the top one was a golden sheet,
        To make those infants sleep.

7   "Take it off, take it off," said the oldest one,
        "Take it off, take it off, I say;
    For yonder stands our Saviour dear,
        And to him we must return."

8   "Rise up, rise up," said the oldest one,
        "The chickens are crowing for day;
    For yonder stands our Saviour dear,
        And him we must obey."

C

"Lady Gay." Contributed by John B. Adkins, Branchland, Lincoln County, February 19, 1916; learned when a child from an old aunt, who learned it from her mother.

1   There lived in London a lady gay,
        And children she had three;
    She sent them away to a North country,
        To learn their grammaree.

2   They had not been there very long,
        Scarcely three weeks and a day,
    Until sweet death came hastening along,
        And stole those babes away.

3 "There is a King in heaven," she cried,
      "Who once did wear a crown;
  I pray send home my three little babes,
      To-night or in the morning soon."

4 She fixed them a bed in the backmost room,
      And on it spread a clean white sheet,
  And over the top a golden spread,
      So that they might sweetly sleep.

5 "Take it off, take it off," said the first oldest one,
      "Take it off, take it off, if you can;
  For woe unto this wicked world,
      When pride it first began!"

6 She set them a table both wide and long,
      And on it put bread and wine;
  Says, "Come eat, come eat, my three little babes,
      Come eat and drink of mine."

7 "We cannot eat your bread, mother,
      Nor can we drink your wine;
  For yonder stands our Saviour dear,
      And to him we must resign."

D

"Three Little Babes." Communicated by Mr. Decker Toney, Queens Ridge, Wayne County, January 20, 1916; learned from his mother, who learned it from her mother, Hannah Moore, and she, from her mother, Hannah Ross, who was born in Virginia. Printed by Cox, XLV, 11.

1 There was a lady, a lady gay,
      And children she had three;
  She sent them away to a North country,
      To learn their grammar.

2 They had not been there very long,
      But scarcely three weeks and a day,
  When death, cruel death, came hastily along,
      And taken those babes away.

3 She prayed God both day and night,
      And she prayed God at noon,
  That he might send those three little babes,
      That night or in the morning soon.

4   She was sitting in her back door,
        Gazing up the road;
    There she spied her three little babes,
        Coming down the road.

5   Her heart leaped forth with loving joy,
        A kiss and a prayer from her lips;
    She sprang forth [with] great joy,
        Her three little babes to meet.

6   She sprang to fold them in her arms,
        The tears flowing fastly away;
    "Stand back, stand back, dear mother,
        Our Saviour we must obey."

7   "What news, what news, my dear little babes,
        What news have you brought to me?
    What news have you brought, my dear little babes,
        From the foreign country?"

8   "Green grass grows at our head, dear mother,
        Cold clay lays at our feet;
    Every tear that rolls down your cheek,
        Wets our winding sheet."

9   She made a bed, a white plush bed,
        Spreaded over it a golden spread;
    Around the spread a golden fringe,
        So her three little babes might sleep.

10   "The table is sitting in the dining room,
        Spreaded over with bread and wine;
    Come eat, come drink, my three little babes,
        Come eat, come drink of mine."

11   "We do not want your bread, dear mother,
        Neither do we want your wine;
    For yonder stands my Saviour dear,
        To him we must resign.

12   "Farewell, farewell, dear mother,
        He is calling us to our fold;
    Yonder stands our Saviour;
        To him we must go."

ℰ

No local title. Communicated by Miss Mary M. Atkeson, Morgantown, Monongalia County, December 20, 1915; obtained from Mr. Joseph H. Spicer, Spring Gap, Hampshire County; learned from his mother, who learned it from her grandmother, who came from Ireland. Printed by Cox, XLIV, 388.

1 Once there was an old woman,
        And very wealthy was she;
    She had three great big boys,•
        And she sent them over the sea.

2 They had only been gone a week from her,
        A week, not more than three,
    When word came to that old woman,
        That her sons she'd never see.

F

"A Lady Gay." Communicated by Mr. C. D. Miller, Sandyville, Jackson County, February 24, 1916; dictated by his mother, who learned it in the time of the Civil War from Sindusky Kollings. A confused and fragmentary text in eight stanzas.

G

No local title. Communicated by Miss Mary M. Atkeson, Morgantown, Monongalia County, December 20, 1915; obtained from Mr. A. G. Springer, Farmington, Marion County; dictated by his mother, who learned it from her mother, a lady of Welsh and English ancestry, who came from Pennsylvania. The first two stanzas of a ballad, practically the same as A.

15

LITTLE MUSGRAVE AND LADY BARNARD

(Child, No. 81)

Diligent search has failed to recover any more of this ballad in West Virginia tradition than the following stanza, contributed by Mr. John Hill, Hughey, Logan County, January 7, 1916 (printed by Cox, XLVI, 22, 64; cf. 145). This was all he could remember except that a person named Matthew Groves, or Mathy Groves, was mentioned in the song.

> The first came down all dressed in red,
>> The next came down in green;
> The next came down Lord Daniel's wife,
>> As fair as any queen.

For Nova Scotia texts see Mackenzie, *Journal*, XXIII, 371, and XXV, 182 (*Quest*, p. 14). Texts from Kentucky (Wyman) and Missouri (Belden) are printed by Kittredge, *Journal*, XXX, 309; from North Carolina, Tennessee, and Kentucky, by Campbell and Sharp, No. 20 (29 B is reprinted by Pound, No. 15). For reports from Virginia, Kentucky, North Carolina, and South Carolina, see references in *Journal*, XXX, 309. Add *Bulletin*, Nos. 6, 7, 9, 11.

From Professor J. H. Combs, West Virginia University, April 12, 1924, the editor received the following version, "Sung by Mrs. Margaret Green, Knott County, Kentucky, and called 'Lord Daniel's Wife'" in 1910.

1   The first came down all dressed in red;
>> The next came down in green;
> The next came down Lord Daniel's wife,
>> She's as fine as any queen, queen,
>> She's as fine as any queen.

2   "Come and go home with me, little Gayly,
>> Come and go home with me to-night;
> For I know by the rings on your fingers
>> You are Lord Daniel's wife, wife," etc.

3   A little foot-spade [1] was standing there,
>> A-hearing all they say;
> He made a vow Lord Daniel should know
>> Before the break of day.

4   He had but sixteen miles to go,
>> And ten of them he run;
> He run till he came to a broken-down bridge,
>> He held his breath and swum.

---

1. Error for *foot-page*.

5 He swum till he came where grass grows green,
 He turned to heels and run;
 He run till he came to Lord Daniel's gate,
 He rattled those bells and rung.

6 "If this be false you bring to me,
 And I believe it to be,
 I'll build a gallows just for you,
 And hangen you shall be."

7 "If this be false I bring to you,
 As you believe it to be,
 You need not build the gallows for me,
 Just hang me on a tree."

8 He travelled over hills and valleys,
 Till he came to his staff stand still; [1]
 He placed his bugle-horn to his mouth,
 And blew most loud and shrill.

9 He took little Gayly by the hand
 And led her through the hall;
 He drew his sword and cut off her head,
 And kicked it against the wall.

[1] A corrupt line.

16

BONNY BARBARA ALLEN

(CHILD, No. 84)

TWELVE variants have been found in West Virginia under various titles. A is a very close reproduction of Child B, stanza for stanza, with an added stanza at the end not found in Child; B, in general, follows Child B, with two stanzas at the beginning not found anywhere in Child; C, D, E, J, agree closely with Child A; the first three stanzas of E are like Child B, the next five, like Child A; the leaving of three rolls of money to Barbara in F indicates some connection with the ballad in Buchan's MS. Cf. Child II, 276, also West Virginia G 3; in H 2 the lover defends himself, an incident not found in Child; for similar stanzas in American texts, see Smith, p. 13; *Journal*, XIX, 286; XIX, 287; XXII, 63; Campbell and Sharp, p. 90; Wyman and Brockway, p. 5; McGill, p. 39; Pound, p. 9. In this connection it is interesting to note that one of the American texts makes the lover acknowledge the charge as a just one (*Journal*, XX, 256).

For American texts, in song-books and in oral circulation, see references in *Journal*, XXIX, 160, XXX, 317; XXXV, 343. Add *Focus*, V, 282; Shoemaker, p. 107; Pound, No. 3; *Bulletin*, Nos. 6–10; Minish MS.

A

"Barbara Allen." Contributed by Mr. Lyndell O. Baker, Belington, Barbour County, January 28, 1915; learned about nine years before from Roy Keller, who learned it from his father in Tucker County. Printed by Cox, XLIV, 305.

1 In Scarlet town, where I was born,
    There was a fair maid dwelling,
Made every youth cry "Well away!"
    Her name was Barbara Allen.

2 All in the merry month of May,
    When green buds they are swelling,
Young Jimmy Green on his death bed lay
    For the love of Barbara Allen.

3 He sent his man unto her there,
    To the town where she was dwelling;
"O you must come to my master dear,
    If your name be Barbara Allen.

4 "For death is printed on his face
    And o'er his heart is stealing;
O haste away to comfort him,
    O lovely Barbara Allen!"

5   "If death is printed on his face
     And o'er his heart is stealing,
Yet little better shall he be
     For the love of Barbara Allen."

6   So, slowly, slowly she came up,
     And slowly she came nigh him;
And all she said when there she came,
     "Young man, I think you're dying."

7   He turned his face unto her straight,
     With deadly sorrow sighing:
"O lovely maid, come pity me!
     I'm on my death bed lying."

8   "If on your death bed you do lie,
     What need the tale you're telling?
I cannot keep you from your death:
     Farewell," said Barbara Allen.

9   He turned his face unto the wall,
     And deadly pains he fell in:
"Adieu, adieu, adieu to all,
     Adieu to Barbara Allen."

10   As she was walking o'er the fields,
     She heard the bell a-knelling;
And every stroke it seemed to say,
     "Unworthy Barbara Allen."

11   She turned herself around about
     And spied the corpse a-coming:
"Lay down, lay down the corpse," said she,
     "That I may look upon him."

12   With scornful eyes she did look down,
     Her cheeks with laughter swelling;
While all her friends cried out amen,[1]
     "Unworthy Barbara Allen!"

13   When he was dead and laid in grave,
     Her heart was struck with sorrow:
"O mother, mother, make my bed,
     For I shall die to-morrow.

1. Error for *amain*.

14   "Hard-hearted creature him to slight,
          He who loved me so dearly!
     O had I been more kind to him,
          When he was alive and near me!"

15   On her death bed as she did lay,
          She begged to be buried by him,
     And sorely repented of that day
          That she e'er did deny him.

16   "Farewell, ye virgins all," she said,
          "And shun the fault I've fell in;
     Henceforward take warning by the fall
          Of cruel Barbara Allen."

B

"Barbara Ellen." Communicated by Miss Lalah Lovett, Bulltown, Braxton County, 1916; obtained from Miss Martha Jenkins, Valley Point, Preston County, who learned it from Miss Callie Long, Morgantown, Monongalia County.

1   In Scotland I was bred and born,
          In London was my dwelling;
     I fell in love with a pretty maid,
          Her name was Barbara Ellen.

2   I courted her for months and weeks,
          Hoping that I might gain her;
     Although she solemnly replied,
          No man on earth should have her.

3   'T was in the merry month of May,
          The flowers and trees were swaying;
     A young man on his death bed lay
          For the love of Barbara Ellen.

4   He sent his servant to his home,
          To the place of Barbara's dwelling;
     "My master he doth call on thee,
          If thy name be Barbara Ellen."

5   Slowly she put on her things,
          And slowly she went to him;
     And all she said, when she got there,
          Was, "Young man, I think you're dying.

6   "And if it be for love of me
          You're on your death bed lying,
     But little better would you be
          For the love of Barbara Ellen.

7   "Do you remember last New Year's Eve,
          Way down at yonder dwelling,
     You drank a toast to all around
          And slighted Barbara Ellen?"

8   He turned his pale face to the wall,
          As death was creeping on him:
     "Farewell, farewell to all around,
          And adieu to Barbara Ellen."

9   As she was walking in the fields,
          She heard the bells a-tolling;
     And every toll it seemed to say,
          "O cruel Barbara Ellen!"

10 As she was walking in the street,
          She saw the corpse a-coming:
     "Lay down, lay down that corpse," she cried,
          "That I may gaze upon him."

11 "Mother, mother, make my bed,
          Make it soft and narrow;
     For Willie was buried for me to-day,
          And I'll die for him to-morrow."

12 One was buried in the high churchyard,
          The other in the choir;
     On one there grew a red rose bush,
          On the other there grew a brier.

13 They grew and they grew to the high steeple top,
          Till they could grow no higher;
     And there they locked in a true-lover's knot,
          For true lovers to admire.

C

"Barbara Ellen." Communicated by Miss Lalah Lovett, Bulltown, Braxton County, 1916; obtained from Mrs. Cora Starkey, Harrison County, who learned it when a child from her parents; they learned it in Virginia from their parents, who were of English descent.

1   Early, early in the spring,
        When the green buds were a-swelling,
    Young Johnnie Green, from a foreign country,
        Fell in love with Barbara Ellen.

2   This young man was taken sick,
        And he lay in a low condition;
    And all he said both night and day,
        Was, "Send for Barbara Ellen."

3   They sent a servant to the town,
        Where Barbara was a-dwelling:
    "Arise you up and quickly go,
        If your name be Barbara Ellen."

4   Slowly, slowly she got up,
        And slowly she drew nigh him;
    And all she said when she got there,
        Was, "Young man, I think you're dying."

5   "O yes, O yes, my pretty fair maid,
        I lay in a low condition;
    But one sweet kiss would comfort me,
        Hard-hearted Barbara Ellen."

6   "Do you remember the long summer day,
        Around the table gathered,
    You treated all other pretty maids
        And slighted Barbara Ellen?"

7   He turned his pale face to the wall,
        He turned his back unto her:
    "Adieu, adieu to all pretty maids,
        And woe to Barbara Ellen."

8   As she went walking through the fields,
        She heard the death bells ringing;
    The more they rang they seemed to say:
        "Hard-hearted Barbara Ellen."

9 As she looked east, as she looked west,
 She spied the corpse a-coming:
"Lay down, lay down that ice-cold corpse,
 Till I may look upon it."

10 She knelt down and kissed his cheek,
 And then rose up a-smiling;
And all her friends cried out, "For shame,
 Hard-hearted Barbara Ellen!"

11 "O mother dear, go make my shroud,
 Go make it long and narrow;
Young Johnnie Green has died for love,
 And I shall die for sorrow."

12 Young Johnnie was in the churchyard laid,
 And Barbara laid beside him;
And out of her grave grew a bright red rose,
 And out of his a green briar.

13 They grew up to the top of the church,
 And then they could grow no higher;
And there they tied in a true-lover's knot,
 For the sake of Barbara Ellen.

𝒟

"Barby Ellen." Communicated by Mrs. Hilary G. Richardson, Clarksburg, Harrison County, 1916; obtained from Mrs. Nancy McDonald McAtee.

1 Early, early in the spring,
 When green buds they was swelling,
This young Johnnie Green on his death bed lay
 For the love of Barby Ellen.

2 He got hisself a waiting boy
 To do his errants in dwelling;
He sent him down to Strawberry Town,
 For to fetch him Barby Ellen.

3 So slow-li, slow-li she got up,
 And so slow-li she drawed near him;
And all she said when she got there,
 "Young man, I think you're dyin'."

4   "Yes, indeed, I know I am,
        Cold death is on me dwellin';
    And never better can I be,
        Till I git Barby Ellen."

5   "Never better could you be,
        If your own heart's blood was spillin';
    Never better can you be,
        For you'll never git Barby Ellen."

6   So slow-li, slow-li she got up,
        So slow-li she did leave him.
    .   .   .   .
        .   .   .   .

7   "You remember the time in Strawberry Town,
        Where we was all a-dwellin',
    You treated all the pretty girls round
        And slighted Barby Ellen?"

8   She had n't got a mile from the place,
        Till she heard the church bell tollin';
    And all it seemed to say,
        "Be woe upon Barby Ellen!"

9   She looked to the east and she looked to the west,
        And she seen the corpse a-comin':
    "Set you down upon this road,
        Till I git one kiss upon him."

10 This young Johnnie Green died on one glad day,
        Barby Ellen died to-morrow;
    Johnnie Green died for the loss of his dear,
        Barby Ellen died for sorrow.

11 Johnnie Green was buried in a churchyard,
        Barby Ellen was buried close by;
    And out of his breast grew a red, red rose,
        And out of his'n there grew a brier.

12 They grew till they came to the top of the church,
        And could n't git any higher;
    And there they tied in a true-lover's knot,
        The red rose round the brier.

$\mathcal{E}$

"Barbary Ellen." Communicated by Professor Walter Barnes, Fairmont, Marion County, July, 1915; obtained from Mr. G. W. Cunningham, Elkins, Randolph County, who learned it many years ago from Ellen Howell, Dry Fork.

1 'T was early in the month of May,
    When the green buds were swelling,
This young man on his death bed lay,
    In love with Barbary Allen.

2 He sent his butler to the place
    Where his true love was dwelling.

    .   .   .   .
        .   .   .   .

3 So slowly, slowly she came there,
    So slowly she drew nigh him;
And all she said when she came near:
    "Young man, I think you're dying."

4 "Yes, I am sick and very sick,
    In love with Barby Ellen;
But one sweet kiss from your tender lips
    Will save me from this dying."

5 "O do you not remember the day,

    .   .   .   .
You drank a health to the ladies all,
    But slighted Barbary Allen?"

6 He turned his face unto the wall,
    His back to Barbary Allen,
And said, "Adieu, adieu to kind friends all,
    But a woe to Barbary Allen!"

7 She scarcely went one mile from town,
    Till she heard his death knell ringing;
And every toll it seemed to say:
    "Hard-hearted Barbary Allen."

8 "O mother, mother, make my bed,
    And make it straight and narrow;
Young Johnnie Green died for me to-day,
    And I'll die for him to-morrow."

9   "O bury him in the churchyard,
        And bury me in the choir;
    And out of him shall a red rose spread,
        And out of me a green brier."

10 They buried him in the churchyard,
        They buried her in the choir;
    And out of him a red rose spread,
        And out of her a green brier.

11 They grew and grew to the church-steeple top,
        Till they could grow no higher;
    And there they twined in a true-love knot,
        With the rose around the brier.

F

"Barbara Allen."   Contributed by Mr. Josiah Keely, Kayford, Kanawha County, December 27, 1917; learned about twenty years before from Geraldine Dickinson, a little girl who sang it in the home of a family named Warner, who lived on Cotton Hill Mountain in Fayette County.

1   'T was early in the month of May,
        The roses all were bloomin';
    Sweet William cou'ted a fair young maid,
        Her name was Barbara Allen.

2   He cou'ted her six mont's or mo',
        An' was 'bout to gain her favor;
    "Young man, young man," she says to him,
        "Young men has mines[1] to waver."

3   He went right home an' taken sick,
        An' he sent for Barbara Allen;
    So slow she walk, so slow she came,
        She found her true love dy-i-n-g.

4   She walked along by his bedside
        An' gazed down upon him;
    "Young man, young man," she says to him,
        "I believe you is a-dy-i-n-g."

5   "In vain, in vain my love has called,
        For love of you I's dy-i-n-g."
    Then he turned his face to the milk-white wall,
        An' his back on Barbara Allen.

1. For *minds.*

6 "Look under my head, when I am dead,
        An' you'll find three rolls of money;
    Go share 'em wid those ladies 'round,
        An' done [1] slight Barbara Allen."

7 "Dear mother, dear mother, go make my bed,
        Go make it soft an' easy;
    Sweet William died to-day for love,
        An' I's gwine die to-morrow.

8 "Dear father, dear father, go dig my grave,
        Go dig it long and norrow,
    To-day Sweet William died for love,
        An' I's gwine die of sorrow."

9 They buried him in the new churchyard,
        An' Barbara in the other;
    An' from his grave there grew a sweet red rose,
        But from her grave a brier.

10 They grew and clumb to the steeple top,
        Tell they could not grow any higher;
    Then they wropped and tied and withered and died,
        The rose wropped round the brier.

G

"Barbara Ellen." Communicated by Miss Mabel Richards, Fairmont, Marion County, October, 1915; obtained from Mrs. P. J. Lang; learned from Mrs. Marjory West, Monongalia County.

1 It was in the early spring,
        When the green buds were swelling;
    I espied a youth on his death bed
        For the love of Barbara Ellen.

2 Now this young man was taken very sad
        And in a low condition;
    And all he could say, both night and day,
        Was, "Send for Barbara Ellen.

3 "O mother, O mother, look under my bed,
        There you'll find gold and silver;
    Take it all, take it all, take it all, I say,
        And give to Barbara Ellen."

1. For *don't*.

4 And slowly, slowly she got there,
      And slowly she approached him;
   And all she could say when she got there,
      Was, "My love, you're surely dying."

5 She looked to the east, she looked to the west,
      She saw his cold corpse coming;
   "Lie him down, lie him down, lie him down, I say,
      Till I gaze awhile upon him."

6 She looked upon his corpse of clay,
      And turned away a-smiling;
   She looked again on his corpse of clay,
      And turned away a-crying.

7 "Mother, O mother, go make my bed,
      And make it long and narrow;
   For little Johnnie Gray has died of love,
      And I shall die of sorrow."

8 They buried her in the old churchyard,
      They buried him beside her;
   And out of his grave there grew a red rose,
      And out of hers a briar.

9 They grew till they came to the tallest church tower,
      And then they could grow no higher;
   And there they entwined in a true-lover's knot,
      The red rose and the briar.

H

"The Love of Barbara Ellen." Communicated by Professor C. E. Haworth, Huntington, Cabell County, 1917; obtained by Miss Virginia Ranson from Mrs. Ranson's maid, who had lived both in Kentucky and West Virginia.

1 "O do you remember down in town,
      All down where you were drinking,
   You drank the health to the ladies in the room,
      And slighted Barbara Ellen?"

2 "O yes, I remember down in town,
      All down where I was drinking,
   I drank the health to the ladies in the room,
      And love to Barbara Ellen."

3   She started to go down in town,
        She heard the death bells ringing;
    She looked due east and looked due west,
        And saw the corpse a-coming.

4   Fold down, fold down, those linen white sheets,
        And let me gaze upon him;
    The more she looked, the more she loved,
        And bursted out a-crying.

*   *   *   *   *   *   *   *   *   *   *   *   *   *

5   They grew in height and grew in tall,
        Till they could not grow no taller;
    And lapped and tied in true-love's knots,
        With the rose around the green brier.

I

"Barbara Allen." Communicated by Miss Susan Montgomery, Kingwood, Preston County, 1922; obtained from Miss Marion Brooks, formerly of Buckhannon, but now of Alarka, North Carolina, whence the ballad came.

1   In Scarland town where I was bound,
        And many fair ladies dwelling,
    I chose me one to be my own,
        And her name was Barbara Allen.

2   If I was a man and many of a man,
        And a man of my own dwelling,
    I would write me a letter of my own heart's blood,
        And send to Barbara Allen.

3   O yes, I'm a man and a many of a man,
        And a man of my own dwelling.
    I'll write me a letter of my own heart's blood,
        And send to Barbara Allen.

4   The month, the month, the month was May,
        The green buds were a-swelling,
    And Sweet William on his death bed lay
        For the love of Barbara Allen.

5   He sent his servant to the town,
        To this young lady's dwelling:
    "My master dear has sent me here
        For the Lady Barbara Allen."

6   Slowly, slowly rose she up
         And went to where he's lying;
     And when she reached him, thus she spoke:
         "Young man, I think you're dying."

7   "O yes, I'm sick, and very sick,
         And feel very much like dying;
     And no better will I ever be,
         Till I get Barbara Allen."

8   "O yes, you're sick, and very sick,
         And feel very much like dying;
     But no better will you ever be,
         For you'll not get Barbara Allen."

9   He turned his pale face to the wall;
         He turned his back upon them:
     "Bedew,[1] bedew, to the friends all round;
         Be kind to Barbara Allen."

10   As she rode out from Scarland town,
         She heard the death bells ringing;
     And as they rung, she thought they sung,
         "Hard-hearted Barbara Allen."

11   Then looked she east, and looked she west,
         Till she saw that cold corpse coming.
     "O hand me down those corpse of clay,
         That I may look upon him."

12   The more she looked, the more she wept,
         Till she cried out in sorrow:
     "Sweet William died for me to-day,
         I'll die for him to-morrow.

13   "O, mother, mother, dig my grave,
         And dig it long and narrow;
     Sweet William died for me to-day,
         I'll die for him to-morrow.

14   Barbara lies in the King's Churchyard,
         Sweet William close beside her;
     And out of her grave sprang a red, red rose,
         And out of his a brier.

1. For *Adieu.*

15 They grew and grew up the old church tower
        Till they could grow no higher;
    And there they twined in a true-love knot,
        The red rose and the brier.

$\mathcal{J}$

"Little Johnnie Green." Communicated by Mrs. Hilary G. Richardson, Clarksburg, Harrison County, March 15, 1916; learned from Mrs. Rachel Fogg, originally from Doddridge County. She learned it from her mother, and she from her mother, "on back into the old country across the sea" (cf. *Journal*, XXXII, 504). Much like C.

$\mathcal{K}$

"Barbara Allan." Communicated by Miss Mabel Richards, Fairmont, Marion County, October, 1915; obtained from Mrs. J. C. Roby of Lowesville; learned about twenty years before from Mrs. Mona Arnett, Fairmont. Practically identical with variant G, but omits stanzas 5 and 6.

$\mathcal{L}$

No local title. Communicated by Miss Emma Boughner, Monongalia County; obtained from Mrs. E. B. Hall. A fragment of three stanzas.

17

LADY ALICE

(CHILD, No. 85)

FIVE variants have been recovered in West Virginia, under various titles. A, B, and E represent one version, C and D another. They all differ widely from the Child versions.

A Pennsylvania version going back almost to 1800 was printed by Child, II, 279. For other American texts see *Journal*, XXVIII, 151 (Perrow; North Carolina); *Focus*, III, 154, and IV, 50 (Virginia); Campbell and Sharp, No. 22 (North Carolina, Tennessee); Campbell, *The Survey*, New York, January 2, 1915, XXXIII, 373 (two stanzas from Georgia). For other American references see *Journal*, XXX, 317. Add *Bulletin*, Nos. 6–10.

A

"Young Collins." Contributed by Mr. J. Harrison Miller, Wardensville, Hardy County, January, 1917; learned from Mr. Lemuel C. Combs about eight years previously; a community song known to various people. Printed by Cox, XLVI, 124.

1   Young Collins rode out from his fields one day,
       While the flowers and trees were in bloom,
   And it was there that he saw his own Fair Ellen,
       A-washing a white marble stone.

2   She screamed, she cried, she changed her mind,
       She waved her lily-white hand,
   Saying, "Come here, come here, Young Collins, my dear,
       Your life is near at hand."

3   He clasped around her slender waist,
       He kissed both her cheeks and her chin,
   Till the stars from heaven came twinkling down,
       To the spot where Young Collins jumped [in].

4   He ran, he ran to his own father's house,
       Till he came to his own father's door,
   Saying, "Father, dear father, I pray let me in,
       I pray let me in once more.

5   "If I should die this very night,
       Which I feel in my mind that I will,
   Go bury me under the white marble stone,
       At the foot of Fair Ellen's green hill."

6 As Ellen was sitting in her own cottage door,
  All dressed up in silk so fine,
 It was there that she spied a casket coming,
  As far as her eyes could shine.

7 "Whose casket, whose casket, whose casket I see?
  Who lies in that casket so fine?"
 "'T is Young Johnny Collins, a cold clay corpse,
  Who lies in that casket so fine."

8 She ordered the casket to be opened right there,
  Till she gazed on his cold clay form,
 Till she took the last kiss from his cold clay lips,
  As oft they had kissed her before.

9 She ordered the curtains to be brought right there,
  Till she trimmed them in lace so fine:
 "To-day they will weep over Collins' grave;
  To-morrow they shall weep over mine."

10 The news went round through Dublin Town,
  It was printed on Dublin gate,
 That six pretty maidens on Saturday's night
  All died for Young Collins' fate.

B

"Young Collins" or "Johnny Collins." Communicated by Mrs. Hilary G. Richardson, Clarksburg, Harrison County, March 9, 1916; obtained from Mrs. Rachel Fogg, originally from Doddridge County; learned from her mother, and she from her mother, "on back into the old country across the sea in Scotch, Dutch, or Jerusalem, she forgets which, but in this country they call 'em Hebrews." Reported by Cox, XLV, 159; printed, *Journal*, XXXII, 500.

1 Young Collins went forth one morning in May,
  All over the fresh blooming flowers;
 And the first that he spied was his Eleanor dear,
  A-washin' a white marble stone.

2 He took her round the slender waist
  And kissed both her cheeks and her chin;
 The stars from heaven came twinkling down,
  At the place where Young Collins jumped in.

3 He swum and he swum and he swu-u-u-um,
  Till he came to his own father's door,
 Says, "Father, dear father, O let me in,
  O let me in once more!

4 "If I should die this very night,
    Which I think in my heart I will,
  Go bury me under the white marble stone,
    At the foot of Fair Eleanor's hill."

5 As she was sitting in her own father's hall,
    All dressed in her silks so fine,
  She spied Young Collins' cold clay corpse:
    "An old true love of mine."

6 She ordered the coffin to be brought right there,
    So she might gaze on his beautiful form once more,
  And get one kiss from those cold clay lips,
    "Which ofttimes has kissed mine before."

7 She ordered a sheet to be brought right there,
    All trimmed in its laces so fine:
  "For to-day it was over Young Collins' grave,
    To-morrow shall wave over mine."

8 The news it went round to Dablin Town,
    All printed on Dablin's gate:
  "Six pretty fair maids all died last night,
    And 't was all for Young Collins' sake."

C

"George Collins." Communicated by Mr. R. C. Kelly; Sutton, Braxton County, January, 1917; obtained from Howard Dent and Lidel Evans, who learned it in the lumber camps.

1 George Collins rode home one cold rainy night,
    George Collins rode home so fine;
  George Collins rode home one cold rainy night,
    And taken sick and died.

2 Little Hattie was sitting in her mother's room,
    A-sewing on silk so fine;
  When she heard poor George had died,
    She laid her silk aside.

3 She followed him up, she followed him down,
    She followed him to his grave;
  And there upon her knees she fell,
    She wept, she moaned, she prayed.

4   She sat down on the coffin: "Take off the lid,
        Fold back the linen so fine,
    That I may kiss his cold, pale lips,
        For I know he'll never kiss mine.

5   "The happiest hours I ever spent
        Were by George Collins' side;
    The saddest news I ever heard
        Was that George Collins had died.

6   "O, don't you see the turtle dove,
        As he flies from pine to pine?
    He weeps, he moans for his own true love,
        Just as I wept for mine."

D

"George Collins." Contributed by Miss Snoah McCourt, Orndoff, Webster
County, March, 1916; learned from Mrs. Lenna Thorpe. Reported by Cox,
XLV, 159.

1   George Collins rode home one cold winter night,
        George Collins rode home so fine;
    George Collins rode home one cold winter night,
        And taken sick and died.

2   Little Mattie sat in her mother's room,
        Sewing on silks so fine;
    But when she heard of George's death,
        She laid her silks aside.

3   "O daughter, O daughter, what makes you weep?
        There's lots of men beside George."
    "O mother, O mother, George had my heart,
        But now he's dead and gone."

4   She followed him up, she followed him down,
        She followed him to the grave;
    'T was there she fell upon her knees,
        She wept, she mourned, and she prayed.

5   "My love is like the turtle dove,
        That flies from pine to pine;
    She mourns and weeps for her lost love,
        Just as I do for mine."

ε

"John Collins." Communicated by Mr. C. R. Bishop, Green Bank, Pocahontas County. Obtained from Miss Valera Ervine.

1 One morning, one morning, one morning in May,
        When the flowers were all in bloom,
    . . . he spied fair Ellen,
        A-washing her marble stone.

2 He caught her around her slender waist,
        He kissed both her cheek and her chin,
    And the stars of heaven came twinkling down,
        The place where Young Collins jumped in.

3 She screamed, she cried, she changed her voice,
        She threw up her lily-white hands,
    Saying, "Come here, come here, Young Collins, my dear,
        Your life is not at an end."

4 He swam, he swam, he swam till he came
        To his own father's door,
    Saying, "Father, dear father, I pray let me in,
        I pray let me in once more.

5 "If I should die this very night,
        Which I feel in my mind I will,
    Go bury me yonder at the white marble stone,
        At the foot of Fair Ellen's green hill."

6 Next morning as she sat at her own cottage door,
        All dressed in her silk so fine,
    She spied a corpse a-coming,
        As bright as her eyes could shine.

7 "Whose coffin, whose coffin, whose coffin," cried she,
        "Whose coffin so bright and fine?
    'T is Young John Collins' clay cold corpse,
        An old true lover of mine."

8 The news went round through Dublin town,
        'T was written on Dublin's gate,
    That six fair ladies were buried next day,
        And it was all for John Collins' sake.

9 She ordered a snow-white sheet to be brought,
        Till she trimmed it in laces so fine:
    "For to-day it shall wave over Collins' grave,
        And to-morrow it shall wave over mine."

18

THE MAID FREED FROM THE GALLOWS

(CHILD, NO. 95)

SEVEN texts have been secured in West Virginia under various titles. The first six of these texts differ from each other but slightly, and are similar to that printed by Child, v, 296. Text G is fragmentary, and differs from the others in that it states the crime for which the maid is to be hanged (see stanza 2). Of the English versions in Child, the language of the West Virginia texts is most like B. The term "hangman" occurs in Child G only.

The first American copy to be printed was that in Child, v, 296 (from Virginia by way of North Carolina). For texts printed since, see *Journal*, XXI, 56 (Reed Smith; West Virginia); XXVI, 175 (Kittredge; from an Irish servant in Massachusetts); XXVII, 64 (Reed Smith; South Carolina); XXX, 319 (Kittredge; New York, Missouri, North Carolina; contributed by Reinhard, Belden, and Hart); Wyman and Brockway, p. 44 (Kentucky; reprinted by Pound, No. 13); Smith, p. 10 (Virginia); Campbell and Sharp, No. 24 (Tennessee, North Carolina, Virginia); cf. Minish MS. (North Carolina); Belden's Missouri collection. Barry gives the tune current in Ireland, from the Hudson MS. (*Journal*, XXIV, 337). For further references see *Journal*, XXX, 318. Add *Bulletin*, Nos. 6, 8–10.

A

"The Hangman's Tree." Communicated by Mr. George Paugh, Thomas, Tucker County, October, 1915; obtained from Mae Cosnor, who says, "When I was a little girl I used to play it." Reported by Cox, XLV, 159.

1   "Hangsman, hangsman, hold your rope,
         And hold it for awhile;
     I think I hear my father coming,
         For many a many a mile."

2   "O father, have you brought me any gold,
         Or have you come to set me free?
     Or have you come to see me die,
         Beneath this gallows tree?"

3   "I have not brought you gold,
         I have not come to set you free;
     But I have come to see you die,
         Beneath this gallows tree."

Repeat the triad, substituting for the word *father* the words *mother, brother, sister,* and *lover.* The last stanza is as follows:

15 "I have not come to see you die,
        Beneath the gallows tree;
    But I have brought a knife to cut the rope,
        And take you home with me."

B

"The Hangman's Tree."   Contributed by Mr. Warren C. Steele, Walker, Wood County, January, 1917; learned from a young man named Richards, in Logan County in 1916.

1 "Hangman, hangman, go slack your rope,
        Go slack it for awhile;
    For yonder comes my father,
        He's come for many a mile."

2 "O father, O father, have you brought me gold,
        Likewise to pay my fee?
    Or have you come for to see me hung,
        Upon the gallows tree?"

3 "I have not brought you any gold,
        Likewise to pay your fee,
    But I have come for to see you hung,
        Upon the gallows tree."

Repeat the triad, substituting *mother*, *brother*, *sister*, and *true-love* for *father*. The last stanza is as follows:

15 "O yes, I have brought you gold,
        Likewise to pay your fee,
    And I did not come for to see you hung,
        Upon the gallows tree."

C

"Down by the Green Willow Tree."   Contributed by Miss Carrie Hess, Spencer, Roane County, August 8, 1916.

1 "O hangsman, hangsman, slack your rope,
        O slack it for a while;
    I think I see my father coming,
        He has come for many a long mile."

2 "O father, father, have you brought any gold,
        Any gold to set me free?
    Or have you come for to see me hung,
        Down by the green willow tree?"

3   "O no, my son, I have brought no gold,
          No gold to set you free,
     But I have come to see you hanged,
          Down by the green willow tree."

Instructions for the remainder of the ballad are as in B.

D

"The Hangman's Tree."   Communicated by Mr. George Paugh, Thomas, Tucker County, August 28, 1915; obtained from Mrs. H. S. Paugh. He writes that he has found nine different persons who sing this song. Reported by Cox, XLV, 159.

1   "Hangman, hangman, hold your rope,
          Hold it for a while;
     I think I see my father coming,
          Coming for many a mile."

2   "Father, father, have you any gold,
          Gold to set me free?
     Or have you come to see me hung,
          Hung to this willow tree?"

3   "No, O no, I have n't any gold,
          Gold to set you free;
     But I have come to see you hung,
          Hung to the willow tree."

Instructions for the remainder of the ballad are as in B.

E

"The Hangman's Tree."   Communicated by Miss Mabel Richards, Fairmont, Marion County, 1916; obtained from Miss Flora Hood, Lowesville, who learned it about twenty-five years before from Mrs. James Wiseman, Fairmont. Reported by Cox, XLV, 159.

1   "Ropeman, ropeman, slack your rope.
          Slack it for a while;
     For I think I see my father a-coming,
          Away off many a mile."

2   "Father, father, have you any gold,
          Gold to set me free?
     Or did you come for to see me hung,
          Beneath this willow tree?"

3   "O no, no, no, I have n't any gold,
      Gold to set you free;
   I came here this morning for to see you hung,
      Beneath this willow tree."

Instructions for the remainder of the ballad are as in B, but substitute *sweetheart* for *true-love*.

F

"The Hangman's Tree." Communicated by Mr. R. E. Quirk, Mannington, Marion County, July 21, 1916; obtained from Miss Hazel K. Black, Pine Grove, Wetzel County, who learned it from the children at school.

1   "Ropemen, ropemen, slack your rope,
      Slack it for a while;
   For I think I see my father a-coming,
      Away off many a mile."

2   "Father, father, have you any gold,
      Gold to set me free?
   Or did you come for to see me hung,
      Beneath this green oak tree?"

3   "No, O no, I have n't any gold,
      Gold to set you free;
   I came here this morning to see you hung,
      Beneath this green oak tree."

Repeat triad for *mother*, *brother*, and *sister*.

13   "Ropeman, ropeman, slack your rope,
      Slack it for a while;
   For I think I see my true-love on yonder shore,
      He's walked for many a mile."

14   "True-love, true-love, have you any gold," etc.

15   "Yes, O yes, I have got gold," etc.

G

"By a Lover Saved." Communicated by Mr. Harold Staats, Ripley, Jackson County, 1921, who writes: "This song was told, or rather sung, to me by some person living on Tug Fork. It is claimed that this song was brought to this country by Captain William Parsons, one of the early settlers. According to legends it was at one time a popular folk song in the British Isles."

1   "Hold up your hands, O Joshua," she cried,
      "Wait a little while and see;
   I think I hear my own father dear,
      Come rambling over the sea."

2 "O father, have you brought any gold for me?
       Or any silver to pay my fee?
   For I have stolen a golden cup,
       And hanging it will be."

3 "No, daughter, no, no, I have no gold for thee,
       Nor silver to pay your fee;
   For I have come to see you hung,
       All on the willow tree."

* * * * * * * * * * * * * *

4 "Yes, true-love, I have some gold for you,
       And silver for to pay your fee;
   For I have come for to pay your fee,
       And take you home with me."

19

SIR HUGH, OR, THE JEW'S DAUGHTER

(Child, No. 155)

Fourteen variants have been found in West Virginia, under various titles (cf. Cox, xlv, 160). They all tell the same brief story and differ in trifling details only. The version agrees closely with Child G and H. Child K of the English versions is very similar. Stanza A 6 and the corresponding stanzas in other variants are most like Child F 4 and N 6.

For American texts see Child, iii, 248, 249 (Philadelphia and Baltimore); Newell, *Games and Songs of American Children*, p. 75 (New York; reprinted by Child, iii, 251); Krehbiel, *New York Tribune*, August 17, 1902 (see *Journal*, xv, 195); Belden, *Journal*, xix, 293 (Missouri; Kentucky); Tolman, *Journal*, xxix, 164 (Indiana; reprinted by Pound, No. 5 A); Kittredge, *Journal*, xxix, 166 (probably from Connecticut); Tolman and Eddy, *Journal*, xxxv, 344 (Ohio); *Focus*, iii, 396, 399 (Virginia); Steger and Morrow, *The University of Virginia Magazine*, December, 1912, p. 115 (Alabama; the same in Smith, p. 16, and Pound, No. 5 B); Campbell and Sharp, No. 26 (North Carolina). For further references see *Journal*, xxix, 164; xxx, 322; xxxv, 344. Add *Bulletin*, No. 7, p. 6; No. 9, p. 7; No. 11, p. 5.

A

"It Rained a Mist." Communicated by Miss Violet Hiett, Great Cacapon, Morgan County, February, 1917; obtained from her father, who learned it when a child from his mother.

1 It rained a mist, it rained a mist,
   All o'er, all o'er the land;
  And all the boys of our town,
    Went out to toss their ball, ball, ball,
    Went out to toss their ball.

2 At first they tossed their ball too high,
   And then again too low;
  And over into the Jew's garden it went,
   Where no one dared to go.

3 One little boy said, "I'll not go in,
   Unless my playmates do;
  For I have heard whoever goes in,
   Shall never come out again."

4 Out came the Jew's daughter, all dressed, all dressed,
   All dressed in red so grand;
  "Come in, little lad," said she,
   "You shall have your ball again."

5 At first she showed him a big red apple,
  And then a gay gold ring,
And then a cherry as red as blood,
  To entice this little boy in.

6 She took hold of his little white hand,
  And through the castle they went;
She penned him in the cellar below,
  Where no one could hear him lament.

7 She pinned him in a napkin,
  And pinned him very tight;
And called for a vessel of brightest gold,
  To catch his heart blood in.

8 "Please lay my Bible at my head,
  My prayer-book at my feet;
And if my playmates ask for me,
  Tell them that I'm asleep.

9 "O lay my prayer-book at my feet,
  My Bible at my head;
And if my playmates ask for me,
  Tell them that I am dead."

$\mathcal{B}$

"It Rained, It Mist." Communicated by Professor Walter Barnes, Fairmont, Marion County, May 19, 1916; obtained from Miss Lelia Withers, Grafton, Taylor County, who got it from her mother.

1 It rained, it mist, it rained, it mist,
  It rained all over the town;
Until the boys of this our town,
  Went out to toss a ball, a ball,
  Went out to toss a ball.

2 At first they throwed it too high,
  And then they throwed it too low;
And then they throwed it into the Jew's garden,
  Where no one was darest to go.

3 Out came a Jew's lady,
  All dressed in rich array:
"Come in, come in, my pretty little boy,
  And get your ball again."

4 "I won't come in, I darest come in,
       Unless my playmates can;
   For they that enter this garden here
       Can never come out again."

5 At first she showed him a mellow apple,
       And then a gay gold ring;
   She showed him a cherry as red as blood,
       To entice that little boy in.

6 She took him by the lily-white hand,
       She led him down in the . . . ,
   She led him down in a cellar deep,
       Where no one could hear him lament.

7 She called for a knife both sharp and keen,
       To pierce his little heart with;
   She called for a basin both wide and deep,
       To catch his heart's blood in.

8 "Go put the Bible at my head,
       The hymn book at my feet;
   And when my playmates call for me,
       Just tell them I'm asleep.

9 "Go put the hymn book at my feet,
       The Bible at my head;
   And when my playmates call for me,
       Just tell them I am dead."

C

"The Jew's Daughter." Communicated by Miss Mildred Joy Barker, Morgantown, Monongalia County, October 2, 1916; obtained from her mother, who says that it has been known in the family for many years.

1 It rained a mist, it rained a mist,
       All over, all over the land;
   And all the boys in our town,
           Went out to toss their ball, ball, ball,
           Went out to toss their ball.

2 At first they tossed their ball too high,
       And then again too low;
   Till over into the Jew's garden it went,
       Where no one dared to go.

3 Out came the Jew's daughter, all dressed,
  All dressed in spangles of gold:
"Come in, come in, my lad," she said,
  "And you shall have your ball."

4 "I won't come nor I shan't come in,
  Unless my playmates do;
For I've heard it said whoever comes in,
  Shall never come out again."

5 At first she showed him a nice red apple,
  And then a gay gold ring,
And then a cherry as red as blood,
  To entice this little boy in.

6 She took him by the lily-white hand,
  And led him through the hall,
And then into the cellar below,
  Where no one could hear him call.

7 "O, lay my Bible at my head,
  My prayer-book at my feet;
And if my playmates ask for me,
  Tell them that I'm asleep.

8 "O, lay my prayer-book at my feet,
  My Bible at my head;
And if my playmates ask for me,
  Tell them that I am dead."

𝓓

"The Jew's Daughter." Communicated by Mr. George Paugh from Ray-wood, Pocahontas County; obtained from Mrs. Charles Young, of Davis, who learned it when a child.

1 It rained a mist,
  All o'er, all o'er the town;
And all the boys and girls went out,
  To toss their ball around.

2 At first they tossed it up too high,
  And then again too low;
Down into the Jew's garden it went,
  Where none would dare to go.

3 Out came the Jew's daughter,
    All dressed in gay apparel:
"Come in, come in, my little lad,
    You may have your ball again," she said.

4 "I won't come in, I shan't come in,
    Unless my playmates do;
I've heard it said that those who came in,
    They never come out again."

5 First she showed him a mellow apple,
    And then a gay gold ring,
And then a cherry as red as blood,
    To entice the little boy in.

6 She took him by the lily-white hand,
    And through the castle they went,
Down in the dark cellar beneath,
    Where none could hear him lament.

7 She pinned him in a napkin tight:
    Now was n't this a sin?
She then called for a basin bright of gold,
    To hold his heart's blood in.

8 "Pray lay my prayer-book at my head,
    My Bible at my feet;
And if my playmates ask for me,
    Just tell them I'm asleep.

9 "Pray lay my Bible at my . . . ,
    My prayer-book at my feet;
And if my parents ask for me,
    Just tell them that I am dead, dead, dead."

$\mathcal{E}$

"The Jew's Lady." Contributed by Miss Snoah McCourt, Orndoff, Webster County, May, 1916, who learned it from her mother.

1 It rains our mist,[1] it rains,
    It rains all o'er the town;
And all the boys that were therein,
    Went out to toss their ball and play, play, play,
    To toss their ball and play.

1. Cf. A 1 for correct reading.

2 First they tossed their ball too high,
    And then again too low;
Then over into the Jew's garden it went,
    Where no man dared to go.

3 Out came a Jew's lady all dressed, all dressed,
    All dressed in riches gay:
"Come in, my little lad," she said,
    "And you shall have your ball, and play."

4 "I can't come in nor I won't come in,
    Unless my schoolmates do;
For it is said that he that goes in,
    Can never come out again."

5 First she showed him a nice mellow apple,
    And next a gay gold ring;
And next a cherry as red as blood,
    To entice this little boy in.

6 She took him by his little white hand,
    And through the castle went,
And placed him in a cellar beneath,
    Where no one could hear him lament.

7 "Go place my prayer-book at my head,
    My Bible at my feet;
And if my schoolmates call for me,
    Pray tell that I'm asleep.

8 "Go place my prayer-book at my feet,
    My Bible at my head;
And if my schoolmates ask for me,
    Pray tell them that I am dead."

F

"The Jew's Daughter." Communicated by Miss Minnie Lee Dickinson, Cheat Haven, Pennsylvania; obtained from Mrs. David Fowler, Cheat Neck, West Virginia, who learned it from her mother.

1 It rained, it mist, it rained, it mist,
    It rained throughout the town;
The girls and boys went out to play,
    Went out to toss their ball, their ball.

2 Sometimes they tossed their ball too high,
    And then again too low;
They tossed it up and over it went,
    Into the Jew's garden did go, did go,
    Into the Jew's garden did go.

3 Out came one of the Jew's daughters,
    All dressed in richest pearl:
"Come in, come in, my sweet little boy,
    Come in and get your ball, your ball,
    Come in and get your ball."

4 "I won't come in, I can't come in,
    For I've often heard them say,
Those who enter the Jew's garden
    Can never get away, away,
    Can never get away."

5 She offered him a mellow apple,
    And then a beautiful ring,
And then a cherry as bright as gold,
    To entice that little boy in, boy in,
    To entice that little boy in.

6 She took him by the lily-white hand
    And through the castle did go;
And down into the cellar she pinned him down,
    Where no one could hear him lament, lament,
    Where no one could hear him lament.

7 She pinned him to a napkin tight:
    O, was n't that a sin?
She called for a basin as bright as gold,
    To take his heart's blood in, blood in,
    To take his heart's blood in.

8 "Go lay my prayer book at my head,
    My Bible at my feet;
If any of my schoolmates inquires for me,
    Just tell them I'm asleep, asleep,
    Just tell them that I'm asleep.

9 "Go lay my prayer book at my feet,
    My Bible at my head;
If either of my parents inquires for me,
    Just tell them that I'm dead, am dead,
    Just tell them that I am dead."

G

"The Jew's Daughter." Communicated by Professor Walter Barnes, Fairmont, Marion County, August, 1915; obtained from Mr. Showan, Roane County, who learned it from his mother. Seven stanzas.

H

"The Jew's Daughter." Communicated by Miss Mabel Richards, Fairmont, Marion County, October, 1915; obtained from Mrs. Lawrence C. Roby; learned about twenty-five years before from Mrs. Arnett, Fairmont. Seven stanzas.

I

"The Jew's Daughter." Communicated by Mr. Richard Elkins Hyde, Martinsburg, Berkeley County, December, 1916; obtained from his mother, who learned it from her mother, who had it from her mother, a lady of good Scotch-Irish stock from Wardensville, Hardy County. Eight stanzas.

J

No local title. Communicated by Miss Mary Meek Atkeson, Morgantown, Monongalia County. Obtained from Mr. Fred M. Smith, Glenville, Gilmer County, who got it from Mr. Harry G. Eubank. Six stanzas.

K

"The Jew's Daughter." Communicated by Mr. George Paugh, Thomas, Tucker County, October, 1915; obtained from Mrs. Stella Thomas, Ben Bush, who learned it about thirteen years previously from Lena Ashfield of St. George. Seven stanzas.

L

"The Jew's Daughter." Communicated by Professor Walter Barnes, Fairmont, Marion County, August, 1915; obtained from Mrs. Snyder, Roane County, who said that she "had always heard it." Six stanzas.

M

"The Jew's Daughter." Contributed by Professor Walter Barnes, Fairmont, Marion County, July 28, 1915; learned, when he was about nine years old, from Miss Straight, an illiterate servant. Fragmentary; six stanzas.

N

"The Jew's Daughter." Communicated by Miss Violet Noland, Davis, Tucker County, March 24, 1916; obtained from her mother.

20

THE BONNIE HOUSE O' AIRLIE

(CHILD, No. 199)

THE excellent version of this ballad found in West Virginia is, as a whole, most like Child C, but has many close likenesses to other versions, especially A. The incident of the search for the lady's dowry and the reference to her bonny sons fail to appear. Stanza 9 does not occur in any of the Child versions.

In *The English Journal*, April, 1918, p. 270, is printed "The Haunted Tower O' Airlie," contributed by Julia Tunnicliffe, "a high-school student born in Scotland, but long resident in this country," Moline, Illinois.

Contributed by Miss Fannie Eagan, Hinton, Summers County, January 12, 1917; learned from Miss Amelia Bruce, who was born and bred in Edinburgh, came to America about twenty years previously, and had recently returned to Scotland to remain there. Reported by Cox, XLVI, 145.

1 It fell on a day, a bonnie summer day,
    When the corn grew green and yellow,
  That there fell out a great dispute
    Between Argyle and Airlie.

2 Argyle he has ta'en a hundred of his men,
    A hundred men and mairly,
  And he's awa' on yon green shaw
    To plunder the bonnie house o' Airlie.

3 The lady looked on fra the castle wa',
    And O but she sighed sairly,
  When she saw Argyle and all his men,
    Come to plunder the bonnie house o' Airlie.

4 "Come down, Lady Margaret," he says,
    "Come down to me, Lady Airlie;
  Or I swear by the brand that I haud in my hand,
    I winna leave a stan'in' stone in Airlie."

5 "I'll no come down, ye proud Argla,
    Until that ye speak mair fairly,
  Though ye swear by the sword that ye haud in your hand
    That ye will not leave a stan'in' stone in Airlie.

6 "Had my ain lord been at his home,
    But he's awa' wi' Charlie,
  There's no a Campbell in a' Argyle
    Dare hae trod on the bonnie green o' Airlie.

7   "But since we can haud out na mair,
      My hand I offer fairly;
  O lead me down to yonder glen,
      That I may na see the burnin' o' Airlie."

8   He's ta'en [her] by the trembling hand,
      But he's na ta'en her fairly;
  For he led her up to a hie hill-top,
      Where she saw the burnin' o' Airlie.

9   Clouds o' smoke and flames sae hie
      Soon left the wa's but barely;
  And she laid her down on that hill to die,
      When she saw the burnin' o' Airlie.

2 1

THE GYPSY LADDIE

(Child, No. 200)

Four variants have been recovered in West Virginia. They resemble Child J. B differs from A and from Child J in that the lady repents and goes back home. Cf. note by Kittredge, *Journal*, xxx, 323. Of the English versions they are most like Child G. Cf. *The American Star Songster*, New York, 1851, p. 54.

For a list of American texts and for references, English and American, see *Journal*, xxx, 323. Add Campbell and Sharp, No. 27 (Tennessee, North Carolina, Virginia); Sharp, *Folk-Songs of English Origin collected in the Appalachian Mountains*, 2d Series, p. 6 (compounded of Campbell and Sharp, No. 27, A and C); Minish MS. (North Carolina); *Bulletin*, No. 8, p. 7; No. 9, p. 7; No. 11, p. 8.

A

"The Gypsy Davy." Contributed by the Editor of this volume; learned about 1880, from hired men, while living on a farm in Illinois. Reported, xliv, 428.

1 The Gypsy Davy crossed the plain,
     He sang so loud and sweetly;
  He sang till he made the green woods ring,
     To charm the heart of a lady.

  Tum-a-roe-eye ink-a-toodle ink-a-toodle-a
    Tum-a-roe-eye ink-a-toodle-a-dy

2 The lord of the house came home at night,
     Inquiring for his lady;
  The servants all made quick reply,
     "She's gone with the Gypsy Davy."

3 "Go saddle me up my milk-white steed,
     The brown he ain't so speedy;
  I've rode all day and I'll ride all night,
     Or overtake my lady."

4 They saddled him up his milk-white steed,
     His milk-white steed so speedy;
  He rode all night and he rode all day,
     To overtake his lady.

5 He rode till he came to the river side,
     That runs so deep and shady;
  The tears came trickling down his cheeks,
     For there he met his lady.

6 "Have you forsaken your house and lands,
        Have you forsaken your baby?
    Have you forsaken your own true-love,
        And gone with the Gypsy Davy?"

7 "Yes, I've forsaken my house and lands,
        And I've forsaken my baby;
    And I've forsaken my own true-love,
        And gone with the Gypsy Davy."

8 The lord of the house rode home that night,
        Rode home without his lady,
    For she remained by the river side,
        In the arms of the Gypsy Davy.

𝓑

"The Gypsy Daisy." Communicated by Miss Violet Noland, Davis, Tucker County, March 24, 1916; obtained from Mr. John Raese; learned in youth and copied down in 1880. Reported by Cox, XLV, 160.

1 Gypsy Daisy crossed the sea,
        Sung a song so sweetly;
    Sung a song so sweetly,
        To charm his little lady.

    Rattle O ding, O ding, O ding,
        Rattle O ding, O Daisy;
    Rattle O ding, O ding,
        I am gone with the Gypsy Daisy.

2 The lord of the house when he came home,
        Inquiring of his lady;
    The servant made a quick reply:
        "She is gone with the Gypsy Daisy."

3 He mounted on his bonny beast,
        His bonny beast so speedy;
    He rode all day and he rode all night,
        And he overtook his lady.

4 "Have you forsaken your house and lands,
        Have you forsaken your baby?
    Have you forsaken your own true love,
        And gone with the Gypsy Daisy?"

5 She mounted on her bonny beast,
     Her bonny beast so speedy;
   She rode all day and she rode all night,
     Till she came to her home and baby.

6 "Last night I slept on the cold, cold ground,
     With all the gypsies all around me;
   To-night I sleep in my own feather bed,
     With my husband and my baby."

C

"The Gypsy Davy." Contributed by Mr. N. E. Cogar, Berryburg, Webster
County, January 12, 1922.

1 Gypsy came riding down this way,
     He looked so neat and handsome;
   He made such a sound to[1] the greenwoods roared,
     And charmed the heart of a lady.

   Raddle lol de ding, de ding, dol day,
     Raddle lol de ding, de ding, dol,
   Raddle lol de ding, de ding, dol day,
     Saying, "I'm for the Gypsy Davy."

2 A lady came tripping down the stairs,
     And in each hand a bottle,
   Saying, "I will drink with all my friends,
     And go with the Gypsy Davy."

3 At night the landlord he came home,
     Inquiring for his lady,
   And all the answer he could get,
     "She is gone with the Gypsy Davy."

4 "Go saddle me up the gray," he said,
     "For the black is not so speedy;
   I've rode all day and I'll ride all night,
     But I'll overtake my lady."

5 He rode till he came to the river's brim,
     It being both deep and muddy;
   The tears came trickling down his cheeks,
     And there he beheld his lady.

---

[1] Error for *till* or *that*.

6   "Have you forsaken your house and land,
        Have you forsaken your baby?
    Have you forsaken your old mother-in-law,
        And gone with the Gypsy Davy?"

7   "Yes, I've forsaken my house and land,
        Yes, I've forsaken my baby;
    Yes, I've forsaken my old mother-in-law,
        And gone with the Gypsy Davy."

8   "Last night I lay in my own feather bed,
        By the side of my little baby;
    To-night I'll lay in the mud and the rain,
        By the side of the Gypsy Davy."

D

"Bill Harman."   Contributed by Mr. A. C. Payne, Barclay, McDowell County, August, 1918.

Mr. Payne said that this song was made by Henry Mitchell about Billy Harman, whose wife had gone off with Tim Wallace, Harman's brother-in-law. Wallace was immensely ugly and the wife very pretty. She never came back; he did. "War" and "Barranshee" are names of local streams in the southern part of West Virginia.

1   Bill Harman came home at night,
        Inquiring for Melindy, O!
    Mandy made him this reply:
        "She's gone with a spurlock laddie, O!"

2   "Go saddle me up old Tice's gray,
        Go saddle me up old Brownie, O!
    I plowed all day and I'll ride all night,
        Or overtake Melindy, O!"

3   He rode till he came to the north of War,
        The water seemed deep and muddy, O!
    He tucked up his bridle reins,
        He forded it most steady, O!

4   He rode till he came to the mouth of Barranshee,
        He stopped and studied, O!
    He rode till he came to Bartley Rose's,
        Inquiring for Melindy, O!

He here inquired if she had gone that road, but, receiving a negative reply, he returned home. The singer could not recall the last stanzas.

22

BESSIE BELL AND MARY GRAY.

(CHILD, No. 201)

COMMUNICATED by Miss Eva Hughes, Spencer, Roane County, December 7, 1915; obtained from her mother, whose maiden name was Elmira Grisell, born near Malaga, Ohio, in 1837. She learned it from her mother, who was Elizabeth Adams, daughter of Ann Hazlett and Jonathan Adams (English) of Massachusetts. Elizabeth's parents died when she was a child, and she was brought up by her aunt, Betsy Adams Horne, Darby, Pennsylvania. Printed by Cox, XLIV, 428.

What seems to be a similar fragment is reported from Virginia (Smith, p. 2; *Bulletin*, No. 5, p. 8; No. 9, p. 7).

The first stanza of the West Virginia text agrees with Child, stanza 1, "Yonburn Bay" being a corruption of "yon burn-brae." Nothing like stanza 2 is found in his text. That stanza resembles "The Gypsy Laddie" (Child, No. 200), G 4, I 7, J 1–2. It should be noted that stanza 1, in some form, has circulated independently of the ballad as a whole, both in a song of Allan Ramsay's and in an English nursery rhyme (see Child, IV, 75).

1   Bessie Bell and Mary Gray,
         They were two bonnie lassies;
     They built their home on Yonburn Bay,
         And thatched it o'er with rushes.

2   They would n't have their shoes of red,
         Nor would they have them yellow;
     But they would have a bonny green,
         To walk the streets of Yarrow.

23

GEORDIE

(CHILD, NO. 209)

OTHER American texts of this ballad have been printed as follows: — by Belden (*Journal*, XX, 319; Missouri); Shoemaker, p. 140 (Pennsylvania); Campbell and Sharp, No. 28 (North Carolina); cf. Pound, p. 11; *Bulletin*, Nos. 7, 9. They all belong to a single version (to which the West Virginia text also belongs), and show particular resemblances, as Belden remarked of his copy, to the eighteenth-century broadside "The Life and Death of George of Oxford" (Child, IV, 141; Ebsworth, *Roxburghe Ballads*, VII, 70). This American version obviously comes from the form still current in England: see Broadwood, *English Traditional Songs and Carols*, p. 32; Sharp and Marson, *Folk-Songs from Somerset*, I, 5; Sharp, *One Hundred English Folksongs*, No. 9; R. Vaughan Williams, *Folk-Songs from the Eastern Counties*, p. 47; *Journal of the Folk-Song Society*, I, 164; II, 27, 208; IV, 89, 332 (tunes); Kidson, *Traditional Tunes*, p. 24. To the same version belong "Maiden's (Maid's) Lamentation for her Georgy" (broadside, Pitts; slip, T. Birt; broadside, W. S. Fortey) and "The Life of Georgey" (broadsides: R. Evans, Chester, ca. 1831; H. Such, No. 80).

Comparison of "George of Oxford" with the current version shows one stanza in the West Virginia text (3) which cannot have come from anything in the black-letter piece, but which is represented in some of the traditional versions in Child (A 12, B 21, C 10, D 16, etc.). The inference is irresistible that "George of Oxford" is a literary rifacimento of a traditional form of the song, and this is confirmed by certain features of the black-letter text (*e. g.*, lines 89–92); perhaps also by the fact that this text was to be sung "to a pleasant New Tune, called, *Poor Georgy*."

No local title. Communicated by Mrs. Hilary G. Richardson, Clarksburg, Harrison County, December 3, 1917; obtained from Mrs. Nancy McAtee. Printed, *Journal*, XXXII, 504.

1 Go saddle me up my milk-white steed,
　　Go saddle it full gaily,
　Until I write[1] to the earthen sires,
　　To plead for the life of Georgie.

2 She rid till she came to the earthen sires' office,
　　So early in the morning;
　She tumbled down on her bended knees,
　　Saying, "Spare me the life of Georgie."

3 There was an old man stepped up to her,
　　He looked as he was pleasing:
　"O pretty maid, if it lays in my power,
　　I'll spare you the life of Georgie."

[1] Or *ride*.

4 The judge looked over his left shoulder,
     He looked as if he was angry;
Says, "Now, pretty miss, you've come too late,
     For Georgie he's condemned already."

5 "If Georgie ever trampled on the king's highway,
     Or did he murder any?"
"He stole sixteen of the milk-white steeds,
     And conveyed them away to the army."

6 Georgie he was hung in a white silk robe,
     Such robes there was not many,
Because he was of that royal blood
     And was loved by a virtuous lady.

24

THE BRAES O' YARROW

(CHILD, No. 214)

THE text found in West Virginia is not derived from any of the English versions printed in Child, but from "The Braes of Yarrow," William Hamilton of Bangour (see Child, IV, 163). Cf. Reed Smith, *Journal*, XXVII, 59, and XXVIII, 200; Cox, XLVI, 145.

"The Braes O' Yarrow." Contributed by Miss Fannie Eagan, Hinton, Summers County, February, 1917; learned from Miss Amelia G. Bruce, who came from Scotland about twenty years before and had recently returned to Edinburgh to live.

1 Busk ye, busk ye, my bonnie, bonnie bride,
    Busk ye, busk ye, my winsome marrow;
  Busk ye, busk ye, my bonnie, bonnie bride,
    And think nae mair o' the braes o' Yarrow.

2 "Where got ye that bonnie, bonnie bride?
    Where got ye that winsome marrow?"
  "I got her where I dasena weel be seen,
    Pu'ing the birks on the braes o' Yarrow."

3 Weep not, weep not, my bonnie, bonnie bride;
    Weep not, weep not, my winsome marrow;
  Nor let thy heart lament to leave,
    Pu'ing the birks on the braes o' Yarrow.

4 "Why does she weep, thy bonnie, bonnie bride?
    Why does she weep, thy winsome marrow?"
  And why daus ye nae mair be seen,
    Pu'ing the birks on the braes o' Yarrow?"

5 Lang maun she weep, lang maun she weep,
    Lang maun she weep wi' dule and sorrow;
  And lang maun I nae mair weel be seen,
    Pu'ing the birks on the braes o' Yarrow.

6 For she has tint her lover, lover dear,
    Her lover dear, the cause of sorrow;
  And I have slain the comeliest swain,
    That e'er pu'ed birks on the braes o' Yarrow.

7 Fair was thy love, fair, fair indeed thy love,
  In flowery bands thou didst him fetter;
 Tho' he was fair and well beloved again,
  Than me, he did not love thee better.

8 Busk ye, busk ye, my bonnie, bonnie bride,
  Busk ye, busk ye, my winsome marrow;
 Busk ye, and lo'e me on the banks o' Tweed,
  And think nae mair o' the braes o' Yarrow.

25

JAMES HARRIS (THE DAEMON LOVER)

(CHILD, No. 243)

TWENTY-ONE variants have been found in West Virginia, under the titles: "The House Carpenter," "The House Carpenter's Wife," and "The Salt Water Sea" (cf. Cox, XLV, 159). The story is virtually the same in all the variants.

In the main, the West Virginia variants agree very closely with Child B, but contain here and there stanzas that show relations to other Child versions. The returned lover has lost all trace of the "Daemon," unless such a trace is found in A 13, 14.

For a list of American texts see *Journal*, XXX, 325; XXXV, 346. Add Campbell and Sharp, No. 29 (North Carolina, Kentucky, Tennessee); Pound, No. 17 (Illinois; same as *Journal*, XXVI, 360); Minish MS. (North Carolina); *Bulletin*, Nos. 6-11.

A

"The House Carpenter." Communicated by Mr. Decker Toney, Queens Ridge, Wayne County, January 20, 1916; obtained from his mother, who learned it from her sister.

1   "Well met, well met, my old true love,
        Well met, well met!" said he;
    "I have come from the rolling salty sea,
        And for all the sake, love, of thee.

2   "I could have married a king's daughter,
        A beautiful dame was she;
    But I have forsaken a rich crown of gold,
        And all for the sake, love, of thee."

3   "If you could have married a king's daughter,
        I'm sure you are to blame;
    I have just married a house carpenter,
        And I think he's a fine young man."

4   "If you will forsake your house carpenter
        And go along with me,
    I'll take you where the grass grows green
        On the banks of Sweet Willie."

5   "If I should forsake my house carpenter
        And go along with you,
    And you'd have nothing to supply me with,
        O Lord, what should I do?"

6 "I have six ships on the ocean, love,
　　Sailing for dry land;
　One hundred and ten of your own countrymen
　　Shall go at your command."

7 She dressed herself in silk so fine,
　　In rings and diamonds and gold;
　And as she walked her rooms all round,
　　She was a beauty to behold.

8 She picked up her tender little babe
　　And gave it kisses three;
　"Lie there, lie there, my tender little babe,
　　And keep your papa company."

9 They had not been on board the ship,
　　Not over two weeks or three,
　This fair lady sat down to weep,
　　And she wept most bitterly.

10 "What are you weeping about, my old true love,
　　What are you weeping about?" said he.
　"Are you weeping about your house carpenter,
　　Whose face you can never more see?

11 "Are you weeping for riches, my love,
　　Or are you weeping for store?
　Are you weeping for your tender little babe,
　　Whose face you'll see no more?"

12 "I am not weeping for riches, love,
　　I am not weeping for store;
　I am weeping for my tender little babe,
　　Whose face I'll see no more."

13 "What hills, what hills are those, my love,
　　That look so bright and high?"
　"It's the hills, it's the hills of heaven, my dear,
　　Where all righteous people lie."

14 "What hills, what hills, are those, my love,
　　That look so dark and low?"
　"It's the hills, it's the hills of hell, my dear,
　　Where you and I must go."

15 They had not been on board of the ship,
　　Not over three weeks or four,
　There sprang a leak in the bottom of the ship,
　　And she sank for to rise no more.

𝓑

"The House Carpenter." Communicated by Mr. Greenland Thompson Federer, Morgantown, Monongalia County, January, 1917; taken from an old manuscript song book owned by Lizzie Kelly, Independence. A name at the end of the ballad seems to indicate that it was taken down from the dictation of Mary Guseman.

1   "Well met, well met, my own true love,
    Well met, well met!" cried he;
  "I have just returned from the salt, salt sea;
    It was all for the love of thee.

2   "I could have married the king's daughter,
    And vain[1] she'd 'a' married me;
  But I refused all her crown of gold,
    'T was all for love of thee."

3   "If you could have married the king's daughter,
    I am sure you are much to blame;
  For now I am married to a house carpenter,
    And I think him a nice young man."

4   "O won't you forsake your house carpenter
    And go to sea with me?
  I will take you down where the grass grows green,
    On the banks of sweet Italy."

5   "If I forsake my house carpenter
    And go to sea with you,
  O what have you to support me on
    And keep me from slavery?"

6   "I've seven ships all on the sea,
    All sailing for dry land;
  I've a hundred and ten of the finest waiting men,
    That shall be at your command."

7   She took her babe up in her arms
    And gave it kisses three:
  "Stay at home, my sweet little babe,
    And keep your papa company."

8   She dressed herself in rich appearl,[2]
    Most beautiful to behold;
  And she walked down by the river-side,
    She shone like glittering gold.

[1] For *fain*.   [2] *Apparel*.

9   She had not been on the sea two weeks,
       I'm sure it was not three,
    Till this fair lady began to weep:
       O she wept most bitterly.

10 "And is it for my gold you weep,
       Or is it for my store?
    Or is it for your house carpenter,
       That you never will see any more?"

11 "It is not for your gold I weep,
       Nor is it for your store;
    But it is for that sweet little babe,
       That I never shall see any more."

12 She had not been on the sea three week,
       I'm sure it was not four,
    Till from the deck she sprang a leak,
       And she sank to rise no more.

13 The captain, crew, tried to save,
       But it was all in vain;
    She sank, O she sank to the bottom of the sea,
       And she sleeps in a watery grave.

14 O now her child is growing up,
       Her husband doing well,
    While this fair lady lies in the bottom of the sea,
       And her soul is doomed to hell.

C

"The House Carpenter."   Communicated by Professor Walter Barnes, Fairmont, Marion County, January, 1917; given to him by Mr. George Gregg, Pocahontas County, who obtained it from Miss Grace Bernard, Durbin.

1   "Well met, well met, my own true love,
       Well met, well met!" said he;
    "For I have just returned from the salt, salt sea,
       And it's all for the love of thee.

2   "I could have married a king's daughter dear,
       And she would have married me;
    But her chains in gold I did refuse,
       And it's all for the love of thee."

3   "If I could forsake my house carpenter
      And go along with thee,
  What would you have to maintain me on
      And keep me from poverty?"

4   "I have six ships on sea
      And seven more on land;
  If you will go along with me,
      They'll be at your command."

5   She dressed herself in scarlet red,
      Most beautiful to behold;
  And as she walked the streets up and down,
      She shone like glittering gold.

6   She picked up her own little babe
      And gave it kisses three,
  Saying, "Stay at home my sweet little babe,
      And keep papa's company."

7   Saying, "Who will shoe your pretty feet,
      And who will glove your hand,
  And who will kiss your red rosy cheek,
      When I'm in a foreign land?"

8   "My papa will shoe my pretty little feet,
      And he will glove my hand;
  And you may kiss my red rosy cheek,
      When returned from the foreign land."

9   She had not been on board two weeks,
      I am sure it was not three,
  Until this lady began to weep,
      And she wept most bitterly.

10   Saying, "Is it for my gold you weep,
      Or is it for my store?
  Or is it for the house carpenter,
      Who you will never see more?"

11   "It's neither for your gold I weep,
      Or is it for your store;
  But it's all for the love of the sweet little babe,
      Who I shall never see any more."

12   She had not been on board three weeks,
  I am sure it was not four,
The ship it sprang a leak,
  And she sank to rise never more,

13   Saying, "Cursed be to a seaman,
  And curse a sailor's life,
For robbing a house carpenter of his wealth
  And stealing away his wife!"

14   The little babe in the churchyard lies,
  And it's mother in the bottom of the sea;
And it's father roams all over the world,
  And still no pleasure can see.

D

"The House Carpenter." Communicated by Mr. George Paugh, Thomas, Tucker County, October 1915; written down for him by Mrs. Stella Thomas, Ben Bush.

1   "Well met, well met, my own true love,
  Well met, well met," said he;
"I have just returned from the salt, salt sea,
  And it's all for the love of thee.

2   "I could have married a queen's daughter fair,
  In fain married would she be;
But I regret of her golden crown,
  And it's all for the love of thee."

3   "You should have married a queen's daughter,
  In fain married would she;
For I have married a house carpenter,
  And a fine young man is he."

4   "If you will forsake your house carpenter,
  And go along with me,
I'll take you where the grass grows green,
  On the banks of a sweet libertee."

5   "If I would forsake my house carpenter,
  And go along with thee,
What have you to maintain me on,
  And keep me from misery?"

6   "Seven ships I have out on the sea,
      Seven more I have at land;
  One hundred and ten, brave jolly young men,
      All to be at your command."

7   "Then I will forsake my house carpenter
      And go along with thee,
  If you will take me where the grass grows green,
      On the banks of the sweet libertee."

8   She called her children to her side,
      And gave them kisses three,
  Saying, "Stay at home with your papa, dear,
      And keep him in company."

9   She dressed herself in rich array,
      Most glorious to behold;
  And every town that she sailed through,
      She shone like the glittering gold.

10   "O do you weep for gold," he said,
      "Or do you weep for fear?
  Or do you weep for the house carpenter,
      That you left and came with me here?"

11   "I do not weep for gold," she said,
      "I do not weep for fear;
  But I do weep for the pretty little babes,
      That I left and came with you here."

12   We had not been at sea three weeks,
      I am sure it was not four,
  Till this fair lillie threw herself overboard,
      And her weeping was heard no more.

13   He turned himself round about,
      With dark and watering eyes,
  Saying, "The nearest and the dearest of this world must
      part,
      And so must you and I."

14   O cursed be those seafaring men,
      O cursed be their lives,
  For the robbing of the house carpenter
      And the stealing away of his wife!

15 They had not sailed half across the main,
  Till the winds began to roar,
 And the ship sprang a leak, and she sank to the deep,
  And she sank to rise no more.

E

"The House Carpenter." Communicated by Mr. George Paugh, Thomas, Tucker County; learned from his mother, whose maiden name was Ida Knapp. Printed by Cox, XLIV, 388.

1 "Well met, well met, my own true love,
  Well met, well met!" cried he;
 "I am just returning home from the sea,
  And it's all for the sake of thee, thee, thee,
  And it's all for the sake of thee.

2 "I could have married the king's daughter dear,
  I'm sure she'd a married me;
 But I forsook her crowns of gold,
  And it's all for the love of thee."

3 "If you could of married the king's daughter dear,
  I'm sure you're much to blame;
 For I have married a house carpenter,
  And I'm sure he's a nice young man."

4 "If you will forsake your house carpenter,
  And go along with me,
 I'll take you where the grass grows green,
  On the banks of the sweet Morea."

5 "If I forsake my house carpenter,
  And go along with thee,
 What have you to support me upon,
  To keep me from poverty?"

6 "I have on sea one hundred ships,
  All sailing for dry land;
 One hundred and ten nice, jolly young men, —
  They shall be at your command."

7 She picked up her sweet little babe,
  The kisses she gave was three,
 Saying, "Stay at home my sweet little babe,
  Keep your father's company."

8   She dressed herself in richery,
        Most beauteous to behold;
    And as they walked along the street,
        She shined like glittering gold.

9   They had not been on the sea two weeks,
        I'm sure it was not three,
    Until this maid began to weep,
        And she wept most bitterly.

10 "Are you weeping for your gold,
        Or for your richery?
    Or are you weeping for your house carpenter,
        That you never again shall see?"

11 "I'm neither weeping for my gold,
        Nor for my richery;
    But I'm weeping for my sweet little babe,
        That I never again shall see."

12 "Cheer up, cheer up, my own true love,
        Cheer up, cheer up," said he;
    "I'll take you where the grass grows green,
        On the banks of the sweet Morea."

13 They had not been on the sea three weeks,
        I'm sure it was not four,
    Until the ship it sprang a leak,
        And it sank for to rise no more.

14 "Cursed be to all seafaring young men,
        Cursed be to the sailor's life,
    Who has robbed me of my house carpenter,
        And taken away my life!"

F

"The House Carpenter." Communicated by Mrs. Hilary G. Richardson, Clarksburg, Harrison County, March 15, 1916; obtained from Mrs. Rachel Fogg, originally from Doddridge County. She learned it from her mother, and she from her mother. Eight stanzas.

G

"The House Carpenter." Contributed by Mrs. J. J. Haines, Parkersburg, Wood County, January, 1916. She writes: "I have heard these old ballads sung from earliest recollections by grandparents and others. My ancestors on both sides came to America in the time of colonization. A variant in ten stanzas, the first one corrupt."

H

"The Carpenter's Wife." Communicated by Professor C. E. Haworth, Huntington, Cabell County. Obtained from Mrs. J. A. Rollyson, who says it is familiar in Clay, Braxton, and Calhoun Counties. Ten stanzas; heroine's name, Ellen.

I

"The House Carpenter." Communicated by Mr. Rex Hoke, Second Creek, Monroe County, February 4, 1916; obtained from his mother, who learned it in 1871 from Cyrus McKinsley. An excellent text in fourteen stanzas.

J

"The House Carpenter." Communicated by Miss Lalah Lovett, Bulltown Braxton County. Obtained from Mrs. Cora Starkey, Clarksburg; learned from her parents, who learned it in Virginia from their parents, who were of English descent. Twelve stanzas. The heroine dressed herself in a "scarlet robe" and "walked the downward road." The ship sails "two links from land."

K

"The House Carpenter." Communicated by Anna Copley, Shoals, Wayne County, December 28, 1915; obtained from Luther Burwell, who learned it from his mother about fifty years previously. Twelve stanzas. The heroine dressed herself in white and trimmed herself in green.

L

"The House Carpenter." Contributed by Professor A. J. Hare, Morgantown, Monongalia County. He learned it when a child from his mother. Ten stanzas.

M

"The House Carpenter." Contributed by Mr. W. T. Ryan, Chicago, Illinois, a native of Monongalia County. Reported August 10, 1915; learned about fifty years before from a relative. Eleven stanzas.

N

"The House Carpenter." Communicated by Mrs. Elizabeth Tapp Peck, Morgantown, Monongalia County, March 31, 1916; obtained from her mother, Mrs. Thomas H. Tapp, who learned it from her mother, Mrs. Elizabeth Wade Mack, who lived in her youth near Bethel Church. A very good text in thirteen stanzas.

O

"The House Carpenter." Communicated by Miss Alice Brake, Webster Springs, Webster County, February 27, 1916; obtained from her mother, who probably learned it from her brothers. Nine stanzas.

P

"House Carpenter." Contributed by Miss Polly McKinney, Sophia, Raleigh County, 1919. Eleven stanzas.

Q

"Salt Water Sea." Communicated by Miss Sallie Evans, Elkins, Randolph County, 1916; obtained from Mr. Guy Marshall, who got it from his mother, who learned it from her mother. Ten stanzas.

R

"The House Carpenter." Communicated by Professor Walter Barnes, Fairmont, Marion County, May 19, 1916; obtained from Miss Daisy Watkins, who learned it from her mother. Ten stanzas, much corrupted.

S

"The House Carpenter." Communicated by Professor Walter Barnes, Fairmont, Marion County, July, 1915; obtained from Mr. C. W. Cunningham, Elkins, Randolph County, who learned it from his father. Seven stanzas.

T

"The House Carpenter's Wife." Contributed by Miss Maud Groves, Deepwell, Nicholas County, August 3, 1915; learned from Mr. Wiley Geho. Twelve stanzas.

U

"The House Carpenter." Communicated by Professor Walter Barnes, Fairmont, Marion County, 1919. It appeared shortly before in a Tyler County newspaper, which says of it in part: "Mrs. Nora V. Ankron of near Kidwell gives us a faded copy of an old ballad that was sung by the old settlers in Tyler and Wetzel counties back prior to the Civil War and had its origin possibly in the romantic adventures of some Saxon seaman. The copy she handed us was written on July 5th, 1869, on old fashioned foolscap paper." An excellent text in twelve stanzas.

26

HENRY MARTIN

(CHILD, No. 250)

THE only version found in West Virginia goes under the title: "Three Brothers of Scotland." It is practically identical with the American version printed by Child, v, 302, with the exception of stanza 8, which is not found in Child. For references to American texts and recent English tradition, see *Journal*, XXX, 327.

"Three Brothers of Scotland." Communicated by Mr. George Paugh, Thomas, Tucker County, January 10, 1916; written down by Mrs. Stella Thomas, Ben Bush, who had learned it about twenty years before from her mother. Reported by Cox, XLV, 160.

1 Three loving brothers in Scotland did dwell,
  Three loving brothers were they;
They each cast lots to see who must go
  To maintain his two brothers and he.

2 The lot it fell on Andrew Bardun,
  The youngest of the three,
That he should go roving around the salt sea
  To maintain his two brothers and he.

3 They had not sailed scarce three winter's nights,
  Till a ship they did espy,
A-sailing far off and a-sailing far off,
  And at last they came sailing along side.

4 "Who's there? Who's there?" cried Andrew Bardun,
  "Who's there that sails so nigh?"
"We are the rich merchants from old England,
  And be pleased if you'd let us pass by."

5 "O no! O no!" cried Andrew Bardun,
  "That thing can never be;
Your ship and your cargo I have, my brave boys,
  And your body I'll drown in the sea."

6 And when the men reached old England,
  It caused the king to frown,
To think that his ship and his cargo had [been] taken,
  And many a man had been drowned.

7 "Go build me a ship," cried Captain Charles Stewart,
    "Go build it strong and sure;
If I don't bring you in Andrew Bardun,
    My life will no longer endure."

8 The ship was built at his command,
    'T was built both strong and sure;
And Captain Charles Stewart was placed thereon,
    For to maintain his crew.

9 They had not sailed scarce three winter's nights,
    Till the ship they did espy,
A-sailing far off and a-sailing far off,
    And at last they came sailing long side.

10 "Who's there? Who's there?" cried Captain Charles
    Stewart,
    "Who's there that sails so nigh?"
"We are the bold robbers from old Scotland,
    And be pleased if you'd let us pass by."

11 "O no! O no!" cried Captain Charles Stewart,
    "That thing can never be;
Your ship and your cargo I have, my brave boys,
    And your bodies I carry with me."

12 "Come on! Come on!" cried Andrew Bardun,
    "I'll value not one pin;
If you can but show me bright brasses without,
    I'll show you good steel within."

13 Now the battle had begun,
    Loud the cannons roared;
They had not fought scarcely a half hour,
    Till Captain Charles gave o'er.

14 "Go home! Go home!" cried Andrew Bardun,
    "Go home and tell your king,
That he can reign king o'er all the dry land,
    I'll reign king over the sea."

27

THE SUFFOLK MIRACLE

(CHILD, No. 272)

THIS famous ballad has found its way through oral transmission to West Virginia, where it was recorded in 1919. In its long journey it has lost its name, and has become somewhat confused at the beginning; many stanzas have dropped out. Moreover, the incident of binding the handkerchief round the dead man's head has disappeared.

For texts from North Carolina and Tennessee, see Campbell and Sharp, No. 31. A Virginia text is reported in *Bulletin*, No. 7, p. 6.

"A Lady near New York Town." Contributed by Miss Polly McKinney, Sophia, Raleigh County, 1919. She writes: "Grandma Lester taught me the song when I was a little child. Grandma is eighty-five years old. She says the song is very old. Her mother taught it to her when she was a little girl." Printed by Cox, XLVII, 86.

1 There was a lady near New York Town,
    She was proper straight and tall;
    She was straight and tall,
    And has a handsome face after all.

2 The boys came courting her far and near,
    But none of them could her favor gain,
    Except the wealthy old Squire's son,
    Who courted her favor and won.

3 But when her father came to know,
    He sent her three hundred miles or more;
    He first declared and then he swore,
    Back home she should never come any more.

4 The young man mourned, he wept, he sighed,
    At length for love this young man died.
    He had not been more than twelve months dead,
    Until he rode on a milk-white steed.

5 "Your mother's cloak, your father's steed,
    I've come after you in great speed."
    As her old uncle understood,
    He thought it was for her own good.

6 She jumped up all behind him,
    They rode rather swifter than the wind,
    In the length of three hours, or a little more,
    He sat her at her father's door.

7 "Go in, go in, go in," said he,
   "While I go put this steed away."
   She knocked at her father's door,
   The sight of him she could see no more.

8 Her father arose, put on his clothes,
   Saying, "My dear child you're welcome home.
   What trusty friend have been with you?
   What trusty friend have brought you here?"

9 "Did you not send my old true love,
   Who I should never love no more?"
   It made the hair rise on his head
   To think he had been twelve months dead.

10 They called old and young and to them did say:
   "In love let your children have their way;
   In love let children have their way,
   Or else their love might them decay."

28

OUR GOODMAN

(CHILD, No. 274)

THREE variants of the same version of this ballad have been recovered in West Virginia under the title of "Home Came the Old Man." This version is the same as Child A. By variation or extension several vulgar stanzas are current in West Virginia and elsewhere. For American texts see *Journal*, XVIII, 294 (Barry; Massachusetts); XXX, 199 (Parsons, North Carolina); Smith, p. 16 (Virginia); Campbell and Sharp, No. 32 (North Carolina); Belden's Missouri collection. For references see *Journal*, XXIX, 166; XXX, 328; XXXV, 348.

A

"Home Came The Old Man." Communicated by Mrs. Elizabeth Tapp Peck, Morgantown, Monongalia County, March 31, 1916; obtained from her mother, Mrs. Thomas H. Tapp, who learned it from her mother, Mrs. Elizabeth Wade Mack. Printed by Cox, XLV, 58.

1   Home came the old man,
         Home came he;
     He went into the parlor,
         A strange coat did see.

2   "My wife, my beloved wife,
         What does all this mean?
     A strange coat here,
         Where my own ought to been?"

3   "You old fool, you blind fool,
         O can you not but see,
     'T is nothing but a blanket,
         My mother sent to me?"

4   "Miles have I travelled,
         Five hundred miles or more,
     But buttons on a blanket,
         I never saw before."

5   Home came the old man,
         Home came he;
     He went into the kitchen,
         A strange gun did see.

6 "My wife, my beloved wife,
      O what does all this mean?
   A strange gun here,
      Where my own ought to been?"

7 "You old fool, you blind fool,
      O can you not but see,
   'T is nothing but a mush-stick,
      My mother sent to me?"

8 "Miles have I travelled,
      Five hundred miles or more,
   But a gun for a mush-stick,
      I never saw before."

9 Home came the old man,
      Home came he;
   He went into the stable,
      A strange horse did see.

10 "My wife, my beloved wife,
      O what does all this mean?
    A strange horse here,
      Where my own ought to been?"

11 "You old fool, you blind fool,
      O can you not but see,
    'T is nothing but a milch cow,
      My mother sent to me?"

12 "Miles have I travelled,
      Five hundred miles or more,
    But a saddle on a milch cow,
      I never saw before."

13 Home came the old man,
      Home came he;
    He went into a bed room,
      A strange face did see.

14 "My wife, my beloved wife,
      O what does all this mean?
    A strange face here,
      Where my own ought to been?"

15 "You old fool, you blind fool,
    O can you not but see,
'T is nothing but a baby,
    My mother sent to me?"

16 "Miles have I travelled,
    Five hundred miles or more,
But whiskers on a baby's face,
    I never saw before."

𝐵

"Home Came The Old Man." Communicated by Mr. Walter M. Duke, Shepherdstown, Jefferson County, May 6, 1916; dictated by Mrs. R. A. Jaques, Hedgesville, who learned it in childhood from her mother. Printed by Cox, XLV, 92.

1 Home came the old man,
    Home came he;
He went into the house,
    Strange boots did see.

2 "My wife, my beloved wife,
    O what does all this mean?
Strange boots here,
    Where mine ought to been?"

3 "You old fool, you blind fool,
    Can you not but see,
'T is nothing but a bootjack,
    That my mother sent to me?"

4 "Miles have I travelled,
    Five hundred miles or more,
But spurs on a bootjack,
    I never saw before."

5 Home came the old man,
    Home came he;
He went into the kitchen,
    A strange hat did see.

6 "My wife, my beloved wife,
    O what does all this mean?
A strange hat here,
    Where my own ought to been?"

7 "You old fool, you blind fool,
        O can you not but see,
    'T is nothing but a dinner pot,
        That mother sent to me?"

8 "Miles have I travelled,
        Five hundred miles or more,
    But crape on a dinner pot,
        I never saw before."

9 Home came the old man,
        Home came he;
    He went into the house,
        A strange shirt did see.

10 "My wife, my beloved wife,
        O what does all this mean?
    A strange shirt here,
        Where my own ought to been?'

11 "You old fool, you blind fool,
        Can you not but see,
    'T is nothing but a table cloth,
        My mother sent to me?"

12 "Miles have I travelled,
        Five hundred miles or more,
    But sleeves on a table cloth,
        I never saw before."

13 Home came the old man,
        Home came he;
    He went into the bed room,
        A strange face did see.

14 "My wife, my beloved wife,
        O what does all this mean?
    A strange face here,
        Where mine ought to been?"

15 "You old fool, you blind fool,
        O can you not but see,
    'T is nothing but a baby,
        My mother sent to me?"

16 "Miles have I travelled,
        Five hundred miles or more,
    But whiskers on a baby's face,
        I never saw before."

C

"Home Came The Old Man." Communicated by Miss Mary Meeks Atkeson, Morgantown, Monongalia County, June, 1917; obtained from Miss Effie Anderson, a student in West Virginia University.

1   Home came the old man,
        Home came he;
    He went into the parlor,
        A strange coat did see.

2   "My wife, my beloved wife,
        O what does this mean?
    A strange coat here,
        Where my own ought to be?"

3   "You old fool, you blind fool,
        O can you not but see,
    'T is nothing but a blanket,
        My mother sent to me?"

4   "Miles have I travelled,
        Five hundred miles or more,
    But buttons on a blanket,
        Did I never see before."

5   Home came the old man,
        Home came he;
    He went into the bed room,
        A strange face did see.

6   "My wife, my beloved wife,
        O what does this mean?
    A strange face here,
        Where my own ought to be?"

7   "You old fool, you blind fool,
        O can you not but see,
    'T is nothing but a baby,
        That my mother sent to me?"

8   "Miles have I travelled,
        Five hundred miles or more,
    But whiskers on a baby's face,
        I ne'er did see before."

29

THE WIFE WRAPT IN WETHER'S SKIN

(CHILD, No. 277)

IN West Virginia, this ballad goes under the titles: "Dandoo," "Bandoo," and "Gentle Virginia." Five variants have been found, A, B, and D practically alike and very similar to the version printed by Belden, *Journal*, XIX, 298. The first four and the last two stanzas in C correspond to stanzas in A or B, but the arrangement is somewhat confused and several stanzas are more or less corrupt. Stanzas 5, 6, 7, and 8 are not to be found in any other American version nor in any of the Child versions. They may point to a different source for this copy, or they may have been deliberately added by some singer to satisfy a whim or to make a local hit. In phraseology and in the burden, E shows a close relationship to the text printed by Newell, *Journal*, VII, 253 (Child, V, 304).

For American texts see *Journal*, VII, 253 (Newell; Massachusetts; reprinted by Child, V, 304); XIX, 298 (Belden; Missouri); XXX, 328 (Kittredge, from Belden; Missouri; reprinted by Pound, No. 6 A); Campbell and Sharp, No. 33 (Virginia and Kentucky); Pound, No. 6 B (Nebraska). For references see *Journal*, XXX, 328. Add *Bulletin*, Nos. 7–10; Reed Smith, *Journal*, XXVIII, 200.

$\mathcal{A}$

"Dandoo." Contributed by Mr. Wallie Barnett, Leon, Mason County, 1915; learned from his grandfather about the year 1898. His grandfather was of English descent, a native of Gilmer County. The last stanza was furnished by some teacher whose name was not secured. It is a reminiscence of the famous nursery rhymes about the man who had naught — "and robbers came to rob him." Reported by Cox, XLV, 159.

1 There was a little man, he lived in the West,
 Dandoo, dandoo
There was a little man, he lived in the West,
 Ham bam gingo
There was a little man, he lived in the West,
He had an old woman that was none of the best.
 With a ham bam berry winkeye doodle jerry comingo
 calla callacum collingo

2 He came in from sowing wheat,
Says, "Old woman, is there anything to eat?"

3 "There lies some bread all on the shelf,
If you want any more you can get it yourself."

4 He went out to his sheepfold,
He killed a ewe both fat and old.

5   He hung her up on two little pins,
     With two little jerks she was skinned.

6   "I'll tan the hide on my wife's back,
     Take two little sticks to make it crack."

7   "I'll tell all my folks and all my kin,
     You whip me on the naked skin."

8   He ran fourteen miles in fifteen days,
     And that's what I call getting away.

ℬ

"Dandoo." Contributed by Miss Courtney, Clay Court House, Clay County, August 8, 1918.

1   There was an old man lived in the West,
       Dandoo
   There was an old man lived in the West,
       Tommy Tim cli clingo
   There was an old man lived in the West,
   He had a little old wife that was none of the best.
       With a hare and a bear liddy I cliddy I Tommy Tim
         cli clingo

2   This old man went out to plow,
     "Hey! old woman, is dinner ready now?"

3   "A piece of dry bread lies on the shelf,
     If you want any more you can get it yourself."

4   This old man went to his sheepfold,
     And the best old wether he strung on a pole.

5   He threw the skin around his wife's back,
     And two little sticks went whickity whack.

6   "I'll tell our neighbors and all our kin,
     The way you tan your wether's skin."

7   This old man then ran away,
     Went fourteen miles in fifteen days.

C

"Dandoo." Communicated by Miss Maud Groves, Deepwell, Nicholas County, April 27, 1916; obtained from Miss Bertie Johnson, who learned it about twenty years before from Russel McMillon in Greenbrier County. Printed by Cox, XLV, 92.

1 Little old man he lived in the West,
        Dandoo dandoo
   Little old man he lived in the West,
        Ham bam jingo
   Little old man he lived in the West,
   And he married a woman she was none of the best.
        And a ham bam by and a winkeye doodle jar and a
        mingo come like a lightning

2 Little old man went out to plough,
   And when he came to his breakfast now,

3 A piece of corn dodger was laying on the shelf:
   "If you want any thing better, you can get it yourself."

4 Little old man he swore he would run away,
   And he run fourteen miles in fifteen days,
   And that's what I call getting away.

5 He run till he came to his father's house:
   "O father, O father, my wife's caught a louse."

6 "O son, O son, if you have took my advice,
   You would have married a woman that had no lice."

7 "Father, O father, hold your tongue!
   You married my mother when she was young,

8 "And hair was thick and lips were thin,
   When she went to stir her puddin' and her nose dipped in."

9 He run till he came to a sheep pen,
   And there he found an old sheepskin.

10 And he cut off a piece and threw it over his back,
    And he made that tail go whickity whack.

11 "Father and mother and all your kin,
    And that's the way I tan my old sheepskin."

D

"Bandoo." Contributed by Mr. B. C. Cutlip, Hacker Valley, Webster County, August, 1921.

1 There was an old man who lived in the West,
  Bandoo tol de day
There was an old man who lived in the West,
And his old wife was none of the best.
  To me arms Barney while I curry Mingo
  Comme comme cannick klice and a clingo

2 O, the old man he went out to plow,
Saying,"O, good wife, is my breakfast ready now?"

3 "There's a piece of bread upon the shelf,
If you want any more you can bake it yourself."

4 O, he killed a wether and hung it on a pin,
And with his knife ripped off the skin.

5 O, he stretched that skin on his wife's back,
And with a withe went whickaty whack.

6 "O, I'll tell dad and mam and all my kin,
What a whipping you gave me."

7 "O, you can tell dad and mam and all your kin,
But I'm just dusting my old wether's skin."

E

"Gentle Virginia." Contributed by Miss Florence Miller, Turtle Creek, Boone County, 1919.

1 I married me a wife,
  Gentle Virginia my Rosy my Lee
And I wish to the Lord I had let her alone.
  As the dew flies over the green valley

2 So the very next day I went out to plow,
I come in, "Is my dinner ready now?"

3 "You triflin' old scamp, you triflin' old whelp,
If you get any dinner, you'll get it yourself."

4 So I went into the kitchen, what I did not choose,
In fear I would spoil my new cloth shoes.

5 So I went out to the barn,
   I cut me a switch as long as my arm.

6 And on my way back [her] I met,
   And around her back went whickity whack.

7 "I'll tell all my people, I'll tell all my kin,
   You beat me up with a hickory limb."

8 "Go tell all your people, go tell all your kin,
   If I take a notion I'll whip you again."

9 And ever since that she has been a good wife,
   And I hope that she will to the end of her life.

30

THE FARMER'S CURST WIFE

(CHILD, No. 278)

ONE copy only of this ballad has been found in West Virginia (reported by Cox, XLVI, 145) and, notwithstanding several prose lines, it is the most interesting of the versions recovered in this country. Notice the Falstaffian touch in stanza 7. In phraseology it shows some likenesses to Child A.

Texts and fragments have been printed from Maine, Massachusetts, Virginia, North Carolina, Kentucky, and Missouri. For references see *Journal* XXX, 329. Add Campbell and Sharp, No. 34 (North Carolina, Virginia); Sharp, *Folk-Songs of English Origin*, 2d Series, p. 12 (Kentucky); *Bulletin*, Nos. 6–10.

Communicated by Mr. Parker C. Black, Parkersburg, Wood County, January 3, 1917; received from his mother, who learned it from "my uncle, W. B. Foley, who learned it from his cousin, M. F. Foley, who learned it from one Mr. Dils, who now resides in Clarksburg."

1 There was an old man lived under the hill,
     Hi ran di dan di da
If he ain't moved away he's living there still.
     So gallop mi ran di dan di da

2 The devil came to the old man at the plow,
Says he, "I want the old woman you promised me now."

3 Says he, "You may have her with all my heart;
If you can't pack her away, I'll lend you my cart."

4 He picked her up all on his back,
And like a gay peddler went packing his sack.

5 He packed her to the gates of hell,
Says he, "Walk in and take a chair."

6 Four little devils came rattling their chains,
She up with her crutch and knocked out their brains.

7 Four more little devils says, "Hoist her up higher!"
She up with her crutch and knocked nine in the fire.

8 Four more little devils jumped upon the wall,
Cried, "Father, take her home or she'll kill us all."

9 So he picked her up all on his back,
And like an old fool went packing her back.

10 He packed her to the house where she was born,
    When she got there the old man was in bed.

11 She called for the mush that was left in the pot,
    Says he, "Old lady, we've eat it all."

12 Says he, "Old lady, did you fare very well?"
    Says she, "Old man, I flattened all hell."

13 Now you see what these old women can do,
    They can whip old men and devils too.

31

THE CRAFTY FARMER

(CHILD, No. 283)

COMMUNICATED by Miss Mary Meek Atkeson, Morgantown, Monongalia County, 1916; obtained by Mr. Fred Smith, Glenville, Gilmer County, from Paul Farnsworth, who got it from his grandmother, Mrs. Sarah Pickens, Weston, Lewis County. It was told to her by a soldier during the Civil War. The ballad has no local title. Barring verbal differences of no special significance, the first fifteen stanzas are the same as the first fifteen stanzas of Child A. Stanzas 17 and 19 are not to be found in any of the Child versions. The other stanzas agree with the remaining stanzas of Child A, but with a slight difference in the order of arrangement. Reported by Cox, XLVI, 145.

No American text of this ballad has been previously printed so far as I know. For American texts of "The Yorkshire Bite," a parallel to "The Crafty Farmer," see Barry, *Journal*, XXIII, 451 (Boston); Kittredge, *Journal*, XXX, 367 (Plymouth, Massachusetts; from Child MSS., XXVII, 188 [1]). For references see *Journal*, XXX, 367. There is an early nineteenth-century broadside of the "Bite" (Providence, Rhode Island), and the piece is reported from North Carolina (F. C. Brown, p. 7), probably from Tennessee (Reed Smith, *Journal*, XXVIII, 199), and from Michigan (Jones).

1   This story I'm going to sing,
        I hope it will give you content,
    Concerning a silly old man,
        That was going to pay his rent.

2   As he was a-riding along,
        Along all on the highway,
    A gentleman-thief overtook him,
        And thus unto him did say:

3   "O, well overtaken, old man,
        O, well overtaken," said he.
    "Thank you kindly, sir," says the old man,
        "If you be for my company."

4   "How far are you this way?"
        It made the old man to smile:
    "To tell you the truth, kind sir,
        I'm just a-going twa mile.

5   "I am but a silly old man,
        Who farms a piece of ground;
    My half-year rent, kind sir,
        Just comes to forty pound.

6 "But my landlord's not been at home,
    I've not seen him this twelve month or more;
It makes my rent to be large,
    I've just to pay him fourscore."

7 "You should not have told anybody,
    For thieves are ganging many;
If they were to light upon you,
    They would rob you of every penny."

8 "O, never mind," says the old man,
    "Thieves I fear on no side;
My money is safe in my bags,
    In the saddle on which I ride."

9 As they were riding along,
    And riding a-down a ghyll,
The thief pulled out a pistol,
    And bade the man stand still.

10 The old man was crafty and false,
    As in this world are many;
He flung his old saddle o'er t' hedge,
    And said, "Fetch it, if thou 'lt have any."

11 The thief got off his horse,
    With courage stout and bold,
To search this old man's bags,
    And gave him his horse to hold.

12 The old man put his foot in the stirrup,
    And he got on astride;
He set the thief's horse in a gallop,
    You need not bid the old man ride.

13 "O stay! O stay!" says the thief,
    "And thou half my share shalt have!"
"Nay, marry, not I," quoth the old man,
    "For once I've bitten a knave."

14 This thief he was not content,
    He thought these must be bags;
So he up with his rusty old sword,
    And chopped the old saddle to rags.

15   The old man galloped and rode,
      Until he was almost spent;
   Till he came to his landlord's house,
      And paid his whole year's rent.

16   He opened the rogue's portmantle;
      It was glorious to behold;
   There was five hundred pounds in money,
      And five hundred in gold.

17   His landlord it made him to stare,
      When he did the sight behold;
   "Where did you get the white money,
      And where get the yellow gold?"

18   "I met a fond fool by the way,
      I swapped horses and gave him no boot
   But never mind," says the old man,
      "I got a fond fool by the foot."

19   "But now you're grown cramped and old,
      Nor fit to travel about."
   "O, never mind," says the old man,
      "I can give those[1] old bones a root.[2]"

20   As he was a-riding hame,
      And a-down a narrow lane,
   He spied his mare tied to a tree,
      And said, "Tile, thou'lt now gae hame."

21   And when that he got hame,
      And told his wife what he'd done,
   She rose and she donned her clothes,
      And about the house did run.

22   She sung and she danced and she sung,
      And she sung with merry devotion:
   "If ever our daughter gets wed,
      It will help to enlarge her portion."

[1] Mistake, probably, for *these*.   [2] For *rout*, a vigorous movement.

32

THE SWEET TRINITY (THE GOLDEN VANITY)

(CHILD, No. 286)

THIS ballad is known in West Virginia as "The Green Willow Tree" and "The Golden Willow Tree." Two variants of the former have been found, practically identical, with the exception that the second has been localized in "North America." A single stanza only under the second title has been recovered. They are very similar to Child C. A and C were reported by Cox, XLV, 160 (*Journal*, XXIX, 400).

For American texts see *Journal*, XVIII, 125 (Barry; Vermont); XXIII, 429 (Belden; Missouri); XXX, 331 (Kittredge, from Belden; Missouri); *Focus*, IV, 158 (Virginia); Wyman and Brockway, p. 72 (Kentucky); McGill, p. 96 (Kentucky); Shoemaker, p. 111 (Pennsylvania); Campbell and Sharp, No. 35 (North Carolina); Pound, No. 10 (Nebraska); Minish MS. (North Carolina); *Singer's Journal*, II, 686. For references see *Journal*, XXX, 330. Add *Bulletin*, Nos. 8–10. A fragment of the ballad, combined with an additional stanza of a comic character, has been popular as a college song: Waite, *Carmina Colligensia* (Boston, cop. 1868), p. 171; *The American College Songster* (Ann Arbor, 1876), p. 101; White, *Student Life in Song* (Boston, cop. 1879), p. 58.

A

"The Green Willow Tree." Contributed by Mr. John B. Adkins, Branchland, Lincoln County, April 1, 1916; learned from a cousin, D. F. Mitchell, who learned it from an old man in Brethett County, Kentucky, by the name of Allen.

1 Once there was a ship and it sailed on the sea,
  Crying, O the lonesome Lowlands low
 Once there was a ship and it sailed on the sea,
 It went by the name of the Green Willow Tree.
  A-sailing in the Lowlands low

2 She had n't been sailing more than weeks two or three,
 Till she was overtaken by a Turkish Travelier.

3 Down stepped the Captain, says, "What shall we do?
 They will overtake us and cut us in two."

4 Up stepped the cabin-boy, says, "What will you give me,
 To stop that ship, that Turkish Travelier?"

5 "I'll give you gold or I'll give you fee,
 Besides, my oldest daughter your wife may she be."

6   So he fell upon his breast and away swame he,
    He swum till he came to the Turkish Travelier.

7   He had instruments fitten for the use,
    He bored nine holes and in poured the juice.

8   Some were playing cards and some were playing checks,
    The first thing they knew they were in water to their necks.

9   Some with their hats and some with their caps,
    Trying to stop them salt-water gaps.

10 So he fell upon his breast and away swame he,
    He swum till he came to the Green Willow Tree.

11 "Say, kind sir, won't you take me on board,
    And be to me as kind as your word?"

12 "No, kind sir, I won't take you on board,
    Neither be to you as kind as my word."

13 "If it was n't for the respect that I have for you men,
    I'd serve you as I served them."

14 He fell upon his breast and away swame he,
    And bid adieu to the Green Willow Tree.

𝓑

"The Green Willow Tree." Communicated by Miss Iva Thornton, Branch-land, Lincoln County, August 31, 1916; obtained from Parker Lucas, a blind man, who learned it when he was a boy from J. W. Adkins, his sister's husband.

1   There was a ship a-sailing off North America,
        Crying, O, 't is lonesome in the Lowlands low
    There was a ship a-sailing off North America,
    And she went by the name of the Green Willow Tree.
        As we're sailing in the Lowlands low

2   She had n't been on sea for more than weeks three,
    Until she was overtaken by the Turkish Revelee [or
        Turkey Sweveltee].

3   Up spoke the Captain, saying, "Who will it be,
    To go and destroy the Turkish Revelee?"

4   Up steps the cabin-boy, saying, "What will you give me,
    If I overtake her and destroy all her crew?"

5   "I will give you gold and I will give you fee,
     Likewise, my eldest daughter your wedded bride shall be."

6   He fell upon his breast and away swam he,
     He swam till he came to the Turkish Revelee.

7   He had a tool just fitted for the use,
     He bored in a hole and let in a sluice.

8   Some were playing cards and some were playing checks,
     And the first thing they knew they were in water to their
       necks.

9   He fell upon his breast and away swam he,
     Swam till he came to the Green Willow Tree.

10   Saying, "Captain, O Captain, won't you take me on board,
     And be as good to me as your word?"

11   "Oh no, sir, oh no, sir, not take you on board,
     Nor be as good to you as my word."

12   He fell upon his breast and down sank he,
     Bidding adieu to the Green Willow Tree.

C

"The Golden Willow Tree." Communicated by Mrs. Elizabeth Tapp Peck, Morgantown, Monongalia County, March, 1916; obtained from her mother, Mrs. Thomas H. Tapp, who learned it from her mother, Mrs. Elizabeth Wade Mack, who formerly lived near Easton.

     There is a ship in the North Countree,
    And she goes by the name of the Golden Willow Tree,
       And she lieth in the Lowlands low, low, low,
       And she lieth in the Lowlands low.

33

THE MERMAID

(Child, No. 289)

One variant has been recovered in West Virginia, under the title: "The Sinking Ship."

This is a reduced version of "The Mermaid." See *Journal*, XVIII, 136, and XXII, 78 (Barry; Vermont); XXV, 176 (Belden; Missouri); *Focus*, III, 447, and IV, 97 (Tennessee); Shoemaker, p. 157 (Pennsylvania); McGill, p. 45 (Kentucky); Luce, *Naval Songs*, 2d ed., 1902, p. 118. It is common in American songbooks and broadsides: as, *The Forget Me Not Songster* (New York, Nafis & Cornish), p. 79; the same (D. & J. Sadlier & Co.), p. 46; *Uncle Sam's Naval and Patriotic Songster*, p. 40; *Singer's Journal*, I, 301; Deming broadside (Boston, ca. 1838); De Marsan broadside, List 14, No. 56. It has long been popular as a college song: see Waite, *Carmina Colligensia* (Boston, cop. 1868), p. 19; *The American College Songster* (Ann Arbor, 1876), p. 56; Waite, *Student Life in Song* (Boston, cop. 1879), p. 47; W. H. Hills, *Students'. Songs*, p. 27; Noble, *Songs of Harvard* (cop. 1913), p. 82. For a broadly burlesque version see *The "We Won't Go Home till Morning" Songster* (cop. 1869), p. 8; *The "Slap-Bang" Songster* (cop. 1870), p. 8.

For Great Britain see Ebsworth, *Roxburghe Ballads*, VIII, 446; Callcott, *The Child's Own Singing Book* (London, 1843), reprinted in part in *Journal of the Folk-Song Society*, III, 48; the same *Journal*, III, 47, 139; V, 227; Baring-Gould, *English Minstrelsie*, VI, 74 (cf. p. vi); Ashton, *Real Sailor-Songs*, 41, 42; Stone, *Sea Songs and Ballads*, p. 17; Buck, *The Oxford Song Book*, 1916, p. 136; Duncan, *The Minstrelsy of England*, I, 266; *The Scottish Students' Song Book*, p. 122. The ballad is common in modern broadsides (as, Pitts; Catnach, Such, No. 53; Harkness, Preston, No. 146; Gilbert, Newcastle, No. 77; Ross, Newcastle, No. 77; J. Arthur, Carlisle; slip, J. & H. Baird). A part of the song is used in a children's game: see Gomme, *Traditional Games*, II, 143, 422.

"The Sinking Ship." Contributed by Miss Sallie Dice Jones, Franklin, Pendleton County, September 23, 1916.

1   Up stepped the captain of our gallant ship,
      A fine looking man was he:
"I've a wife and a child in my own native land,
      Who this night are looking out for me, for me,
      Who this night are looking out for me."

Chorus

O the stormy winds do blow,
      And the raging seas o'er they flow,
While we poor sailors are toiling in the tower below,
      And the landsmen are lying down below,
      And the landsmen are lying down below.

2 Up stepped a youth of our gallant ship,
  A brave looking lad was he:
 "I've a father and a mother in my own native land,
  Who this night are looking for me,
  Who this night are looking for me."

3 Three times around sailed our gallant ship,
  Three times around sailed she,
 And when she was going the fourth time around,
  She sank to the bottom of the sea, the sea,
  She sank to the bottom of the sea.

34

ROBIN HOOD

COMMUNICATED by Miss Sallie D. Jones, Hillsboro, Pocahontas County, January, 1917; obtained from Mr. Edward Fenwick, a very old gentleman, who came to this country from England about forty years previously. He learned the song, some thirty years before he came to America, from Mr. William Sedgewick.

"Bold Robin Hood" (broadside: George Walker, Jun., Durham, No. 12; W. Carbutt, Tadcaster; J. Harkness, Preston, No. 242) has stanza 1 but not stanza 2. A text almost identical with that here printed was taken down recently in the Thames valley by Alfred Williams, who says that it is "of great popularity with the more aged men" (*Folk-Songs of the Upper Thames*, p. 237).

1 O Robin Hood was a forrester good
    As ever drew bow in a merry greenwood,
        And the wild deer will follow, will follow.

2 Little John with his arms so long,
    He conquered them all with his high ding dong,
        And the bugles did echo, did echo.

35

JOHN HARDY

THE ballad of "John Hardy," although known and sung far beyond the boundaries of West Virginia, without doubt had its origin and development in this state. Its hero was a negro whose prowess and tragic end are well remembered and reported by men, both white and black, who saw him and knew him when he was alive. There are no printed or written records concerning him except the following order for his execution on file in the court house at Welch, McDowell County:

STATE OF WEST VIRGINIA
vs.   *Felony*
JOHN HARDY

This day came again the State by her attorney and the Prisoner who stands convicted of murder in the first degree was again brought to the bar of the Court in custody of the Sheriff of this County; and thereupon the Prisoner being asked by the Court if any thing he had or could say why the Court should not proceed to pass sentence of the law upon him in accordance with the verdict of the jury impanelled in this cause, and the Prisoner saying nothing why such sentence should not be passed upon him by the Court; It is therefore considered by the Court that the Prisoner John Hardy, is guilty as found by the verdict of the jury herein and that the said John Hardy be hanged by the neck until he is dead, and that the Sheriff of the County, on Friday the 19th day of January 1894, take the said John Hardy from the jail of the County to some suitable place to be selected by him in this County and there hang the said John Hardy by the neck until he is dead, and the prisoner is remanded to jail.

In a letter dated Charleston, West Virginia, February 16, 1916, addressed to Dr. H. S. Green of that city and written by the Hon. W. A. McCorkle, Governor of West Virginia from 1893 to 1897, occurs the following passage:

"He [John Hardy] was a steel-driver and was famous in the beginning of the building of the C[hesapeake] & O[hio] Railroad. He was also a steel-driver in the beginning of the extension of the N[orfolk] & W[estern] Railroad. It was about 1872 that he was in this section. This was before the day of steam drills and the drill work was done by two powerful men who were special steel drillers. They struck the steel from each side and as they struck the steel they sang a song which they improvised as they worked. John Hardy was the most famous steel-driver ever known in southern West Virginia. He was a magnificent specimen of the genus homo, was reported to be six feet two, and weighed two hundred and twenty-five or thirty pounds, was straight as an arrow and was one of the handsomest men in the country, and, as one informant told me, was as black as a kittle in hell.

"Whenever there was any spectacular performances along the line of drilling, John Hardy was put on the job, and it is said that he could drill more steel than any two men of his day. He was a great gambler and was notorious all through the country for his luck at gambling. To the dusky sex all through the country he was 'the greatest ever,' and he was admired and beloved by all the negro women from the southern West Virginia line to the C. & O. In addition to this he could drink more whiskey, sit up all night and drive steel all day to a greater extent than any man ever known in the country. . . . His story is a story of one of the composite characters that so often arise in the land. A man of kind heart, very strong, pleasant in address, yet a gambler, a roué, a drunkard, and a fierce fighter."

The following statement was made to the Editor in person in the summer of 1918 by Mr. James Knox Smith, a negro lawyer of Keystone, McDowell County, who was present at the trial and also at the execution of John Hardy:

"Hardy worked for the Shawnee Coal Company, and one pay-day night he killed a man in a crap game over a dispute of twenty-five cents. Before the game began, he laid his pistol on the table, saying to it, 'Now I want you to lay here; and the first nigger that steals money from me, I mean to kill him.' About midnight he began to lose, and claimed that one of the negroes had taken twenty-five cents of his money. The man denied the charge, but gave him the amount; whereupon he said, 'Don't you know that I won't lie to my gun?' Thereupon he seized his pistol and shot the man dead.

"After the crime he hid around the negro shanties and in the mountains a few days, until John Effler (the sheriff) and John Campbell (a deputy) caught him. Some of the negroes told them where Hardy was, and, slipping into the shanty where he was asleep, they first took his shotgun and pistol, then they waked him up and put the cuffs on him. Effler handcuffed Hardy to himself, and took the train at Eckman for Welch. Just as the train was passing through a tunnel, and Effler was taking his prisoner from one car to another, Hardy jumped and took Effler with him. He tried to get hold of Effler's pistol, and the sheriff struck him over the head with it and almost killed him. Then he un-handcuffed himself from Hardy, tied him securely with ropes, took him to Welch, and put him in jail.

"While in jail, after conviction, he could look out and see the men building his scaffold; and he walked up and down his cell, telling the rest of the prisoners that he would never be hung on that scaffold. Judge H. H. Christian, who had defended Hardy, heard of this, visited him in jail, advised him not to kill himself or compel the officers to kill him, but to prepare to die. Hardy began to sing and pray, and finally sent for the Reverend Lex Evans, a white Baptist preacher, told him he had made his peace with God, and asked to be baptized. Evans said he would as soon baptize him as he would a white man. Then they let him put on a new suit of clothes, the guards led him down to the Tug River, and Evans baptized him. On the scaffold he begged the sheriff's pardon for the way he had treated him, said he had intended to fight to the death and not be hung, but that after he got religion he did not feel like fighting. He confessed that he had done wrong, killed a man under the influence of whiskey, and advised all young men to avoid gambling and drink. A great throng witnessed the hanging.

"Hardy was black as a crow, over six feet tall, weighed about two hundred pounds, raw-boned, and had unusually long arms. He came originally from down eastern Virginia, and had no family. He had formerly been a steel-driver, and was about forty years old, or more."

Mr. H. S. Walker, from Fayette County, through which the C. & O. runs, reports the following as a current belief where he lives:

"John Hardy, a negro, worked for Langhorn, a railroad contractor from Richmond, Va., at the time of the building of the C. & O. Road. Langhorn had a contract for work on the east side of the Big Bend Tunnel, which is in the adjoining county of Summers, to the east of Fayette County, and some other contractor had the work on the west side of the tunnel. This was the time when the steam drill was first used. Langhorn did not have one, but the contractor on the other side of the tunnel did, and Langhorn made a wager with him that Hardy could, by hand, drill a hole in less time than the steam drill could. In the contest that followed, Hardy won, but dropped dead on the spot."

For a complete account of the biographical data of John Hardy and a full discussion of the genesis and development of the ballad, see *Journal*, XXXII, 505; also, a doctor's dissertation by the Editor of this volume on "Folk-Songs from West Virginia," deposited in the Harvard University Library. The following men living in Welch and vicinity gave special help in establishing the facts about John Hardy: Ernest Kyle, W. T. Tabor, H. J. Grossman, R. L. Johnson, Charles V. Price, Judge Herndon, A. C. Payne, and W. C. Cook.

Two versions of the ballad, with a total of nine variants, have come to hand. Version A has something of the very atmosphere of the construction camp, its rough gang of illiterate negroes, its profanity, and its glorification of a gambler, a drunkard, and a murderer. The greatest prominence is given to the episode of the hanging, in which the name of the place, Shawnee Camp, is correctly given, but the number of men killed is two, and the murderer is caught because he refuses to run. The gambling element is also introduced, and the incident of the steel-drilling contest is clearly remembered and vigorously expressed. H is entirely about the steel-drilling incident and may represent a form of the ballad made about John Hardy before he committed the murder. If so, it is the descendent of a version older than A.

In version B the steel-driver has dropped out of memory entirely. Shawnee Camp has become a Chinese camp, an easy change, and consequently, the man killed is a Chinaman. The yellow girl with her money is still in the game, and a man is killed in a gambling brawl. The reference to the Big Bend Tunnel is probably introduced from another West Virginia ballad, "The Wreck on the C. & O. Road" (No. 47). The conventional ballad element of having the hero's mother and sweetheart come to see him appears.

C, D, E, F, G, and I are variants of version B. In C the negro gambling dive is exalted into a Wild-West Show, and the conventionalizing is carried further by giving the hero a pretty little wife. In D the yellow girl becomes a less shadowy personage upon whom is bestowed the high-sounding name of Rozella. The refusal of the court to give bond to a "murderen" man is a good bit of realism with which no doubt the negro singers were fairly familiar   The reference to the baptism fails to appear. In E the conventionalizing goes on apace. The father is introduced, the hero is blessed with three children, and two stanzas (7 and 8) from "The Lass of Roch Royal" are inserted. Variant I shows close similarities to D and E.

West Virginia A–E have already been printed by Cox, *Journal*, XXXII, 505 (E also by Cox, XLIV, 216, and *Journal*, XXVI, 180). For other texts see *Journal*, XXII, 247 (Bascom; North Carolina); XXVI, 163 (Perrow; Tennessee, Indiana, Mississippi, Kentucky); XXVIII, 14 (Lomax; Kentucky, West Virginia); *Berea Quarterly*, October, 1910, XIV, No. 3, p. 26 (Kentucky); Campbell and Sharp, No. 87 (North Carolina); Talley, *Negro Folk-Rhymes*, p. 105. Cf. *Journal*, XXVII, 249 (Davis; South Carolina); XXIX, 400 (Cox); Shearin and Combs, p. 19; Cox, XLV, 160; *Berea Quarterly*, October, 1915, p. 20; F. C. Brown, p. 12.

A

Communicated by Dr. H. S. Green, Charleston, Kanawha County, February 21, 1916; obtained from Ex-Governor W. A. McCorkle, who said he had known it about twenty years.

1 John Hardy was a bad, bad man,
     He came from a bad, bad land,
   He killed two men in a Shawnee Camp,
       Cause he's too damn nervy for to run, God damn!
       Too damn nervy for to run.

2 John Hardy went to the rock quarry,
     He went there for to drive, Lord! Lord!
   The rock was so hard and the steel was so soft,
       That he laid down his hammer and he cried, "O my God!"
       He laid down his hammer and he cried.

3 John Henry was standing on my right hand side,
     The steel hammers on my left, Lord! Lord!
   "Before I'd let the steamer beat me down,
       I'd die with my hammer in my hand, by God!
       I'd die with my hammer in my hand."

4 John Hardy was standing at the dice-room door,
     So drunk he could not see, Lordy, Lord!
   Long come his woman, five dollars in her hand,
       Said, "You count John Hardy in the game, God damn!
       You count John Hardy in the game!"

5 John Hardy went to playing in the game of cards,
     The pot was broken, says he stays, Lordy, Lord!
   He drawed the nine of diamonds to a diamond bob,
       And he says, "I'll let the whole damn bill play, by God!"
       He says, "I'll let the whole damn bill play."

6 John Hardy went staggering by the jail-house,
     As drunk as he could be, Lordy, Lord!
   Up stepped a [p]leaceman, catched him by the arm,
       Says, "John Hardy, come an go with me, poor boy!
       John Hardy, come and go with me."

7 Friends and relatives standing around,
     Crying, "John Hardy, what have you done? poor boy!"
   "I've murdered two men in a Shawnee Camp,
       Was too damn nervy for to run, God damn!
       Now I'm standing on my hanging ground."

ℬ

Communicated by Mr. E. C. Smith, Weston, Lewis County, 1913; obtained from Miss Maude Rucks, Heaters, Braxton County.

1   John Hardy was but three days old,
        Sitting on his mama's knee,
    When he looked straight up at her and said,
        "The Big Bend Tunnel on the C. & O. Road
    Is bound to be the death of me,
        The Big Bend Tunnel on the C. & O. Road
    Is bound to be the death of me."

2   John Hardy was standing in a dice-room door,
        Not taking any interest in the game,
    When a yellow girl threw ten dollars on the board,
        Saying, "Deal John Hardy in the game, poor boy,
        Deal John Hardy in the game."

3   John Hardy drew his pistol from his pocket,
        And threw it down on the tray,
    Saying, "The man that uses my yellow girl's money,
        I'm going to blow him away, away,
        I'm going to blow him away."

4   John Hardy drew to a four-card straight,
        And the Chinaman drew to a pair;
    John failed to catch, and the Chinaman won,
        And he left him sitting back dead in his chair,
        And he left him lying dead in his chair.

5   John started to catch the east-bound train,
        So dark he could not see;
    A police walked up and took him by the arm,
        Saying, "John Hardy, come and go with me, poor boy,
        John Hardy, come and go with me."

6   John Hardy's mama came to him,
        Saying, "John, what have you done?"
    "I've murdered a man in a Chinese camp,
        And now I'm sentenced to be hung, O Lord!
        And now I'm sentenced to be hung."

7   John Hardy's sweetheart came to him,
        She came to go his bail;
    They put her on a west-bound train,
        And shoved John Hardy back in jail, poor boy,
        And shoved John Hardy back in jail.

8 "I've been to the East and I've been to the West,
      I've travelled this wide world round;
   I've been to the river and I've been baptized,
         And now I'm on my hanging ground, O Lord!
         And now I'm on my hanging ground.

9 "I don't care a damn for the C. & O. Road,
      And I don't care a damn what I say;
   I don't care a snap for the police!"
         But they let John Hardy get away, poor boy,
         They let John Hardy get away.

C

Communicated by Mr. Lee C. Wooddell, Durbin, Pocahontas County
October 4, 1915; obtained from Mr. Ernis Wright, Hosterman.

1 John Hardy he was two years old,
      Sitting on his mother's knee:
   "The Big Ben Tunnel on the C. & O. Road
      Is going to be the death of me, poor boy,
      Is going to be the death of me, poor boy."

2 John Hardy went into a Wild West show,
      Playing at a fifty-cent game:
   "Whoever wins my fifty cents,
      I'm going to blow out his brains, poor boy,
      I'm going to blow out his brains, poor boy."

3 John Hardy laid down a twenty dollar bill,
      And he did n't ask for change:
   "All I want is a forty-four gun,
      To blow out another nigger's brains, poor boy,
      To blow out another nigger's brains, poor boy."

4 John Hardy went to New Port,
      Expecting to be free;
   The detective patted him on the back:
      "John Hardy, go along with me, poor boy,
      John Hardy, go along with me, poor boy."

5 "I've been to the East, I've been to the West,
      And I've been all over the world;
   I've been to the river to be baptized,
      But I'm on my hanging ground, poor boy,
      But I'm on my hanging ground, poor boy."

6 John Hardy had a pretty little wife,
  He kept her dressed in blue;
When she heard that John was dead,
  "John Hardy, I've been true to you, poor boy,
  John Hardy, I've been true to you, poor boy."

D

Communicated by Mr. John B. Adkins, Branchland, Lincoln County, March, 1917; obtained from David Dick, an old banjo player.

1 John Hardy was a desperate man,
  He roved from town to town,
Saying, "The man that wins my money this time,
  I'm going to blow his life away,
  And lay him in his lonesome grave."

2 John Hardy was standing in the dice-room door,
  He was not concerned in the game;
Rozella threw down one silver dollar,
  Saying, "Deal John Hardy in the game, poor boy,"
  Saying, "Deal John Hardy in the game."

3 John Hardy threw down one half-dollar,
  Saying, "One half of this I'll play,
And the man that wins my money this time,
  I'm going to blow his life away,
  And lay him in his lonesome grave."

4 John Hardy was making for the station that night,
  It was so dark he could hardly see;
A policeman took him by the arm,
  Saying, "John, won't you come and go with me, poor
    boy,
  John won't you come and go with me?"

5 Every station that they passed through,
  They heard the people say:
"Yonder goes John Hardy making his escape,
  John Hardy is getting away, poor boy,
  John Hardy is getting away."

6 They brought John Hardy out before the judge,
  And bond they offered him;
No bond was allowed a murderen man,
  So they put John Hardy back in jail, poor boy,
  They put John Hardy back in jail.

7 John Hardy's wife went mourning along,
    Went mourning along in blue,
  Saying, "O John, what have you done?
    I've always been true to you, poor boy,
    I've always been true to you."

ℰ

Communicated by Mr. E. C. Smith, Weston, Lewis County, March, 1913; obtained from Walter Mick, Ireland, West Virginia, who learned it from hearing it sung by people in his community.

1 John Hardy was a little farmer boy,
    Sitting on his father's knee;
  Says he, "I fear the C. & O. Road
    Will be the ruination of me, poor boy,
    Will be the ruination of me."

2 John Hardy got to be a desperate man,
    Carried a pistol and a razor every day;
  Shot a nigger through the heel in a Chinese camp,
    And you ought of seen that nigger get away, poor boy,
    And you ought of seen that nigger get away.

3 John Hardy's mother ran up to him,
    Saying, "Son, what have you done?"
  "I murdered a man in a Chinese camp,
    And now I'm sentenced to be hung, poor boy,
    And now I'm sentenced to be hung."

4 John Hardy's father went to the judge,
    Saying, "What do you think will be done?"
  The judge he answered with a quick reply,
    "I'm afraid John Hardy will be hung, poor boy,
    I'm afraid John Hardy will be hung."

5 John Hardy was standing in a dice-room door,
    He did n't have a nickel to his name;
  Along came a yaller gal, threw a dollar on the board,
    Saying, "Deal John Hardy in the game, poor boy,"
    Saying, "Deal John Hardy in the game."

6 John Hardy was standing in a railroad station,
    As drunk as he could be;
  A policeman came up and took him by the arm,
    "John Hardy, come along with me, poor boy,
    John Hardy, come along with me."

7 "O, who will shoe your pretty little feet,
    And who will glove your hands,
And who will kiss your sweet rosy lips,
    When I'm in a foreign land, poor boy,
    When I'm in a foreign land?"

8 "My father will shoe my pretty little feet,
    My mother will glove my hands;
John Hardy will kiss my sweet rosy lips,
    When he comes from a foreign land,
    When he comes from a foreign land."

9 John Hardy married a loving wife,
    And children he had three;
He called to him his oldest son,
    Saying, "Son, make a man like me, poor boy,
    Saying, "Son, make a man like me."

10 John Hardy married a loving wife,
    And children he had three;
He cared no more for his wife and child,
    Than the rocks in the bottom of the sea, poor boy,
    Than the rocks in the bottom of the sea.

F

Communicated by Miss Virginia Foulk, Huntington, Cabell County, April, 1923. It was printed in "The Sunday Advertiser," April 29, 1923. Text furnished by Mr. J. Roy Fuller.

1 John Hardy was a desperate boy,
    He carried a gun and a razor every day;
He killed him a man for a rowdy young girl,
    And you ought to have seen Johnny get away, poor boy.

2 John Hardy was standing at the bar-room door,
    Showing no interest in the game;
Up stepped a woman with a dollar in her hand,
    Saying, "Deal John Hardy in the game, poor boy."

3 John Hardy took that yaller gal's money,
    And then began to play,
Saying, "The man that wins my yaller gal's dollar,
    John Hardy will blow him away, poor boy,
    And lay him in his lonesome grave."

4 John Hardy made for the Coalburg train,
    It was so dark he could hardly see,
When a constable took him by the arm and said,
    "Johnny, won't you come and go with me, poor boy,
    Johnny, won't you come and go with me?"

5 John Hardy was standing in the jail-room door,
    The tears came rolling down,
Saying, "I've been to the East and I've been to the West,
    I've been the wide world round,
I've been to the river and I've been baptized,
    And now I'm ready for my hanging grounds."

6 John Hardy had a pretty little girl,
    She always dressed in blue,
She threw her arms around his neck,
    Saying, "Have n't I been true, poor boy?"
    Saying, "Have n't I been true?"

7 "O, pay me back my fifteen cents,
    O, pay me back my change,
For all I want is a forty-four gun,
    And I'll shoot John Hardy through the brains."

8 They took him to the scaffold,
    They hung him there to die;
The last word John Hardy said, poor boy,
    "My forty-four gun never lies,
    My forty-four gun never lies."

G

Communicated by Mr. C. Woofter, Glenville, Gilmer County, December, 1923; obtained from Miss Talitha Brown, Rosedale, in 1915. The last stanza was also communicated by Mrs. Olive Tallman Dowdy, 1918.

1 John Hardy was only three days old,
    Sitting on his mother's knee;
He looked right up in his mamma's face,
    Saying, "A big ban tunnel on the C. & O. Road,
    Bound to be the death of me."

2 John Hardy had a pretty little wife,
    And children he had three,
But he cared no more for his wife and his babes,
    Than rocks in the bottom of the sea,
    Lord! Lord! than rocks in the bottom of the sea.

3 John Hardy was a desprit man,
    He carried two guns every day;
He shot a nigger in a China camp,
    And to see John Hardy get away, poor boy,
    To see John Hardy get away!

4 John Hardy's wife came to the jail,
    She always dressed in blue,
She threw her arms around his neck,
    Saying, "Johnny, I've been true to you, poor boy,
    John Hardy, I've been true to you."

5 "I've been to the East, I've been to the West,
    I've been the wide, wide world around;
I've been to the river and been baptized,
    And now I am on my hanging ground,
    And now I am on my hanging ground."

H

Contributed by Professor J. H. Combs, West Virginia University, April 30, 1924. Obtained in Knott County, Kentucky.

1 When John Henry was a little babe,
    A-holding to his mama's hand,
Says, "If I live till I'm twenty-one,
    I'm going to make a steel-driving man, my babe,
    I'm going to make a steel-driving man."

2 When John Henry was a little boy,
    A-sitting on his father's knee,
Says, "The Big Bend Tunnel on the C. & O. Road
    Is going to be the death of me, my babe," etc.

3 John he made a steel-driving man,
    They took him to the tunnel to drive;
He drove so hard he broke his heart,
    He laid down his hammer and he died, my babe, etc.

4 O now John Hardy is a steel-driving man,
    He belongs to the steel-driving crew,
And every time his hammer comes down,
    You can see that steel walking through, etc.

5 The steam drill standing on the right-hand side,
    John Henry standing on the left;
He says, "I'll beat that steam drill down,
    Or I'll die with my hammer in my breast," etc.

6 He placed his drill on the top of the rock,
    The steam drill standing close at hand;
He beat it down one inch and a half
    And laid down his hammer like a man, etc.

7 Johnny looked up to his boss-man and said,
    "O boss-man, how can it be?
For the rock is so hard and the steel is so tough,
    I can feel my muscles giving way."

8 Johnny looked down to his turner and said,
    "O turner, how can it be?
The rock is so hard and the steel is so tough
    That everybody's turning after me."

9 They took poor Johnny to the steep hillside,
    He looked to his heavens above;
He says, "Take my hammer and wrap it in gold
    And give it to the girl I love."

10 They took his hammer and wrapped it in gold
    And gave it to Julia Ann;
And the last word John Hardy said to her
    Was, "Julia, do the best you can."

11 "If I die a railroad man,
    Go bury me under the tie,
So I can hear old Number Four,
    As she goes rolling by.

12 "If I die a railroad man,
    Go bury me under the sand,
With a pick and shovel at my head and feet,
    And a nine-pound hammer in my hand."

I

Contributed by Professor J. H. Combs, West Virginia University, April 30, 1924. Obtained in Knott County, Kentucky.

1 John Hardy was a brave little man,
    He carried a pistol every day;
He killed a man in Shallow Town,
    'T was a sight to see John Hardy get away, Lord, Lord,
    'T was a sight to see John Hardy get away.

2 John Hardy was standing at the gambling bar
  And was not concerning the game;
Up stepped a lady, threw down half a dollar,
  Said, "Deal John Hardy in the game," etc.

3 John Hardy picked up the half a dollar
  And threw it against the ground,
Saying, "The very first man that wins my money,
  I sure will blow him down."

4 A big buck nigger he won the money
  And picked it up from the ground;
John Hardy he drew out his pistol
  And shot that nigger down.

5 John Hardy got on an old freight train,
  The old freight train was too late;
And if the old train had n't a-been behind time,
  John Hardy would have made his escape.

6 John Hardy was a-standing at the station bars,
  So dark he could not see;
Up stepped a policeman and took him by the arm,
  Says, "Johnny, come and go with me."

7 The policeman he arrested John
  And brought him on to jail;
They no bail allowed for a murderer,
  And they locked John Hardy up in jail.

8 John wrote for his father and mother to come
  And get him out on bail;
They no bond allowed for murdering crime,
  So they kept John Hardy in jail.

9 John's father and mother crossed the deep blue sea,
  To get him out on bail;
Says, "There's no bond for a murdering man."
  So they kept John Hardy in jail.

10 John Hardy had a pretty little wife,
  She always went dressed in green;
And coming down on the hanging ground,
  Says, "Johnny, you were always too mean."

11   John Hardy had a true little boy,
          He was all dressed in black;
      As coming down on the hanging ground,
          Says, "Papa, I wish that you were back."

12   John Hardy had a true little girl,
          She always dressed in red;
      As coming down on the hanging ground,
          Says, "Papa, I would rather be dead."

13   "I've been to the East and I've been to the West,
          I've been the wide world round;
      I've been to the river and I've been baptized,
          And now I'm on my hanging ground."

36

THE ASHLAND TRAGEDY

CONTRIBUTED by Mrs. Hannah Bradshaw, Matewan, Mingo County, July, 1918; learned about thirty years before from a printed copy in Ashland, Kentucky; dictated to the Editor at the time and place named above.

The authority for the following data is Mr. James Hunter, the father of Mrs. Bradshaw. He is an old soldier who lived at the time at Matewan, but formerly lived in Ashland, Kentucky. It was at that place, in his home, that the song was composed by one Elijah Adams. Mrs. Hunter had made a tune for the verses at the time of their composition, but none of the family could remember it.

The crime consisted in the murder of two Gibbons children, Fannie and Robert, and a Miss Emma Charcoóla, who was staying with them. The perpetrators of the deed were George Ellis, William Neal, and Ellis Craft. George Ellis was hanged by a mob, and the other two, having been tried and convicted, were hanged by the sheriff.

According to Mr. W. E. Boggs, of Matewan, Craft and Neal were hanged in 1884. He said that he witnessed the execution and that Lige Adams had a *stack* of ballads on the day of the hanging, stood on a big rock, and sold them as fast as three men could hand them out. The hanging took place at Grayson, Carter County, Kentucky. Ellis confessed and was hanged by a mob. The people of Mount Sterling, Montgomery County, were brought into the song, so Mr. Boggs said, because the prisoners had at one time been taken there to prevent the mob from taking vengeance on them. He gave the name of the murdered children as Gibson and seemed to think that the young woman also belonged to the family. He recited a fragment of the song, concluding as follows:

> The people of Mount Sterling,
> Who are themselves so high,
> Say they are in favor of justice,
> But say they [the murderers] sha'n't die.

1 Dear father, mother, sister, come listen while I tell
All about the Ashland tragedy, of which you know full well.
'T was in the town of Ashland, all on that deadly night,
A horrible crime was committed, but soon was brought to light.

2 Three men who did the murder, was Craft, Ellis, and Neal;
They thought the crime they had concealed, but God the same
  revealed.
George Ellis, one of the weakest, who could not bear the pain,
To J. B. Powell, trembling, revealed the horrid stain.

3 Ellis Craft, who was the leader, and had an iron heart,
Caused a son and two lovely daughters from their mother's
  embrace to part.
Poor Neal, he may be innocent, but, from what George Ellis
  tells,
The crime he has committed will send his soul to hell.

4 He dragged poor Emma from her bed and threw her on the
       floor,
   Crushed her head with an iron bar, her blood did run in gore.
   In my own imagination I can see her little hands
   Upheld, crying for mercy, murdered by cruel hands.

5 Those little white hands so tender, upheld in prayer to him,
   Falls useless at her bleeding side, her eyes in death grow dim.
   Craft committed the same offence, and murdered the other two;
   While their forms were cold in death, Craft says, "What shall we
       do?"

6 Then Neal proposed to burn them up, to hide their bloody stain,
   While some other three might arrested be, and them not bear the
       blame.
   Then, in tones of thunder, Craft told Ellis to get to camp,
   And pour oil on the children, while they stood with bloody hands.

7 Then Craft he lit a match and touched it to their clothes,
   The flame loomed up with melting heat, and away the wretches
       goes.
   Then off they went, I have no doubt, as fast as they could go,
   And thought no one their bloody crime would ever, ever know.

8 Then early the next morning the town in mourning wept,
   To see the children's burning forms, the sight they can't forget:
   Such screams and bitter weeping of friends that stood around,
   Their heart strings torn and bleeding, tears falling to the ground.

9 Poor little Robert Gibbons, a helpless orphan child,
   Died in defence of his sister; to her he was loving and mild.
   For their three forms are buried, they sleep beneath the sod,
   Murdered while defending their virtues, and their souls are at
       rest with God.

10 At rest in the golden city, where God himself gives light,
   Where crystal streams are flowing, in the city where there is no
       night;
   They 're with the white-robed angels, whose harps are made of
       gold,
   Whose crowns are set with brilliant stars, forever in the dear
       Lord's hold.

11 There is one thing yet I do remember well:
   Major Allen with his bloody hounds caused tears and tide to
      swell;
   They hovered round those dreadful fiends that sent death knell
      through town,
   Caused other friends from friends to part; for hell such men are
      bound.

12 The people of Mt. Sterling, who rate themselves so high,
   Ought to be in favor of justice and say that he should die.
   I suppose they have forgotten that they have daughters too,
   And law and right should be their aim, to protect their children
      too.

13 May law and justice be dealt out, and spread from plain to
      plain,
   And in the future day enjoy a moral land again!
   Now all dear fathers and mothers, a warning take by this,
   Stay at home with your children, and guard against crimes like
      this.

14 Remember the advice I give you is from a true and loving heart;
   I hope you'll take its earnest heed, from its teachings never part.
   Remember the world is wicked, no mortal you can trust;
   Trust God, who is all wisdom and doeth all things just.

37

McAFEE'S CONFESSION

Six texts of this song have been found in West Virginia, under the titles of "McAfee," "McAfee's Confession," and "McAtee's Confession." They do not differ materially.

Texts have been printed as follows: — from Ohio by Tolman (*Journal*, XXIX, 185, (with references); from West Virginia by Cox, XLVII, 668: A, below); from Iowa by Pound (No. 68). Lomax publishes a version in his *Cowboy Songs*, p. 164. The song has also been reported from Missouri (Belden, No. 24) and Kentucky (Shearin and Combs, p. 16). Mrs. Soners, of Warren, Indiana, the source of Tolman's copy, heard it from her mother in Ohio about 1866. She states that the poem records an actual occurrence, and that her mother knew Hettie Stout well.

A

"McAfee's Confession." Learned by the Editor when he was a youth, in Illinois, from hearing it sung by a relative, Mr. George McMahon.

1   Draw nigh, young men, and learn from me
    My sad and mournful history,
    And may you ne'er forgetful be
    Of what this day I tell to thee.

2   Before I reached my fifth year,
    My father and my mother dear
    Were both laid in their silent grave
    By Him who them their beings gave.

3   But Providence, the orphan's friend,
    A relief did quickly send,
    And snatched from want and penury
    Poor little orphan McAfee.

4   Beneath my uncle's friendly roof,
    From want and danger far aloof,
    Nine years was I most tender reared,
    And oft his kind advice I heard.

5   But I was thoughtless, young and gay,
    And sometimes broke the Sabbath day,
    In wickedness I took delight,
    And ofttimes did what was not right.

6   And when my uncle would me chide,
    I'd turn away dissatisfied,
    And join again my wickedness,
    And Satan serve with eagerness.

7 At last there came the fatal day,
When from my home I ran away,
And to my sorrow since in life,
I took unto myself a wife.

8 And she was kind and good to me
As any woman need to be,
And now alive would be no doubt,
Had I ne'er seen Miss Hettie Shout.

9 O, well I recollect the day
When Hettie stole my heart away;
'T was love for her controlled my will,
And causèd me my wife to kill.

10 'T was on a pleasant summer night,
When all was still, the stars shone bright,
My wife was lying on the bed,
When I approached and to her said:

11 "Dear wife, here's medicine I brought,
Which for your sake this day I bought,
And I do hope it will cure you,
From those vile fits; pray, take it, do."

12 She gave to me a tender look
And in her mouth the poison took;
Then by her babe upon the bed
Down to her last long sleep she laid.

13 But, fearing that she was not dead,
My hand upon her throat I laid,
And there such deep impressions made,
Her soul soon from her body fled.

14 Then was my heart filled full of woe,
I cried, "O, whither shall I go?
Or how to quit this mournful place,
The world again how can I face?"

15 I'd freely give up all my store,
Had I ten thousand times much more,
If I could bring again to life
My dear, my darling murdered wife.

16 Her body lies beneath the sod,
    Her soul I hope is with its God,
    And soon into eternity,
    My guilty soul will also be.

17 The moment now is drawing nigh
    When from this world my soul must fly,
    To meet Jehovah at the bar,
    And there my final sentence hear.

18 Young men, pray take advice from me,
    And shun all evil company;
    Walk in the ways of righteousness,
    And God your soul will surely bless.

19 Kind friends, I bid you all adieu;
    No more on earth shall I see you;
    On heaven's bright and flowery plain
    I hope we all shall meet again.

ℬ

"McAfee's Confession."   Contributed by Mrs. J. S. Thurmond, Alderson,
Monroe County, March, 1917; learned from her father, Jackson B. Huddleston,
more than thirty years previously.

1 Draw near young men and learn from me
   My sad and mournful history,
   And may you ne'er forgetful be
   Of all this day I tell to thee.

2 Before I reached my full fifth year,
   My father and my mother dear
   Were both laid in their silent grave
   By Him who did their beings give.

3 No more was I a father's joy,
   But a poor little orphan boy;
   No more a father's voice I heard,
   No more a mother's love I shared.

4 Then to my uncle's friendly roof,
   From want and danger far aloof;
   For nine long years it sheltered me,
   As safe and good as need to be.

5 But I was thoughtless, young and gay,
And often broke the Sabbath day;
In wickedness I took delight,
And often did what was not right.

6 And when my uncle did me chide,
I turned from him dissatisfied,
And turned again to wickedness,
And Satan served with eagerness.

7 At length arrived the fatal day
When from my home I ran away,
And to my sorrow since in life,
I took unto myself a wife.

8 And she was kind and good to me,
As any woman need to be,
And living yet would be no doubt,
Had I not seen Miss Hetty Shout.

9 Ah! well I recollect the day
When Hetty stole my heart away;
'T was love for her controlled my will
And causèd me my wife to kill.

10 'T was on a pleasant summer's night,
All things were still, the stars shone bright,
My wife was lying on the bed,
When I approached her and said:

11 "My dear, here's medicine I brought,
This very day for you I bought;
My dear, I know it will cure you,
Of those vile fits; pray, take it, do."

12 She gave to me a tender look
And in her mouth the poison took,
And by her baby on the bed
Down to her last long sleep she laid.

13 My heart was then filled full of woe;
I cried, "Ah, whither shall I go?
How can I quit this mournful place!
The world again how can I face?"

14   I'd freely give up all my store,
      Had I ten thousand worlds or more,
      If I could bring again to life
      My dear, my darling murdered wife.

15   Young men, young men, be warned by me,
      And shun all evil company,
      And walk in ways of righteousness,
      And God your souls will surely bless.

16   The moment now is drawing nigh
      When from this world my soul must fly,
      And meet Jehovah at the bar,
      And hear my final sentence there.

17   To all my friends I bid adieu;
      No more on earth shall I see you,
      But upon heaven's flowery plain
      I hope we all may meet again.

C

"McAfee's Confession." Communicated by Mr. C. R. Bishop, Green Bank, Pocahontas County, 1917; obtained from Miss Ruth Sutton. Eighteen stanzas.

D

"McAfee." Contributed by Mr. John B. Hagar, Madison, Boone County, July, 1918. An abbreviated story with a good text in eleven stanzas.

E

"McAfee's Confession." Contributed by Mr. W. E. Boggs, Matewan, Mingo County, July, 1918, who says that the hero of the song was hanged in Magoffin County, Kentucky, for the crime of killing his wife. Eleven stanzas, text somewhat corrupt.

F

"McAtee's Confession." Communicated by Mrs. Hilary G. Richardson, Clarksburg, Harrison County, 1917; obtained from Mrs. Nancy McAtee, whose name is no doubt responsible for the first word of the title. Nine stanzas, more or less confused.

G

"McAphee's Confession." A fragment of eight lines; contributed by Mr. Sam Turman, Buchanan, Boyd County, Kentucky, July, 1918.

38

THE JEALOUS LOVER

EIGHT variants of this song have been found in West Virginia under the titles: "The Jealous Lover," "Blue-Eyed Ella," and "Pearl Bryan." These do not differ greatly except in the arrangement of stanzas, and the story is in all essentials the same as that in the ballad previously reported by other collectors. For a list of versions see Kittredge, *Journal*, XXX, 344. Add Shoemaker, p. 49; Pound, No. 43; *Boston Transcript*, January 13, 1912. Professor Jay B. Hubbell has recovered "Pearl Bryan" from eastern Texas.

The title "Pearl Bryan" and certain incidents and names found in the variants under that title are without doubt due to the following facts, for which I am indebted to Mr. Clifford R. Meyers, State Historian and Archivist of West Virginia. In a letter dated March 23, 1920, he wrote:

"I tried to secure the words of the song but failed. It seems that the song was very popular for a few years after the punishment of the criminals and I believe it was one of the ephemeral songs composed by some music hall singer. I remember hearing it many times and in it was a couplet which ran: —

> 'O, Pearl Bryan, she's dead,
> And they can't find her head.'

"The murder occurred near Fort Thomas, Kentucky, Friday night January 31, 1896, and was the result of a criminal operation. The girl apparently died, her head was taken off, and the body placed in the woods. After being found it was identified by the feet — Miss Bryan being 'web-footed.' Two young doctors, Scott Jackson and Alonzo M. Walling, were arrested and later convicted. A young man by the name of Woods was implicated, but later released. The two were hanged, but I do not know the exact date. Miss Bryan was from Greencastle, Indiana."

On April 1, 1920, he wrote as follows: "A letter to the Cincinnati Enquirer failed to obtain the words of the song, but the following is what the paper sent me:

"'Pearl Bryan was a Greencastle, Indiana girl. She is said to have appealed to Scott Jackson and Alonzo Walling, students at the dental college in Cincinnati, to have her given medical attention after she arrived in this city. Her body was found, minus her head, near Fort Thomas, Kentucky, February 1, 1896. Her identity was established through marks found in her shoes, which were sold in Greencastle. Jackson and Walling, charged with first degree murder, were tried in Newport, Ky. They were found to be guilty, and were hanged on March 20, 1897. The girl's head was never found.'

"The enclosed data were published in the various parts of the country the day after the hanging and were sent out by some news agency:

"'Pearl Bryan, the daughter of a wealthy farmer near Greencastle, Indiana, was a belle of that town, and had been indiscreet, presumably with William Wood (or Woods) as Jackson and Walling alleged. On January 27, Pearl Bryan left her home ostensibly to visit friends in Indianapolis, but instead came direct to Cincinnati to meet Scott Jackson, then a student in the Ohio College of Dental Surgery. Jackson failed to keep his appointment with the girl and after wandering about the city she went to the Indiana house and registered under an assumed name.   The next day Jackson called to see her.   On Wednesday, January 29, she left the Indiana house with Jackson and a fellow student, Alonzo Walling, and from that day until her headless body was found at Fort Thomas, nothing is positively known of the movements of the trio.   It was testified at the trial that George Jackson, a negro cabman, had driven the three to near Fort Thomas, where the girl was decapitated.   Her head was never found. Jackson and Walling were arrested at their boarding house, in Cincinnati, and were charged with the murder.   At the preliminary examination of the prisoners, and later, while standing over the girl's corpse, each accused the other of having killed the girl.   Jackson admitted that he was acquainted with Pearl Bryan, but denied any knowledge of the murder.   Walling said he did not know her.   The trials were sensational and resulted in separate convictions.   Each made numerous confessions and statements, the last one a joint effort to place the blame upon a doctor of Bellevue, Kentucky, who had been insane.   This, as were the others, was disbelieved.'"

May 8, 1920: "My visit included a conference of the directors of the Enlarged Program of the American Library Association at Indianapolis . . . and a visit to Depauw at Greencastle.   While there I saw Pearl Bryan's grave.   The grave stone had been damaged somewhat by relic hunters."

A

"The Jealous Lover."   Communicated by Mr. John B. Adkins, Branchland, Lincoln County, May 1, 1916; "copied from an old ballad written by hand for Albert Adkins, several years ago, by Mrs. Mary Harless."

1 Down in yon lonely meadow, where the violets fade and bloom,
    There lies my own fair Ella, in her cold and silent tomb;
    She died not broken-hearted, nor from diseases fell,
    But in one instant parted from the home she loved so well.

2 One night as the moon shone brightly, and the stars were shining too,
    Up to her cottage window her jealous lover drew;
    He says, "Dear, let us wander down in yon meadow gay,
    And while that we are pondering, we'll name our wedding day."

3 So deep into the forest he led his love so fair,
    Says she, "It's for you only, that I am wandering here;
    For the night is dark and dreary, and I am afraid to stay,
    Now I am growing weary, and would like to retrace my way."

4 "Retrace your way? No never! No more this earth you'll roam;
    So bid adieu to parents, and to kind friends at home;
    For here in the wilds I have you, from me you cannot fly,
    No mortal arms can save you, fair Ella, you must die."

5 Down on her knees before him she pleaded for her life,
But deep into her bosom he plunged the fatal knife:
"Dear Edward, what have I done, that you should take my life?
I always have been faithful, and would have been your wife.

6 "So adieu, my friends and parents; you ne'er shall see me more,
Though long you will wait my coming at the little cottage door.
Dear Edward I'll forgive you, is my last enduring breath,
I never have deceived you." And she closed her eyes in death.

7 The birds sang in the morning, but mournful were their song;
A stranger found her body in a cold and lifeless form.
Come all you fair young ladies, who choose to look this way,
Don't put your trust in young men, for they will lead you astray.

$\mathcal{B}$

"Blue-Eyed Ella." Communicated by Mr. E. C. Smith, Weston, Lewis County, December 18, 1915; obtained from a copy belonging to Miss Maude Rucks and Ella Cunningham.

1 Way down in yonder valley, where the early violets bloom,
There lies my blue-eyed Ella, so silent in the tomb.
She died not broken-hearted, nor sickness caused her death;
But she was cruelly murdered by one that she loved best.

2 One night when the moon shone brightly, the stars were shining too,
Up to a lonely cottage a faithless lover drew:
"Come, Ella, let us wander to some far meadow gay,
And there we'll sit and ponder and appoint our wedding day."

3 "O Edward, I'm so lonely, I care not far to roam;
O Edward! I'm so lonely, I pray you take me home."
"Now down to this I've got you, you have no wings to fly;
No mortal hand can save you, so, Ella, you must die."

4 On bended knees before him, she pleaded for her life;
But into her lily-white bosom he plunged the fatal knife.
"Your parents must forgive me for the crime I now have done;
And I'll go into some foreign country and never more return."

5 "Yes, Edward, I'll forgive you," she spoke in a dying breath;
Then closed her eyes forever, and her voice was stilled in death.

C

"The Jealous Lover." Communicated by Mr. C. R. Bishop, Green Bank, Pocahontas County, 1917; obtained from Miss Fannie Kerr.

1 One night the moon shone brightly, the stars were shining too,
Into her cottage lightly her jealous lover drew.
"Come, love, with me let's wander into the fields so gay,
And as we wander, we'll ponder upon our wedding day."

2 Deep, deep into the forest he led his love so dear:
"'T is for you and you only that I do wander here."
"O the way grows dark and dreary, and I'm afraid to stay;
Oft, ofttimes I am weary, let us retrace our way."

3 "Retrace your way? No, never! No more this world you'll roam;
You may bid farewell forever to parents, friends, and home."
Down on her knees before him she pleaded for her life;
Deep, deep into her bosom he plunged the fatal knife.

4 "Farewell, kind, loving parents, you may never see me more;
You may watch and wait my coming, at the little cottage door.
"Dear Willie, I'll forgive you!" was her last and dying breath;
"I never have deceived you"—and she closed her eyes in death.

5 The buzzards hovered o'er her, and loud did the bugle sound;
The stranger came and found her, lying lifeless on the ground.
O she died not broken-hearted, or of disease she fell,
But in one moment parted from all she loved so well.

D

"Pearl Bryan." Communicated by Miss Nellie Donley, Morgantown, Monongalia County, December, 1915; obtained from Miss Marion Rennar, who first heard it in 1912, one winter night, while gathered about a great wood fire in the country near Morgantown. Miss Debbie Bolyard sang the song and her brother, Winfield, played it on a mouth-harp.

1 Down in a low green valley, where the fairest flowers grow,
There lies poor Pearl Bryan, lies mouldering in her tomb.
She died not broken-hearted, nor by disease she fell;
One moment's parting took her from the ones she loved so well.

2 One night when the moon was shining, and the stars were shining too,
Down to Pearl Bryan's cottage, her jealous lover flew.
"Come, Pearl, O let us wander all through these woods so gay;
While wandering we will ponder upon our wedding day."

3 The way was dark and dreary, poor Pearl was afraid;
  She said, "I am so weary, let us return our way."
  "Retrace your way? No never! For in these woods you'll die;
  So bid farewell forever to your loved ones left at home."

4 Down, down she kneeled before him and pleaded hard for life;
  But into her snowy-white bosom he plunged the fatal knife.
  "Dear Jackson, I'll forgive you," she cried in dying breath;
  "For you know I never deceived you." And she closed her eyes
    in death.

5 White flowers growing about her, close by a mossy mound
  A stranger found Pearl Bryan, cold, lifeless on the ground.

&

"Pearl Bryan." Communicated by Professor Walter Barnes, Fairmont,
Marion County, May 18, 1916.

1 Down in a low green valley, where the fairest flowers grow,
  There's where poor Pearl Bryan lies mouldering in her tomb.
  She died not broken-hearted, nor from diseases fell,[1]
  But just one moment took her from the one she loved so well.

2 One night the moon was shining, the stars were shining too,
  Down to poor Pearl's dwelling Jackson and Walling flew.
  "Come, Pearl, say let us wander all through these woods so gay,
  While roaming we will ponder upon our wedding day."

3 The woods were dark and dreary, Pearl was afraid to stay;
  Said she, "I am so lonely! Let us retrace our way."
  "Retrace our way? No, never! For in these woods your doom;
  So bid farewell forever to parting friends and home."

4 Down, down she knelt before him and pleaded for her life,
  But in her snow-white bosom he plunged his fatal knife.
  "Dear Jackson, I'll forgive you," she said in dying breath;
  "You know I never deceived you"; and she closed her eyes in
    death.

5 While farmers plowing o'er her, shrill was the tempest sound;
  A stranger found poor Pearl, cold, headless on the ground.

[1] Supplied from A.

F

"Pearl Bryan." Communicated by Professor Walter Barnes, Fairmont, Marion County, January 12, 1916. It was written down by Miss Janet Cook and given to Mr. H. M. Hart of the Watson School. It agrees closely with E, but concludes thus: —

White banner floating o'er her, her thrills in triumph sound;
A stranger found poor Pearl lying cold, headless, on the ground.

G

"The Jealous Lover." Communicated by Mr. J. Harrison Miller, Wardensville, Hardy County. It agrees closely with D, but has lines corresponding to A 6 [1,2] and concludes as follows:

Her body was found next morning and placed into a grave,
'Way down in yonder valley, where the weeping willows wave.
Young Edward was convicted; on the gallows he was swung
For the murder of blue-eyed Ella, so silent in the tomb.

It has no stanza corresponding with D 5.

H

No local title. Communicated by Miss Julia E. Otto, Wheeling, Ohio County, 1916. A condensed version; the victim is called "my sweet Luella."

39

A TOLLIVER–MARTIN FEUD SONG

CONTRIBUTED by Mr. C. H. Ellis, Williamson, Mingo County, 1918. His mother was a Hatfield, and died when he was three months old. Joseph Hatfield, son of Ali Hatfield, took charge of him and brought him up in the east end of Mingo County. About two years after his mother died, his father moved back to Morehead, Rowan County, Kentucky, where he was still living at the time these data were given. The place is in the midst of the Tolliver-Martin feud country. He furnished the facts concerning the affair after Martin had been sent to jail, as follows:

A man named Bowling was one of the men who went after Martin, whose wife happened to be visiting him at the time. They brought them back together, but removed her before the killing occurred. Bowling just stepped up to Martin and shot him several times.

Martin lived a mile east of Morehead, where, some years later, a big lumber company located. Martin had two sons, lads at the time of his murder, and one of them went West. Bowling left the country, too, but after a number of years he came back. He got a job with the lumber company as an inspector of timber, and one day, while he and some others were looking at Martin's grave, which they could see from the camp, Bowling said to them, "I shot that . . . and I wish he were alive so that I could shoot him again."

Martin's younger son overheard the remark, went home, and tried to get his father's pistol, but his mother would not let him have it. Then he sent a telegram to his brother out West, who came home, waited in the wood, shot Bowling, and then went back. The body was rotten before it was found. No one ever knew who shot Bowling, but really everybody knew.

This song is cited by Shearin and Combs, p. 18, as "The Rowan County Tragedy." A note by W. A. Bradley ascribes it ("The Rowan County Trouble") to "the blind Day Brothers" (*Berea Quarterly*, October, 1915, XVIII, No. 4, p. 10). The next piece in the present collection (No. 40) is, in fact, a rewording of this song to fit a similar occurrence.

1 Come all you fathers and mothers, brothers and sisters too,
   And I'll relate to you a history of the Rowan County crew.
   It was in the month of August, all on election day,
   John Martin he was wounded; they say by John Day.

2 But he did not believe it; he did not think it so;
   He thought it was Floyd Tolliver who struck the fatal blow.
   Martin did recover; some months had come and passed,
   When in the town of Morehead these two men did meet at last.

3 Tolliver, with a friend or two, about the streets did walk;
   He seemed to be uneasy, with no one wished to talk.
   He stepped into Judge Carety's grocery[1] and stepped up to the bar,
   But little did he think he had met the fatal hour.

---

[1] For *bar-room*.

4 . . . Martin stepped in at the door,
And a few words passed between them concerning the [trouble]
before.
The people were excited, began to rush out of the room,
When a shot from Martin's pistol laid Tolliver in the tomb.

5 Martin was arrested, and taken to Winchester jail

. . . .

They killed the deputy sheriff, Baumgardner was his name

. . . .

6 . . . his life may never be forgot,
His body was pierced and torn by thirty-three buck shot.
They shot and wounded young Ad Sizemore, his life was luckily
saved;
He seems to shun all grogshops, since he stood so near the grave.

7 Some parties forged an order, their names I do not know,
. . . and for Martin they did go.
"It is a plan to kill me," to the jailer Martin said.
(The jailer gave him up.) . . .

8 When the train arrives at Farmer's, . . .
A mob approached the engineer, and bade him not to move.
Martin was in the smoking car, accompanied by his wife;
They did not want her present, when they took her husband's
life.

9 . . . .
She cried, "O Lord, they've killed him, I heard the pistol fire."
In the bottom of the whiskey glass the lurking devil dwells,
It burns the breast of those who drink it and sends their souls to
hell.

40

A WEST–VIRGINIA FEUD SONG

COMMUNICATED by Mr. T. M. Martin, Marlinton, Pocahontas County, June 12, 1916; obtained from Miss Pearl Carter, who received it from Mr. S. S. Workman, Seebert. In a letter to the editor of this volume, Mr. Workman gives the following data:

The fight, out of which this song grew, occurred, as near as he could remember, in 1890, at the house of George Fries, eleven miles east of Hamlin, Lincoln County, and the trial took place at Hamlin. The trouble between the factions was of long standing. The McCoy mentioned was a close relative of the McCoys that fought with the Hatfields. George Pack helped Mr. Workman get the song together. They never saw it in print.

1 Come all you young men and ladies, and fathers and mothers too;
I'll relate to you the history of the Lincoln County crew;
Concerning bloody rowing, and a many a threatening deed;
Pray lend me your attention, and remember how it reads.

2 It was all in the month of August, all on a very fine day,
Ale Brumfield he got wounded, they say by Milt Haley;
But Brumfield he recovered; he says it was not so,
He says it was McCoy that fired the fatal shot.

3 Two months have come and passed, now those men have met at last,
Have met at George Fries' house, at George Fries' house at last;
McCoy and Milt Haley, it's through the yard did walk,
They seemed to be uneasy, with no one wished to talk.

4 They went into the house, sit down by the fire,
But little did they think they had met their fatal hour.
As the mob came rushing on them, the ladies left the room;
A ball from some man's pistol lay McCoy in his tomb.

5 They shot and killed Boney Lukes, a sober and innocent man,
And left his wife and children to do the best they can;
They wounded old Ran Sawyers, although his life was save[d];
He seems to shun the drugshops, since he stood so near the grave.

6 Tom Feril was soon arrested and confined in jail;
He was put in jail in Hamlin to bravely stand his trial;
The Butchers threatened to lynch him, and that was all his fears;
The trial day it came on, Tom Feril he came clear.

7 There is poor old Perries Brumfield, he died among the rest;
  He got three balls shot through him, they went through his
    breast.
  The death of poor old Parris so lately has been done,
  They say it was a hired deed, it was done by his son.

8 So go tell the nation around you it will never, never cease;
  I would give this whole world around me to reach my home in
    peace;
  In the bottom of the whiskey glass there is a lurking devil dwells,
  It burns the breath of those who drink it and sends their souls to
    hell.

41

THE VANCE SONG

THIS song is widely known throughout the southern part of West Virginia, and two copies have come to hand. The first was furnished on a printed slip by Mr. D. K. Vance, Wilsondale, Mingo County, a great-grandson of Abner Vance, the man who is celebrated in the ballad. The story as told the Editor by Mr. Vance is as follows:

Some hundred years ago, Abner Vance, a Baptist preacher, was hanged at Abingdon, Virginia, for the killing of Lewis Horton, who had abused Vance's family in his absence. Horton tried to escape, jumped on his horse, and attempted to swim across a river near Vance's house. Vance got his gun and shot him while he was fording the river. After conviction, Vance lay in prison for some time, during which he made a ballad about himself. From his prison window he looked out and saw them erect the scaffold and make the coffin upon which he stood on the day of his execution and preached his own funeral sermon. His son-in-law, Frank Browning, was present, and Vance asked him to turn his back when the trap should fall. A reprieve had been granted the doomed man, but the men who had him in charge hanged him a few minutes before it arrived. Mr. Vance said that his grandmother, Elizabeth Deal, had often talked to him about this affair.

A second copy of the song was given to the editor by Mr. James Knox Smith, a colored lawyer, who lives at Keystone. He told the following story about the case:

Horton, a wealthy farmer, owned what is now called Russel County, Virginia. Vance was a native of what is now West Virginia, a hunter, and a Baptist preacher, quick tempered, but a good man. Horton had seduced one of his daughters, and Vance was talking to him and trying to get him to marry her. Horton, after having used vulgar language, ran outside the house, jumped on his horse, and tried to get across the river. Vance levelled on him with a flintlock rifle, and Horton fell into the river. He had leaned over on his horse and the bullet struck him in the hip and came out at his shoulder.

Vance escaped and was gone three years, and finally a reward of one hundred dollars was offered for him. Getting tired of being a fugitive, he persuaded his son to deliver him up to justice and get the reward. He was indicted, tried, convicted, and hanged in Russel County, Virginia. The judge who tried him was named Johnson, who had a son-in-law named Elliott. Elliott had killed a man, and Vance, who was on the jury that tried him, hung it; in a second trial, Elliott came clear. Vance thought Johnson would save his life, but instead, he sent him to the gallows. Vance preached his own funeral sermon.

Four stanzas of this song (C) were recited to the editor by Mr. Sam Turman, who lives in Kentucky, just across the Big Sandy from Prichard, West Virginia. His story is as follows:

A man, not named, had taken away Vance's daughter. Some time later, he brought her back home, dumped her in the yard, and said he had brought back their heifer. Vance got his gun and shot him while he was trying to get across the river. Mr. Turman added that Vance should not have been hanged.

Version A is printed by Cox, XLVII, 638.

A

In the version immediately following, the title, note of explanation, **and** ballad proper appear exactly as they are printed on the slip above-mentioned. The Rev. A. M. Lunsford is evidently the person who gave the song to **the** printer.

A Poem

This song was composed and sung by Elder Abner Vance, under the gallows, at Abingdon, Virginia, about ninety years ago.   Given by Rev. A. M. Lunsford, October 14, 1897.

1 Green are the woods where Sandy flows,
        And peace it dwelleth there;
    In the valley the bear they lie secure,
        The red buck roves the knobs.

2 But Vance no more shall Sandy behold,
        Nor drink its crystal waves;
    The partial judge pronounced his doom,
        The hunter has found his grave.

3 The judge said I was an incarnate fiend,
        For Elliott I tried to save;
    I agreed as a juryman Elliott's life to save,
        Humanity belongs to the brave.

4 That friendship I have shown to others,
        Has never been shown to me;
    Humanity it belongs to the brave,
        And I hope it belongs to me.

5 'T was by the advice of McFarlin,
        Judge Johnson did me call;
    I was taken from my native home,
        Confined in a stone wall.

6 My persecutors have gained their request,
        Their promise to make good;
    For they ofttimes swore they would never rest,
        Till they had gained my heart's blood.

7 Daniel Horton, Bob, and Bill,
        A lie against me swore,
    In order to take my life away,
        That I might be no more.

8   But I and them together must meet,
         Where all things are unknown,
     And if I've shed the innocent blood,
         I hope there's mercy shown.

9   Bright shines the sun on Clinch's Hill,
         And soft the west wind blows,
     The valleys are covered all over with bloom,
         Perfumed with the red rose.

10   But Vance no more shall Sandy behold,
         Nor smell its sweet perfume;
     This day his eyes are closed in death,
         His body confined in the tomb.

11   Farewell, my friends, my children dear;
         To you I bid farewell;
     The love I have for your precious souls
         No mortal tongue can tell.

12   Farewell to you, my loving wife;
         To you I bid adieu,
     And if I reach fair Canaan's shore,
         I hope to meet with you.

B

"The Vance Song."   Contributed by Mr. James Knox Smith, Keystone, McDowell County, July, 1918, who wrote it down as he learned it by hearing it repeated in his community.

1   Green are the woods where Sandy flows,
         Peace it dwelleth there,
     Secure the red buck roams the wood,
         In the valley the bear lies.

2   Sandy no more will Vance behold,
         Nor drink of its crystal waves,
     The partial judge pronounced his doom;
         The hunter has found his grave.

3   It was by the advice of James McFarland,
         Judge Johnson did me call;
     I was taken from my native home,
         And confined in a stone wall.

4   The judge he said he was my friend,
       Though Elliott's life I saved;
     A juryman I did become,
       That Elliott he might live.

5   The friendship I have shown to others
       Has never been shown to me;
     But humanity it belongs to the brave,
       I hope it shall remain to me.

6   There was Daniel, Hoston,[1] Lewis, and Bill,
       All three a lie against me swore,
     In order to take my life away,
       That I might be no more.

7   Them and I together shall meet,
       When Gabriel's trumpet shall blow;
     Perhaps I will rest in Abraham's breast,
       While they roll in the gulf below.

8   I killed the man, I do not deny,
       But he threatened to kill me first,
     And for this I am condemned to die,
       The jury all agreed.

9   Them and I together must meet,
       Where all things are well known;
     And if I have shed the innocent blood,
       I hope there is mercy shown.

10 Bright shines the sun on Clinch's hill,
       So soft the west wind blows,
     The valleys are covered all over with bloom,
       Perfumed with the red rose.

11 Sandy no more will Vance behold,
       Nor smell of its sweet perfume;
     This day his eyes will close in death,
       His body confined in the tomb.

12 Farewell, my friends, my children dear,
       To you I will bid farewell;
     The love I have for your precious souls
       No mortal tongue can tell.

[1] Mistake for *Daniel Horton.*

13 Farewell, my true and loving wife,
        To you I will bid adieu,
    And when I reach fair Cannian's shore,
        I hope to meet with you.

C

"The Vance Song."   A fragment contributed by Mr. Sam Turman, Buchanan, Boyd County, Kentucky, July, 1918.

1   I've killed a man and I don't deny it,
        He first threatened it to kill me;
    The judges said that I must hang,
        The jurors did agree.

2   There's Bill and Ike and Lewis, too,
        A lie against me swore,
    In order for to take my life,
        That I should be no more.

3   But I and them will meet again,
        When the last trump shall blow;
    I will rest in Abraham's breast,
        They'll burn in the gulf below.

4   Where the black bear hides in the valley,
        The red buck roves the hill secure,
    No more Vance will roam Sandy's banks,
        Nor drink her crystal waves.

42

LOGAN COUNTY COURT HOUSE

Four variants of this song have been reported. No doubt there were many such songs as this made and lost concerning persons and happenings of local interest. In the course of time it becomes impossible to distinguish what of them is truth and what is fiction. Some stanzas of the song appear in two of Lomax's *Cowboy Songs* — "Root Hog or Die" (p. 254) and "The Lone Star Trail" (p. 310).

A

"Logan County Court House." Contributed by Mr. J. D. James, Williamson, Mingo County, July, 1918, who did not know anything about the events that gave rise to it.

1 O, when I was a little boy, I worked in Market Square;
  I used to pocket money, I did not make it fair.
  I rode upon the lakes, to learn to rob and steal,
  And when I made a big haul, how happy I did feel!

2 I used to wear the white hat, my horse and buggy fine;
  I used to court that pretty girl, I always called her mine.
  I courted her for beauty, her love to me was great,
  And every time I'd go to see her, she'd meet me at the gate.

[The part of the song that told about the crime is missing.]

3 As I lay down the other night, I dreamt a mighty dream;
  I dreamt I was a rich merchant, lived on the golden stream.
  As I woke up broken-hearted, in Logan County jail,
  Not there around me was a friend to go my bail.

4 Down came my darling, with the keys in her hand:
  "O, my dearest darling, I'll help you all I can!
  May the angels help you, wherever you may go,
  And the devil take the jury, for sending you below!"

5 Down came the jailer about ten o'clock,
  His hands full of keys, and rushing toward the lock.
  "Cheer up, cheer up, my prisoner," I thought I heard him say,
  "Bound for the penitentiary, seven long years to stay."

6 A pocketful of wheat, and a pocketful of rye!
  We'll take a drink of whiskey, and let all things pass by.

B

"Logan County Jail." Contributed by Miss Snoah McCourt, Orndoff, Webster County, May, 1916.

1 When I was a little boy, I worked on Market Square,
O money I did pocket, but I never did it fair.
I rode upon the lakes and learned to rob and steal,
And when I made a great haul, how happy I did feel!

2 I used to wear the white hat, my horse an' buggy fine;
I used to court a pretty girl, I always thought was mine.
I courted her for beauty, her love for me was great,
And when I'd go to see her, she'd meet me at the gate.

3 One night as I lay sleeping, I dreamed a mighty dream,
That I was marching down on the golden stream.
I awoke all broken-hearted, in Logan County jail,
And not a friend around me for to go my bail.

4 Down came the jailer about ten o'clock,
And with the key in his hand he shoved against the lock:
"Cheer up, cheer up, my prisoner!" I thought I heard him say,
"You're going around to Moundsville, seven long years to stay."

5 Down came my true-love, ten dollars in her hand:
"O my dearest darling, I've done all that I can!
And may the Lord be with you, wherever you may go,
And Satan snatch the jury for sending you below!"

6 Sitting in the railroad, waiting for the train,
I am going away to leave you, to wear the ball and chain.
I'm going away to leave you; darling, don't you cry;
Take a glass of whiskey and let it all pass by.

C

No local title. Communicated by Mrs. Hilary G. Richardson, Clarksburg, Harrison County, 1917; obtained from Mrs. Nancy McAtee.

1 When I was the age of sixteen, I rode the Madison Square;
I used to pocket money, but I did n't get it square;
And when I rode the lake, to learn to rob and steal,
When I made a rich haul, how happy I did feel!

2 I used to wear that white hat, with horse and buggy fine,
And go to see that little girl, I used to think was mine;
And when she saw me coming, she'd meet me at the gate;
She'd throw her arms around me and kiss me unaware.

3 .   .   .   .
   .   .   .   .
Next morning when I woke up, I was in the prison county jail,
Without a cent of money, and no one to go my bail.

4 Down came my true-love, about eight o'clock,
   Said she, "My dearest darling, what sentence have you got?"
   "The judge has found me guilty, and the clerk has wrote it
      down;
   "We've got to go to Moundsville, for seven long years to stay."

5 Down came my true-love, with ten dollars in her hand;
   Said she, "My dearest darling, I've done for you all I can,
   And may the Lord be with you, wherever you do go,
   And the devil take the jailer, for sending you below!"

6 Down came the jailer about ten o'clock,
   With a bunch of keys all in his hand, and shoved agin the lock:
   "Cheer up, cheer up, my prisoner!" I thought I heard him say,
   "You have to go to Moundsville, for seven long years to stay."

7 Now I'm settin' on the railroad, a-waitin' for the train,
   To ride around to Moundsville, to wear the ball and chain:
   "Do shut up, dear sweetheart, and don't be grievin' so!
   Just take a glass of liquor, and let it all pass by;
   For I'll be back next Saturday night, I'm a-comin' back or die."

D

No local title. Communicated by Mr. Fred Smith, Glenville, Gilmer County,
1916; obtained from Hu Summers. A fragment of four stanzas.

43

BLACK PHYLLIS

COMMUNICATED by Miss Florence Crane, Morgantown, Monongalia County, July, 1916; obtained from her mother, who learned it about forty years before from a very old washerwoman in Sistersville, Tyler County.

1 And then came black Phyllis, his charger astride,
   And took away Annie, his unwilling bride.
   It rainèd, it hailèd, and I sat and cried,
   And wished that my Annie that day had then died.

2 I sat all alone, sad and forlorn,
   And waited the coming of that Sunday morn.
   It rainèd, it hailèd, and I in the storm;
   Ten thousand around me had never been born.

3 And then came her true-love from over the moor,
   And left them a-cursing his cross on the door.
   It rainèd, it hailèd, I waited no more;
   I knew that my Annie he soon would restore.

* * * * * * * * * * * * *

4 He fell on Black Phyllis with wild lion's roar;
   They fought and they struggled for hour after hour.
   It rainèd, it hailèd, though wounded and sore,
   He left Phyllis a-dead on the moor.

5 Then swift as a bird to his true-love he fled,
   Found the cabin in ashes, the ground all a-red.
   It rainèd, it hailèd, though swift he had sped,
   He found he was too late; his Annie was dead.

44

JESSE JAMES

Of this song but one fragmentary and confused text has been received. It was communicated by Mrs. Hilary G. Richardson, Clarksburg, Harrison County, 1917. For texts and fragments (from North and South Carolina, Kentucky, Tennessee, Mississippi, Georgia, Missouri, Indiana, and Iowa) see Pound, p. 34; Pound, No. 64; *Journal*, XXII, 246 (Bascom); XXV, 17 (Belden, No. 75); XXV, 145 (Perrow); XXXIV, 124 (Redfearn). Odum prints a three-stanza negro song on Jesse James (*Journal*, XXIV, 387; cf. Perrow, *Journal*, XXV, 149). For other references and remarks see Tolman, *Journal*, XXIX, 178.

1   Jesse James was a robber he robbed many a man,
    He robbed the demill [1] train;
But the dirty little coward, that shot Mr. Howard,
    And laid Jesse James in his grave.

2   Jesse was a robber, but he robbed it from the rich
    And gave it to the poor;
O, where is such a man as Jesse James?

3   Poor Jesse had a wife, he knew her all his life,
    And three children, they were brave;
But the dirty little coward, that shot Mr. Howard,
    And laid Jesse James in his grave.

4   Poor Jesse went to the depot, the agent for to see,
    And fell upon his knees and delivered up the keys
To Frank and his brother, Jesse James.

5   Poor Jesse's wife was standing by, but did n't seem to cry,
    Just to arrest Robert Ford in time.

6   Poor Jesse now is dead and buried in his grave,
    And is gone to the sweet by-and-by;
His money still is clear, passing year by year,
    By the grave that they laid Jesse James in.

[1] For *Danville*.

45

YE SONS OF COLUMBIA

CONTRIBUTED by Mr. Sam Turman, Buchanan, Boyd County, Kentucky, July, 1918.

For this song, otherwise known as "Fuller and Warren," see Lomax, p. 126; Pound, No. 49 (Nebraska); Belden, No. 16 (cf. *Journal*, XXV, 12; *Modern Philology*, II, 574).

1   Ye sons of Columbia, your attention I do crave
    While my sorrowful ditty I tell,
Which happened here of late in Indiana state
    Of a hero that none could excel.

2   Like Samson he courted the choice of the fair,
    Intending to make her his bride;
Just like a lily fair she did his heart ensnare,
    And she robbed him of his honor and his life.

3   With his bosom full of woe unto Warren he did go:
    "You reported I left a prudent wife."
With one fatal shot, he killed Warren on the spot;
    With a smile he is now to lose his life.

4   Old Fuller was condemned by the honors of the law,
    In Lawrenceburg to be hung;
It's an ignominious death to hang above the earth,
    Like a gambler on a gallows so high.

5   Ten thousand spectators all smote upon their breasts,
    And the tears from their eyes they did flow;
Like an angel he did stand, for he was a handsome man,
    On his breast he wore ribbons so blue.

6   Of all the histories that we now-a-days do read,
    Our Bible it must be true;
For whiskey and women are the downfall of all men,
    Since old Adam was beguiled by old Eve.

7   O marriage is but lottery,
    Both pleasing to the heart and to the eye;
O he that never marries may be called wise:
    So ladies, excuse me, good-bye.

46

MAGGIE WAS A LADY

THESE are versions of the negro ballad of "Frankie" or "Frankie Baker," current also among whites. See Odum, *Journal*, XXIV, 366; Perrow, *Journal*, XXVIII, 178 (Mississippi); Thomas, *Some Current Folk-Songs of the Negro* (Folk-Lore Society of Texas, 1912), p. 12; *Spectator*, London, December 25, 1920, p. 845 (reprinted in the *Boston Herald*, January 20, 1921); Gordon, *Adventure* (magazine), August 20, 1923, p. 191; Wyman MS., No. 59 (North Carolina); Kittredge MSS., XI, 129 (sung in logging camps near the Virginia-Tennessee line); N. I. White MS., II, 216; Shearin, p. 28 (Kentucky). Belden reports privately two texts, one from Maryland, the other a composite from Missouri.

A

"Maggie was a Lady." Communicated by Mr. J. Carl Cox, Cox's Mills, Gilmer County, September 18, 1918; obtained from Frank Reaser, who learned it from lumbermen in the mountains near Richwood, Nicholas County.

1 Maggie was a lady,
  A money-making girl;
 She made all the money she could rake and scrape,
  And she gave it to her darling Pearl.
  O he's my man, but he done me wrong.

2 Miss Maggie went down to the bar-room,
  She called for a glass of beer:
 "Say, Mr. Greeda, will you tell me no lie?
  Has my darling Walter been here?"
  O he's my man, but he did me wrong.

3 "Miss Maggie, I'll tell you no story,
  Miss Maggie, I'll tell you no lie:
 Your Walter left here about an hour ago
  With a girl called Lily Fry."
  O he's my man, but he did me wrong.

4 Miss Maggie went down to the Hock joint,
  She did n't go there for fun;
 Under her apron she kept concealed
  Walter's long, black, forty-four gun,
  Saying, "I want my man, but he did me wrong."

5 Miss Maggie went down to the depot,
  Along came Number One;
 Up stepped Walter with his Lily Fry,
  And she shot him with his forty-four gun,
  Saying, "You're my man, but you did me wrong."

6 O Walter began to holler,
       O Walter began to cry:
   "Say, Miss Maggie, don't you murder me,
       For I'm not prepared to die.
       I was your man, and I did you wrong."

7 They took up Maggie for to hang her,
       Not many tears were shed;
   Pull the black cap over her head,
       And the words that Maggie said,
       "He was my man, and he did me wrong."

ℬ

"Maggie was a Good Little Girl."   Communicated by Mrs. Hilary G. Richardson, Clarksburg, Harrison County, 1916.

1 Maggie was a good little girl,
       Everybody know;
   She threw down a hundred dollar bill
       For to buy little Albert close,
       For he's the man, but he done me wrong.

2 Maggie went down to the bar-room
       To get a glass of beer:
   "Hello! Mr. Bartender,
       Has Albert been here?"
       For he's the man, but he done me wrong.

3 "O no, O no! I'll tell you no story;
       I'll tell you no lie;
   He left here 'bout an hour ago
       With a girl named Rachel Fry."
       For he's the man, but he done me wrong.

4 Maggie went down to the pawnshop,
       Feeling very sore;
   She threw down a hundred-dollar bill
       For blue steel forty-four,
       For to kill that man that done her wrong.

5 Maggie loaded up her forty-four,
       Started through the door,
   Shot little Albert in his left side,
       Stood and seen him fall.
       For he's the man, but he done me wrong.

6 "O turn me over, Maggie,
   Turn me over slow;
Turn me on my right side,
   So my heart won't overflow;
   For I am your man, but I've done you wrong."

7 "Rubber-tired is my buggy,
   Rubber-tired is my hack,
To haul poor Albert to the graveyard,
   Never to bring him back."
   For he's the man, but he done me wrong.

8 Maggie went up to the graveyard,
   Fell down on her knees;
And all that I could hear her say was,
   "Nearer my God to Thee."
   For he's the man, but he done me wrong.

9 Maggie was sitting in a pailas [1]
   Under the electric fan,
Teaching her youngest daughter
   To marry no gambling man.
   For he's the man, but he done me wrong.

[1] *Palace.*

47

THE WRECK ON THE C. & O.

THIS ballad, like that of "John Hardy," was made in West Virginia. Ten variants have been found, all very much alike. The facts out of which the song grew were obtained from Miss Margaret Alley and Mr. Ernest N. Alley, Alderson, West Virginia, sister and brother of George Alley, the man killed in the wreck, and from Mr. R. E. Noel, Hinton, formerly an engineer on the Chesapeake & Ohio Railroad

George Alley was born in Richmond, Virginia, July 10, 1860, was married November 10, 1881, and had four children. The wreck on the C. & O. in which he was killed occurred at 5.40 A.M., October 23, 1890. He was running train No. 4, the F. F. V. (Fast Flying Vestibule), engine No. 134. He lived five hours after being hurt. The wreck occurred three miles east of Hinton, and was caused by a landslide. Lewis Withrow, the regular fireman, was firing the engine. He had been "laying off," but, on the morning of the wreck, took his run back at Hinton. Jack Dickinson was not on the engine, but Robert Foster was. He had been working in Withrow's place, and his run being out of Clifton Forge, he was deadheading back home that morning. Neither he nor Withrow jumped into the New River: he went out of the window on the left side of the engine, that being the side away from the river, and Withrow went out of the gangway on the same side. The engine turned over on the opposite side from which they jumped, that is, toward the river. Withrow was badly hurt, and for a long time it was thought he would not live. Hinton is an important town on the C. & O. in Summers County. Sewell is forty miles west of Hinton; the Big Bend Tunnel is eight miles east of Hinton; Stock Yards, then, is now Pence's Spring, fourteen miles east of Hinton; and Clifton Forge, a terminal, or division point, where train crews change, is eighty miles east of Hinton.

George Alley was six feet tall, weighed about one hundred seventy pounds, had a dark complexion, black eyes, and straight black hair. At the time of the wreck, his home was at Clifton Forge. His father and stepmother lived at Alderson, West Virginia, his own mother having died many years before, when the family was living at White Sulphur Springs, in the same state. Mr. Ernest N. Alley thinks the ballad was first started on its way by a negro engine-wiper, who worked in the roundhouse at Hinton. Mr. H. S. Walker, a former student in West Virginia University, told the Editor that the ballad was composed by a negro who worked in the roundhouse at Hinton.

The ballad and the facts agree as follows: (1) The F. F. V., train No. 4, running east on the C. & O. Railroad, was wrecked near Hinton by a landslide. (2) The regular engineer, George Alley, was killed. (3) The fireman saved his life by jumping from the engine. As in "John Hardy," certain fundamental facts are retained in an atmosphere of verisimilitude, but the details are entirely untrustworthy.

For American references see Cox, XLV, 160, and *Journal*, XXIX, 400; Shearin and Combs, p. 20 ("The F. F. V.," "Stockyard Gate").

A

"The Wreck on the C. & O." Communicated by Mr. E. C. Smith, Weston, Lewis County, December 18, 1915; obtained from Miss Maude Rucks, Braxton County.

1 Along came the F. F. V., the fastest on the line,
Running o'er the C. & O. Road, a quarter behind time;
As she passed Sewell, 't was quarters on the line,
Waiting to get orders at Hinton, late, behind time.

2 When she got to Hinton, the engineer was there;
George Alley was his name, with bright and golden hair;
Jack Dickerson, a faithful man, was standing by the side,
Waiting to get orders; both in the cab did ride.

3 Georgie's mother came to him with a bucket on her arm;
Gave him a letter and said, "My boy, be careful how you run;
For many a man has lost his life in trying to make lost time,
But if you run your engine right, you'll seldom be behind."

4 Georgie said, "Dear mother, to your warning I'll take heed;
I know my engine is all right, I know that she will speed;
But if I had a local train, the truth to you I'd tell,
I'd run her into Clifton Forge or drop her into hell."

5 Georgie said, "Now listen, Jack, it must be known to all,
I'm going to blow for the Big Bend Tunnel; they'll surely hear my call."
Then he cried, "O look, look, Jack! a rock ahead I see!
I know that death is waiting there, to grab both you and me."

6 "So, from the cab, Jack, you must fly, your darling life to save,
For I want you to be the engineer when I'm in my grave."
"No, no, George, I cannot go! on that we can't agree."
"Yes, yes, Jack, you must! I'll die for you and me."

7 So from the cab poor Jack did fly; the river it was high;
Farewell, he kissed the hand of George; old No. 4 flew by;
Up the road she darted, just like an angry bull;
To get her back in action, the lever he did pull.

8 Against the rock the engine crashed, and upside down she lay;
The best engineer on the C. & O. Road went to his grave that day;
Brave and strong he held his grip; at last she made the crash,
Knocked poor George upon his face, his tender breast did smash.

9 . . . .
. . . .

The firebox fell against his head and burning flames rolled out,
[He said], "I'm glad I was born an engineer to die on the C. & O.
    Road."

10 Georgie's mother came again; with sorrow she did sigh,
When she looked upon her darling boy and knew that he must die;
She prayed for every engineer to take warning from her son,
In making any schedule to be careful how they run.

11 The doctor said, "Now Georgie, my darling boy, be still;
Your life may be saved, if it be God's precious will."
"No, no, Doc, I want to die! I'm ready now to go,
I said I'd die on my engine, No. 134."

B

"Georgie Allen." Contributed by Mr. John B. Adkins, Branchland, Lincoln
County, April 1, 1916.

1 Along came the F. F. V., the fastest on the line,
Came running o'er the C. & O. Road, just twenty minutes behind;
Came running into Sewell, lies quartered on the line,
And then received strict orders for Hinton, away behind.

Chorus

Many a man's been murdered by the railroad,
By the railroad, by the railroad;
Many a man's been murdered by the railroad,
And is sleeping in his lonesome grave.

2 When she got to Hinton, her engineer was there,
Georgie Allen was his name, with blue eyes and curly hair;
His fireman, Jack Dickinson, was standing by his side,
Waiting for his orders, and in his cab to ride.

3 Georgie's mother came to him with a basket on her arm,
Saying, "Now, my darling son, be careful how you run;
For many a man has lost his life trying to gain lost time,
And if you run your engine right, you'll get there yet on time."

4 "Mother, I know your advice is good; to your letter I'll take heed;
I know my engine is all right and I know that she will speed;
And o'er this road I mean to fly with a speed unknown to all,
And when I blow for the Big Bend Tunnel, they will surely hear
    my call."

5 Georgie said to his pal, "Jack, just a little more steam;
I mean to pull old No. 4 the fastest ever seen;
And o'er this road I mean to fly with a speed unknown to all,
And when I blow for the Stock Yard Gate, they will surely hear
my call."

6 Georgie said to his pal, "Jack, a rock ahead I see;
I know that death is waiting to grasp both you and me;
So from this cab you must fly, your darling life to save,
For I want you to be an engineer when I am sleeping in my
grave."

7 "O no!" said Jack, "that will not do; I want to die with you."
"O no!" said Georgie, "that will not do; I'll die for me and
you."
So from the cab, poor Jack did fly; the river it was high,
And as he kissed his hand to George, old No. 4 flew by.

8 Up the road she darted; against the rock she crashed;
Upside down the engine turned, upon his breast it crashed;
His head upon the firebox door, the burning flames rolled o'er:
"I'm glad I was born an engineer to die on the C. & O. Road."

9 Georgie's mother came to him, "My son what have you done?"
"Too late, too late my doom is almost run."
The doctor said to Georgie, "My son, you must lie still;
Your precious life may yet be saved, if it be God's holy will."

10 "O no, doctor, O no! I want to die so free;
I want to die with my engine, old 143."
His last words were, "Nearer, my God, to Thee, nearer to Thee,
Nearer, my God, to Thee, nearer to Thee."

C

"The Wreck on the C. & O." Communicated by Mrs. Walter M. Parker,
Hinton, Summers County, October 4, 1915; obtained from Miss Ruth Keatly.

1 Along came the old F. F. V., the fastest on the line,
Running over the C. & O. Road, twenty minutes behind time;
Running into Sewell, she was quartered on the line,
And there received strict orders: Hinton, away behind time.

Chorus

Many a man's been murdered by the railroad,
By the railroad, by the railroad;
Many a man's been murdered by the railroad,
And sleeping in his lonesome grave.

2 When she got to Hinton, that engineer was there,
George Allen was his name, with bright and golden hair;
His fireman, Jack Dickinson, was standing by his side,
Waiting for strict orders, and in his cab did ride.

3 George's mother came to the train with a bucket on her arm,
Says she to him, "My darling son, be careful how you run;
For many a man has lost his life in trying to make lost time,
And if you run your engine right, you'll get there yet on time."

4 "Mother, I know your advice is good; to the letter I'll take heed;
I know my engine is all right, and sure that she will steam;
But over this road I mean to fly with a speed unknown to all,
And when I blow for the Stock Yard Gates, they'll surely hear
    my call."

5 Then he said to his fireman, "Jack, a rock ahead I see;
I know that death is waiting there to grab both you and me;
And from the cab you must fly, your darling life to save,
For I want you to be an engineer when I'm sleeping in my
    grave."

6 "No, no!" said Jack, "I will not go, I want to die with you!"
"No, no!" said George, "I'll die, I'll die for you and me."
And from the cab poor Jack did fly, the river it was high,
And as he kissed his hand to George, old No. 4 flew by.

7 Down the road she darted; against the rock she crashed;
Upside down his engine turned, upon his breast she smashed;
His head upon the firebox door, the rolling scenes rolled o'er:
"I'm glad I was born an engineer and died on No. 4."

8 George's mother came to him: "My son, what have you done?"
"Too late, too late! the dome [1] is almost done.
But if I had a local train, the truth to you I'll tell,
I'd pull her into Clifton Forge, or bid you all farewell."

9 The doctor said to George, "My darling son, lie still;
Your life may yet be saved, if it's God's own blessed will."
"No, no!" said George, "I want to die so free;
I want to die with my engine, 143."

[1] Cf. B 9, 2.

D

"George Alley." Communicated by Professor Walter Barnes, Fairmont, Marion County, May, 1916; obtained from George W. Gregg, Durbin, Pocahontas County, who learned it from Addison Collins.

1 Along came the F. F. V., the fastest on the line,
 Running o'er the C. & O. Road, twenty minutes behind the time;
 Running into Sewell yard, was quartered on the line,
 Awaiting for strict orders and in the cab to ride.

Chorus

Many a man has been murdered by the railroad,
By the railroad, by the railroad;
Many a man has been murdered by the railroad,
And laid in his lonesome grave.

2 And when she blew for Hinton, her engineer was there,
 George Alley was his name, with bright and wavery hair;
 His fireman, Jack Dixon, was standing by his side,
 Awaiting for strict orders and in the cab to ride.

3 George Alley's mother came to him with a basket on her arm,
 She handed him a letter, saying, "Be careful how you run;
 And if you run your engine right, you'll get there just on time,
 For many a man has lost his life in trying to make lost time."

4 George Alley said, "Dear mother, your letter I'll take heed,
 I know my engine is all right and I know that she will speed;
 So o'er this road I mean to run with a speed unknown to all,
 And when I blow for Clifton Forge, they'll surely hear my call."

5 George Alley said to his fireman, "Jack, a little extra steam;
 I intend to run old No. 4 the fastest ever seen;
 So o'er this road I mean to fly like angels' wings unfold,
 And when I blow for the Big Bend Tunnel, they'll surely hear my call."

6 George Alley said to his fireman, "Jack, a rock ahead I see,
 And I know that death is lurking there for to grab both you and me;
 So from this cab, dear Jack, you leap, your darling life to save,
 For I want you to be an engineer while I'm sleeping in my grave."

7 "Oh no, dear George! that will not do, I want to die with you."
  "O no, no, dear Jack! that will not be, I 'll die for you and me."
  So from the cab dear Jack did leap, old New River was running
      high,
  And he kissed the hand of darling George as No. 4 flew by.

8 So in the cab dear George did leap, the throttle he did pull;
  Old No. 4 just started off, like a mad and angry bull.

  . . . .
  . . . .

9 So up the road she dashed; against the rock she crashed;
  The engine turning over and the coaches they came last;
  George Alley's head in the firebox lay, while the burning flames
      rolled o'er:
  "I am glad I was born an engineer, to die on the C. & O. Road."

10 George Alley's mother came to him and in sorrow she did sigh,
   When she looked upon her darling boy and saw that he must die.
   "Too late, too late, dear mother! my doom is almost o'er,
   And I know that God will let me in when I reach that golden
       shore."

11 The doctor said, "Dear George, O darling boy, keep still;
   Your life may yet be spared, if it be God's precious will."
   "O no, dear Doc, that can not be, I want to die so free,
   I want to die on the engine I love, 143."

12 The people came from miles around this engineer to see.
   George Alley said, "God bless you, friends, I am sure you will
       find me here."
   His head and face all covered with blood, his eyes you could not
       see,
   And as he died he cried aloud, "O near, my God, to Thee!"

E

"George Alley." Communicated by Mr. Guy Dowdy, Union, Monroe
County, January 21, 1916; obtained from R. S. Miller, Wikel, Monroe County,
who got it from Bert Ellison, an old railroad man, who learned it while living at
Hinton.

1 Along came the old F. F. V., the swiftest on the line,
  Running into Sewell, twenty minutes behind time.

  . . . .
  . . . .

Chorus

Many a man has been murdered by the railroad,
    By the railroad, by the railroad;
Many a man has been murdered by the railroad,
    And a-sleeping in their lonesome graves.

2 And when she got to Hinton, this engineer was there,
  George Alley was his name, with his bright and golden hair;
  His fireman standing by his side, Jack Dickison was his name,
  Awaiting for his orders, and in his cab did ride.

3 George's mother came to him, with a bucket on her arm,
  Saying, "George, my darling son, be careful how you run;
  For many a poor man has lost his life by trying to make lost time,
  But if you'll run your engine right, you'll get there yet on time."

4 "Yes, mother, I know your advice is good, and to your letter I'll take heed;
  But I know my engine is all right, and sure that she will steam;
  I mean to run her over the road with a speed unknown to all,
  And when I blow for the Big Ben Tunnel, they will surely hear my call."

5 Georgie said to his fireman, "Jack, a little more extra steam!
  For I mean to run old No. 4 the swiftest ever seen;
  I mean to run her over the road with a speed unknown to all,
  And when I blow for the Stock Yard Gates, they will surely hear my call."

6 Georgie said to his fireman, "Jack, a rock ahead I see,
  And I know that death is waiting there, to grab both you and me;
  And from this cab you must fly, your darling life to save,
  For I want you to be an engineer, when I'm sleeping in my grave."

7 "O no!" said Jack, "that won't do! I want to die with you."
  "O no!" said Georgie, "that won't do! I'll die for you and me."
  But from this cab poor Jack did fly; the river it was high;
  He kissed his hand to Georgie, while No. 4 flew by.

8 Up the road she darted; against the rock she crushed;
  Upside down his engine went, upon his breast did crush;
  With his head against the firebox door, while the roaring flames rolled over,
  Saying, "I'm glad I was born an engineer, to die on the C. & O. Road."

9 When Georgie's mother came to him: "Too late, mamma, too
   late!

  .   .   .   .

   But mamma, if I had a local train, the truth to you I would tell,
   I would run her in on time to Clifton Forge, or drop her into
      hell."

F

"George Alley." Communicated by Mr. R. F. Noel, Hinton, Summers
County, January 28, 1916; obtained from Miss Maggie Alley, a sister of the
engineer who was killed, Alderson, Monroe County.

1 Long come the F. F. & V., the fastest on the line,
   Running on the C. & O. Road, thirty minutes behind the time;
   When she run into old East Sewell, quartered on the line,
   There to receive orders: 't is Hinton, behind time.

Chorus

   Many a man's been murdered by the railroad,
      By the railroad, by the railroad;
   Many a man's been murdered by the railroad,
      And laid in his lonesome grave.

2 When at Hinton she made her stop, the engineer was there;
   George Alley was his name, with his curly golden hair;
   And his fireman, Jack Dickinson, was standing by his side,
   Ready to receive his orders and in his cab to ride.

3 Georgia's mama came to him, with a bucket on her arm:
   "Pray to God, George, my dear son, be careful how you run;
   Many a man has lost his life, trying to make up lost time;
   If you'll run your engine right, you'll get there just in time."

4 "Dear mama, your advice is good; to it I will take heed;
   But my engine she's all right, and I know that she will speed;
   It's over the road I mean to fly with speed unknown to all;
   When I blow at the Big Ben Tunnel, you'll surely hear my
      call."

5 Said George to his fireman: "A rock ahead I see;
   I tell you death is awaiting there, to snatch both you and me;
   From this cab you now must fly, your darling life to save;
   I want you to be an engineer, when sleeping in your grave."

6 "No, no, George! I cannot go, I want to die with you."
"No, no, Jack! that will not do! I'll die for me and you."
From this cab poor Jack did fly; New River it was high;
As he struck the water, old No. 4 flew by.

7 Up the road she darted; upon the rock she crashed;
Upside down his engine turned, and upon his breast it smashed;
His head upon the firebox door, the burning flames rolled o'er;
"I'm glad I was born an engineer, to die on the C. & O. Road."

8 The people to the engine run, to see the engineer;
Georgia said, "God bless you, friends! You'll surely find me
    here."
There never was a braver man than Georgia Alley born
To die upon the C. & O. Road, one reckless July morn.

9 The doctor said, "Now Georgia, my darling boy, be still;
Your precious life may yet be saved, if it is God's blessed will."
"No, no, Doc! I want to die so free;
I want to die with my engine, One Hundred and Forty-three."

G

"C. & O. Wreck." Communicated by Mr. C. A. Prickett, Fayetteville, Fayette County, March, 1917; obtained from Mrs. Bessie Vaughn, Wriston. Eleven stanzas, somewhat corrupt.

H

"The Wreck on the C. & O. Road." Contributed by Miss Snoah McCourt, Orndoff, Webster County, May, 1916; learned from a Mr. Simms. Seven stanzas.

I

No local title. Communicated by Mr. Fred Smith, Glenville, Gilmer County, who received it from D. L. Williams. A fragment of two stanzas.

J

"George Alley." Communicated by Mr. C. R. Bishop, Green Bank, Pocahontas County, 1917; obtained from Miss Lila Orndoff. A good text.

K

"The Wreck on the C. & O." Communicated by Mr. Sam Turman, Buchanan, Boyd County, Kentucky, July, 1918; taken from a manuscript written by his son Paul. Mr. Turman said this song was made by an engineer on the C. & O.

48

MACK McDONALD

COMMUNICATED by Mr. J. Harrison Miller, Wardensville, Hardy County, 1917; an adaptation of "Casey Jones." For "Casey Jones" see Pound, No. 59, with note, p. 250.

1   It was Mack McDonald owned a big saloon;
    He runs a local freight on the C. V. Q.;
    He's a fast freight hauler and he's never behind,
    For he has the reputation of making the time.

2   Mack pulled into Keyser just thirty minutes late,
    With thirty-five cars heavy loaded down with freight;
    He stepped on the engine and looked all about,
    Gave a toot from his whistle, and the train pulled out.

3   Mack told his fireman never to fear,
    For he was as brave a man as ever did steer;
    While stand at the front board and shovel in the coal,
    While hang at the right and watch the drivers roll.

4   The fireman, being of a weary mind,
    Said, "Mack, you're running on another's time."
    He pulled out his watch and then shook his head,
    Saying, "Mack might make it, but we'll all be dead."

5   It was down the road just a mile or so,
    You ought to have heard Mack McDonald blow;
    He blew a long blast for to clear off the track,
    And the smoke from his engine came a-rolling back.

6   It was round a curve they ran in a whirl,
    It was then that the accident did occur;
    Mack threw on the air and broke his train in two:
    It killed Mack McDonald and all his crew.

7   "O mamma, O mamma, did you hear the news?
    My father was killed on the C. V. Q."
    "O baby, O baby, why do you hold your breath?
    For we will all draw a pension from your father's death."

8   Mack told his wife just the night before he died,
    There were two more roads that he longed to ride;
    The people all wondered where those roads might be:
    It was up the Gulf of Colorado and the Santa Fe.

49

THE DYING CALIFORNIAN

"The Dying Californian or The Brother's Request — Ballad — Poetry
from *The New England Diadem*—Music by A. L. Lee" was published in Boston by Ditson in or about 1855 (the date of the copyright) and is still in Ditson's
list.   The book or periodical called *The New England Diadem* has not been
found, but the words circulated widely during the fifties and sixties in broadsides and song-books and appear in one of these little volumes as late as 1910
(for details see Kittredge, *Journal*, xxxv, 365). Miss Pound, who prints a copy
from an Iowa MS. of 1856 (No. 90), remarks that "the model for this piece was
evidently the 'I am dying, Egypt, dying' of William Haines Lytle's well-known
poem, 'Antony to Cleopatra'" (*Journal*, xxvi, 359).   See also Tolman and
Eddy, *Journal*, xxxv, 364.   H. A. Franz included the poem in his *American
Popular Songs*, Berlin, 1867, p. 15.
    Communicated by Mr. George W. Cunningham, Elkins, Randolph County,
July 26, 1916; obtained from Mrs. Ida Harding Caplinger, who learned it from
her mother while living in Baltimore, Maryland.

1 Lay up nearer, brother, nearer,
       For my limbs are growing old,
   And thy presence seemeth dearer
       Whilst thine arms around me fold.

2 I am going, surely going,
       But my faith in God is strong;
   I am willing, brother, knowing
       That he doeth nothing wrong.

3 Tell my father when you greet him,
       That in death I prayed for him;
   Prayed that I one day might meet him
       In a world that's free from sin.

4 Tell my mother (God assist her,
       Now that she is growing old!)
   That her child would glad have kissed her
       When his lips grew pale and cold.

5 Tell my sister (closer listen,
       Don't forget a single word!)
   That in death my eyes did glisten
       With the thoughts her memory stirred.

6 Listen, brother, catch each whisper,
       'T is my wife I speak of now;
   Tell, O tell her how I missed her
       When the fever burned my brow.

7 Tell her she must kiss my children,
       Like the kiss I last impressed;
   Hold them as when I last held them
       Folded closely to my breast.

8 O my children, heaven bless them!
       They were dear as life to me;
   Would I could once more caress them,
       E'er I sink beneath the sea!

9 'T was for them I crossed the ocean;
       What my hopes were, I'll not tell;
   But I've gained an orphan's portion,
       Yet, "He doeth all things well."

50

JOE BOWERS

FOR "Joe Bowers" as orally current, see Lomax, *Journal*, XXVIII, 5 (Idaho), and
Cowboy Songs, p. 15; Shoemaker, p. 39; Pound, p. 32 and No. 88 (Nebraska);
Shearin and Combs, p. 32 (Kentucky); Belden, No. 63 (Missouri); N. I. White
MS., II, 599; Professor Roland P. Gray reports it from Maine; Lomax from
Wyoming, California, Arizona, and Oklahoma. It was popular, Lomax notes,
among Confederate soldiers in the Civil War. Belden remarks that "the rush
for the California gold-fields in 1849–50 gave birth to 'Joe Bowers,' which everybody knows" (*Journal*, XXV, 16). Miss Pound says that it was in existence as
early as 1854 (*Ballads*, p. 254).

"Joe Bowers" was popular on the comic stage in the fifties and sixties. Mr.
Kittredge refers me to De Marsan broadside (New York), List 11, No. 48;
Wehman broadside (New York), No. 455; A. W. Auner broadside (Philadelphia); *Singer's Journal*, I, 143; *Howe's Comic Songs* (Boston), p. 98; *Carncross
and Sharpley's Minstrel* (Philadelphia, 1860), p. 38; *Tony Pastor's Comic and
Eccentric Songster* (cop. 1862), p. 28; *Bob Hart's Plantation Songster* (cop. 1862),
p. 39; *J. S. Berry's Comic Song Book* (cop. 1863), p. 60; *Allan's Lone Star Ballads*, p. 36; *Gus Williams' Old-Fashioned G. A. R. Camp-Fire Songster*, p. 9;
"Joe Bowers's Sister Kitty" occurs in *The Lanigan's Ball Comic Songster* (cop.
1868), p. 35.

Communicated by Mrs Hilary G. Richardson, Clarksburg, Harrison County,
1917.

1 My name it is Joe Bowers, I have a brother Ike,
   I came from old Missouri, and all the way by pike;
   I'll tell you how I came there, and how I came to roam
   And leave my poor old mamma so poor away from home.

2 I once courted a girl there, her name was Sally Black;
   I asked her if she'd marry me, she said it was a whack;
   Said she to me, "Joe Bowers, before we hitch for life,
   You'd better get a home for your little wife."

3 "O Sally, dearest Sally, and Sally for your sake,
   I'll go to California and try to raise a rake!"[1]
   And when I got to that country, I hadn't nary red,
   . . . I wished that I were dead.

4 .   .   .   .
   .   .   .   .
   But thoughts of my dear Sally soon made those feelings get,
   Whispers to me, "Joe Bowers," I wish I had them yet.

[1] For *stake*.

5 I went to work upon the . . .
  The pelting rain came down upon my head just like a thousand
      of brick;
  I worked both late and early, through heat and rain and snow,
  I was working for my Sally, but 't was all the same to Joe.

6 At length I got a letter, it was from my brother Ike,
  He said that Sally's love for me had fled;
  Sally had married a butcher, and the butcher's hair was red,
  And more than that, he said that Sally had a baby, and the
      baby's head was red.

51

THE JAM AT GERRY'S ROCK

Four excellent variants of this song have been recovered in West Virginia, under the titles, "The Jam at Gerry's Rock," "The Jam on Jerry's Rock," and "Jack Monroe." They are all very close in story and phraseology.

Texts have been printed by Lomax, p. 174 ("Foreman Monroe"); by Shoemaker, pp. 72, 74; in *Focus*, IV, 428 (from Michigan); by Jones, p. 4 (a few lines); and by Gray, *Songs and Ballads of the Maine Lumberjacks*, p. 3. It has been reported from Michigan by Dr. Alma Blount (Kittredge MSS., XI, 109). By way of Canada it has crossed the sea to Scotland: see "The Lumbering Boys" in Greig's *Folk-Song of the North-East*, CXXXII. The song originated in Maine and is founded on fact. Gerry's Rock, since blown up, was on the West Branch of the Penobscot River. See Gray's introduction, p. xi.

A

"The Jam at Gerry's Rock." Communicated by Mr. E. C. Smith, Weston, Lewis County, 1915; obtained from Miss Maude Rucks, Heaters, Braxton County, whose brother learned it in a lumber camp at Richwood, Nicholas County.

1 Come all of you bold shanty-boys and list while I relate,
  Concerning a young shanty-boy and his untimely fate;
  Concerning a young river man, so manly, true, and brave;
  'T was on a jam at Gerry's Rock, he met a watery grave.

2 It was on a Sunday morning, as you will quickly hear,
  Our logs were piled up mountains high, we could not keep them clear;
  Our foreman said, "Turn out, brave boys, with hearts devoid of fear,
  We'll break the jam at Gerry's Rock and for Eganstown we'll steer."

3 Now some of them were willing, while others they were not;
  For to work on jams on Sunday they did not think we ought;
  But six of our Canadian boys did volunteer to go
  And break the jam at Gerry's Rock, with the foreman, Young Monroe.

4 They had not rolled off many logs when they heard his clear voice say,
  "I'd have you boys be on your guard, for the jam will soon give way."
  These words were scarcely spoken when the mass did break and go,
  And it carried off those six brave youths, and their foreman, Jack Monroe.

5 When the rest of our brave shanty-boys the sad news came to
hear,
In search of their dead comrades to the river they did steer;
Some of the mangled bodies a-floating down did go,
While crushed and bleeding near the bank was that of Young
Monroe.

6 They took him from his watery grave, brushed back his raven
hair;
There was one girl among them whose sad cries rent the air;
There was one fair form among them, a maid from Saginaw
Town,
Whose moans and cries rose to the skies for her true-love who'd
gone down.

7 Fair Clara was a noble girl, the river-man's true friend;
She, with her widowed mother, lived at the river's bend;
The wages of her own true-love the boss to her did pay,
And the shanty-boys for her made up a generous purse that day.

8 They buried him with sorrow deep; 't was on the first of May:
"Come all of you bold shanty-boys and for your comrade pray."
Engraved upon a hemlock tree that by the grave did grow
Was the name and date of the sad, sad fate of the shanty-boy,
Monroe.

9 Fair Clara did not long survive, her heart broke with her grief;
And scarcely two months afterward death came to her relief;
And when this time had passed away and she was called to go,
Her last request was granted, to be laid by Young Monroe.

10 Come all of you bold shanty-boys, I would have you call and see
Those green mounds by the river side, where grows the hemock
tree;
The shanty-boys cleared off the wood, by the lovers there laid
low,
'T was the handsome Clara Vernon and her true-love, Jack
Monroe.

B

"The Jam at Gerry's Rock." Contributed by Mrs. H. A. Walkup, Hartford,
Mason County. A good text, agreeing very closely with A.

C

"The Jam on Jerry's Rock." Communicated by Mr. J. Campbell Floyd, Sutton, Braxton County, November 14, 1916; obtained from Mr. Thomas E. Foley, who says that it is a familiar song among the rivermen. Practically identical with A and B.

D

"Jack Monroe." Communicated by Mr. John Adkins, Branchland, Lincoln County, May 1, 1916. He writes: "I understand that this ballad originated in the Northern lumber camps some fifty years ago and was composed to be sung in contests of ballad singing, which was a popular pastime among the lumbermen of Northern New York. Each 'shanty' had its particular song, commemorating incidents of the logging camps or the virtues of the 'bosses' of their respective camps." He obtained the song from Mr. Albert Adkins. It is practically identical with A and B.

52

AN ARKANSAW TRAVELLER

THREE variants of this satirical song have been found in West Virginia, one with the title of "Bill Stafford." For other texts see Perrow, *Journal*, XXVI, 173 (Tennessee: "The State of Arkansaw"); Lomax, p. 226 (same title); N. I. White MS., II, 597 (Alabama: "Bill Stafford"). Cf. Belden, No. 110 (Missouri: "The Arkansaw Traveller"; "Bill Stafford"); Shearin and Combs, p. 15 ("The Arkansaw Traveller"; "Santford Barnes").

A

"An Arkansaw Traveller." Communicated by Miss Sallie Evans, Elkins, Randolph County. She received it from Eleanor Kline, who got it from Lawson Ketterman, who learned it from his father.

1 My name it is Bill Stafford, I came from Buffalo Town;
   I've travelled this wide world over, I've travelled this wide
      world round;
   I've had my ups and down in life, but better days I've saw;
   I never knew what misery was till I came to Arkansaw.

2 It was in eighteen hundred and two, in the early month of June;
   I landed in Hot Springs one sultry afternoon;
   Up steps a walking skeleton and gives to me his paw,
   Inviting me to his hotel, the best in Arkansaw.

3 I followed my conductor into his dwelling place,
   And poverty was pictured in his melancholy face;
   His bread it was corn dodgers, and his beef I could not chaw;
   And that's the kind of hash I got in the state of Arkansaw.

4 I rose quite early next morning, to catch an early train,
   He says, "You'd better work for me, I have some land to drain;
   I'll give you fifty cents a day, your washing, board, and all;
   You'll find that you're a different man when you leave Arkan-
      saw."

5 I worked six weeks for this gentleman, Jess Harold was his name;
   He stood nine feet in his stocking feet, as tall as any crane;
   His hair hung down in ringlets o'er his lean and lanken [1] jaws;
   He was a photograph of all the gents that were raised in Arkan-
      saw.

[1] Error for *lantern*.

6 He fed me on corn dodgers, as hard as any rocks;
My teeth became all loosened, and my knees began to knock;
I got so lean on sage and sassafras tea that I could hide behind
    a straw;
Indeed I was a different man when I left Arkansaw.

ℬ

No local title. Communicated by Mrs. Hilary G. Richardson, Clarksburg,
Harrison County, 1917; obtained from Mrs. Nancy McAtee.

1 My name it is Bill Staffato, I'm just from Buffalo Town;
Nine long years and over, I've travelled this wide world round,
And, with all my ups and downs in life, but few good days I've
    saw;
I never knew what misery was till I struck Arkansaw.

2 I landed in Van Buren one sweltry afternoon . . .
  . . . .
Up stepped this walking skeleton, with his long and lantern jaw;
He led me to his hotel, for the best in Arkansaw.

3 I follered after this big bluff unto his dwelling place,
While milintary [1] providence was deplected [2] on his face.
He fed me on corn dodgers, since beef I could not chaw;
I tell you, boys, I was a different man when I left Arkansaw.

4 I started out next morning to ketch an early train:
"You'd better stay and work for me, for I've got land to drain.
I'll give you fifty cents a day, your wash and boardin' free,
And you will be a different man when you leave Arkansaw."

5 I worked six months for this big bluff, Jess Carvus was his name;
He stood ten seven in his boots, and thin as any crane;
His hair hung down like rat-tails, and his long and lantern jaw,
He was the telephone (?) for all the gents that lives in Arkansaw.

6 He fed me on corn dodgers, such beef I could n't chaw,
Till all my teeth got loose and my knees began to rock.
I got so thin as [3] sassafras I could hide behind a straw;
I tell you boys I *was* a different man when I left Arkansaw.

7 I started out next morning, a quarter after five;
I staggered into the saloon, half dead and half alive;
I called for whiskey merrilie, I called for liquor raw;
I jumped the train for Chicago, and good-bye to Arkansaw!

[1] Probably for *melancholy*.   [2] For *depicted*.   [3] Error for *on*

C

"Bill Stafford." Communicated by Mr. Fred Smith, Glenville, Gilmer County, 1916; obtained from Miss Lenore Powell.

1 My name 't is Bill Stafford, I'm from a Western town;
For nine long years and over I've travelled this wide world
    round;
I've had my ups and down of life, and a few good days of[1] saw,
But I never knew what misery was till I struck Arkansaw.

2 I landed in Van Buren one sultry afternoon,
. . . .
Up stepped a walking skeleton, with long and lantern jaw,
Asked me to his hotel, for the best in Arkansaw.

3 I followed up that wide street unto his dwelling place;
Melancholy and poverty were pictured on his face.
I started out next morning, to catch the early train,
Says he, "You'd better work for me, I have some land to drain.

4 "I'll give you fifty cents a rod, your washing, board, and a';
You'll find yourself a different man when you leave Arkansaw."
He fed me on corn dodgers and beef I could hardly chaw,
And taxed me fifty cents a meal in the state of Arkansaw.

5 . . . .
. . . .
If ever I see that land again, I'll give to you my paw,
It'll be through a telescope, from here at Arkansaw.

[1] For *I've*.

53

THE DYING COWBOY

"The Dying Cowboy" ("The Cowboy's Lament"), as Barry pointed out, is "a communal re-creation" of the English broadside song known as "The Unfortunate Rake" or "The Unfortunate Lad" (*Journal*, XXIV, 341); cf. *Journal of the Folk-Song Society*, I, 254; III, 292. For the American song see Lomax, p. 74; *Journal*, XXII, 258 (Will; North Dakota); XXV, 153 (Perrow; Mississippi and West Virginia), 277 (Barry; Massachusetts); XXVI, 356 (Pound; Nebraska); Pound, No. 77 (Illinois by way of Wyoming); Wister, *Lin McLean*, 1898, p. 217. Cf. Belden, No. 68 (Missouri); Shearin and Combs, p. 15 (Kentucky); Jones, p. 4 (Michigan); Minish MS., I, 19 (North Carolina). The piece is to be found in a New York broadside published by Wehman, No. 952: "The Cowboy's Lament" (copyright 1887).

Another adaptation of "The Unfortunate Lad" is "The Young Girl Cut Down in her Prime": see *Journal of the Folk-Song Society*, IV, 325; V, 193.

Compare also the English broadside song usually known as "Wild and Wicked Youth" (Catnach; Paul; T. Birt; Such, No. 174; Cadman, Manchester, No. 188; Bebbington, Manchester, No. 189; George Walker, Jun., Durham, No. 86; C. Croshaw, York), which is still in oral circulation in England and America; Barrett, *English Folk-Songs*, No. 19 ("Flash Lad"); Baring-Gould and Sheppard, *A Garland of Country Song*, p. 39; Sharp, *One Hundred English Folksongs*, No. 83 ("The Robber"); Sharp, *English Folk Songs*, II, 79; *Journal of the Folk-Song Society*, I, 114; II, 291; American broadsides of the early nineteenth century ("The Irish Robber": Ford, *Massachusetts Broadsides*, Nos. 3187, 3188, 3282; see also *Paddy's Own Song Book*, New York, ca. 1860, p. 65); R. W. Gordon, *Adventure* (magazine) for April 20, 1924, p. 191; also "Sarah Wilson" (broadside, C. Paul, London). Cf. Belden's Missouri collection.

A

"The Wild Cowboy." Communicated by Mr. J. Harrison Miller, Wardensville, Hardy County, 1916.

1 As I passed by Tom Sherman's bar-room,
   Tom Sherman's bar-room, quite early one morn,
   I spied a young cowboy all dressed in his buckskins,
   All dressed in his buckskins, all fit for his grave.

Chorus

"Then beat the drum lowly and play the fife slowly,
   Beat up the death marches as they carry me along;
   Take me to the prairie and fire a volley o'er me,
   For I'm a young cowboy and dying alone."

2 "Once in my saddle I used to go dashing,
   Once in my saddle I used to ride gay;
   But I just took up drinking and then to card-playing,
   Got shot by a gambler, and dying to-day.

3 "Go gather around me a lot of wild cowboys,
      And tell them the story of a comrade's sad fate;
   Warn them quite gently to give up wild roving,
      To give up wild roving before it's too late.

4 "Some one write to my gray-headed mother,
      And then to my sister, my sister so dear;
   There is another far dearer than mother,
      Who would bitterly weep if she knew I were here.

5 "O bury beside me my knife and my shooter,
      My spurs on my heels, my rifle by my side;
   Over my coffin put a bottle of brandy,
      That the cowboys may drink as they carry me along.

6 "Some one go bring me a drink of cold water,"

   .   .   .   .

   As they turned the soul had departed,
      He had gone on a round-up and the cowboy was dead.

ℬ

"The Dying Cowboy." Communicated by Miss Ora B. Dowler, Loudens-
ville, Marshall County, who obtained it from Mrs. Lloyd Burton, McMechen.

1 It was down in the valley so early one morning,
      So early one morning, so early one morn,
   I spied a young cowboy, all dressed in white linen,
      All dressed in white linen, as fair as the day.

Chorus

   "So beat the drums slowly and play the fife lowly,
      And sound the dead marches, to carry me away;
   Take me to some churchyard, and roll the sod o'er me,
      For I am a cowboy, and I know I must die."

2 "Go write a long letter to my gray-headed mother;
      And one to my sister, my sister so dear;
   And one to another, who loves me much better:
      I know they will weep when they hear of my death.

3 "Go bring to my bedside a glass of cold water,
      A glass of cold water," the poor fellow said;
   But when it was brought in, the spirit had departed,
      The spirit had departed, the cowboy was dead.

C

"The Cowboy." Communicated by Mr. Greenland Thompson Federer, Morgantown, Monongalia County, January, 1917; taken from an old manuscript song book owned by Miss Lizzie Kelly, Independence. Apparently received from Kate Bucy.

1 My friends and relatives in Boston I left them,
　　My parents knew not where this poor boy had gone;
　I first came to Texas to hire to a rich man,
　　For hell is my doom, for I know I have done wrong.

Chorus

　Go beat the drum lowly and play the fife sadly,
　　Go play the death marches that carry me on;
　Go lie me in the graveyard and roll the sod o'er me,
　　For I am the young cowboy and I know I've done wrong.

2 "'T was once in my saddle I used to be dashing,
　　'T was once in my saddle I used to be gay;
　'T was first to hard drinking and then to card-playing,
　　Now I'm shot in the breast, and I know I must die.

3 "Don't write to my mother, O please don't inform her
　　Of the wicked condition that death caught me in;
　For I know she would be grieved o'er the loss of her darling —
　　O could I return to my childhood again!

4 "Go gather around me a crowd of young cowboys;
　　Go tell my brothers and sisters so dear;
　And there is another, more sweet than all others,
　　And in all the wild roamings I wish she was here.

5 "Don't tell my mother, for I know it would grieve her,
　　For I know that she loves me, wherever I roam;
　My heart it is with her, I fain would not forget her;
　　I am the poor cowboy and a long way from home."

𝒟

"The Dying Cowboy." Communicated by Miss Lalah Lovett, Bulltown, Braxton County, 1916; obtained from Mrs. Cora Starkey, Clarksburg; learned from her parents, who learned it from their parents in Virginia.

1 As I rode up to McFinegan's bar-room,
    McFinegan's bar-room so early one morn,
  ' T was there I spied a handsome cowboy,
    All dressed in fine linen, prepared for the tomb.

Chorus

"Go beat the drum softly and play the fife slowly,
    And sing the death march as you bear me away;
And in the grave lower me and roll the sod o'er me,
    For I'm a young cowboy and know I've done wrong."

2 "O once in my saddle I used to go dashing,
    Once in my saddle I used to ride gay;
  I first took to drinking and then to card-playing;
    Got shot last night and must die to-day.

3 "Go write to my mother, when I am buried,
    And tell her the Saviour has come;
  But never tell my youngest sister
    I received a death wound from John Thurman's grandson.

4 "Perhaps there's another more dear than a sister,
    Who will bitterly weep when she hears I am gone;
  There's another more worthy may win her affections,
    Who once loved a cowboy, although I've done wrong."

ℰ

"The Cowboy." Communicated by Professor C. E. Haworth, Huntington, Cabell County, 1917; obtained from Mrs. J. A. Rollyson.

1 "I am a cow-herder . . .
    It was only last night I drove up the trail;
  And if I had stayed away from Dodge City,
    I need not be telling this sad, mournful tale.

Chorus

"Go beat your drum slowly and play the fife lowly,
    Go beat the dead march as you carry me down;
As you carry me down and roll the sod o'er me,
    I'm only a herder and I know I've done wrong.

2 "O, once in the saddle I used to go dashing,
    O, once in the saddle I used to be gay;
I first took to drinking and then to card-playing,
    Last night I was shot, and to-day I must die.

3 "Go write to my mother when I am buried,
    And tell her that the dear Saviour has come;
But never tell my young sister
    I received my death wounds in John Sherman's dance-hall.

4 "But there's another more dear than a sister,
    Who'll weep most bitterly when she hears I am gone;
Perhaps another will win her affection,
    For I was only a cowboy, and I know I've done wrong."

54

THE LONE PRAIRIE

THE two variants of this song found in West Virginia go under the title of "The Dying Cowboy."

Barry (*Journal*, XXII, 372, note 2) pointed out that the song is an adaptation of "The Burial at Sea" ("The Ocean Burial"); see p. 250. Pound, who prints a text from Montana (No. 78; cf. Pound, p. 26), remarks that the words of "The Ocean Burial" are by W. H. Saunders, the music by G. N. Allen (p. 253). For texts of "The Lone Prairie" see Lomax, p. 3; *Journal*, XIV, 186 (Ellis; Texas); XXV, 278 (Barry, Belden; Kansas); XXVI, 357 (Pound; Nebraska); Pound, No. 78 (Montana); Thorpe, *Songs of the Cowboys*, p. 62. Cf. Belden, No. 67 (Missouri); Shearin and Combs, p. 15 (Kentucky).

A

"The Dying Cowboy." Contributed by Mr. Decker Toney, Queens Ridge, Wayne County, January 26, 1916; learned from his mother who learned it from Lewis Workman.

1   "O bury me not in the lone prairie!"
These words came low and mournfully
From the youthful lips, where the pallet lay,
On his dying bed at the close of day.

2   He lay and pointed unto his brow;
Death's shadows are closely gathering now;
He thought of his home, and friends so nigh;
The cowboys gathered in, to see him die.

3   "Pray bury me not in the lone prairie,
Where the wild coyote can howl over me,
Where the buffalo roves and the winds sport free;
Pray bury me not in the lone prairie!

4   "It makes me think of my mother now;
She has curled these locks and kissed this brow;
For among these locks a rattlesnake hissed;
These lips she has pressed with a cold grave-kiss.

5   "I want to be laid by my mother's prayer;
Where sister's tears can mingle there;
Where friends can come and weep over me;
O bury me not in the lone prairie!

6   "I want to be laid by my father's side,
     In the old churchyard, on the green hillside,
     Where friends can come and sing over me;
     Pray bury me not in the lone prairie!

7   "It's mother's tears whose will be shed
     For the lonely grave on the prairie bed;
     My dying heart is filled with grief;
     My mother's prayer would give relief."

8   And as he spoke, his voice failed him there;
     We heeded not to his lonely dying prayer;
     In a narrow grave just six by three
     We buried her boy in the lone prairie.

𝓑

"The Dying Cowboy." Communicated by Mr. A. C. Stone, Charleston, Kanawha County, December, 1916; obtained from his grandfather, Mr. A. N. Gatch, who learned it many years before in Ohio.

1   "O bury me not on the lone prairie!"
     These words came low and mournfully,
     From the pallid lips of a youth, who lay
     On his dying bed at the close of day.

2   He had wasted and pined till on his brow
     Death's cold shade was gathering now,
     As he thought of his home and his friends so nigh,
     As the cowboys gathered in to see him die.

3   He had fancied and listened to the well-known words,
     As the free wild wind bore the song of the birds,
     As he thought of his home in the cottonwood bower,
     The same he had loved in his boyhood hours.

4   "I had hoped to be laid thus when I died,
     In the old churchyard 'neath the green hillside,
     Where friends might meet and weep over me;
     O bury me not on the lone prairie!

5   "I had hoped to be laid where a mother's prayer
     And a sister's tears might mingle there;
     By the side of my father, O, let my grave be!
     O bury me not on the lone prairie!

6   "And there is another whose tears will be shed
    O'er the lonely grave on the prairie bed;
    It breaks my heart to think of her now;
    She has curled these locks and kissed this brow.

7   "Through these locks the rattlesnake will hiss,
    These lips she has pressed [with] the cold grave-kiss;
    For the sake of loved ones waiting for me
    O bury me not on the lone prairie!

8   "O bury me not on the lone prairie,
    Where the wild-eyed coyote will howl over me,
    Where the buffalo roams and the wind roars free,
    O bury me not on the lone prairie!

9   "O bury me not" and his voice failed there,
    And we heeded not to his dying prayer,
    But in a narrow grave just six by three
    We buried our boy on the lone prairie,

10 Where the coyote howls and the butterfly did rest,
    Where the wild flowers bloomed on the prairie crest,
    Where the buffalo roams and the wind blows free,
    "O bury me not on the lone prairie!"

55

THE OCEAN BURIAL

"Ocean Burial," music by George N. Allen, was copyrighted in 1850 (Harvard College, sheet music). It may be found in *The Shilling Song Book* (Boston, cop. 1860), p. 126; *Beadle's Dime Song Book No. 5* (cop. 1860), p. 61; *The Pleasant Fellows' Songster* (cop. 1869), p. 27; *The "Oh, How is That for High?" Songster* (cop. 1870), p. 28; Andrews broadside (New York), List 4, No. 38; *Singer's Journal*, I, 55; *Journal*, xxv, 278 (Barry; Pennsylvania). Cf. Barry, No. 61; Shearin and Combs, p. 16; Pound, p. 42. Miss Pound ascribes the words of the song to W. H. Saunders (*Poetic Origins*, p. 207, note 11).

"The Ocean Burial." Communicated by Mr. J. R. Waters, Morgantown, Monongalia County, 1915; obtained from Mrs. F. W. Brown, Belington, Barbour County, who learned it more than fifty years before in Delaware, Ohio.

1　"O bury me not in the deep, deep sea!"
　　Those words came slow and mournfully,
　　From the pallid lips of a youth who lay,
　　On his cabin couch at the close of day.

2　He had wasted and pined till o'er his brow
　　Death's shade had slowly passed, and now,
　　As the land and his fond loved home drew nigh,
　　They gathered around to see him die.

3　"O bury me not in the deep, deep sea,
　　Where the ocean billows will roll o'er me;
　　Where no light can break through those dark cold waves,
　　And no sunbeams rest upon my grave.

4　"Yet it matters not, I oft have been told,
　　Where the body lies when the heart is cold;
　　But grant, O grant, this boon to me,
　　That you 'll bury me not in the deep, deep sea!

5　"Let my death-chambers be where a mother's prayer
　　And a sister's tear may be blended there.
　　O it will be sweet, ere the heart throb is o'er,
　　To know that its fountains will gush once more,

6　"And that those it so fondly hath yearned for will come,
　　And plant the first wild flowers of spring on my tomb.
　　Let me lie where those loved ones will weep over me;
　　O bury me not in the deep, deep sea!

7   "And there is another whose tears will be shed
For him who lies in an ocean bed;
In hours that it pains me to think of now,
She has twined these locks and pressed this brow.

8   "In the locks she has twined, shall the sea snake hiss,
And the brow she has pressed shall the cold wave kiss.
For the sake of that loved one that is waiting for me,
O bury me not in the deep, deep sea!

9   "She has been in my dreams — " His voice failed there;
They gave no heed to his dying prayer;
They lowered him low o'er the vessel's side,
And o'er him closed the dark, cold tide.

10   There to dip the light wing, the sea birds rest,
And the blue waves dance o'er the ocean's crest;
Where the billows bound and the waves roll free,
They buried him there in the deep, deep sea.

56

THE DYING HOBO

For other texts of this parody of "Bingen on the Rhine" see Gray, *Songs and Ballads of the Maine Lumberjacks*, p. 102; Webb, *Publications of the Texas Folk-Lore Society*, II, 40.

Communicated by Mr. E. C. Smith, Weston, Lewis County, December 18, 1915; obtained from Mr. George Conley, living near Charleston.

1 Behind a Western water tank a dying hobo lay,
   Inside an empty box-car, one cold November day;
   His comrade sat beside him with low and drooping head,
   Listening to the dying words this poor dying hobo said.

2 "I am going to a better land, where everything is bright,
   Where hand-outs grow on bushes, and you can sleep out every
       night.
   Tell my sweetheart back in Denver no more her face I'll view,
   For I have caught the fast train and now I'm going through.

3 "Tell her not to weep for me, no tears in her eyes must lurk,
   For I have gone to a land where hoboes don't have to work,
   Don't have to work at all, not even have to change your socks,
   Where little streams of alcohol come tingling down the rocks.

4 "Hark! I hear the whistling; I must catch her on the fly;
   Just one drink of 9–5 booze — it's not so hard to die."
   His voice grew weak, his head fell back, he's sung his last refrain;
   His partner swiped his coat and hat and caught the east-bound
       train.

57

A COMICAL DITTY

COMMUNICATED by Miss Lalah Lovett, Bulltown, Braxton County, 1917; obtained from John N. Wine, who learned it from B. P. Williams.

An elaborated version of much interest is "The Arizona Boys and Girls" (Lomax, p. 211).

1   Come all you good people, I pray you draw near;
    Tolay, fo laddy, fo lay
  A comical ditty you shortly shall hear.
    Tolay, fo laddy, fo lay

2   The boys of the country, they try to advance,
  By courting the ladies and learning to dance.

3   Their old rusty stirrups they'll brush and they'll rub;
  Their old dirty boots they'll black and they'll scrub.

4   A gentleman's neat, and their own conceit,
  And value those ladies at a very low rate.

5   I'm done for the lads now, I'll sing for the ladies;
  In their own way they're equally as bad.

6   They'll dress themselves up; they'll look in the glass,
  Saying, "Tee, he, he, he!   What a fine bonny lass!"

7   Just let their old parents be ever so poor,
  They must have a little hat with a feather before.

8   They will dress themselves up, put on a false hair,
  And then in the glass like an owl they will stare.

9   The girls of this country will give the boys a slap;
  They are always a-laughing and don't know what at.

10   They're always a-laughing, in vain to be wise!
  They couldn't get married to save their lives.

11   I think it is time my story should end,
  For fear there's some one I might offend.

12   But if there's any one here that would take offence,
  They can go to the devil and seek recompense.

58

THE TUCKY HO CREW

THIS piece agrees in part with "Mississippi Girls" (Lomax, p. 108), other versions of which are "Cheyenne Boys" (Pound, p. 25 and No. 81), "The Texas Boys" (Belden, No. 111), and "Arizona Boys and Girls" (Thorpe, *Songs of the Cowboys*, p. 1). With the second stanza cf. the "Ground Hog Song" (No. 176). Lomax's text and Baldwin's have passages in common with Campbell and Sharp, No. 75.

Communicated by Mr. R. C. Newman, Spencer, Roane County, January 17, 1916; obtained from Miss Lucky Goff, Grace, Roane County, who got it from an old man in the community.

1   I'll sing you a song, the best song yet;
      It's all about the half-famine set,
      The ragged, the ugly, that dwell down below,
      Called by the Irish the poor Tucky Ho.

2   When they go a-hunting, they call up the dog,
      Run an old hare in an old hollow log;
      "Bow wow! I've got him," and it's "Bow wow! I declare
      I never seen a fatter nor a finer old hare."

3   When we get home, jerk off the skin;
      Pot is open ready to put him in;
      Scarce give him time to stew or to thaw:
      All a force out, we'll eat him done or raw.

4   When they go to eat him, the table looks so bare,
      Nothing on it but a stewed double hare,
      Hare and a ho and a raw cake of dough:
      Hop around a-grinning like a poor Tucky Ho.

5   When they go to dress, I'll tell you how they dress:
      Old hunting shirts, and they are the best;
      The old socks' legs, they wore the winter round,
      The old leather hats with the high brimmed crown.

6   They'll take you out to the black jack hills,
      Leave you there contrary to your will,
      Leave you there to perish and starve:
      That's the only way I ever saw 'em do,
      Since I've belonged to the Tucky Ho Crew.

59

IMMORTAL WASHINGTON

TEXT A was communicated, along with Nos. 60 and 107, by Mr. R. H. Jarvis, Salem, Harrison County, February 2, 1916. The three songs were taken from an old manuscript owned by his father, W. M. Jarvis. The Samuel Brown, whose name appears at the end of A, was the great-grandfather of R. H. Jarvis, and was born in Lewis County. His father, Samuel Brown, was born in Virginia, and his father came from England. The Jarvises have for three generations lived in Harrison County. Mr. W. M. Jarvis writes of the manuscript, "Maybe it is a hundred years old. Nothing is known of Sarah Wells, whose name appears at the end of A, and who, apparently, wrote it down for Samuel Brown." The handwriting of No. 107 is the same as that of No. 59. No. 60 is in a different handwriting, and nothing is known of the persons whose names appear at the end of it. Titles, modernized spelling, verse arrangement, and punctuation have been supplied by the Editor.

A

Text A is a strangely corrupted version of "Immortal Washington," a lament written soon after Washington's death. To make the song intelligible, as well as to illustrate the vagaries of tradition, I append a correct text (B). See also *The American Songster*, ed. by Kenedy (Baltimore, 1836), p. 173; *The American Minstrel* (Cincinnati, 1837; Philadelphia, 1844), p. 87; *The Rough and Ready Songster* (New York, Nafis & Cornish), p. 115.

1 Columbia's greatest glory
 Is our love chief for Freedom's friend;
  His name renowns in story,
 Shall last till time itself shall end.
   You muses tune
   Your harps, and sing
 Sweet joys that in smooths numbers run,
  In praise of our loved hero,
 The great, the godlike Washington.

2 His name through future ages,
 Columbia's free-born son, shall raise
  The theme all hearts enjoys,
 All tongues shall join to sing his praise,
   With joy sound forth
   His wondrous works,
 And tell of the glorious acts he has done,
  Of all mankind the greatest
 Was our beloved Washington.

3 And, O Thou, great Creator,
The guide, the guardian of our song,
 Since thou, in course of nature,
Has called his from his earthly stage,
  Ye powers above
  Enrolled in loved,
Have was before the world begun
  Received into His bosom,
The great, the matchless Washington.

B

"Immortal Washington." From McCarty's *Songs, Odes, and Other Poems,
on National Subjects* (Philadelphia, 1842), I, 249.

1 Columbia's greatest glory
Was her loved chief, fair Freedom's friend;
 Whose fame, renown'd in story,
Shall last till time itself shall end.
  Ye muses, bring
  Your harps, and sing
Sweet lays that in smooth numbers run,
  In praise of our loved hero,
The great, the godlike Washington.

2 His fame, through future ages,
Columbia's free-born sons shall raise;
 The theme each heart engages,
All tongues shall join to sing his praise.
  With joy sound forth
  His virtuous worth,
And tell the glorious acts he's done,
  Of all mankind, the greatest
Was our beloved Washington.

3 And, O! thou great Creator,
Who form'd his youth, and watch'd his age,
 Since thou, in course of nature,
Hast call'd him from his earthly stage,
  Great Power above,
  Enthroned in love,
Who was, before this world began,
  Receive into thy bosom
Our virtuous hero — Washington.

60

THE CONSTITUTION AND THE GUERRIERE

(HULL'S VICTORY)

THE battle between the *Constitution* (Captain Hull) and the *Guerriere* (Captain Dacres) was fought on August 19, 1812, and this song was written soon after, to the tune of "A Landlady of France." Harvard College has an undated broadside copy (printed at Boston) which is almost contemporary with the event (Ford, *Massachusetts Broadsides*, No. 3027; cf. No. 3326), and another ("Printed and Sold by John Low, No. 17 Chatham-street," New York) is in the library of the New York Historical Society. The song has been often reprinted: see, for example, *The American Star*, 2d ed. (Richmond, 1817), p. 122; *Grigg's Southern and Western Songster* (Philadelphia, 1829), p. 44; *The Minstrel Boy* (Philadelphia, 1830), p. 135; *The Singer's Own Book* (Woodstock, Vermont, 1837), p. 24; Eggleston, *American War Ballads*, I, 115; Firth, *Naval Songs and Ballads*, pp. 309, 361; *Bulletin of the Essex Institute*, XX, 88–89; Stevenson, *Poems of American History*, p. 288. The song was imitated at the time of the Civil War in "Yankee Boys so Handy, O!" (broadside, Partridge, Boston, No. 520).

The text given below is from the manuscript described on p. 255, in which it has no title. At the end are two names: "S Pascal" (at the left) and "I Young" (at the right); nothing is known of these persons. The spelling has been regulated by the Editor and the verses adjusted. The interest of this text consists in its illustration of the vagaries of oral tradition. The readings in the footnotes (correcting some of the most glaring errors) are from the text in *The American Star*.

1 It often has been told that the British seamen bold
    Could thrash the tars of France quite neat and handy-O;
    But they never met their match till the Yankees they did tach,[1]
    For the Yankee tars at fighting are the dandy-O.

2 The Guerriere so bold on the ocean foaming rolled,
    Commanded by proud Decer, the grandee-O;
    With his choice of British crew, as roamer ever drew,[2]
    He could slash the Frenchmen two to one quite handy-O.

3 The ship hove in sight;[3] says proud Decer to his crew,
    "Prepare your ship for action, lads; be handy-O!"
    To the weathergauge gutter,[4] to make his men fight better,
    Then he gave them gunpowder and brandy-O.

---

[1] MS. illegible. *Star* has: *did them catch.*   [3] *When this frigate hove in view*

[2] *As a rammer ever drew.*   [4] *On the weathergauge, boys, get her.*

4 Our boatswain chiefly cries,[1] "Make this Yankee ship your prize!
You can do it in thirty minutes quite handy-O.
In twenty-five, I'm sure.   If you'll do it in a score,
I'll give you all a double share of brandy-O."

5 The British balls flew hot, yet the Yankees answered not,
Till they came within the distance quite handy-O.
Says brave Hull unto his crew, "Let us see what you can do!
If we take this boat of Britain, it will be the dandy-O."

6 The first broadside we poured brought the mizzen to the board,
Which made this lofty vessel look so handy-O.[2]
Then Decer deeply sighed and to his Lieutenant cried,
"God! I did not think the Yankees were so handy-O!"

7 The second told so well that their main and foremast fell,
Which brought this British ship in sight so handy-O.[3]
"God," [said] he, "we're done!"[4] and he fired his lee gun,
And your drummers struck up Yankee Doodle Dandy-O.

8 When proud Decer came on board to deliver up his sword,
It grieved him to the heart, it was so handy-O.
"You may keep it," says brave Hull; "pray what makes you
look so dull?
Cheer up, and take some more of the brandy-O."

9 Come fill your glasses full, and drink to valiant Hull;
So merrily we'll toss about the brandy-O.
Johnny Bull may boast his full, let the world say what it will,
But the Yankee tars at fighting are the dandy-O.

[1] *Now this boasting Briton cries.*   [3] *Which dous'd the royal ensign so handy-O.*
[2] *Look abandon'd-O.*   [4] *By George, says he, we're done.*

61

THE BATTLE OF BRIDGEWATER

THE BATTLE OF BRIDGEWATER (or Lundy's Lane) was fought on July 25, 1814. Major General Jacob Brown commanded the Americans; Brigadier General Winfield Scott commanded a brigade. "Royalist" in stanza 2 is an error for "Riall," the name of the British commander.

"Bridgewater." Communicated by Miss Laura Brake, Webster Springs, Webster County, February 27, 1916; obtained from her mother, who learned it from her father, the Rev. E. L. Snodgrass.

1 On the twenty-fifth of July, as you may hear them say,
　We had a short engagement on the plains of Chippewa;
　Bridgewater was the fighting ground, as you will understand,
　And brave General Brown, of high renown, our army did command.

2 At four o'clock brave General Scott the enemy espied,
　And with firm and manly countenance along our lines did ride;
　He viewed them from an eminence and, to his men did say,
　"Lo, yonder comes bold Royalist! remember Chippewa!"

3 We formed our lines for battle, the conflict soon began;
　The cannons loud did rattle, while many a valiant man
　Lay bleeding in his purple gore: heart-rending were their cries,
　While the clouds of sulphur, tinged with blood, ascended to the skies.

4 To paint the horror of that night is far beyond my power;
　Our lines appeared in a blaze of light for more than three long hours;
　Each hero stood well shod in blood, and gave such dreadful fire
　That the Redcoats dressed in crimson red by hundreds did expire.

5 Eight thousand chosen British troops we had for to oppose;
　Our number was inferior, as you may well suppose;
　They reinforced from every quarter and thought to make us yield,
　But the Columbians made such slaughter we forced them from the field.

6 Brave General Brown was wounded, both in his side and thigh;
　It grieved his men both one and all when he made this reply:
　"Fight on, ye brave Columbians! we soon shall gain the field;
　I'll die with my brave countrymen before that I will yield."

7 And Scott, that noble general, was most severely bruised;
It grieved his men both one and all when they received the news;
Two horses were shot under him, but still he gave command,
Saying, "Play them home, my countrymen! much longer they
   can't stand."

8 Six hundred British rank and file soon fell into our lot,
And thirty British officers were taken on the spot;
Then we removed our wounded and to our camp returned,
While the trumpets loudly sounded, each man his bosom burned.

62

JAMES BIRD

JAMES BIRD, after fighting valiantly in the Battle of Lake Erie (1814), deserted. He was tried by court-martial and shot. There is a long ballad on his fate, of which the fragment here printed was communicated by Mr. Sam Turman, Buchanan, Boyd County, Kentucky, July, 1918. See *Journal*, XXXV, 379.

1   Where is Bird? The battle rages,
        Is he in the strife or no?
    Now the cannons roar tremendous:
        Dare he meet his hostile foe?

2   Ay, behold! see him and Perry!
        In the selfsame ship they fight;
    Though his messmates fall around him,
        Nothing can his soul affright.

3   Ay, behold! a ball has struck him,
        See the crimson current flow:
    "Leave the deck," exclaimed brave Perry;
        "No," cries Bird, "I will not go.

4   "Here on board I tuck my station,
        Ne'er will Bird his colors fly;
    I'll stand by you, gallant captain,
        Till we conquer, lest we die."

5   Still he fought, though faint and bleeding,
        Till our Stars and Stripes arose,
    Victory having gained our efforts,
        All triumphant o'er our foes.

    [Bird deserts; he is court-martialed and shot.]

6   See him kneel upon his coffin;
        Sure his death can do no good:
    Spare him! Hark! O God, they've shot him!
        See, his bosom streams with blood.

7   Farewell, Bird; farewell, forever;
        Friends and home you'll see no more;
    Now his mangled corpse lies buried
        On Lake Erie's distant shore.

63

WAR SONG

THIS is an imperfect text of "The Texas Ranger(s)": see Lomax, p. 44; Shoe-maker, p. 78; Pound, p. 28 and No. 73 (Missouri); Barry, No. 66; Belden, No. 60, and *Journal*, XXV, 14 (Missouri); Wehman broadside, No. 748; *Boston Transcript*, April 18, 1911. In *Allan's Lone Star Ballads* (Galveston, 1874), p. 38, the piece appears as a Confederate song, "the Yankees" taking the place of "the Indians" whom, in the regular version, the Rangers have to fight.

Contributed by Mr. A. C. Payne, Barclay, McDowell County, August, 1918.

1 About the age of sixteen I joined this jolly band,
Marched from Old Virginia to the Rio Grande;
Our Captain he informed us perhaps he thought 't was right,
Before we reached the station, "I guess we'll have to fight."

2 I saw the glittering bayonets, the bullets round me hailed,
I feel that at the moment my courage almost failed:
I saw the smoke arisin', appeared to reach the sky;
I feel that at this moment it is my time to die.

3 I thought of my old mother, with tears to me did say:
"You're going off with strangers; at home you'd better stay."
I thought that she was childish, or else she did not know,
My mind was placed on rovin', and I was bound to go.

4 We fought on full nine hours, until the strife was over;
The like of dead and wounded I never saw before.

. . . .
. . . .

5 Perhaps you have a mother, likewise a sister, too;
Perhaps you have a sweetheart, to weep and mourn for you.
If this be your condition, . . .
I advise you by experiment, you'd better stay at home.

64

THE DYING RANGER

COMMUNICATED by Mrs. Hilary G. Richardson, Clarksburg, Harrison County, 1917. Text confused and in places unintelligible. An excellent text is given by Lomax, *Cowboy Songs*, p. 214.

1 The sun was slowly sinking, and filled with brightest ray;
In the branches of a forest a dying ranger lay;
Down by the old plantation, and beneath the southern sky,
Far away in old Texas, this wee lad lay down to die.

2 A group had gathered round him, with the conerds [1] in the land,
And the tears ran down each nandels [2] cheeks, as he bid them all good-night.
One dear and loved commander was kneeling by his side,
Trying to stop the life-blood, but at last in vain it died.

3 It cheered his heart with pity, when he saw it was in vain,
And o'er this dear commander's face the tears rolled down like rain.
"Far away in good old Texas, that good old slave state,
There is one who for my coming with a merry heart will wait.

4 "I am dying, comrades, dying! she will never see my face no more,
But with patience she'll be waiting by the lonely cottage door.
My mother she lies sleeping beneath the churchyard sod;
It's many and many a year that's past since her spirit went to God.

5 "My father he lies sleeping beneath the deep blue sea;
I have no other kinfolks; there is only Nell and me.
Come, comrades, gather round me, and listen to my prayer:
Who will be to Nell a brother and shelter her with care?"

6 Up spoke a forest ranger, with a voice that seemed to fail:
"We will be to Nell a brother and shelter her with brother's care."
Far away in old Texas this lad lay down to rest,
With a saddle for a pillow and a gun across his breast.

[1] Error for *comrades*.   [2] Error for *manly*.

65

THE BATTLE OF MILL SPRINGS

COMMUNICATED by Miss Violet Noland, Davis, Tucker County, March 24, 1916; obtained from Mr. John Reese, who learned it when a boy and wrote it down in 1880.

Perrow, *Journal*, XXVIII, 165, prints a version from North Carolina under the title "Young Edwards."

The battle was fought at Mill Springs, Kentucky, on January 19, 1862.

1 There lies a wounded soldier on the batt efield,
His comrades gathered round him and by his side did kneel,
And then this wounded soldier did raise his head and said:
"Who will care for mother when her wounded boy is dead?

2 "I was my parents' only son to comfort their old age;
My heart is like a captive bird a-fluttering in its cage;
I was my father's only son, a mother's only joy,
And they will weep in tears for me, their dying soldier boy.

3 "O tell my dear old father that in death I prayed for him,
That one day I might meet him in a world that is free from sin;
And tell my dear old mother not to mourn and cry,
For her son was a soldier and a soldier he did die.

4 "And tell my little sister not to weep for me;
I'll sit no more by the fireside and nurse her on my knee,
And sing to her them good old songs she used to have me sing,
For her brother now lies wounded at the Battle of Mill Springs.

5 "O when I was a little boy I used to hear them tell
About the gallant soldiers, how lonely they did feel;
Then I came to be a servant, it was my country's call,
Fighting for the Union, for the Union I did fall.

6 "O listen, comrades, listen! 't is a girl I speak of now,
If she was only here this night to cheer my aching brow!
But little does she know of the battle as she sings,
That her true love now lies wounded at the Battle of Mill Springs.

7 "Alas! and now I'm wounded, no more of her I'll see,
But I hope one day to meet her in a world that is free from sin;
Tell her that in death I murmured her sweet name;
That she was just as dear to me as when from her I came.

8 "O listen, comrades, listen! I have something more to tell."
  They stopped to hear him speak again and he only said "Fare-
      well."
  He kissed the Stars and Stripes and he laid them by his side,
  Gave three cheers for the Union and bowed his head and died.

9 And then this Battle of Mill Springs it was over,
  And thousands of wounded soldiers lie in a crimson grave,
  And many a wounded soldier did raise his head and tried,
  To gaze upon young Edward, who prayed before he died.

66

THE VICTORY WON AT RICHMOND

COMMUNICATED by Mrs. Hilary G. Richardson, Clarksburg, Harrison County, 1917; obtained from Mrs. Nancy McAtee. Printed, *Journal*, XXXI, 276.

1   The Southers boys may longer lie,
    On the first and fourth of sweet July,
    Our General Beauregard resound,
        For his Southern boys at Richmond.

2   That night we laid on *the* cold ground,
    No tents nor shelter could be found,
    With rain and hail was nearly drowned,
        To cheer our hearts at Richmond.

3   Next morn the burning sun did rise
    Beneath the cloudy eastern skies;
    Our general viewed the forts and cried,
        "We'll have hot work at Richmond."

4   As soon as the height we strove to gain,
    Our balls did fly as thick as rain;
    I'm sure the plains they did run red
        With the blood that was shed at Richmond.

5   As soon as the heights we did command,
    We fought the Yankees hand to hand,
    And many a hero there was slain
        On the plains at Richmond,

6   And many a pretty fair maid will mourn
    For her lover who will never return,
    And parents mourn beyond control
        For their sons they lost at Richmond.

7   Thirty thousand Yankees, I heard them say,
    Was slain all on that fatal day,
    And seven thousand Southerners lay
        In the bloody gore at Richmond.

8 Their guns and knapsacks they threw down
And ran like hares before the hound;
I'm sure the plains they did run red
    With the blood that was shed at Richmond.

9 Cease, you Southerner, from your hand,
Which from Yankees we cannot stand;
Go spread the news throughout the land
    Of the victory that was won at Richmond.

67

THE YANKEE RETREAT

COMMUNICATED by Mrs. Hilary G. Richardson, Clarksburg, Harrison County, 1917; obtained from Mrs. Nancy McAtee (printed in *Journal*, XXXI, 277).

1 The very next morning we marched very slow,
We wakened those Yankees, their bugles did blow,
Fighting through briers, fighting through thorn,
Such fighting I never saw since I was born.

2 Up rode General Averil, his moustache on his face:
"Pitch in, my Virginians, we'll soon win the race."
But Jackson overheard him, he thought it was best,
To take keer of hisself, and care naught for the rest.

68

BULL RUN

COMMUNICATED by Mrs. Hilary G. Richardson, Clarksburg, Harrison County, 1917.

1 Away down in Belden Green,
Where the like was never seen,
    The whole earth shook in a quiver;
Every devil had done his best
To outrun the rest,
    To get back to Washington to shelter.

2 O there they mowed them down
Like grass upon the ground,
    And when we got back to Washington
Old Abe Linken jumped up
And pulled his hair and said:
    "O boys, you have lost all your cannons and I have to
        pay

"The debt in the land and I have no money. . . ."

69

WAR SONG

CONTRIBUTED by Mr. A. C. Payne, Barclay, McDowell County, August, 1918.
Mr. Payne said that he rode on a horse in a parade on Election Day in Breathitt County, Kentucky, played his fiddle and sang this song. Henry Combs was the Captain of the regiment.

Down in Bowling Green, such a sight was never seen,
    The earth all stood in a quiver;
We run 'em twelve miles, and the devils laid in piles,
    Besides what we drowned in the river.

Chorus

Fol de rol de day, fold de rol de day,
    The Black Horse cavalry a-coming;
You need n't mind the weather, we 'll git damned together,
    And spree around the Happy Land of Canaan.

70

JEFF DAVIS

COMMUNICATED by Mr. Fred Smith, Glenville, Gilmer County, 1916; obtained from Miss Evelyn Matthews, who writes: "Grandfather, who was a Union captain, used to sing it to me."

This is a single stanza of "That Southern Wagon," a Northern parody of a favorite Confederate song, "The Southern Wagon." For the latter, in various forms, see Frank Moore, *The Rebellion Record*, III, 67, and IV, 85 (*Poetry and Incidents*); the same, *Anecdotes, Poetry and Incidents of the War* (New York, 1866), p. 397; *Allan's Lone Star Ballads* (Galveston, 1874), p. 13; cf. "The Southern Wagon in Kentucky," *War Lyrics and Songs of the South* (London, 1866), p. 190. For the parody see De Marsan broadside, List 16, No. 87; Belden, No. 122.

1 Jeff Davis built a wagon and on it put his name,
  And Beauregard was driver of Secession's ugly fame.[1]
  Their horse would get hungry, as most of horses do;
  They had to keep the collar tight to keep from pulling through.

[1] Error for *frame*.

7 1

OLD GLORY

COMMUNICATED by Mr. Fred Smith, Glenville, Gilmer County, 1916; obtained from Miss Evelyn Matthews, who writes: "This was given to me by an aunt, who received it from her aunt, Mrs. George Heckert of Troy, who lived during the war."

1 Say, have you heard the joyful news of Burnside's expedition,
    Giving treacherous Jeff the blues?   There's hope of his contrition.
    That other day at Roanoke, and I'll pay for song and story,
    The boys, to play a Union joke, ran up the flag of Glory.

2 The rattlesnake came out and fought, but only to surrender;
    The eagle in his talons caught the reptile on a bender;
    And by a little suasion made of powder and of ball
    That ugly thing of Caroline again was forced to crawl.

3 Three cheers then for the gallant men!   We're pushing on to
    save
    The glories of our children from an ignominious grave.
    All hail the flag whose starry folds we're fighting to maintain!
    And when we hang the traitor, he'll never trait again.

72

BROTHER GREEN

In addition to the variants given below, a fragment was received from Mrs Hilary G. Richardson, Clarksburg, Harrison County, 1917. She obtained it from Mrs. Nancy McAtee.

Wyman and Brockway, p. 18, give words and music of an excellent version from Kentucky ("Brother Green," or "The Dying Soldier"). Belden has found the song in Missouri.

A

Contributed by Mr. John B. Adkins, Branchland, Lincoln County, May 1, 1916.

1 O come to me, my brother Green, for I am shot and bleeding;
Now I must die, no more to see my loving wife and children.
The Southern foe has laid me low, on this cold ground to suffer;
Stay, brother, stay, and put me away, and write my wife a letter.

2 I know that she has prayed for me, I know her prayers are answered;
She prayed that I might be prepared, if I should fall in battle.
Tell her that I am prepared, and hope we'll meet in heaven;
For I believe in Jesus Christ, my sins are all forgiven.

3 My dear wife, you must not grieve, to kiss my little children;
For they will call for me in vain, when I am gone to heaven.
Dear Mary, you must treat them well, and train them up for heaven;
Teach them to love the Lord, and they will be forgiven.

4 My little babes I love them both; if I could once more see them,
I'd bid them both a long farewell, until we meet in heaven.
But here I am in Tennessee, and they are in Ohio,
And now I am too far away to hear their silvery voices.

5 Sister Nancy, you must not grieve o'er the loss of your dear brother;
I am going home to Jesus Christ, to meet my blessed mother.
I am dying, brother Green! O I do die so easy!
I know that death has lost its sting, because I love my Jesus.

6 Dear father, you have suffered long, and prayed for my salvation;
Now I must leave you all at last, so fare-you-well, temptation.
Two brothers yet I can't forget are fighting for the Union;
For this, dear wife, I've lost my life, to put down this rebellion.

$\mathcal{B}$

Communicated by Mr. J. Harrison Miller, Wardensville, Hardy County, January, 1917; obtained from his mother, who learned it from her husband, who got it in a bark-camp in New Hampshire, about 1892.

1　O brother Green, do come to me, for I am shot and bleeding;
　Now I must die, no more to see my wife and my dear children.
　The Southern folks have laid me low, on this cold ground to
　　　suffer;
　O brother, stay and lay me away, and write my wife a letter.

2　Tell her I am prepared to die, and hope to meet her in heaven;
　That I believe on Jesus Christ, my sins are all forgiven.
　Tell dear father he suffered long, and prayed for my salvation;
　Now I shall beat him home at last, to see my blessed mother.

3　Tell sister Molly not to weep for the loss of one dear brother,
　For I am going home at last to see my blessed mother.
　O sister Martha has gone too, she lives and dwells with angels;
　And Jefferson, he died when young: I know I see their faces.

4　Go tell my wife not to weep; go kiss my little children;
　For they will call their pa in vain, when he has gone to heaven.
　My eyes are dim, my ears are deaf, but O this world 's a story!
　When I get home to that bright world, I will sing "Glory!
　　　glory!"

5　O brother, I am dying now!　O I do die so easy!
　I know that death has lost its sting, because I love my Jesus.
　O brother, I must leave you now, for this is all I 'm given;
　But don't forget, when I am gone, to meet me up in heaven.

73

THE SOLDIER'S POOR LITTLE BOY

THIS is a version of "The Soldier's Homeless Boy," a song ascribed in a Phila-
delphia broadside (J. H. Johnson) to Charles Bender. Other texts may be found
in Shoemaker, p. 61; *Singer's Journal*, I, 32; De Marsan broadside, List 18,
No. 66; Belden's Missouri collection; English broadsides ("The Soldier's Boy":
Ryle; Such, No. 96). The song may have been imitated from "The Poor
Fisherman's Boy" ("The Fisherman's Boy"), common in English broadsides
and known in America (*Journal*, xxxv, 366); cf. "Poor Smuggler's Boy"
(Catnach; Bebbington, Manchester, No. 394); Ashton, *Modern Street Ballads*,
p. 240.

A

"The Soldier's Poor Little Boy." Communicated by Miss Violet Noland,
Davis, Tucker County, March 24, 1916; obtained from her mother, who
learned it from an older sister during the Civil War. It was a popular song in
the community in which they lived in Morgan County.

1 The snow was fastly falling,
    The wind did loudly roar,
When a poor little boy, 'most frozen,
    Came up to a rich lady's door.

2 He spied her at the window so high,
    It filled his heart with joy,
Saying, "For mercy sake, some pity on me take,
    I'm a soldier's poor little boy.

3 "My mother died when I was young,
    My father's gone to the war;
A many a battle brave he's fought,
    He's covered with wounds and scars.

4 "A many a mile on his knapsack
    He's carried me with care;
But now I'm left quite parentless,
    I'm a soldier's poor little boy."

5 She then arose from the window so high
    And opened the door unto him;
Saying, "Come in, come in, you unfortunate child!
    You never shall wander again.

6 "My own dear son in the battle was slain,
    My own, my life, my joy;
So long as I live, some shelter I'll give
    To a soldier's poor little boy."

B

"A Soldier Boy." Contributed by Mr. Elmer K. Merinar, Sherrard, Marshall County, November 9, 1915, who says that all he knows about it is: "When a child, I often wandered off into dreamland with it ringing in my ears."

1 The snow was fastly falling,
    The night was coming on,
When a poor little boy nigh frozen
    Came up to a rich lady's door.

2 He spied her at the window so high,
    Which filled his heart with joy:
"For mercy sake, some pity on me take!
    I'm a soldier's poor little boy.

3 "My mother died when I was small;
    My father went to war,
And many a battle he fought brave,
    He's covered with wounds and scars.

4 "Many a mile on his knapsack
    He's carried me with joy;
But now I'm left quite parentless,
    I'm a soldier's poor little boy.

5 "The snow is fastly falling,
    The night is coming on;
If you do not protect me,
    I'll perish before the morn.

6 "And would n't that grieve that heart of thine,
    That peaceful heart of thine,
To find me cold and frozen
    Next morning at your door?"

7 She quickly arose from her window so high
    And opened unto him:
"Come in, come in, my unfortunate little boy!
    You ne'er shall roam any more.

8 "My only son in battle was slain,
    My love, my pride, my joy;
As long as I live, some shelter I will give
    To a soldier's little boy."

74

JUST BEFORE THE BATTLE, MOTHER

THIS is a not quite complete copy of a well-known song of the Civil War composed, both words and music, by George Frederick Root (1820–95) and published by Root and Cady, Chicago (cop. 1862). It was carried to England by Christy's Minstrels, and was published in London as "No. 68 of Hopwood and Crew's Authorized Edition of Christy's Songs." It has sometimes been mistaken for an English song and taken to refer to the Crimean War. See Root's autobiography, *The Story of a Musical Life* (Cincinnati [1891]), pp. 243–245; *Notes and Queries*, 10th Series, IV, 208; De Marsan broadside, List 18, No. 42.

Contributed by Mr. A. C. Payne, Barclay, McDowell County, August, 1918.

1   Just before the battle, mother,
    I am thinking most of you,
While upon the fields we're watching,
    With the evening [1] in view.

2   Comrades brave around me lying,
    Filled with thoughts of home and God,
For well they know that on the morrow
    Some will sleep beneath the sod.

3   Farewell, mother! you may never
    Press me to your breast again;
But O do not forget me, mother,
    If I'm numbered with the slain.

4   Hark, I hear the bugle sounding!
    'T is the signal for the fight;
Now may God protect us, mother,
    As he ever does the right.

5   Hear the battle cry of freedom,
    How it swells upon the air!
O yes, we'll rally round the standard,
    Or we'll perish nobly there.

[1] Error for *enemy*.

75

MOTHER, IS THE BATTLE OVER?

THIS song was equally popular in the North and (without the last stanza) in the South during the Civil War. See broadsides published by De Marsan of New York (List 13, No. 47), A. W. Auner of Philadelphia, and Partridge of Boston (No. 570), as well as by Ryle of London; *Allan's Lone Star Ballads* (Galveston, 1874), p. 111; sheet music "composed by B. E. Roefs" (Cincinnati and St. Louis, Peters); Ellinger, *The Southern War Poetry of the Civil War*, p. 125.

Contributed by Mr. W. E. Boggs, Matewan, Mingo County, 1918.

1 "Mother, is the battle over?
    Thousands have been slain, they say.
  Is my father come? and tell me,
    Has the army gained the day?

2 "Is he well, or is he wounded?
    Mother, do you think he's slain?
  If he is, pray will you tell me,
    Will my father come again?

3 "Mother, I see you always sighing
    Since that paper last you read;
  Tell me why you are crying:
    Is my dearest father dead?"

4 "Yes, my boy, your noble father
    Is one numbered with the slain;
  Though he loves me very dearly,
    Ne'er on earth we'll meet again.

5 "Fighting for the glorious Union,
    Like a hero he is slain;
  Still the day may not be distant
    When in heaven we'll meet again."

76

THE REBEL SOLDIER

For other versions see *Allan's Lone Star Ballads* (Galveston, 1874), p. 80 ("The Rebel Prisoner"); Lomax, p. 292 ("Jack o' Diamonds"); Sharp, *Folk-Songs of English Origin Collected in the Appalachian Mountains*, 2d Series, p. 52 ("The Rebel Soldier"; from Virginia). Stanza 2 (with "Rebels" for "Yankees" occurs in "A Roving Soldier" (a Union version of "The Guerilla Boy") in Belden's Missouri collection. "The Rebel Soldier," as Kittredge has noted (*Journal*, XXX, 345), is an adaptation of "The Forsaken Girl," which in its turn resembles the English song of "The Poor Stranger." The first five stanzas of B belong to quite a different piece.

A

"The Rebel Soldier." Contributed by Mr. A. C. Payne, Barclay, McDowell County, August, 1918.

1 One morning, one morning in May,
   I heard a poor soldier lamenting and say:
   "I am a Rebel soldier and far from my home;
   Adieu to Old Kentucky, no longer can I stay.

Chorus

The Union men and Yankees have forced me away,

. . . .

The Union men and Yankees have forced me to roam;
I am a rebel soldier and far from my home.

2 I'll eat when I'm hungry and drink when I get dry;
   If those Yankees don't kill me, I'll fight till I die.
   Miss Marley, Miss Marley, you've caused me to roam,
   To follow John H. Morgin, and in his arms I'll roam.

3 I'll build myself a castle, all on the mountains high,
   Where my true love will see me, as she is passing by,
   Where the turtle dove may harkle, and help me to mourn;
   I am a Rebel soldier, and far from my home.

4 There's a bottle of good old whiskey, a glass of good old wine;
   You can drink to your true love, and I will drink to mine:
   I am a Rebel soldier, and the Rebels they can shine.

B

"The Bright Sunny South." Contributed by Mr. Sam Turman, Buchanan, Boyd County, Kentucky, July, 1918.

1 In the bright sunny South, where in peace and content,
　Where the days of my boyhood was carelessly spent,
　From the bright spreading plains to the deep flowing streams,
　Ever dear to my memory, has been since in my dreams.

2 I have the refinements and comforts of life,
　To endure privations, starvation, and strife.
　I have counted the cost, I have pledged my word,
　I have shouldered my musket, I have belted my sword.

3 O father, dear father, for me do not weep,
　For in some foreign country, I expect for to sleep:
　To the dangers of war, I expect for to bear;
　As to sickness and death, I expect for to share.

4 O mother, dear mother, for me do not weep,
　For your good advice I shall forever keep:
　You have taught me for to be brave, from a boy to a man;
　Now I've started in defence of my own native land.

5 My friends and relations, I once had to part;
　My wife and my children were dear to my heart.
　I never shall forget when I tuck them by the hand,
　And I started in defence of my own native land.

6 Here adieu to old Kentucky, I can no longer stay,
　Hard times and the Yankees have forced me away,
　Hard times and the Yankees have caused me to roam;
　I am a poor soldier, I am a long way from home.

7 I'll eat when I'm hungry, I'll drink when I'm dry;
　If the Yankees don't kill me, I'll live till I die.
　If Miss Mollie forsakes me and causes me to roam,
　I am a poor soldier, a long way from home.

77

I'M A GOOD OLD REBEL

ELLINGER, *The Southern War Poetry of the Civil War*, p. 134, cites this song from Davidson, *Cullings from the Confederacy* (Washington, 1903), as " 'O! I'm a Good Old Rebel.' Respectfully dedicated to Thad. Stevens, 1862. Sung by Harry Allen, Washington Artillery, New Orleans, La." In Fagan's *Southern War Songs* (New York, 1890), p. 360, it is ascribed to "J. R. T." But the song is included in *Poems by Innes Randolph*, compiled by his Son from the Original Manuscript (Baltimore [1898]), p. 30: See Pound, *Poetic Origins*, p. 228. For current oral variants see Lomax, *Journal*, XXVIII, 11; *Cowboy Songs*, p. 94.

Contributed by Mr. E. C. Smith, Weston, Lewis County, 1915, who writes, "The song is found in *Gems of The Confederacy*, published at Salem, West Virginia, in 1903 for a Confederate monument benefit."

1   O I'm a good old rebel,
     Now that's just what I am;
For the "fair land of freedom,"
     I do not care a damn;
I'm glad I fit against it,
     I only wish we'd won,
And I don't want no pardon,
     For anything I done.

2   I hate the Constitution,
     This great republic too;
I hate the freedman's buro,
     In uniforms of blue.
I hate the nasty eagle,
     With all his brags and fuss;
The lyin' thievin' Yankees,
     I hate 'em wuss and wuss.

3   I hate the Yankee nation
     And everything they do;
I hate the Declaration
     Of Independence, too.
I hate the glorious Union,
     'T is dripping with our blood;
I hate the striped banner,
     I fit it all I could.

4   I followed old Marse Robert
        For four years near about,
    Got wounded in three places,
        And starved on Point Lookout.
    I cotch the roomatism
        A-campin' in the snow,
    But if I killed a chance of Yankees,
        I'd like to kill some mo'.

5   Three hundred thousand Yankees
        Is stiff in Southern dust;
    We got three hundred thousand
        Before they conquered us;
    They died of Southern fever,
        And Southern steel and shot,
    I wish it was three million
        Instead of what we got.

6   I can't take up my musket
        And fight 'em now no more;
    But I ain't a-goin' to love 'em,
        Now that is certain sure.
    And I don't want no pardon
        For what I was and am;
    I won't be reconstructed,
        And I don't give a damn.

78

CORPORAL SCHNAPPS

THIS song was composed (words and music) about 1864 by Henry Clay Work (1832–84) and published by Root and Cady, Philadelphia (cop. 1864). See his *Songs*, edited by Bertram G. Work [1920], p. 124; cf. G. F. Root, *The Story of a Musical Life*, p. 137.

Communicated by Miss Mildred Boggess, West Liberty, Ohio County, March, 1917; obtained from Mr. J. R. Collock, who learned it during the Civil War.

1 Mine heart is proken into little pits;
    I tells you, friend, what for:
  Mine schweetheart, von coot patriotic kirl,
    She trives me off mit der war.
  I fights for her the pattles of the flag,
    I strikes so prave ash I can;
  But now long time she nix remembers me,
    And coes mit another man.

Chorus
  Ah, mine fraulein!
    You is so ferry unkind!
  You coes mit Hans to Zhermany to live
    And leaves poor Schnapps behind.

2 I march all tay, no matter of [1] der schtorm
    Be worse ash Moses' flood;
  I lays all night, mine head upon an schtump,
    And sinks to schleep mit ter ghost;
  I wakes next morning frozen in der ground,
    So stiff as one schtone post.

3 They kives me hard pread, toughern as a rock,
    It almost preaks mine zhaw;
  I schplits him sometimes mit an iron wedge
    And cut him up mit a saw.
  They kives me peef so ferry, ferry salt,
    Like Sodom's wife, you know;
  I surely dinks they put him in der prine
    Von hundred years ago.

[1] Error for *if*.

4   Py'n-py we takes one city in the South;
    We schtay there one whole year;
  I gits me sourkrout much as I can eat
    And plenty lagger beer.
  I meets von lady Repel in der schtreet,
    So handsome effer I see;
  I makes to her von ferry callant pow,
    But ah! she schpits on me.

5   "Hart times!" you say, "What makes you folunteer?"
    I told you, friends, what for:
  Mine schweetheart, von coot patriotic kirl,
    She trove me off mit der war.
  Alas! Alas! mine pretty little von
    Will schmile no more øn me;
  Put schtill I fights der pattles of der flag,
    To set mine countries free.

79

OLD JOE CAMP

Communicated by Mrs. Hilary G. Richardson, Clarksburg, Harrison County, 1917; obtained from Mrs. Nancy McAtee. Already printed (*Journal*, xxxi. 277).

1   Old Joe Camp when he came to town,
    He enlisted under Captain Brown;
    Brown swore him on the very first slap,
    And sent him off to Manassas Gap.

2   Brown he was a-walking around,
    He found Joe sleepin' on the ground;
    Brown said to Joe, "It is your lot,
    We'll take you out and have you shot."

3   Said Joe to Brown, "Fightin' was not my intent,
    . . . .
    And now I can't do you no dirt,
    Fur I 'low to desert."

4   The ammunition gittin' thin,
    They wound Joe up and poked him in;
    They fired him off at the very first round,
    And fired him back to Captain Brown.

80

FAIR CHARLOTTE

Six good texts and one fragment of this fine American ballad have been found in West Virginia. The general agreement of the complete copies in length, arrangement, and phraseology is remarkable.

Barry gives a full account of this song, with texts and tunes. He ascribes it to William Lorenzo Carter, of Benson or Bensontown, Vermont, before 1833 (*Journal*, XXII, 367, 442; XXV, 156). It has spread throughout the United States and to Nova Scotia. For references, see also *Journal*, XXV, 13; XXVI, 357; XXIX, 191; XXXV, 420; Shoemaker, p. 62; Gray, p. 94; F. C. Brown, p. 12; Belden's Missouri collection. It is interesting to note that variant F has travelled into West Virginia from Ohio, where it was learned about the year 1858, at which time the author, William Lorenzo Carter, was living at Kirkland, in that state.

A

"Young Charlotte." Communicated by Miss Sallie D. Jones, Franklin, Brooke County; obtained from Katherine Johnson, who got it from Fred Eye, Pendleton County.

1　Young Charlotte lived on a mountain side
　　In a wild and lonely spot;
　There were no dwellings for three miles wide,
　　Except her father's cot.

2　And yet on many a winter's night
　　Young swains were gathered there,
　For her father kept a social board,
　　And she was very fair.

3　One New Year's eve, as the sun went down,
　　Far looked her wishful eye
　Out from the frosty window pane,
　　As the merry sleighs dashed by.

4　At the village, fifteen miles away,
　　Was to be a ball that night,
　And though the air was piercing cold,
　　Her heart was warm and light.

5　How brightly beamed her laughing eye
　　As a well-known voice she heard,
　And, dashing up to the cottage door,
　　Her lover's sleigh appeared!

6 "O daughter dear," the mother cried,
      "This blanket round you fold;
  For 't is a dreadful night abroad,
      And you will get your death of cold."

7 "O nay, O nay!" young Charlotte cried,
      As she laughed like a gypsy queen;
  "To ride in blanket muffled up
      I never would be seen.

8 "My silken cloak is quite enough,
      You know 't is lined throughout;
  And there is my silken scarf to twine
      My head and neck about."

9 Her bonnet and her gloves were on,
      She jumped into the sleigh,
  And swift they sped down the mountain side
      And o'er the hills away.

10 With muffled beat so silently
      Five miles at last were passed,
  When Charles with few and shivering words
      The silence broke at last.

11 "Such a dreadful night I never saw;
      My reins I scarce can hold."
  Young Charlotte faintly replied,
      "I am exceeding cold."

12 He cracked his whip and urged his steed
      Much faster than before,
  And thus five other dreary miles
      In silence were passed o'er.

13 Spoke Charles, "How fast the freezing ice
      Is gathering on my brow!"
  And Charlotte still more faintly said,
      "I'm growing warmer now."

14 Thus on they rode through the frosty air
      And the glittering, cold starlight,
  Until at last the village lamps
      And the ballroom came in sight.

15   They reached the door, and Charles sprang out
        And held his hand to her:
    "Why sit you like a monument
        That hath no power to stir?"

16   He called her once and he called her twice,
        She answered not a word;
    He asked her for her hand again,
        But still she never stirred.

17   He took her hand in his,
        'T was cold and hard as any stone;
    He tore the mantle from her face,
        And the cold stars o'er it shone.

18   Then quickly to the lighted hall
        Her lifeless form he bore;
    Young Charlotte's eyes had close for aye,
        And her voice was heard no more.

19   And there he sat down by her side,
        While bitter tears did flow,
    And cried, "My own, my charming bride,
        You never more shall know!"

20   He twined his arms around her neck
        And kissed her marble brow,
    And his thoughts flew back to where she said,
        "I'm growing warmer now."

ℬ

"The Frozen Girl." Communicated by Mr. Ernest Hersman, Grantsville, Calhoun County; obtained from Mrs. D. E. Stutler, whose husband learned it in early manhood and wrote it down for her, November 3, 1883. The present version is taken from that manuscript.

1   Young Charlotte lived by the mountain side
        In a wild and lonely spot;
    No dwelling there for three miles around
        Except her father's cot.

2   A many lonely winter's night
        Young swain would gather there:
    Her father kept a social abode,
        And she was very fair.

3 Her father loved to see her dress
    Gay as a city belle,
For she was the only girl he had,
    And he loved his daughter well.

4 It was New Year's eve, the sun was down,
    Yet beamed her restless eye,
As she to the frozen window went,
    For to see the sleighs go by.

5 Yet restless beamed her restless eye,
    As his well-known voice she heard;
Come driving up to the cottage door,
    Young Charlie's sleigh appeared.

6 "There is a merry ball to-night
    Within fifteen miles away;
The air is freezing cold as death,
    But our hearts are light and gay."

7 "Now, Charlotte dear," her mother said,
    "This blanket around you fold,
For it's a dreadful night above,
And you'll catch your death of cold."

8 "O no, O no," Charlotte said,
    For she felt like a gypsy queen;
"For to ride in a blanket all muffled up
    I never can be seen.

9 "My silken cloak is enough for me,
    You know it's lined throughout;
Beside I have my silken shawl
    To tie my neck about."

10 Her bonnet and her shawl was on,
    She stepped into the sleigh;
Away they rode to the mountain side
    And o'er the hills away.

11 There is music in the sound of bells,
    As o'er the hills they go;
What a squeaking noise the runners make,
    As they leave the drifted snow!

12   "It is a dreadful night," said Charles,
        "Those reins I scarce can hold."
    When Charlotte said in these few words,
        "I am exceeding cold."

13   He cracked his whip, he urged his team
        Much faster than before,
    Until five more merry miles
        In silence they passed o'er.

14   "How fast," said Charles, "the ice and snow
        Is freezing on my brow!"
    When Charlotte said in these few words,
        "I am growing warmer now."

15   As o'er the hill the frosty air,
        And in the cold starlight,
    Until at length at the village ball
        They both appeared in sight.

16   He drove up to the door, jumped out,
        He gave to her his hand;
    He asked her for her hand again,
        But still she did not stir.

17   He took her by the hand, O God!
        It was cold and hard as stone;
    He lifted the mantle from off her brow,
        While the stars above them shone.

18   Then quickly to the lighted hall
        Her lifeless corpse he bore;
    Young Charlotte was a frozen girl,
        And she never spoke no more.

19   It was there he sat down by her side,
        As the bitter tears did flow;
    Saying, "My young and charming bride,
        You never more shall know!"

20   He twined his arms around her neck,
        He kissed her marble brow,
    While his thoughts went back to where she said,
        "I am growing warmer now."

C

"Charlotte." Contributed by Mrs. E. A. Hunter, Belington, Barbour County, February 21, 1916; learned from her mother. Nineteen stanzas.

D

"Young Charlotte's Fate." Contributed by Mr. H. S. White, Piedmont, Mineral County, December 20, 1915; learned from his mother, who learned it when a little girl. Seventeen stanzas.

E

"Charlotte." Communicated by Mr. J. Harrison Miller, Wardensville, Hardy County, June, 1917; obtained from Mr. Abraham Wilkins. A good text in sixteen stanzas.

F

"Fair Charlotte." Communicated by Mrs. R. G. Barger, Charleston, Kanawha County, April 9, 1916; obtained from her father, Mr. A. N. Gatchell, Pinchton, who learned it from a schoolmate, Martha Dunleavy, a girl of Scotch parentage, in Tuscarawas County, Ohio, about the year 1858. A good version in thirteen stanzas.

G

"Young Charlotte." Communicated by Professor Walter Barnes, Fairmont, Marion County, September, 1916; received from Miss Edith Williams, New Cumberland, who obtained it from Miss Carrie Price of Nebraska. Fragment of seven stanzas.

81

SPRINGFIELD MOUNTAIN

THE only version of this famous song found in West Virginia bears no local title. It was contributed by Mr. M. F. Morgan, Ravenswood, Jackson County, November 9, 1915. He reports that the song was sung extensively in Wetzel County between the years 1895 and 1900. It is especially interesting to students of folk-lore, because here may be traced the genesis and development of an American folk-song.

The tragic incident recorded took place at Wilbraham, Massachusetts, in 1761, and the song seems to have been composed soon after. It has spread all over the country. References are collected in *Journal*, XXIX, 188; XXXV, 415. See also Shoemaker, p. 126; *The William and Mary Literary Magazine*, April, 1922, XXIX, 524; *Folk-Lore Primer published by the Folk-Lore Committee, Alabama Association Teachers of English*, p. 9; Belden's Missouri collection; N. I. White MS., II, 596; Minish MS. (North Carolina).

1 A charming youth in Conway dwelled,
   A charming youth that I knew quite well.

   Too-da-nica-da-li, too-da-nica-dali, too-da-nica, too-da-nica,
   Too-da-nica-da-li, too-da-nica, too-da-nica, too-di-a

2 That charming youth one day did go
   Down in the meadow for to mow.

3 He mowed along, but at length did feel
   A great big serpent bite him on the heel.

4 They carried him to his Sallie dear,
   Now don't you bet it made her feel queer?

5 "O Johnnie dear, why did you go,
   Down in yon meadow for to mow?"

6 "Why, Sallie dear, and I thought you knowed
   'T was granddaddie's meadow, and it must be mowed."

7 At length he died, gave up the ghost;
   In Abraham's bosom he was post.

8 Now all ye people this warning take,
   To shun the bite of a great big snake.

82

THE DRUMMER BOY OF WATERLOO

A WELL-KNOWN English song (broadside, H. Such, No. 168). See *The American Songster* (Philadelphia, 1850), p. 145; *The Star Song Book* (New York, Richard Marsh), p. 145; *The Forget Me Not Songster* (New York, Nafis & Cornish), p. 202; De Marsan broadside, List 14, No. 19; *Singer's Journal*, 1, 186. Cf. F. C. Brown, p. 11.

Communicated by Mr. J. R. Waters, Morgantown, Monongalia County, November 1, 1915; obtained from Mrs. F. M. Brown, Belington, Barbour County, who learned it more than fifty years before in Delaware County, Ohio.

1 When battle roused each warlike band,
    And carnage loud her trumpet blew,
  Young Edwin left his native land,
    A drummer boy for Waterloo.

2 His mother; when his lips she pressed
    And bade her noble boy adieu
  With wringing hands and aching heart,
    Beheld him marching for Waterloo.

3 He took his drum upon his arm,
    His knapsack o'er his shoulder threw,
  And cried, "Dear mother, dry those tears,
    Till I return from Waterloo."

4 But ere before the set of sun,
    The march began, the foe subdued,
  The flash of death, the murderous gun,
    Had laid him low at Waterloo.

5 "O comrades, comrades!" Edwin cried,
    While proudly beamed his eye of blue,
  "Go tell my mother Edwin died
    A soldier's death at Waterloo."

6 They laid his head upon his drum
    Beneath the moonlight's mournful hue;
  The night has stilled the battle drum;[1]
    They dug his grave at Waterloo.

[1] Read *battle's hum*.

83

THE SHEFFIELD APPRENTICE

"The Sheffield Apprentice" is common in English broadsides (H. Such, No. 333; Catnach; J. Cadman, Manchester, No. 185; Walker, Durham, No. 32; Pitts slip), and is still orally current in England and Scotland: see references in Campbell and Sharp, p. 334: add Murison MS., 26 (Harvard College); Gillington, *Eight Hampshire Folk-Songs*, p. 14.

For American texts from oral sources, see Perrow, *Journal*, XXVIII, 164 (North Carolina); Shearin, *Sewanee Review*, XIX, 320 (Kentucky); Campbell and Sharp, No. 97 (North Carolina; tunes from North Carolina and Tennessee); Belden's Missouri collection; cf. Child MSS., II, 158. It was printed as a chapbook at Philadelphia about 1825 (Harvard College Library, 25276.43.81). There are broadsides by H. De Marsan (New York), List 9, No. 91, and without imprint (Ford, *Massachusetts Broadsides*, No. 3307: "The 'Prentice Boy"). See also *The Forget Me Not Songster* (New York, Nafis & Cornish), p. 244; same (Boston, Locke and Bubier), p. 244; *Elton's Songs and Melodies for the Multitude* (New York, T. W. Strong), p. 318. "The New-York Apprentice Boy. Air: The Sheffield Apprentice. Composed and sung by Harry Greenwood, the Champion Balladist at the Chatham Theatre" is one of De Marsan's broadsides (List 11, No. 70). In Campbell and Sharp. No. 97 A, "The Sheffield Apprentice" has borrowed two stanzas from "The Boston Burglar" (see p. 265).

Communicated by Mrs. Hilary G. Richardson, Clarksburg, Harrison County, 1917; obtained from Mrs. McAtee (see *Journal*, XXXII, 499). Title supplied.

1 I was brought up in Sherefield, not of high degree;
   My parents thought much on me, they had no child but me.
   I rode in such pleasures, just where my fancies led,
   Till I was bound in 'prentice, and then my joys were fled.

2 I did not like my master, he did not serve me well;
   I formed a resolution not long with him to dwell;
   Unknown to my poor parents, from them I ran away;
   I steered my course for London; I did not like the day.

3 They happened a rich lady from Holland was there;
   She offered me great wages, If I'd serve her for one year;
   And after long persuading, at last I did agree
   To serve her in Holland to prove my disperlee.[1]

4 I had n't been in Holland more than one year, two, or three,
   Before my young mistress grew very fond of me;
   Her gold and her silver, her houses and free land,
   If I would say I'd marry her, should go at my command.

---

[1] Unintelligible.

5 Said I, "Dear, honored lady, I cannot wed you both;
  I lately have been promised, and took a solemn oath,
  To wed with none but Polly, your pretty chambermaid;
  Excuse me, dear mistress!   She has got my heart betrayed."

6 She being full of angerlee, from me she turned away;
  She swore that she would have revenge before another day.

  . . . .
  . . . .

7 One day as we was walking, all in the month of June,
  A-viewing of wild flowers, as they was all in bloom,
  A gold ring from her finger, just as I passed her by,
  She slipped into my pocket, and for this I must die.

8 She swore that I had robbèd her by taking of her gold,
  Before the brave old justice, to answer for my fault.
  A long time I pled innocent, but that was no avail;
  She swore so hard against me, till I was put in jail.

9 Come all of you young men that stand around me now,
  Don't glory in my downfall, I pray that you pity me;
  And believe I am innocent, I'll bid this world ajew;[1]
  Farewell, my loving Polly! I'll die in love with you.

[1] For *adieu.*

84

THE BOSTON BURGLAR

"THE BOSTON BURGLAR" is a slightly Americanized version of the English "Botany Bay." A text may be found in Lomax, p. 147, and two more in Pound, No. 23 (Iowa and Wyoming); still another is printed by R. W. Gordon in *Adventure*, March 10, 1924. Two stanzas (corresponding to 3 and 4 of West Virginia A) occur intrusively in a North Carolina variant of "The Sheffield Apprentice" (Campbell and Sharp, No. 97 A: see p. 294, above). "The Boston Burglar. Sung by Dan MacCarthy" was copyrighted in 1881 by H. J. Wehman (New York) and published by him as a broadside (No. 480) and in *The Vocalist's Favorite Songster* (cop. 1885), p. 179. The American text has crossed the sea to Scotland and, as "The Boston Smuggler," appears in Greig, *Folk-Song of the North-East*, CXXXII.

For "Botany Bay" see Pitts and Catnach broadsides ("The Transport"); broadside printed by H. Such, No. 499; Ashton, *Modern Street Ballads*, p. 359; Barrett, *English Folk-Songs*, No. 52, p. 90; Sharp, *One Hundred English Folk-Songs*, No. 86; Sharp, *English Folk Songs*, II, 90; *Journal of the Folk-Song Society*, V, 85. It is well preserved in a text printed by Sturgis and Hughes, *Songs from the Hills of Vermont*, p. 32. "Botany Bay" coincides in part with another English convict ballad known as "Henry's (or Young Henry's) Downfall" or "Young Henry the Poacher." See broadsides by Catnach; Such, No. 499; Bebbington, Manchester, No. 163; J. Cadman, Manchester, No. 132; W. R. Walker, Newcastle, No. 27.

A

"The Boston Burglar." Communicated by Mr. C. R. Bishop, Green Bank, Pocahontas County, 1917; obtained from Miss Leone Oliver, who learned it from her companions in high school. Variants almost identical were furnished him by Miss Vesta Sharp and Mr. Bruce Brown.

1 I was born in Boston, a city you all know well,
  Brought up by honest parents, the truth to you I'll tell;
  Brought up by honest parents, and reared most tenderly,
  Till I became a sporting man, at the age of twenty-three.

2 My character was taken, and I was sent to jail,
  My friends thought it was in vain to get me out on bail;
  The jury proved me guilty, the clerk he wrote it down,
  The judge he passed my sentence: it was off for Charles Town.

3 They put me on an east-bound train one cold December day,
  And every station that I passed I heard the people say:
  "There goes that Boston Burglar! for iron bars he's bound,
  For some bad crime or other he's off for Charles Town."

4 If you could have seen my father, a-pleading at the bar,
Likewise my aged mother, a-pulling out her hair,
A-pulling out those old gray locks, while tears were streaming
   down:
"My darling boy, what have you done, that you're off for
   Charles Town?"

5 Young people who have your liberty, pray keep it as long as you
   can,
And don't go prowling round the streets to break the laws of
   man,
For if you do you'll surely lose, and find yourself like me,
Serving out twenty-one years in the penitentiary.

6 There lives a girl in Boston, a girl I love so well,
And e'er I gain my liberty, along with her I'll dwell;
And e'er I gain my liberty, bad company I'll shun;
Adieu to all bad company! adieu to all bad rum!

B

"The Jail at Morgantown." Communicated by Miss Marie Rennar, Morgantown, Monongalia County; obtained from Mrs. Dayton Wiles, who learned
it from her mother. This is a good example of the localization of a popular
song.

1 I was born in West Virginia, a place we all know well,
Brought up by honest parents, the truth to you I'll tell,
Brought up by honest parents, and raised most tenderly,
Till I became a roving lad, which proved my destiny.

2 My friends would ofttimes say to me, and ofttimes would relate,
A home of thieves or drunkards would sometime be my fate.
But I paid no regards to them, and in bad company roamed,
And now to-day I may be found in the jail at Morgantown.

3 My character was taken, and I was sent to jail;
My friends tried to bail me out, but it proved no avail;
The judge he heard the evidence, and the clerk he wrote it down,
The jury found me guilty, and I was sent to [Morgan]town.

4 You ought to have heard my father, a-pleading at the bar;
Likewise my angel mother, tearing out her hair,
A-tearing out her silver locks, and the tears from her eyes
   dropped down:
"O son! O son! what have you done that you're going to
   Morgantown?"

5 They took me away on an eastern train on a cold and stormy
   day,
   And every station we passed through, you could hear the people
   say:
   "There goes a noted burglar, in chains he's bound down;
   For some bad crime or other he's going to Morgantown."

6 'T is you have the liberty, pray keep it while you can,
   And don't go out, my boy, to-night, and break the laws of man;
   For if you do, you'll surely find in chains they'll bind you down,
   And you'll be spending the best of your days in the jail at
   Morgantown.

C

"The Boston Burglar." Communicated by Mr. E. C. Smith, Weston, Lewis
County, December 18, 1915; obtained from the singing of a servant girl of that
community.

1 I am a Boston burglar, the truth to you I'll tell,
   For I was born in Boston, a city you all know well;
   Brought up by honest parents, and raised most tenderly,
   Till I became a sporting lad at the age of twenty-three.

2 My character being taken, they sent me off to jail;
   My friends they found it difficult to get me out on bail;
   The jury found me guilty, the clerk he wrote it down;
   The judge he passed my sentence and sent me to Charlestown.

3 To see my aged father a-standing by the bar,
   Likewise my aged mother a-tearing of her hair,
   A-tearing of her old gray locks as the tears came rolling down,
   Crying, "Son, dear son, what have you done, you're sent to
   Charlestown."

4 They put me on an east-bound train one cold December day;
   At every station I rode past I heard the people say:
   "There goes the Boston burglar, in an iron chain he's bound;
   For some crime or another he is sent to Charlestown."

5 I have a girl in Boston, a girl that I love well,
  And if I get my liberty, at home with her I'll dwell;
  And if I get my liberty, bad company I will shun,
  Likewise street walks and gambling, and also drinking rum.

6 You men who have your liberty, pray keep it if you can,
  And don't go rambling through the streets to break the laws of
    man;
  For if you do you're sure to rue and find yourself like me
  A-serving out your twenty-one years in the penitentiary.

85

MY PARENTS REARED ME TENDERLY

THIS text is very close to "The Maid I Left Behind" in *The Forget Me Not Songster* (New York, Nafis & Cornish), p. 220, running line for line with that song and showing only trifling variations in phraseology. It will be noted that the man is false in this version. A modified form, in which the girl marries during her lover's absence, occurs in English broadsides as "The Girl I Left Behind" (Bebbington, Manchester, No. 306; George Walker, Jun., Durham, No. 204), and has been found in Scotland by Greig (*Folk-Song of the North-East*, LXXXIII). For American versions in oral circulation (based on a text similar to the broadsides) see Perrow, *Journal*, XXVIII, 161 (North Carolina); Wyman and Brockway, p. 76 ("Peggy Walker"; Kentucky); Campbell and Sharp, No. 96 (North Carolina); Lomax, p. 244 ("The Rambling Cowboy"); Belden's Missouri collection; cf. Shearin and Combs, p. 23. An interesting *rifacimento* is "Lackey Bill" (Lomax, p. 83).

Contributed by Mr. T. J. Doolittle, Fairmont, Marion County, 1917.

1 My parents reared me tenderly, they had no child but me;
My mind being bent on rambling, with them could not agree;
So I became a rover soon, which grieved their hearts full sore;
I left my aged parents to be seen no more.

2 There was a wealthy gentleman who lived in this part;
He had a lovely daughter, and I had gained her heart.
And she was noble-minded too, tall, beautiful, and fair,
And with Columbia's fairest daughters she truly could compare.

3 I told her my intention was quite soon to cross the main,
And saying, "You prove faithful, love, till I return again."
Large drops of tears were in her eyes, her bosom heaves with sigh:
"Dear you," said she "Fear not for me; my love can never die."

4 But said the maid, "I've dreamed a dream that I cannot believe,
That distance breaks the link of love, and leaves the maid to grieve."
I fondly pressed her cheek a kiss, saying, "Loved one, have no fear,"
And swore by Him who rules above that I would live sincere.

5 Her heart was generous, she believed, her eyes were once more
        calm;
   Her lovely arms around my neck, I felt her bosom warm.
   O then said she, "My prayer shall be for health and prosperity!
   May heaven grant you sweet return to the maid you left behind."

6 According to agreement, I went on board the ship:
   First to Glasgow town I went; I had a pleasant trip;
   I found that gold was plenty and the girls was true and kind:
   My love began to cool a bit for the girl I left behind.

7 Then for Guffers [1] Town we set out, for that hospitable land;
   My lovely Jennie forges on,[2] and took me by the hand,
   Saying she, "I have gold in plenty, and my love is true and
        kind!"
   And my love began to cool a bit for the girl I left behind.

8 Then says she, "If you will marry me, and say no more you'll
        rove,
   The gold I now possess is yours, and I will faithful prove.
   My parents dear and other friends, that I have left behind,
   If you ever marry me, again must bear in mind."

9 To this I soon consented, and owned to my shame
   That man can be happy when he knows himself to blame.
   It's true I've gold in plenty, and my love is true and kind,
   Yet my pillow is haunted by the girl I left behind.

10 My father's in his winding sheets, my mother to appear;
    That lovely girl stands by my side, a-weeping off the tears,
    And then to this, they all did die, and now too late to find
    That God has seen my cruelty to the girl I left behind.

---

[1] Error for *Dumfries*.   [2] Error for *Ferguson*.

86

JACKISON AND DICKISON

WHAT follows is a fragment of the American text. A good version ("The Three Butchers") from Tennessee and one stanza from North Carolina may be found in Campbell and Sharp, No. 50. It is ultimately derived from the seventeenth-century black-letter ballad (of 102 lines) "The Three Worthy Butchers of the North," which is signed by Paul Burges (*Roxburghe Ballads*, ed. Ebsworth, VII, 59). Between Burges's long ballad and the American text comes another eighteenth-century broadside, "A New Ballad of the Three Merry Butchers" (Ebsworth, VII, 62), an heroically reduced adaptation, which is common in modern English broadsides ("The Three Butchers") and still circulates as a folk-song in England and Scotland: see broadsides printed by Such (No. 463), Pitts, Forth of Pocklington (No. 143), Bebbington of Manchester (No. 387), and George Walker, Jun., of Durham (No. 83); Ashton, *Modern Street Ballads*, p. 403; references in Campbell and Sharp, p. 330. Add Alfred Williams, *Folk-Songs of the Upper Thames*, p. 275.

Communicated by Mrs. Hilary G. Richardson, Clarksburg, Harrison County, 1917; obtained from Mrs. McAtee.

1 Jackison and Dickison walked out one morning in May,
  A-traveling over mountains ten thousand pounds to pay;
  They traveled five of their long miles, six miles along their way,
  Till seven of they brave soldiers came walking out so gay.

2 Said Jackison to Dickison, "Will you fight or run?"
  Said Dickison to Jackison, "I'll die before I fly."
  They fit from eight o'clock in the morning till in the evening at
    one;
  They killed six of they brave soldiers, but the seventh took heels
    and run.

3 Said Jackison to Dickison, "I hear some human cry."
  They turned their eyes around, and the Irish girl they spy;
  Jackison, being kind-hearted, so very, very kind,
  He wrapped her up in his overcoat and he put her on behind.

4 And then she said to Jackison, "You are condemned to be hung,
  For you've killed as brave a soldier as old England ever sprung."

87

THE ANFORD-WRIGHT

"ANFORD-WRIGHT" is for *Amphitrite*. This ballad, "Loss of the Amphitrite," occurs in an English broadside ("Sold by J. Livsey, 43 Hanover-Street, Shudehill, Manchester," No. 231) with the note: "The above ship was lost off Boulogne, August 31, 1833, having on board 108 female convicts, who perished, together with 12 children, and 13 of the crew!" Under date of August 30, *The Gentleman's Magazine* for September, 1833 (CIII, ii, 268) gives a vivid account of the disaster:

"This evening we were visited by one of the most violent storms, accompanied by torrents of rain, that has occurred for many years. It continued for thirty-six hours, and has produced the most devastating effects both by sea and land. The accounts received from the coast have been most distressing. The loss of vessels with their passengers, on our own coasts and those of France and Holland, has been unusually great. . . . The Amphitrite, with female convicts bound to Botany Bay, went on shore near Boulogne, and out of 130 persons only three were saved. The captain, John Hunter, is stated to have forcibly prevented any communication with the shore; otherwise it is clear that the whole of those on board might have been saved, as the vessel, when the tide was out, lay within a furlong of the multitude collected on the spot. When the tide returned the danger was irremediable. The violence of the storm continued unabated; and as the ship did not float, the perilous condition of the crew could no longer be concealed, the waves broke through the poop, and swept away in an instant every soul in the cabin. The work of destruction was soon completed; in a few moments the ship went to pieces, and out of 130 persons on board only three escaped to land! and one of these died a few hours afterwards. The bodies of 65 women and one man were washed on shore in the course of Saturday night."

Contributed by Miss Fannie Egan, Hinton, Summers County, January 12, 1917; learned when she was a child, from some Canadian settlers who came into West Virginia when the lumber business first opened up.

1 Come all ye jolly sailors brave that wear the jackets blue,
   While I relate the dangers great and hardships of the sea;
   It's of a ship called the Anford-Wright, with a hundred and eight
      females,
   With cargo and crew and passengers too, bound out for New
      South Wales.

2 It was on the eighteenth day of June, from the city we set sail,
   Leaving our friends behind us, it grieved our hearts full sore.
   And as we bore along the shore, till our friends got out of sight,
   Saying, "Adieu unto you blue-eyed girls on board of the
      Anford-Wright."

3 About twelve o'clock on the third day, we were all put to a stand,
When our goodly ship she ran aground, all on a bank of sand;
And the children around their parents flocked and tore their
   hair with fright,
For to think they must end their days on board of the Anford-
   Wright.

4 When our captain found he was aground, both anchors he let go,
Saying, "Go reef your fore and main-top sails, or soon our fate
   we'll know!"
When our ship she gave one dreadful reel, and soon went out of
   sight,
And the shriek and cries would reach the skies, on board of the
   Anford-Wright.

5 All that reached the shore out of our crew were two poor lads and
   me;
We reached the shore all on a spar, we swam the briny sea.
One was exhausted by the waves, he died that very night;
That left only two out of our crew on board of the Anford-
   Wright.

6 Now the Anford-Wright is lost and gone, both passengers and
   crew,
Besides thirty-five as brave sailor lads, as ever wore jackets blue.
God grant relief to those poor souls, and to those lamenting quite;
God grant relief to those poor souls on board of the Anford-
   Wright.

88

THE BRAMBLE BRIAR

Two fairly good copies of the ballad have been found in West Virginia under the titles, "The Bamboo Briers" and "The Bomberry Brier." In story they do not differ materially.

For a full discussion of this song, known in England as "In Bruton Town," and its Old World connections see Belden's paper, "Boccaccio, Hans Sachs, and The Bramble Briar" (*Publications of the Modern Language Association*, XXXIII, 327). See also *Journal*, XXIX, 168; XXXV, 359; Pound, No. 22; Payne, *Publications of the Texas Folk-Lore Society*, II (1923), 6.

A

"The Bamboo Briers." Contributed by Mr. Decker Toney, Queens Ridge, Wayne County, January 20, 1916; learned from his mother, Hannah Moore, who learned it from her mother, Hannah Ross, a native of Virginia.

1 Across Bridgewater a rich man lived,
  He had three sons and a daughter fair;
  He divided up their equal portion,
  Seven thousand pounds was his daughter's share.

2 Seven thousand was his daughter's portion,
  The maid being brisk and a comely dame;
  She fancied a young man who plowed the ocean,
  And unto him she bestowed the same.

3 One night, as they were setting courting,
  Her two brothers chanced to overhear;
  They vowed the courtship should be broken,
  Or send him headlong to his grave.

4 So early next morning they forced him hunting,
  Over high hills and lofty mountains,
  Through silent places quite unknown,
  Until they came to bamboo briers,
  Where they did him kill and slay.

5 As soon as they returned from hunting,
  She quickly asked for the servant-man:
  "You seem to whisper, what makes me ask you,
  Pray, brothers, tell me, if you can."

6 "We lost him in our game of hunting,
  His face again you will nevermore see;
  We lost him in the bamboo briers,
  His face, his face, you'll see no more."

7   Early next morning she started to hunt him,
        Over hills and lofty mountains,
        Through silent places quite unknown,
    Until she came to the bamboo briers,
        There she found him killed and slain.

8   Three days and nights she stayed there with him,
        Kissing him just as he lay:
    "One grave will bury us both, my darling;
        I'll stay here with you until I die."

9   Three days and nights she stayed there with him,
        Seeking life for her sad mourn;
    She felt sharp hunger come creeping o'er her,
        And back home she was forced to return.

10 When she returned from where they were hunting,
        They quickly asked, "Where's the servant-man?"
    "You cursed villains did that murder,
        And for the crime you both shall hang."

11 Then they both darkened their faces,
        They walked slowly off down by the seaside;
    The fearful waves rushed from the ocean,
        And caused their faces from this world to hide.

ℬ

"The Bomberry Brier." Communicated by Mr. S. L. Moore, Burton, Wetzel County.

1   A rich man once lived near Bridgewater,
        He had two sons, one daughter fair;
    From life to death he did believe in,
        To crown his children's life with care.

2   A certain man bound by the mansion,
        All for to plow the raging main;
    O he was of a fair complexion,
        Neat and handsome every limb.

3   On him their sister placed her affections,
        Unawares to any of them;
    She told the secret to her oldest brother,
        Who chanced to see them sport and play.

4 "Now maybe he's of some poor family,
    And thinks our sister he will have;
But we'll put an end to all his courtship,
    And quickly send him to his grave."

5 Now to begin their cruel murder,
    A game of hunting they must go;
With him they did both coax and flatter,
    A game of hunting for to go.

6 When they came near a leafy woodside,
    Where harmless birds did sport and play,
At length they came to the bomberry brier,
    Where they took his sweet life away.

7 When they came home, their sister asked them,
    "What have you done with your servant-man?"
"We lost him in the game of hunting;
    No more of him you'll see again."

8 She rose early, early the next morning,
    Travelled all day alone, alone, alone;
At length she came to the bomberry brier,
    Where his cold body there was thrown.

9 She stayed there three days and nights,
    All alone, alone, alone;
Until she felt sharp hunger creeping,
    Which did oblige her to go home.

10 When she came home her brothers asked her,
    "What makes you look so pale and worn?
The reason is you are offended,
    Now why not leave, leave him alone?"

11 "Now maybe you think I'll hide this murder,
    But I will do no such a thing;
Now since you've robbed me of my jewel,
    For him alone you both shall swing."

12 Now they are confined in prison,
    Now they are condemned to die;
And she lay in her chamber weeping,
    And giving up herself to die.

89

COME, PRETTY POLLY

THE three West Virginia texts represent "Polly's Love, or, The Cruel Ship Carpenter," an English song in eleven stanzas, which is a condensation of "The Gosport Tragedy; or, The Perjured Ship Carpenter," a long broadside ballad that goes back at least to the middle of the eighteenth century (Ebsworth, *Roxburghe Ballads*, VIII, 143, 173). Polly's lover is a ship carpenter. After the murder he goes to sea, but the ship "cannot sail on," because he is on board. The captain suspects that there is a murderer among the crew. William, like the rest, protests innocence, but he is torn to pieces by Polly's ghost. In "The Gosport Tragedy" the ghost appears before the ship sails, and the captain is afraid to leave port with a murderer as shipmate; the ghost causes the guilty man to die raving distracted. For references see Kittredge, *Journal*, XX, 261. Add Ashton, *Real Sailor-Songs*, 86, and *A Century of Ballads*, p. 101; Sharp, *Folk-Songs from Somerset*, IV, 8; broadsides by Catnach, Such (No. 142), Dalton (York, No. 17), Gilbert (Newcastle, No. 59), Cadman (Manchester, No. 213), Bebbington (Manchester, No. 343). A comic version of "Polly's Love" called "Molly the Betrayed, or The Fog-bound Vessel" was popular on the English stage about the middle of the last century (broadsides by Bebbington, Manchester, No. 477; W. S. Fortey; *Sam Cowell's Budget from Yankee Land*, p. [12]; cf. Ebsworth, *Roxburghe Ballads*, VIII, 143).

For American texts from oral tradition see *Journal*, XX, 262 (Kentucky); Campbell and Sharp, No. 39 (Kentucky, North Carolina, Tennessee); Mackenzie, p. 55 (Nova Scotia: "The Gaspard Tragedy"). "The Gosport Tragedy" was printed in this country as a chapbook (at Philadelphia?) in 1816, and again (at Philadelphia) in 1829 (Harvard College Library, 25276, 43, 81). It occurs also in *The New American Song Book* (Philadelphia, 1817), p. 69, in *The Forget Me Not Songster* (New York, Nafis & Cornish), p. 232, and elsewhere. There is an American broadside of about 1820, "The Ship Carpenter, or, The Gosport Tragedy" (Harvard College Library).

A

"Come, Pretty Polly." Contributed by Miss Esther M. Jarrell, Van, Boone County, June, 1916; learned from her sister, Miss Gladys Jarrell.

1   "Come, pretty Polly, come go with me,
    Come, pretty Polly, come go with me,
    Come, pretty Polly, come go with me,
    Before we get married some pleasure to see."

2   He led her o'er hills and dark valleys so deep,
    He led her o'er hills and dark valleys so deep,
    He led her o'er hills and dark valleys so deep,
    And then pretty Polly began to weep.

3 "O Willie, O Willie, I'm afraid of your way,
   O Willie, O Willie, I'm afraid of your way,
   O Willie, O Willie, I'm afraid of your way,
   I'm afraid you are leading me astray."

4 "Polly, pretty Polly, you've guessed just right,
   Polly, pretty Polly, you've guessed just right,
   Polly, pretty Polly, you've guessed just right,
   For I dug on your grave a part of last night!"

5 No time to study, no time to stand,
   No time to study, no time to stand,
   No time to study, no time to stand,
   He drew his knife out all in his right hand.

6 He stabbed her to the heart, and the blood did flow,
   He stabbed her to the heart, and the blood did flow,
   He stabbed her to the heart, and the blood did flow,
   And into her grave pretty Polly did go.

7 He threw some dirt o'er and turned to go home,
   He threw some dirt o'er and turned to go home,
   He threw some dirt o'er and turned to go home,
   Leaving no one but the birds to mourn.

8 Come, gents and ladies, I bid you good-night,
   Come, gents and ladies, I bid you good-night,
   Come, gents and ladies, I bid you good-night,
   And raving distracted he died that same night.

𝓑

"Polly and Sweet William." Contributed by Miss Polly F. McKinney,
Sophia, Raleigh County, 1919.

1 "O Polly, O Polly, O Polly," said he,
   "You had better consent and be married to me."
   "O William, O William, O William," said she,
   "I am too young to be married to thee."

2 He took her by the hand and away he did go,
   He led her over the mountains and the valleys so low;
   He led her a little farther and she began to cry;
   The grave was ready dug, and the spade a-standing by.

3   She threw her arms around him, saying, "I am in no fear.
How could you kill a poor girl who loves you so dear?"
He pulled out her breast, just as white as any snow,
He pulled out his knife and the blood began to flow.

4   Now down in the grave this poor lady did go,
Left nothing but a small bird to tell poor Polly's woe;
"I once loved as pretty a woman as ever the sun shone on;
I once enjoyed her beauty, but now my fair one's gone."

C

"Young Beeham." Contributed by Professor Walter Barnes; obtained
from Mr. G. W. Cunningham, Elkins, Randolph County.

I   .   .   .   .
.   .   .   .
"O pity your infant and spare my sweet life,
And I'll go distressed and not be your wife."

2   He stepped up to her with a knife in his hand,
Saying, "Come, fairest Polly, no time for to stand."
He pierced her to the heart, the blood it did flow;
He covered her over and home he did go.

3   Charles Green, a bold sailor, of courage so brave,
Was hunting one night and he stepped on her grave,
And a beautiful woman to him did appear,
And she in her arms held a baby so fair.

4   "O captain, O captain, some murder's been done!
Far away from this harbor our ship ne'er can run;
For a beautiful woman to me did appear,
And she in her arms held a baby so fair."

90

THE WEXFORD GIRL (THE CRUEL MILLER)

In West Virginia this ballad is known as "The Tragedy" and as "Johnny McDowell." It has been found in oral circulation in Virginia and Tennessee (*Focus*, IV, 370), Missouri (Belden, *Journal*, XXV, 11), and Kentucky (Shearin and Combs, pp. 13, 28). Belden has noted that it is "a reduction of 'The Wittam Miller.'" Of "The Berkshire Tragedy, or, The Wittam Miller" the Harvard College Library has English broadsides of the eighteenth and the early nineteenth century (Stonecutter-street, Fleet Market; J. Evans; Howard & Evans; Turner, Coventry; Pitts; cf. *Roxburghe Ballads*, ed. Ebsworth, VIII, ii, 629). According to an Edinburgh chapbook of 1744 (catalogued by Halliwell, *Notices of Fugitive Tracts*, Percy Society, XXIX, 90), the miller's name was John Mauge and he was hanged at Reading (Berkshire) in that year. An American broadside of the early part of the nineteenth century (Boston, Corner of Cross and Fulton Streets) affords a condensed version of "The Wittam Miller" under the title of "The Lexington Miller." A condensed text, "The Cruel Miller," substantially like the West Virginia version, is found in modern English broadsides (Catnach; Ryle; Such, No. 622); see also *Journal of the Folk-Song Society*, VII, 23, and cf. Baring-Gould and Sheppard, *Songs of the West*, IV, xxx.

A

"The Tragedy." Communicated by Miss Marie Rennar, Morgantown, Monongalia County; obtained from Mrs. Dayton Wiles, who learned it from her mother, who lived many years in the mountains near Rowlesburg, Preston County.

1 There was a rich old farmer in Wexford divine,
Who had two charming daughters; for my love they did pine.
I went to see those charming girls just eight o'clock at night;
Little did poor sister dear, when I left her in great spite.

2 I asked the other to take a walk and view the meadow o'er,
So we might have a chance to talk, and appoint our wedding
hour.
We strolled along both hand in hand, till we came to the level
ground;
I drew a stake out of the hedge and knocked my fair one down.

3 She fell upon her bended knees, and for mercy she did cry:
"O Johnny, dear, don't murder me here, for I'm not prepared
to die!"
I took her by the curly locks, and dragged her o'er the ground,
And threw her into the waters that ran through Wexford town.

4 Straight home, straight, poor Johnny went at twelve o'clock
    that night,
  Which caused his aged mother to wake up in great fright:
  "O Johnny dear, what have you done?   There are bloodstains
    on your hands!"
  The answer that he gave her was, "Bleeding at the nose."

5 He asked her for a candle to light him up to bed,
  While the groans and moans of the Wexford girl went roaming
    through his head.
  Six or seven days afterward the Wexford girl was found,
  A-floating on the waters that run through Wexford town.

6 Marshall came and arrested me and dragged me off to jail;
  There was no one to pity me, no one to go my bail.
  Now come, all you tender-hearted men, and warning take in
    time;
  Never murder a poor girl, or your fate will be like mine.

ℬ

"Johnny McDowell."   Contributed by Miss Snoah McCourt, Orndoff, Webster County, May, 1916.

1 'T was in the town of Woxford, where I did live and dwell,
  'T was in the town of Woxford I owned a flowery dell.
  'T was there I courted a pretty fair miss with a dark and rolling
    eye;
  I asked if she'd marry me; these words she did comply.

2 'T was on one Saturday evening, I came to her sister's house;
  I asked her if she'd walk with me, and the wedding day appoint.
  We walked along together, till we came to the level ground;
  I drew a stake from the fence and knocked this fair miss down.

3 All on her bended knees, how for mercy she did cry!
  "Johnny McDowell, don't murder me, for I'm not prepared to
    die."
  I hated for to kill her, but I beat her all the more;
  I beat her till her body lay a-bleeding in the gore.

4 I took her by her yellow locks and dragged her o'er the sand,
  And threw her in the water that flowed through Woxford town.
  'T was twelve o'clock that very same night, when I came to my
    mother's house,
  I asked for a candle to light me up to bed, also for a handkerchief
    to bind my aching head.

5 "Son, O son, what have you done?   How came this blood upon
      your clothes?"
  The answer that I made to her was, "The bleeding of my nose."
  I rolled and kicked and tumbled, but no rest could I find;
  The flames of hell so brightly then before my eyes did shine.

6 Her sister swore my life, for reasons I've no doubt;
  She swore I was the very identical man that led her sister out.

.   .   .   .

.   .   .   .

91

ROSE CONNOLEY

WHAT seems to be a different version of this song is cited by Shearin and Combs, p. 28, as "Rose Colalee." The girl is murdered on the bank of a river, by her lover, who, intoxicated with Burgundy wine, is persuaded to slay her, by his father's promise of money.

A

Communicated by Mr. M. F. Morgan, Ravenswood, Jackson County, October 15, 1915; obtained from Mr. F. A. Morgan. It was popular in the oil fields of Wetzel County about 1895.

1 Rose Connoley loved me as dearly as she loved her life,
And many's the time I've told her I'd make her my lawful wife.
But Satan and Satan's temptation have overpowered me,
And caused me to murder that fair young maid they called Rose
  Connoley.

2 One night down there by the garden my love and I did meet,
And there we sat discoursing, till at length she fell asleep.
I had a bottle of merkley[1] wine, and this she did not know;
So there I poisoned my own true love, down there by the river
  below.

3 I ran my skeever through her — it was a bloody knife —
And threw her into the river — it was a shocking sight.
I threw her into the river, the worst now you may see,
For my name it is Patsey O'Railly, who murdered Rose Con-
  noley.

4 My father has often told me that money would set me free,
If ever I murdered that fair young maid they call Rose Con-
  noley,
My father may stand in his cottage door with many a watering
  eye,
And gaze upon his own dear son, swinging on the gallows high.

5 .   .   .   .
   .   .   .   .
O my race is run below the sun, and hell it is gaping for me;
For my name it is Patsey O'Railly, who murdered Rose Con-
  noley.

[1] Error for *Burgundy?*

B

Contributed by Mr. Warren C. Steele, Walker, Wood County, January, 1917; learned from Mr. D. L. Plumley, Logan County.

1 Come all young men and pretty fair ladies, and warning take
        from me;
  And never go a-courting down under the willow tree.

2 Down under the willow garden, me and my true love was to
        meet;
  It was there we talked about courting, until she fell asleep.

3 I had a bottle of burglar's wine, which my true love did not know;
  It was then I poisoned my own true love, down under the banks
        below.

4 My father had often told me that his money would set me free,
  If I would murder the pretty, fair lady who they called Rosie
        Condoley.

5 My name is . . . Morrison, my name I'll never deny,
  Who murdered that pretty fair lady, who now does dwell on
        high.

92

A PRETTY FAIR MAIDEN

THIS song is regularly entitled "The Sailor's Return" in English broadsides. Sharp calls it "The Broken Token." For American texts see *Journal*, XXII, 67 (Beatty; Kentucky), 379 (Barry; Massachusetts, from Ireland); XXIX, 201 (Rawn and Peabody; Georgia); Belden, *Herrig's Archiv*, CXX, 64, 65; Wyman and Brockway, p. 88 (Kentucky); Campbell and Sharp, No. 98 (North Carolina); Child MSS., II, 161 (Massachusetts, ca. 1800); Mackenzie, p. 133 (Nova Scotia); Kittredge MSS., IV, 53 (New York); VII, 183, 195 (Indiana, Virginia); XIII, 60 (Virginia). Cf. Shearin and Combs, p. 27.

For British references see Campbell and Sharp, p. 334. Add *The Vocal Library* (London, 1822), p. 525; Catnach broadside ("The Sailor's Return"); Such broadside, No. 126 ("Young and Single Sailor").

A

No local title. Communicated by Mr. Guy Overholt, Erwin, Preston County, who obtained it from Mr. Ralph Buckley, Buckeye, Pocahontas County.

1 A pretty fair maid out in a garden,
    A brisk young man she chanced to see;
  As he stepped o'er a style to view her,
    Saying, "Pretty maid, won't you marry me?"

2 "Indeed, kind sir, you're a man of honor;
    A gentleman you seem to be;
  How can you press a poor young woman,
    Who is not fit your bride to be?

3 "My true love is in the army;
    Three long years he's been from me;
  Seven more I will wait for him;
    If he's alive, he will return to me."

4 "Your true love he may be married,
    Or in some battlefield been slain;
  Your true love he may be drowned,
    And never return to you again."

5 "If he is married, I love him dearly,
    I love the girl he is married to;
  If he is drowned, I hope he is happy,
    No other man shall enjoy me."

6 He slipped his hand into his pocket,
      His fingers being long and slim;
   He pulled the ring that was broken between them,
      And at her true love's feet she fell.

7 He picked her up for to embrace her,
      And gave to her those kisses three,
   Saying, "I am the poor single soldier,
      Just come from the war to marry thee."

B

"A Fair Maiden." Communicated by Mr. George Paugh, Thomas, Tucker County, October, 1915; obtained from Mrs. George Yankee. Stanzas 6 and 7 are borrowed from another song (see p. 465).

1 A fair maid all in the garden,
      A gay soldier came riding by;
   Says he, "Pretty fair maid, won't you marry me?
      O pretty fair maid, won't you marry me?"

2 "O no, kind sir! you are a stranger;
      You're not the man I took you to be;
   I have a fair-way [1] single soldier,
      It's seven long years he's been gone from me.

3 "I love that man and I love him only;
      Still I wonder if he's true;
   And if he's gone the seven years longer,
      No man on earth shall marry me."

4 "O he may be in some battle slain;
      O he may be in some ocean drowned;
   O he may be to some fair girl married,
      A-living well at his command!"

5 "O if he's in some battle slain;
      O if he's in some ocean drowned;
   O if he's to some fair girl married,
      I love the girl that married him!"

6 "O maiden, I have gold and silver,
      O maiden, I have house and land;
   O maiden, I have the world of pleasure,
      And you may have it at your command."

[1] Possibly for *far-away.*

7 "O what do I care for gold and silver,
  O what do I care for house and land?
  O what do I care for the world of pleasure?
   It's all I want is a nice young man!"

8 "O maiden, don't you stand on beauty,
  For beauty is a fading flower;
  For the fairest rose in yonder garden,
   Will fade away in half an hour."

9 He put his arms around her body,
  He gave her a kiss, 't is one, two, three;
  Says, "I am your fair-away single soldier,
   Returning home for to marry thee."

C

"A Pretty Fair Maiden All in the Garden." Communicated by Mr. J. Harrison Miller, Wardensville, Hardy County, January 24, 1916; obtained from his mother, who learned it from her mother, who had it from her grandmother, Mrs. Strawnsnider. Five stanzas.

D

"The Fair Damsel." Communicated by Professor C. E. Haworth, Huntington, Cabell County; obtained from Mrs. J. A. Rollyson, who says it is familiar down on the Big Sandy River. Four stanzas.

E

No local title. Communicated by Mrs. Hilary G. Richardson, Clarksburg, Harrison County, 1917; obtained from Mrs. Nancy McAtee. Six stanzas.

F

"Pretty Fair Maid." Communicated by Mr. C. R. Bishop, Morgantown, Monongalia County; obtained from Mrs. E. E. Harris. Two stanzas.

93

THE BROKEN RING

THIS is the English "Fair Phœbe and her Dark-eyed Sailor"; see Ashton, *Real Sailor-Songs*, 71; Baring-Gould and Sharp, *Folk-Songs for Schools*, No. 40, p. 82; *Journal of the Folk-Song Society*, IV, 129; Greig, *Folk-Song of the North-East*, CXII; broadsides (Catnach; W. S. Fortey; Such, No. 2; W. R. Walker, Newcastle, No. 8; John Livsey, No. 79; G. Jacques, No. 71; Cadman, No. 133; Bebbington, No. 73 — (the last four printed at Manchester).

It is common in American songbooks: *Uncle Sam's Naval and Patriotic Songster*, p. 6; *Home Sentimental Songster* (New York, T. W. Strong), p. 160; *Marsh's Selection* (New York, 1854), III, 69; *De Witt's "Forget-Me-Not" Songster* (cop. 1872), p. 80; *Partridge's New National Songster*, I, 5; *Singer's Journal*, I, 39; J. Andrews broadside, List 3, No. 71; Wehman broadside, No. 406. A text from Maine is given by Gray, *Songs of the Lumberjacks*, p. 109.

Communicated by Miss Mildred Joy Barker, Morgantown, Monongalia County; obtained from her mother, who learned it from her father, Martin Brookover.

1 'T is of a comely young lady fair,
  Who was walking out to take the air;
    She met a soldier upon the way,
  So I paid attention, so I paid attention,
    To hear what they would say.

2 "Fair maid," said he, "why roam along,
  The night is coming and the day's far gone?"
    She said, while tears from her eyes did fall,
  "It's my dark-eyed sailor, it's my dark-eyed sailor,
    That's proving my downfall.

3 "It's three long years since he left this land,
  Then a golden ring he took off my hand;
    He broke the token, here's half with me,
  And the other half is rolling, and the other half is rolling,
    At the bottom of the sea."

4 Cried William, "Drive him from your mind;
  As good a sailor as him you'll find;
    Love turned aside once, cold does grow,
  Like a winter morning, like a winter
    When hills are clad with snow."

5 These words did Phœbe's fond heart inflame;
  She cried, "On me you shall play no game;
    Genteel he was, no rake like you,
  To advise a maiden, to advise a maiden,
    To slight the jacket blue."

6 When William did the ring unfold,
  She seemed distracted with joy untold,
    Crying, "William, William, I have lands and gold,
  For my noble sailor, for my noble sailor,
    So manly, true and bold."

7 In a cottage down by the river side,
  In unity and love they now reside;
    So girls be true, while your lover 's away,
  For a cloudy morning, for a cloudy morning,
    Oft brings a pleasant day.

94

THE BANKS OF CLAUDIE

"THE BANKS OF CLAUDY" is well known in England, Scotland, and Ireland; several American texts and one from Nova Scotia have been recovered. It circulated widely in songbooks. A droll parody was popular on the minstrel stage in the fifties and sixties of the last century. For full references see *Journal*, XXVI, 362; XXXV, 351; add Pound, No. 30.

A

Contributed by Anna Copley, Shoals, Wayne County, December 28, 1915; learned when she was a child, from Julia Stephenson Luther. A second text, B, the same as A with some omissions, was contributed by Miss Lalah Lovett, Bulltown, Braxton County, May, 1917; obtained from John N. Wine, of Napier, who learned it from Stanley Conrad ("Clody Banks").

1 As I walked out one evening, all in the month of May,
   Down by the flowery garden, where Betsey she did stray,
   I overheard this damsel in sorrow to complain,
   About her absent lover, who plowed the raging main.

2 I stepped up to this fair maid; I put her in surprise;
   She owned she did not know me, me being in disguise:
   "My only dearest darling, my soul and heart's delight,
   How far have you to wander this dark and stormy night?"

3 "Is this the banks of Claudie, or would you please to show?
   Pity a maid distracted, for I am forced to go
   In search of a young man, and Johnny is his name,
   And on the banks of Claudie I'm told he does remain."

4 "This is the banks of Claudie, the banks on which you stand;
   But do not believe in Johnny, for he's a false young man.
   Do not believe in Johnny, for he'll not meet you here,
   But stay with me till morning, no danger need you fear."

5 "Oh, if Johnny was here to-night, he'd keep me from all harm;
   But he's in the field of battle, all in his uniform;
   He's in the field of battle, his foes he defies;
   Like some bright king of honor, he's gone the war to try."

6 "It's been six weeks and better, since Johnny left the shore;
   He's sailing the wild ocean, where foaming billows roar;
   He's sailing the wide ocean for honor and great gain;
   The ship's been lost, so I've been told, along the coast of Spain."

7 When she heard this sad news, she fell into despair,
A-wringing of her hands and a-tearing of her hair;
Saying, "Since he's gone and left me, no other will I take,
But in some lonesome valley I'll wander for his sake."

8 When he saw her love was loyal, he could no longer stand,
But sprang into her arms, saying, "Betsey, I'm your man!
I am that faithful young man, the cause of all your pain,
And since we've met on Claudie's banks, we ne'er shall part
    again."

95

GEORGE REILLY

THE West Virginia ballad reproduces, with a remarkable degree of accuracy, the text printed in *The New American Songster* (Philadelphia, 1817), p. 9; *The Forget Me Not Songster* (New York, Nafis & Cornish), p. 150; *The New American Song Book and Letter Writer* (Louisville), p. 130; *The American Songster*, edited by John Kenedy (Baltimore, 1836), p. 40; same (N. Y., 1851), p. 40; *The American Songster* (Philadelphia, 1850), p. 149; *The Popular Forget Me Not Songster, Popular Songs*, p. 130; *March's Selection* (New York, 1854), III, 149. The song was printed as a broadside at Boston very early in the nineteenth century ("George Riley": Ford, Massachusetts Broadsides, No. 3125). It may be found, under the style of "The Constant Damsel," in a little Dublin songbook of 1791, *The Vocal Enchantress*, p. 22.

The short song printed as "George Reilly" by Campbell and Sharp, No. 82, and as "John Riley" by Wyman and Brockway, p. 37, is identical in situation, but differs in meter and phraseology. This "George Reilly" is a modified form of the "Young Riley" of modern broadsides (Catnach; Such, No. 83; Fortey; Harvard College, 25242.17, VI, 186, No. 341). In the last stanza the Wyman text shows the influence of "The Sailor's Return" (No. 92, above). Kittredge has a copy without this stanza ("The Coast of Garba") from an American MS. of the early nineteenth century: the lover is "one young Reilly."

A

"George Reily." Communicated by Miss Sallie Evans, Elkins, Randolph County; obtained from Mr. Orra G. Workman, who got it from his grandmother, Mrs. Lucinda Waldo.

1 One bright summer morning, the weather being clear,
   I strolled for recreation, the better for to hear,
   Where I overheard a damsel most grievously complain,
   All for her absent lover, who plowed the raging main.

2 I, being unperceived, did unto her draw near,
   Where I lay me down in ambush, the better for to hear.
   With doleful lamentations and melancholy cries,
   Whilst sparkling tears like crystal were streaming from her eyes,

3 Crying, "O cruel fortune to me has proved unkind!
   As my true love has left me, no comfort can I find."
   While she was lamenting, and grieving for her dear,
   I saw a gallant sailor, who unto her drew near.

4 With eloquence most complacent he did address the fair,
   Crying, "Sweet and lovely fair one, why do you mourn there?"
   "All for an absent lover," the maiden did reply,
   "Which causes me to wander, for to lament and cry.

5 "It's three long years and more his absence I have mourned,
   And now the way is ended, he has not yet returned."
   "Why should you grieve for him alone?" the sailor he did say;
   "Perhaps his mind is altered, or changed some other way.

6 "If you will but forget him, and fix your heart on me,
   To you I'll faithful prove, . . .
   To which the fair one answered, "Sir, that can never be;
   I never can admire any other man but he.

7 "He is the darling of my heart, none else can I admire;
   So take this for an answer, and trouble me no more."
   Then said the gallant sailor: "What is your true-love's name?
   Both that and his description, I wish to know the same.

8 "It really is most surprising that he was so unkind
   As to leave so fair a creature in sorrow here behind."
   "George Reily I do call him, a lad both neat and trim;
   So manly in deportment that few can excel him.

9 "His amber locks with ringlets, his sturdy shoulders bare,
   And his skin far exceeding the fragrant lily fair."
   "Fair maid, I had a messmate, George Reily was his name;
   I'm sure from your description that he must be the same.

10 "Three years we spent together on board the old Belflew,
   And such a gallant comrade before I never knew.
   It was on the twelfth of April, near to Port Royal Bay,
   We had a tight engagement before the break of day,

11 "Between the Rodney and DeGrasse, where many a man did
   fall;
   Your true love he fell by a French cannon ball.
   Whilst wallowing in his blood your generous lover lay,
   With faltering voice and broken sighs, these are the words I
   heard him say:

12 "'Farewell, my dearest Nancy! were you but standing by,
   To gaze your last upon me, contented would I die.'"
   This melancholy story wounded her so deep,
   She wrung her hands in anguish and bitterly did weep,

13 Crying, "My joys now are ended, if what you say is true;
   Instead of having pleasures, I've naught but grief in view."
   On hearing which, his person no longer he concealed;
   He flew into her arms, his person he revealed.

14 Now these constant lovers did each other embrace;
   He kissed her bright tears from her cheeks and wiped her lovely
      face,
   Crying, "My dearest Nancy, with you I'll ever stay;
   I'll never more depart till my mainmast's cut away."

ℬ

"John Reilly." Communicated by Professor Walter Barnes, Fairmont, Marion County, July, 1915; obtained from Mr. G. W. Cunningham, Elkins, Randolph County, who learned it from Solomon Rhodeman, Pendleton County. Imperfect version in eight stanzas.

C

"John the German." Communicated by Mr. Fred Smith, Glenville, Gilmer County; obtained from Mr. Roy Turner. Fragment of six stanzas.

96

WILLIAM HALL

THE longer of the two texts found in West Virginia is somewhat confused and the shorter is a fragment. The theme is that of the returned sailor or soldier. For American texts see Wyman and Brockway, p. 100 (Kentucky); Belden, *Herrig's Archiv*, CXX, 65 (Missouri); Pound, No. 29 ("The Rich Young Farmer"); Sharp, *Folk-Songs of English Origin Collected in the Southern Appalachians*, 2d Series, p. 32 (Kentucky). Cf. Pound, p. 15 (*Journal*, XXVI, 355); Shearin and Combs, pp. 11, 12; Shearin, *Sewanee Review*, XIX, 322; Belden, *Journal*, XXV, 7.

A

Communicated by Professor Walter Barnes, Fairmont, Marion County, July, 1915; obtained from Mr. G. W. Cunningham, Elkins, Randolph County, who learned it from Solomon Rhodeman of Pendleton County.

1   There was a jolly, brisk young farmer,
    Round Alexandria town,
Who courted a fair and handsome lady
    Of credit and renown.

2   It grieved his parents' hearts to know,
    It grieved his parents' hearts full sore;
They said they would send him over the ocean,
    Where he'd see his love no more.

3   He sailed around and over the ocean,
    Till he came to his own native land,
Saying, "If Molly is alive and I can find her,
    I'll make her my own sweet bride."

4   'T was early, 't was early the next morning,
    While he was walking on the strand,
A golden ranger, just as it happened,
    Meets Miss Molly walking along.

5   "O good-morning, good-morning, my fair pretty lady!
    O do you think you could fancy me?"
"O no, kind sir! my fancy is a farmer,
    Who has lately crossed the sea."

6   "Describe him, describe him, my fair pretty lady,
    O describe him unto me;
Perhaps I saw the sword go through him,
    As I lately crossed the sea."

7 "My true love is tall and slender,
   My true love is handsome too;
He has dark hair and wears it curlèd
   In most graceful ringlets fall.

8 "O cruel, cruel-hearted parents,
   O cruel-hearted parents!" cried she;
"O now we are parted, broken-hearted,
   O my heart shall burst in three!"

9 "Cheer up, cheer up, my fair pretty maid!
   Perhaps I am the very man."
She ran, she flew, she ran unto him,
   And embraced him in her arms.

ℬ

Communicated by Mrs. Elizabeth Tapp Peck, Morgantown, Marion County, March 26, 1916; obtained from her mother, who learned it from her mother, Mrs. Elizabeth Wade Mack.

1 "Good-morning, good-morning, my fair pretty maid!
   Do you think you could fancy me?"
"O no, kind sir, my fancy's a farmer,
   And he's lately crossed the sea."

    .   .   .   .

2 "My love, he is fair in every feature;
   He is proper, straight and tall;
His hair is black and he wears it parted,
   With the most graceful ringlets fall."

3 "O yes, I know him, I have seen him,
   And his name is William Hall;
I saw a cannon ball go through him,
   As I lately crossed the sea."

Mrs. Tapp could remember no more of the words, but the questioner finally revealed himself as the lover.

97

JOHNNY GERMANY

AMERICAN texts are reported by Belden, No. 31, and F. C. Brown, p. 10. Belden prints a copy from Missouri in *Herrig's Archiv*, cxx, 63. Mr. Kittredge informs me that two lines of the song, with a summary of the story, were reported from Virginia in 1907. The West Virginia text is almost word for word identical with that printed in a Boston broadside of about 1820 ("Johnny Jarman") with "The Lexington Miller."

Communicated by Anna Copley, Shoals, Wayne County, December 28, 1915; obtained from Mr. Luther Burwell, who learned it when he was a child, from his mother.

1 'T was of a brisk young sailor, as I have heard it said;
He met a pretty fair damsel, her countenance looked sad;
He asked her the reason what made her look so down;
So modestly she answered, without one smile or frown:

2 "'T is for the loss of my true love, since from me he has gone,
And I have no love token, that ever he 'll return."
"Perhaps I saw your true love when I was last at sea;
And I 'll relate it over, if this you 'll answer me:

3 "He belonged to the Rainbow, and was under Captain Lowe,
By the name of Johnny Germany. Is this the name or no?"
"He belonged to the Rainbow, and was under Captain Lowe,
By the name of Johnny Germany." "He's been dead five months or more."

4 She turned her back unto him and not one word did say;
She turned her back unto him, and straight she went away;
She went unto her chamber, and there she wept and cried,
And sorely she lamented and wished that she might die.

5 He dressed himself in scarlet and back to her he came,
With a jovial resolution to comfort her again:
"Cheer up, cheer up, pretty Polly, and leave your tears behind;
Cheer up, cheer up, pretty Polly, and comfort you shall find."

6 "My loving Johnny Germany, what made you serve me so?"
"O hold your tongue, pretty Polly! I 'll serve you so no more.
I only did it for to try you, to see how true you were.

. . . .

7 "You are truer than the turtle dove; you are redder than the
     rose;
  You are like some blooming blossom; your love and beauty
     flows."
  Polly lived an honest life, all bad company she's shunned;
  Polly's lived in Johnny's favor, till at length his heart she's won.

8 "Farewell unto the Rainbow, since Polly's won my heart!
  And we will now be married before we do part.
  Farewell unto the Rainbow, since Polly's won my heart!
  We will live together till death us part."

98

JACKIE FRAISURE

Two good copies of this well-known ballad have been found in West Virginia, the second going under the title of "The Merchant's Daughter." Belden (*Journal*, XXV, 9) characterizes stanzas 6, 7 (of A) as the "poetic core" of the song and believes they are borrowed from "William and Polly" (Belden, No. 15; Mackenzie, p. 135; Campbell and Sharp, No. 68).

The song ("Jack Munro," "Jackaro," "Jacky Frasier") is common in Great Britain. For British and American references see *Journal*, XX, 269; XXXV, 377.

A

"Jackie Fraisure." Contributed by Mr. John B. Adkins, Branchland, Lincoln County, April 1, 1916.

1   There once lived a rich merchant,
        In London he did dwell;
    He had an only daughter,
        The truth to you I'll tell,
        Ah, the truth to you I'll tell.

2   She had beaus a-plenty,
        To count both day and night,
    And none but Jackie Fraisure
        Could gain her heart's delight,
        Ah, could gain her heart's delight.

3   He called to his daughter;
        So quickly she stepped in;
    Said, "Good morning, Mrs. Fraisure,
        If that's your sweetheart's name,
        Ah, if that's your sweetheart's name.

4   "Ah daughter, ah daughter!
        I say you had better mind;
    I'll lock you in the dungeon,
        Your body there confine,
        Ah, your body there confine."

5   "You can lock me in the dungeon,
        My body there confine,
    But none but Jackie Fraisure
        Can ever suit my mind,
        Ah, can ever suit my mind."

6   "Your waist is slim and tender,
        Your fingers are too small,
    Your cheeks too red and rosy,
        To face a cannon ball,
        Ah, to face a cannon ball."

7   "I know my waist is slim and tender,
        My fingers are quite small,
    But my heart is large a-plenty
        To face a cannon ball,
        Ah, to face a cannon ball."

8   And now poor Jackie's sailing
        All o'er the deep blue sea,
    And now poor Jackie's sailing,
        With his darling girl behind,
        Ah, with his darling girl behind.

9   And now poor Jackie's landed,
        All o'er the deep blue sea,
    And now poor Jackie's landed
        In the wars of Germany,
        Ah, in the wars of Germany.

10 And now poor Mary is sailing,
        All o'er the deep blue sea,
    And now poor Mary is sailing
        To the wars of Germany,
        Ah, to the wars of Germany.

11 And now poor Mary is landed,
        All o'er the deep blue sea,
    And now poor Mary is landed
        In the wars of Germany,
        Ah, in the wars of Germany.

12 She hunted the battle-ground
        All over and over again;
    Among the dead and wounded
        Her darling boy she found,
        Ah, her darling boy she found.

13   She picked him up all in her arms
         And carried him to town,
      She sent the physician
         To heal his deadly wounds,
         Ah, to heal his deadly wounds.

14   And now Miss Mary's married
         And living at her ease,
      And now Miss Mary's married,
         And why not you and me?
         Ah, and why not you and me?

B

"The Merchant's Daughter." Communicated by Mr. J. Harrison Miller, Hardy County, January 29, 1916; obtained from his mother, who learned it when a child from her parents. She thinks her father learned it in Massachusetts, where he lived before he came to West Virginia.

1   There was a rich merchant, in London he did dwell;
     He had a lovely daughter; the truth to you I'll tell.
     This daughter had been courted by many lords and kings;
     But none but Jack the sailor, who has this heart of mine.

2   Young Jack he's going a-sailing with trouble on his mind:
     The leaving of his country, his darling girl behind.
     "If this be true, dear daughter, of which I hear of thee,
     O Jack he shall be banished, and you confined shall be."

3   "You may confine, dear father; my heart you cannot confine;
     There is none but Jack the sailor who has this heart of mine."
     O now upon the deck, to convey herself away,

     .   .   .   .

4   "Your waist is very slender, your fingers are very small,
     Your cheeks too red and rosy, to face the cannon ball."
     "My waist is very slender, my fingers are very small,
     My cheeks are red and rosy to face the cannon ball."

5   The drum began to beat and the fife began to play,
     And off to field of battle young Jack he marched away;
     And after the battle was over, she hunted over the ground,
     Among the dead and wounded, her darling lover found.

6   She took him in her arms and off to sea did go,
     And called for a doctor, to quickly dress his wounds.
     O now they are married, and well they do agree;
     O now they are married and why not you and me?

C

"Jackie was a Sailor." Communicated by Mr. A. B. Shock, Falls Mill, Braxton County, June, 1923; obtained from Mr. J. C. Shock.

1 Poor Jackie was a sailor with trouble on his mind;
   He left his native country and darling girl behind.
       Sing, carry me away,
       Sing, carry me away.

2 There was a rich merchant, in London he did dwell,
   He had a fair daughter whom no one could excel.

3 She had been courted by men, and by men of high degree,
   But none could win her affection but Jackie from the sea.

4 Pretty Polly was left at liberty with money at her command;
   She formed a resolution to see some foreign land.

5 She went into a tailor shop and dressed in men's array;
   Then she bargained with a captain to carry her far away.

6 "Your waistband is too slender, your fingers, too, are small,
   Your face is much too pretty to face a cannon ball."

7 "I know my waistband is slender, my fingers, too, are small,
   But I am not afraid, sir, to face the cannon's ball."

8 The captain put to sea, sir, and sailed for many a day;
   You see he kept his promise, to carry her far away.

9 She travelled over low land, she travelled over mound,
   Till among the dead and wounded, her Jackie boy she found.

10 She gathered him in her arms and she carried him to the town,
   She called in a physician to heal his bloody wound.

11 This couple they got married, so well did they agree;
   This couple they got married, so why not you and me?

99

THE SILK–MERCHANT'S DAUGHTER

COMMUNICATED by Miss Iva Thornton, Branchland, Lincoln County, August 31, 1916; obtained from Parker Lucas, who could remember a few verses only, but the outline of the story he still retained:

> "The silk-merchant's daughter of London I be,
> Oh, see what I 've come to by the loving of thee."

The silk-merchant's daughter loved a sailor who did not return her affection. He went to sea and she took passage on the same ship. During a storm, lots were cast to determine who should be killed, presumably to lighten the vessel's load. It fell to the silk-merchant's daughter to die, and her sailor was the executioner, but he wished to take her place:

> "Love, for the sake of your long life, I 'll die first."

He points the knife at his own breast, but she said:

> "Love, hold your hand, for I 'm sure we 're near ship or land."

Perrow (*Journal*, XXVIII, 160) prints a good text from North Carolina. The hero is sent away to prevent marriage, and the heroine follows him disguised as a merchant. On the way she falls in with two "barbarous Indians," both of whom she kills. Eventually she finds her lover and they sail for London. In a storm the ship goes to the bottom, they all take to a boat. Provisions give out, lots are cast as to who shall die to feed the rest, and the silk-merchant's daughter is the victim. Lots are now cast as to who shall be the executioner, and it falls to her lover. The captain urges him to "quicken the business," but a gun is heard and in half an hour a ship comes and carries them to London, where the lovers are married.

Campbell and Sharp, No. 54, print two North Carolina variants (see also F. C. Brown, p. 10). Cf. Shearin and Combs, p. 12 (Kentucky). For the Old Country, see "The Banks of Sweet Willow": Sharp and Marson, *Folk-Songs from Somerset*, I, 28; *Journal of the Folk-Song Society*, II, 33; III, 292.

In plot the song resembles (though with a happy ending) the tragic ballad of "Bonnie Annie" (Child, No. 24). For the casting of lots see Child, II, 13, 510; V, 463; V, 292.

I OO

THE ORPHAN GYPSY GIRL

THIS is a chastened version of "The Gypsy Girl" (or "The Little Gypsy Girl")
— a song common in English broadsides (as Ryle; Harkness, Preston); cf. Ebsworth, *Roxburghe Ballads*, VIII, ii, 853. See also De Marsan broadside, List 9,
No. 30; *Singer's Journal*, I, 146.

Communicated by Miss Violet Noland, Davis, Tucker County, March 24,
1916; obtained from Mr. John Raese, who learned it when a boy and wrote it
down in 1880. Cf. *The American Star Songster*, New York, 1851, p. 45 (good
text).

1 My father is king of the gypsies, my mother is queen of the Jews;
   My father he died and left me some travelling to do;
   So I packed up my dresses, my friends they wished me well,
   Then I set out for London, some fortunes for to tell.

2 As I was a-walking up the street one day,
   I chanced for to meet a young squire upon his way;
   He viewed my blue eyes, my looks they pleased him well,
   Says he, "My orphan gypsy girl, can you my fortune tell?"

3 "O yes, kind sir, please give me your hand:
   You have houses and fair ladies all under your command;
   You have houses and fair ladies and lay them all aside,
   For I am the orphan gypsy girl that is going to be your bride."

4 He took me to his houses, there were carpets on the floor,
   And maidens for to wait on him and open every door;
   The bells they rang so merrily and through the streets . . .
   Saying, "There goes the orphan gypsy girl that is now a squire's
      bride."

5 Farewell to this world, farewell to roam!
   No more in this wide world does little Nella roam;
   So now my song is ended, I hope to please you well,
   If ever I come this way again your fortune to tell.

I O I

WILLIAM REILLY

THERE are three ballads of "William Reilly." The first is "William Reilly's Courtship," which tells of his meeting with his Coleen Bawn, of his taking service with her father, of the elopement, and of Reilly's arrest and imprisonment. The second, "Reilly's Trial," begins with Coleen Bawn's invitation to the hero to elope; it tells of his arrest, imprisonment, and trial, and ends with the lady's request that he wear a ring of hers when he is in a foreign land (that is, transported). The third, "Reilly's Answer, Releasement, and Marriage with Coleen Bawn," is a continuation of the second and ends with happiness for all concerned. All three ballads are often printed together, affording a three-part text of more than forty stanzas, though it should be noted that in this arrangement the Second Part repeats a portion of the story contained in the First.

For full texts printed in America see *The American Songster*, edited by John Kenedy (Baltimore, 1836), p. 178 (a book several times reprinted, and also included as Volume III in *Marsh's Selection, or, Singing for the Million*, New York, 1854); *The Forget Me Not Songster* (New York, Nafis & Cornish), p. 181; the same (Boston, Locke & Bubier), p. 181; De Marsan, four broadsides (New York), List 16, Nos. 75–78; *Singer's Journal*, I, 135. An American chapbook (*Paddy Carey*, etc.) printed in 1826 (probably at Philadelphia) begins with Part II and finishes the story (Harvard College, 25276. 43. 81). Cf. Shearin, *Sewanee Review*, XIX, 327; Shearin and Combs, p. 13; Barry, No. 54; Belden, No. 81; Pound, No. 38.

See "The Trial of Willy Reilly" (or "Riley and Colinban") in broadsides (Pitts; Catnach; Such, No. 101; Livsey, Manchester, No. 107; John Ross, Newcastle, No. 16; Bebbington, Manchester, No. 367).

"William Riley." Communicated by Mr. Decker Toney, Queens Ridge, Wayne County, January 20, 1916; learned from his mother, who learned it from her father, Mr. Thomas Moore, who learned it when a small boy from George Stephens.

1　As I walked out one morning, all in the bloom of spring,
　　And as the cheerful songsters in concert sweet did sing;
　　The primrose and the daisies were spangled over the lawn,
　　And in the harbor I espied O my fair Coolin Bond.

2　I trembled and I 'dressed her: "Hail, matchless this fair maid!
　　O you will grief oppress me, which I am much afraid."
　　His hair it curled around his head; he's a beauty to behold;
　　He's a match for Squire Ford's daughter, if she were a bride in
　　　　gold.

3　She shot such killing glances, my heart away was drawn:
　　"You've distracted all my senses, O my fair Coolin Bond."
　　I hired to her father and left my home and land,
　　So with pleasure I might gaze on her, O my fair July Anne.

4 I valued not my wages, and would not them demand,
   For I could live for ages with my fair Coolin Bond.
   I and her father, as we walked out alone,
   I asked him for his daughter, saying, "Sir, it is well known,

5 "I have a well-stocked farm, and ten thousand pound in hand;
   I'll share it with your daughter, O my fair July Anne."
   Her father, full of anger, most scornfully did frown:
   "Nothing but a rich squire shall wed my July Anne."

6 And still he increased his anger, and bade me quick "Begone!"
   Saying, "Here is your wages; O now depart the town."
   I went in to his daughter, and told her my sad tale;
   Oppressed with grief and anger, we both did weep and wail.

7 "The thoughts of this, dear Riley, O I can never stand;
   I'll go along with you, my love, and be your July Anne.
   I'll forsake my father's dwelling, fine houses and rich lands;
   I'll go along with you, my love, and be your July Anne."

8 A horse we soon got ready, in the silence of the night;
   We had no other remedy, so quick we made our flight.
   The horse it seemed to stumble and threw us both alone,
   Confused and sorely bruised me and my fair Coolin Bond.

9 Our horses soon we mounted and swiftly rode away;
   Over high hills and mountains, along each lonesome dale.
   We climbed the rugged woods rough, we rode the silent land,
   When Riley was overtaken with his fair Coolin Bond.

10 They hurried him to prison; his hands and feet they bound;
   Confined him like a murderer; they chained him to the ground:
   "All this cruel treatment so freely will I stand,
   Ten thousand deaths I'll suffer for my fair Coolin Bond."

11 The morning of the trial, down came the jailer's son:
   "Dress yourself, young Riley, to-day you must be hung.

   .   .   .   .
   .   .   .   .

12 "Dress yourself, young Riley, you must appear to-day;
   The lady's oath will hang you, or else will set you free."
   "If this be so," said Riley, "some hopes begin to dawn;
   I never can be injured by pretty Coolin Bond."

13 Up stepped the noble Fox, who stood attent to buy: [1]
  "Gentlemen or [2] jury, for justice we apply.
  To hang a man for love, foul murder you may seek;
  Spare the life of Riley, and banished let him be."

14 "O stop, my Lord, he stol'd from her bright jewels and gold
      rings,
  Gold watches, diamond buckles, and many costly things.
  I gave them to my daughter they cost me a thousand pound;
  When Riley was overtaken, those things were with him found."

15 "The miss was young and tender, and tender in her youth;
  If Riley has deluded her, she will declare the truth."
  Just like a spotless angel, before him she did stand:
  "You're welcome here, my heart's delight, my fairest Riley
      man.

16 "If you have got them, Riley, pray hand them unto me."
  "I will, my generous lady, with many thanks," said he.
  "Here is a ring among them, I wish for you to wear;
  It's set with costly diamonds, and braided with my hair.

17 "In token of true friendship, wear it on your right hand;
  Think of my broken heart, my love, when you're in some foreign
      land."
  This young lady was taken home and in her closet bound;
  Young Riley he was taken and confined in Slago town,

18 With twenty other criminals, to double and march away,
  To enter on board the transport, bound straight for Botney's
      Bay.
  Her chains she loudly rattled, she did both weep and wail:
  "For me, poor William Riley, is treated like a slave."

[1] For *attentive by.*   [2] For *of the.*

102

MOLLIE VAUGHN

THREE fairly good copies of this song have been found in West Virginia under the titles, "Mollie Vaunders," "Molly Vaunder," and "Mollie Vaughn."

The earliest known record of this ballad is Jamieson's printed circular letter of 1799. The piece was published, in an incomplete text, in his *Popular Ballads*, 1806, I, 194 ("Peggy Baun"). A variant ("Molly Whan") was issued by Pitts as a slip-song very early in the nineteenth century. An American broadside ("Polly Wand") is among the ballads purchased "from a Ballad Printer and Seller in Boston" by Isaiah Thomas in 1813 (II, 122, American Antiquarian Society). Barry prints a four-stanza medley from Maine which contains four lines of the ballad (*Journal*, XXII, 387). Kittredge prints three versions (*Journal*, XXX, 358), one from a very old lady in Massachusetts, the others from Wyman's MS. Kentucky collection. Pound, No. 33, reprints the third of these. Campbell and Sharp, No. 40, give a text from North Carolina and a fragment from Tennessee. For British and American references see *Journal*, XXX, 358. Add *Journal of the Folk-Song Society*, II, 59; VII, 17; *Journal of the Irish Folk-Song Society*, III, 25.

A

"Mollie Vaunders." Communicated by Miss Violet M. Hiett, Great Cacapon, Morgan County, February, 1917; obtained from Mrs. D. S. Stump, Hampshire County, who learned it in Ohio about 1885.

1 Come all ye young fellows who delight in a gun,
Beware of late shooting, after the sun's down.
I'll tell you a story which happened of late,
Concerning Mollie Vaunders, whose beauty was great.

2 Mollie Vaunders was out walking, when a shower came on;
She stopped under a beech tree, the shower to shun.
Jimmie Randolph was a-hunting, a-shooting in the dark;
He shot at his true love and he missed not his mark.

3 He ran unto her and he picked her up,
Saying, "Uncle, dearest uncle, I've shot Mollie Vaun!
I've killed the dearest being, O the joy of my life,
For I always intended to make her my wife."

4 Jimmie's uncle came stepping up, with locks so very gray,
Saying, "Jimmie, dearest Jimmie, don't run away!
Stay at home with your father till your trial day's here;
By the rights of your country I know you'll count clear."

5 On the day of Jimmie's trial, Mollie's ghost did appear,
Saying, "Uncle, dearest uncle, Jimmie Randolph counts clear;
With an apron turned over my head, he took me for a faun;
He shot and he killed me, and my name is Mollie Vaun."

6 All the girls in the city, they seemed very glad
When they heard the sad tidings, Mollie Vaunders was dead.
Take all of those pretty girls, and place them in a row,
Mollie Vaunders shone among them, like a mountain of snow.

B

"Molly Vaunder." Communicated by Professor Walter Barnes, Fairmont, Marion County, February, 1917; obtained from Mr. George Gregg, Pocahontas County, who learned it from his mother.

1 Come all you jolly sportsmen who delight in a gun,
But beware of late hunting, after down-setting sun.
Molly Vaunders was walking, when a shower came on;
She ran to yonder leech[1] tree, the shower to shun.

2 Jimmy Randall was hunting, was hunting near dark;
He shot at his true love and missed not his mark.
With a white apron pinned round her, he took her to be a swan;
But Providence being against him, he shot Molly Vaun.

3 He ran up to her and found that she was dead;
A fountain of tears on her bosom he shed.
Then he picked up his rifle, to his uncle he did run,
Saying, "Uncle, dearest uncle, I have shot Molly Vaun!

4 "She's the fairest young damsel, and the joy of my life,
And I always intended to make her my wife."
Up stepped Jimmy's father, whose locks were turning gray,
Saying, "Jimmy, dearest Jimmy, don't you run away!

5 "Stay here for your trial, your trial to attend,
And you shall be cleared by the laws of our land."
On the day of Jimmy's trial, Molly's ghost did appear,
And it said to the judge and jurymen, "Jimmy Randall goes
clear."

[1] For *beech*.

C

"Mollie Vaughn." Communicated by Mr. C. R. Bishop, Green Bank, Pocahontas County, 1917; obtained from Miss Valera Ervine, who got it from her mother, who had it from her mother, who got it from an aunt, who got it from her grandfather, all natives of West Virginia and untravelled.

1 Mollie Vaughn was a-walking, when a shower came on;
   She ran under a tree, the shower to shun.
   Jimmie Randells was a-hunting, a-hunting in the dark;
   He shot at his true love and he missed not his mark.

2 He picked up his gun, to his uncle did run,
   Saying, "Uncle, dearest uncle, I killed Mollie Vaughn!
   I've killed that fair damsel, the joy of my life,
   And I always intended to make her my wife."

3 Up stepped Jimmie's father, with his locks turning gray,
   Saying, "Jimmie, dearest Jimmie, do not run away!
   Stay with your country till your trial comes on;
   You ne'er shall be hurt for killing Mollie Vaughn."

4 On the day of Jimmie's trial, Mollie's ghost did appear:
   "Say, ye gentlemen of the jury, young Jimmie goes clear.
   With a white apron round me, he took me for a swan,
   And Jimmie shall ne'er be hurt for killing Mollie Vaughn."

103

CHARMING BEAUTY BRIGHT

AMERICAN texts have been printed as follows: *Journal*, XXVI, 176 (Kittredge; taken down in 1877 or 1878 from an old lady born in Boston in 1799); XXVIII, 147 (Perrow; Mississippi); XXIX, 184 (Tolman; Indiana); XXX, 334 (Kittredge; Kentucky [Wyman]; Campbell and Sharp, No. 57 (North Carolina, Tennessee, Virginia). The first stanza of Campbell and Sharp's A (cf. E and No. 59) appears in "The Forsaken Girl," a Kentucky variety of "The Poor Stranger" (*Journal*, XX, 268; cf. XXX, 344).

Contributed by Miss Myrtle Linger, Waverly, Wood County, November 16, 1916; learned when she was a little child, from her grandmother, of Scotch-Irish descent, who came with her parents from Virginia.

1 Once I courted a fair beauty-bride;
  I courted her by day and I courted her by night;
  And I courted her for love, and her love I did obtain;
  I'm sure she had no reason at all to complain.

2 Then her father came this to know,
  Why I was courting his daughter also,
  And he locked her up so high, and he kept her so severe,
  O how happy would I be to get sight of my dear!

3 Then I thought to the war I would go,
  To see whether I could forget my love or no;
  But when I came in sight, the army shone so bright,
  It put me in fresh mind of my own heart's delight.

4 For seven long years I served my king;
  In seven long years I came home again,
  With my heart so full of woe, and my eyes so full of tears,
  O how happy would I be, to get sight of my dear!

5 Then I thought to her parents I would go,
  To see whether I could see my love or no;
  But when her mother saw me, she wrang her hands and cried:
  "Say, my daughter loved you dearly, and for your sake she
        died."

6 Then I was struck like a lamb that was slain;
  Tears poured from my eyes like showers of rain;
  Come all ye true lovers, come pity, pity me;
  Come pity my misfortune and sad misery.

104

THE RICH MERCHANT

THIS piece is common in English broadsides under the title of "William and Harriet." Harvard College has broadsides by Catnach, Such, Ryle & Co., Bebbington (Manchester, No. 96), W. R. Walker (Newcastle-upon-Tyne, No. 176), Harkness (Preston, No. 306), Forth (Pocklington, No. 62), and Elias Keys (Devonport). For stanza 1 see *Journal of the Folk-Song Society*, I, 222.

Communicated by Miss Nellie Donley, Morgantown, Monongalia County, 1917; obtained from Mr. Jesse Fox, who received it from Miss Sina Morgan McElroy.

1 There was a rich merchant, in London did dwell,
   He had an only daughter, the farmer loved well;
   Because she was so handsome, he liked her so well;
   Her father he wanted her to bid him adieu.

2 "O, father, O father, I hain't so inclined,
   To turn my dear William quite out of my mind."
   As William was rambling for something to spy,
   Upon his lovely Harriet he cast a wishful eye.

3 "O William, O William, O William," said she,
   "Your father and mine have both agreed to send you a-sailing
       far over the sea.
   I'll dress like a ship maid; I'll do what I can;
   And with William I'll venture, like some jolly young man."

4 As they were sailing to some foreign shore,
   The wind of the ocean began to roar;
   The ship it sank down to the bottom of the sea,
   And cast upon an island, with Harriet and me.

5 We had nothing to eat, and nowhere to lie,
   . . . .
   We both lay together all on the cold ground,
   And the wind from the ocean blew a dismal sound.

6 Come all ye young people, who drop by the way,
   Drop one tear of pity, and point by the way
   Where William and Harriet in slumbers both lay.

105

VILIKINS AND HIS DINAH

THIS well-known song is a comic stage-version of the English broadside ballad of "William and Dinah." Both the serious and the comic form have circulated widely. The history of "Vilikins" has been much discussed but never fully elucidated. See *Journal*, XXIX, 190; XXV, 418.

"The Merchant's Daughter." Communicated by Mrs. Hilary G. Richardson, Clarksburg, Harrison County, September, 1916.

1 There was a rich merchant in London did dwell,
   Who had for his daughter a very fine girl;
   Her name it was Dinah, just sixteen years old,
   Had a very large fortune in silver and gold.

2 As Dinah was walking in the garden one day,
   Her father came to her and thus he did say:
   "Go dress yourself, Dinah, in gorgeous array,
   For I've brought you a lover both gallant and gay."

3 "Ah, papa, dear papa! I've not yet made up my mind;
   To marry just yet I do not feel inclined;
   All my fortune in gold I'll gladly give o'er,
   If you'll let me stay single a year or two more."

4 "Go, boldest daughter," the parent replied,
   As he frowned dark upon her and her he did chide:
   "All the fortune I'll give to the nearest of kin,
   And you shan't reap the benefit of one single pin."

5 As Vilikins was walking the garden around,
   He saw his dear Dinah lying dead on the ground,
   And a cup of cold pizen a-laying by her side,
   And a billet-doux a-stating 't was of pizen she died.

6 He kissed her cold corpus a thousand times o'er,
   He called her his Dinah, though she was no more;
   Then drunk up the pizen like a lover so brave,
   And Vilikins and his Dinah both lay in one grave.

7 As the merchant was walking in the garden one day,
   He saw two tall ghosts, who threatening did say,
   "We both should be living, if it were not for you."
   'T was Vilikins and his Dinah both looking very blue.

106

YOUNG EDWIN IN THE LOWLANDS LOW

THIS English song has been found in West Virginia, North Carolina, Kentucky, Georgia, Tennessee, Missouri, Michigan, and Nova Scotia. For English and American references see *Journal*, XX, 274; XXXV, 421, 422.

"Low Lands Low." Communicated by Anna Luther Copley, Shoals, Wayne County, December 19, 1915; written with the help of Mr. Luther Burwell.

1 Come all you feeling lovers, come listen to my song,
While I unfold concerning gold, that leads so many wrong.
Young Mary was a serving maid; she loved a sailor boy,
Who plowed the main, much gold to gain for her, so I've been told.

2 "My father keeps a public house down by the seashore side,
Where you can go and enter in, and there this night abide.
I'll meet you in the morning; don't let my parents know
That your name it is young Edward Bowl, who plows the Low
Lands Low."

3 Young Edward he sat drinking till time to go to bed;
But little was his intention, such sorrow around his head.
Then he arose and went to bed, but scarcely fell asleep
Till Mary's cruel father into his room did creep.

4 He stabbed and dragged him from his bed, down to the beach
did go,
And plunged his body bleeding into the Low Lands Low.
Young Mary she lie sleeping, she had a frightful dream:
She dreamed she saw her true love's blood all appear to her in
streams.

5 Then she arose, put on her clothes, down to her friends did go,
Because she loved him dearly who plowed the Low Lands Low.
Then she arose, put on her clothes, just at the break of day,
Saying, "Father, where is that young man came here last night
to stay?"

6 "O he is dead, no tales he'll tell, but his gold will make a show;
I plunged his body bleeding down in the Low Lands Low."
"Now," said Mary, "cruel father, you shall die a public show,
For taking the gold from him so bold who plowed the Low Lands
Low."

7 Now Mary's cruel father neither night nor day could rest,
For the crime that was guilty on his trial he confessed.

. . . .

. . . .

107

A POOR STRANGER FAR FROM HOME

THIS is the English song known as "The Poor Stranger," "The Happy
Stranger," and "Sweet Europe." It has influenced "The Forsaken Girl" or
"The Onconstant Lovyer" (*Journal*, XX, 268; XXX, 345; McGill, p. 50), which,
in its turn, was adapted as "The Rebel Prisoner" (*Allan's Lone Star Ballads*,
p. 80; Sharp, *Folk-Songs of English Origin Collected in the Appalachian Moun-
tains*, 2d Series, p. 52). See, for references, Kittredge, *Journal*, XXX, 344. Add
Gardiner, *Folk-Songs from Hampshire*, p. 35; Joyce, *Ancient Irish Music*, p. 73;
Journal of the Folk-Song Society, III, 243.

For the source of the present text see note on No. 59.

1 I walked out one morning in spring,
  To hear the birds whistle and the nightingale sing;
  I heard a fair maid a-making sad moan,
  Says, "I am a poor stranger and so far from my home."

2 I stepped up to her and made a low gay,[1]
  And asked her pardon for making so free;
  Says, "I've taken pity on hearing your moan,
  As you are a poor stranger and so far from your home."

3 Her cheeks blusht like roses and she shed a tear;
  "Kind sir, I wonder on seeing you here;
  I hope you'll not use me ill, in the deserts alone,
  As I am a poor stranger, and so far from my home."

4 "As for to ill use you, I never will,
  But for to save you, my heart's blood I'll spill;
  I will try to relieve you and ease all your moans,
  I will try to convey you safe back to your home.

5 "If ever you and me can agree,
  If ever you marry, you marry with me;
  I will be your guardian through the deserts alone,
  And unto your parents I'll leave you at home."

6 "As for your country, I'd wish for to know,
  And what misfortune you did undergo,
  Which made you to wander so far from your home,
  Which made you meet strangers in the deserts alone."

[1] Error for *congee.*

7 "O dear madam, the truth I will tell:
It was near Manory I use for to dwell;
And as for misfortunes, from my love I was prone,
Which makes a many hero go far from their home."

8 "The young men in Manory, they're all roving blades,
They take great delight in courting fair maids;
They'll hug them and kiss them and call them their own,
And perhaps their own darling is moaning at home."

9 "Dear madam, the case is not so;
I never was married, the truth you must know."
But now they're both married and the case it is known,
And I wish them both happy and safe to their home.

108

THE DROWSY SLEEPER

Two variants of this song have been recovered in West Virginia, one having the title, "The Silver Dagger," probably because the last two stanzas of it belong to that song (see p. 350, below).

"The Drowsy Sleeper" an interesting variant of a song known, in a Nithsdale version, to Allan Cunningham, and given in part in a note to "O, my luve's like a red, red rose" in his edition of Burns, 1834, IV, 285 (Kittredge, *Journal*, XX, 260).

For American texts see *Journal*, XX, 260 (Kentucky), XXIX, 200 (Georgia); XXX, 338 (Missouri, Kentucky, Indiana, Michigan, Nebraska or Utah); XXXV, 356 (Ohio); Belden, *Herrig's Archiv*, CXIX, 430 (Missouri, Arkansas); Campbell and Sharp, No. 47 (North Carolina); Sturgis and Hughes, *Songs from the Hills of Vermont*, p. 30; Pound, No. 21 (A, Nebraska; B, the same as *Journal*, XXX, 342); Sharp, *Folk-Songs of English Origin Collected in the Appalachian Mountains*, 2d Series, p. 48; Minish MS., II, 63 (North Carolina); broadside, H. J. Wehman (New York), No. 518 (mixed with "The Silver Dagger").

For English and Scottish references see *Journal*, XX, 260; XXX, 338; XXXV, 356; Campbell and Sharp, p. 330. See also the Hudson MS. of Irish airs, Volume I, No. 181 (Boston Public Library).

There is an extremely interesting paper on "English Songs on the Night Visit," by Baskervill, in the *Publications of the Modern Language Association*, XXXVI, 565–614 (see p. 585 for the present piece).

A

"The Drowsy Sleeper." Communicated by Miss Violet Noland, Davis, Tucker County, March 24, 1916; obtained from Mr. John Raese, who learned it when a boy and wrote it down in 1880.

1   "Rouse up, rouse up, you drowsy sleeper;
         Rouse up, 't is almost day;
     Open your doors, let down your window,
         What your true love has to say."

2   "Go away from my window, you 'll waken my mother;
         This thing you call courting, she does despise;
     Go way, go way, and court some other,
         For what I say, I mean no harm."

3   "I won't go way nor court no other,
         For you are the one that I love best;
     For you are the one that I love dearly,
         And in your arms I hope to rest."

4 "Go way from my window, you'll waken my father,
      Who is taking of his rest;
   For under his pillow there lies a weapon,
      To kill the one that I love best."

5 "Down in yon meadow there lies a sharp arrow;
      I'll draw it across my peaceful breast;
   It will cut off all love and sorrow,
      And send my peaceful soul to rest."

B

"The Silver Dagger." Communicated by Miss Maud I. Jefferson, West
Liberty, Ohio County, 1917; obtained from Miss Roberts.

1 "O Mary, go and ask your mother
      If you my wedded bride may be;
   And if she says no, pray come and tell me,
      And I'll no longer trouble thee."

2 "I dare not go and ask my mother,
      For she said she would part us;
   Then, Willie, go and ask another,"
      She gently whispered in his ear.

3 "Then, Mary, go and ask your father
      If you my wedded bride may be;
   And if he says no, pray come and tell me,
      And I'll no longer trouble thee."

4 " I dare not go and ask my father,
      For at night he lies at rest,
   Close to his side there lies a dagger,
      To pierce the heart that I love best."

5 Then William drew a silver dagger,
      And pierced it to his aching heart,
   Saying, "Here's farewell, my own true lover,"
      Saying, "Here's farewell, for we must part."

6 Then Mary drew that bloody dagger,
      And pierced it in her snow-white breast,
   Saying, "Here's farewell to father and mother;
      Farewell to all that I love best."

109

THE SILVER DAGGER

THREE good copies of this song have been recovered in West Virginia, one of them going under the title of "The Warning Deaths." A and C are almost exactly alike in arrangement and phraseology. B is different from the other two in that the crossing of the lovers is due to the girl's parents.

For texts and references see *Journal*, XX, 267 (Kentucky); XXX, 362 (Missouri); Pound, Ballads, No. 52 (Wyoming and Illinois). For contamination of "The Silver Dagger" with "The Drowsy Sleeper" see *Journal*, XXX, 388. The text of the latter published by Wehman as a broadside (New York, No. 518: "Who's at my Bedroom Window?") shows this mixture, and the same is true of "The Shining Dagger" in Sturgis and Hughes, *Songs from the Hills of Vermont*, p. 30, of Campbell and Sharp's No. 47 C, and Pound's, No. 21 B (*Ballads*, p. 52).

A

No local title. Communicated by Mr. W. H. S. White, Piedmont, Mineral County, January 21, 1916; obtained from Mr. S. G. Yoke, Morgantown, who says that it was a favorite among the young folks of Stone Coal Creek, Lewis County, more than sixty years previously.

1   Young men and maidens lend attention,
        While unto you these lines I write,
    Of a comely youth that I will mention,
        Who courted a lady bright.

2   But when his parents came to know it,
        They strove against him night and day;
    To keep their son from a mesalliance,
        "She's a poor girl," they oft did say.

3   But this fair damsel being handsome,
        She knew the grief that he went through;
    She wandered away and left the city,
        Some pleasant fields and groves to view.

4   She rambled down by a flowing river,
        She leaned her back against a tree,
    And then she sighed, "O shall I ever,
        Ever my true love see?"

5   She then pulled out a silver dagger,
        And pierced it through her snow-white breast;
    These words she spake and as she staggered:
        "Farewell, my love! I'm going to rest."

6 He being low down in the city,
       And hearing of this female voice,
   He ran, he ran like one distracted,
       Saying, "Alas, alas, I am undone!"

7 But when he came just up unto her,
       Her coal-black eyes like stars did shine;
   She says, "My love, O come and meet me,
       Where joy and love are both combined."

8 He then picked up the bloody weapon,
       And pierced it through his tender heart,
   Saying, "Let our ends be a dreadful warning,
       To all who do true lovers part."

ℬ

"The Silver Dagger." Communicated by Anna Copley, Shoals, Wayne County, December 28, 1915; obtained from Mr. Luther Burwell, who learned it when a child from his mother.

1 Pray, men and maids, all lend attention
       To these few lines I'm going to write;
   It is something concerning a youth whom I'll mention;
       He courted a lady, beauty bright.

2 And when her parents came to know it,
       They strove to part them, both night and day;
   They strove to part them from her own dearest jewel,
       "He's poor, he's poor," they often cried.

3 Her bended knees to them she bowed,
       Crying, "Father, O pray pity me!
   And don't let my true lover go denial,
       For without him what's this world to me?"

4 She turned her back unto the city,
       To view those fields and meadows round;
   She wandered away to some clear, broad river,
       And under the shade of a tree sat down,

5 Saying, "Will I now or shall I ever,
       Shall ever I enjoy my true love's charms?
   Shall ever I enjoy my own dearest jewel,
       Or see the man whom I love best?"

6   Then she pulled out a silver dagger,
         And pierced it through her milk-white breast;
     And under those few lines she began to stagger,
         Saying, "Fare you well, I'm going to rest."

7   Her true love not being far behind her,
         He heard her make her love-sake moan;
     He ran on like a man distracted,
         Saying, "I'm ruined, lost, I'm left undone."

8   Her deep-blue eyes to him she opened,
         Crying, "True love, you have come too late!
     But prepare to meet me on Mount Zion,
         Where all our joys will be complete."

9   Then he picked up this bloody weapon,
         And pierced it through his poor tender heart,
     Saying, "Let this day be a dreadful warning,
         To all who doth true lovers part."

C

"The Warning Deaths." Communicated by Mr. E. C. Smith, Weston, Lewis County, December 18, 1915; obtained from an old manuscript in the possession of Mr. J. W. Smith, who lives near Weston. Eight stanzas, almost identical with A.

110

SWEET WILLIAM

(THE SAILOR BOY)

THE majority of the nine variants found in West Virginia are more or less incomplete. There is little variation in story but a good deal in phraseology.

Of this favorite English song texts have been printed or reported from Georgia (*Journal*, XXIX, 199), Tennessee (XXX, 363), Ohio (XXXV, 410), North Carolina (Campbell and Sharp, No. 106; cf. F. C. Brown, p. 10), Missouri (Belden, No. 20), Nebraska (Pound, pp. 42, 69), Canada (*Journal*, XXXI, 170). An interesting copy from the MS. of a Confederate soldier is printed by Frank Moore, *Anecdotes, Poetry, and Incidents of the War* (New York, 1866), p. 180. For references see *Journal*, XXX, 363; XXXV, 410; Campbell and Sharp, p. 334. Add Greig, *Folk-Song of the North-East*, LXIV; *Journal of the Irish Folk-Song Society*, XVII, 18; broadside ("The Sailor Boy and his Faithful Mary"), Harkness, Preston, No. 317.

A

"Moment's River Side." Communicated by Mr. Fred Smith, Glenville, Gilmer County, 1917; obtained from Miss Lucretia Collins.

1 Way down on Moment's river side
  The wind blew fair with gentle guide;
  A pretty maid that sat and mourned:
  "What shall I do? My true love's gone.

2 "His rosy cheeks, his coal-black hair,
  Has drawn my heart all in a snare;
  His ruby lips so soft and fine,
  Ten thousand times I've thrust in mine.

3 "And if ten thousand were in a row,
  My love would make the brightest show,
  The brightest show of every one;
  I'll have my love or I'll have none.

4 "I'll build myself a little boat,
  And on the ocean I will float,
  And every ship that I pass by,
  I'll inquire for my sweet sailor boy."

5 She had not sailed far on the deep,
  Until a ship she chanced to meet:
  "O captain, captain, tell me true,
  Does my sweet Willie sail with you?"

6   "O no, kind miss, he is not here;
    He lies in yonder deep, I fear."
    She [w]rang her hands, she tore her hair,
    Just like a lady in despair.

7   The wind did blow and the waves did roll,
    Which washed his body to the shore;
    She view[ed] him well in every part,
    With melting tears and bleeding heart.

8   With pen and ink she wrote a song,
    She wrote it large, she wrote it long;
    On every line she dropped a tear,
    And every verse cried, "O my dear!"

9   Six weeks from then this maid was dead,
    And on her breast this letter laid:
    "Go dig my grave both wide and deep,
    And strew it well with roses sweet.

10   "Plant by my side a willow tree,
    To many years wave over me,
    And on my breast a turtle dove,
    To tell the world I died for love."

ℬ

"The Sailor Boy." Communicated by Mr. J. Harrison Miller, Wardensville, Hardy County, June, 1917; brought into the community sixteen years
before by Matilda Heishman.

1   Way down on Moment's river side,
    The wind blew fair a gentle glide;
    A very pretty maid sat there a-moan,
    "O what shall I do?   My true love's gone.

2   "If ten thousand were enrolled,
    My love would make the brightest show,
    The brightest show of every one;
    I'll have my true love or else have none.

3   "It was early in the spring,
    He went on sea to serve his king;
    The day was clear, the wind blew fair,
    Which parted me and my dearest dear.

4   " I'll build myself a little boat,
     And on the ocean I will float;
     And every ship that I pass by,
     I'll inquire of my sweet sailor boy."

5   She had not been sailing long on the deep
     Before a ship she chanced to meet;
     She cried, "Captain, captain, tell me true,
     Does my sweet Billy stay with you?"

6   "O no, kind miss, he is not here;
     He is lost in the deep, O I do fear;
     On Greenland's Isle, as we passed by,
     Here we lost a fine sailor boy."

7   She wrung her hands into her hair,
     Just like one who is in despair;
     Against a rock she ran her boat:
     "O what shall I do?   My true love's gone."

8   The water did wave and the sea did roar,
     It washed his body on the shore;
     She viewed his body on every part,
     With melting tears and a broken heart.

9   With pen and paper she wrote a song;
     She wrote it wide and she wrote it long;
     At the end of every line she dropped a tear,
     At the end of every word cried, "Billy, my dear!"

C

No local title. Communicated by Professor Walter Barnes, Fairmont, Marion County; obtained from Miss Daisy Watkins, who got it from her mother.

1   Away down on yon river side,
     There where the waters so swiftly glide,
     I heard a lovely lady mourn,
     Saying, "What shall I do?   My true love's gone."

2   She built herself a little boat,
     That on the ocean she might float;
     And every ship that she drew near,
     She inquired for her William dear.

3   As she was sailing out from Maine,
    She spied three ships coming from Spain;
    She hailed them all as they drew near,
    To inquire for her William dear.

4   "O captain, captain, tell me true,
    Does my sweet William sail with you?
    Tell me quick and give me joy,
    For none will I have but my sweet sailor boy."

5   "O no, kind miss, he is not here;
    He is in yonder deep, I fear;
    On Rocky Island as we drew nigh,
    There we left your sweet sailor boy."

6   She rowed her boat against a rock,
    Just like some lady whose heart was broke.

    . . . .
    . . . .

7   She called for a chair to set upon,
    And paper and ink to pen it down;
    And at the end of every line she dropped a tear,
    And at the end of every verse she cried, "O my dear!"

8   "Dig my grave both wide and deep;
    Place marble stones at my head and feet;
    And on my breast you may place my dove,
    To tell the world that I died of love."

D

"Down by the River Side." Communicated by Mrs. Walter Parker, Keyser, Mineral County; obtained from Mr. F. A. Hoff, who learned it from his mother. Seven stanzas.

E

Communicated by Mrs. Elizabeth Tapp Peck, Morgantown, Monongalia County; obtained from her mother, who learned it from her mother. Fragmentary; seven stanzas.

F

"The Sailor's Sweetheart." Communicated by Mr. George Paugh, Thomas, Tucker County; obtained from Mrs. George Yankee. Six stanzas.

G

"Sailor Boy." Contributed by Mr. J. Harrison Miller, Wardensville, Hardy County, June, 1917; learned five years before from Bessie Budy. Four stanzas and a chorus.

H

"Sweet Willie." Communicated by Miss Mary Meek Atkeson, Morgantown, Monongalia County; obtained from Mr. Fred Smith, Glenville, Gilmer County, who got it from Mr. Harry G. Eubank. Five stanzas.

I

"The Lost Lover." Communicated by Miss Mildred Joy Barker, Morgantown, Monongalia County; obtained from her mother, who learned it from her father, Martin Brookover. Fragmentary; six stanzas.

I I I

EARLY IN THE SPRING

For American texts see Campbell and Sharp, No. 72 (North Carolina). Belden, *Herrig's Archiv*, cxx, 69 (Missouri); for British references see Campbell and Sharp, p. 332. "The Trail to Mexico" (Lomax, p. 132) is an extraordinarily interesting example of adaptation: it is "Early, Early" transformed into a cowboy song. Stanzas A 11, B 10–11, D 9, do not belong to this piece. They are adapted from "A Brisk Young Sailor," perhaps by way of "The Butcher Boy." See No. 145; cf. *Journal*, XXIX, 170, and notes 1, 7.

A

Contributed by Mr. Decker Toney, Queens Ridge, Wayne County, January 20, 1916; learned from his mother, who had it from Hester Burton, who learned it from her mother, Delilah Horn.

1   So early, early in the spring,
    I went on board to serve my king,
    Leaving my dearest dear behind,
    Who to me was always so unkind.

2   My true love she takes me by the hand,
    Saying, "If ever I marry you'll be the man";
    Ten thousand vows and kisses sweet,
    Saying, "We'll get married next time we meet."

3   All the time I sailed the sea,
    My heart could not get one moment's ease;
    Writing letters to my dearest dear,
    Not one word from her could I hear.

4   At last I sailed out to Glady Town;
    I walked the streets both up and down,
    Inquiring for my dearest dear,
    Not one word from her could I hear.

5   I walked straight out to her father's hall,
    And for my true love I did call;
    "Your true love's married, she's a rich man's wife;
    She's married to one much better, for life."

6   I walked straight up and her hand did take,
    Saying, "All false promises are made to break;
    Since you've proved false and I've proved true,
    I'll forever and ever bid adieu.

7 "I'll go back on board again,
  I'll go back and serve my king;
  I'll go back where the bullets fly,
  I'll sail the sea till the day I die.'

8 "If there's a letter came to this town,
  I never received a single one;
  It is my father's fault, you'll find;
  Pray, don't blame this poor heart of mine.

9 "O don't go back on board again!
  O don't go back and serve your king!
  Don't go back where the bullets fly!
  There is other girls much fairer than I."

10 "Yes, I'll go back on board again;
   Yes, I'll go back and serve my king;
   Yes, I'll go back where the bullets fly;
   I'll sail the sea till the day I die."

11 "There is a river flows through this town,
   And in it my body will be found;
   Bury me beneath yon weeping willow tree,
   To show the world I died for thee."

ℬ

Contributed by Mrs. E. A. Hunt, Belinton, Barbour County, January 12, 1916; learned when she was a child, from her mother, Mrs. E. E. Bennett.

1 It was early in the spring,
  I was pressed on board to serve my king;
  I left my dearest dear behind,
  Who ofttimes told me her heart was mine,

2 And when I held her in my arms,
  I thought I held ten thousand charms;
  With promises and vows and kisses sweet,
  Saying, "We'll get married next time we meet."

3 And all the time I sailed the sea,
  I could not see one moment's ease,
  For writing to my dearest dear,
  And not one word from her could I hear.

4 I sailed the sea back to Glasgow Town;
  I walked the streets both up and down,
  Inquiring for my dearest dear,
  And not one word from her could I hear,

5 Until I came to her father's hall,
And for my true love I did call:
"Your true love 's married, she is a rich man's wife;
She is married to one that is better, for life."

6 I went to her, her hand did take;
My forms to her my vows did make;
Saying, "You've proved false, and I've proved true;
Forever and ever I'll bid you adieu.

7 "I'll go on board the ship again;
O yes! I'll go and serve my king;
I'll sail the sea till the day I die;
I'll strike the waves flying mountains high."

8 "O do not go on board again!
O do not go and serve your king!
There's many a fairer girl than I,
O do not go where the bullets fly!

9 "If you wrote letters to this town,
I never received a single line;
It's all my father's fault, you'll find;
O do not blame this poor heart of mine.

10 "There is a river in this town;
Therein my body shall be drown,
And it shall be buried beneath yond tree;
Remember love, that I died for thee.

11 "Go dig my grave both wide and deep,
Place a marble stone at my head and feet,
And upon my heart a turtle dove,
To testify that I died for love."

C

Communicated by Professor Walter Barnes, Fairmont, Marion County, 1915; obtained from Mrs. Charles Snider, Spencer, Roane County.

1 Early, early in one spring,
I was pressed on board to serve my king;
I left my dearest dear behind,
Who oft had told me her heart was mine.

2 When I had started off for sea,
Said I, "Dear love, remember me."
"I will not have no other man,
To love another is more than I can."

3   .   .   .   .
     .   .   .   .
     I wrote a letter back to my dear,
     But nothing from her could I hear.

4   I returned into her father's hall
     And for my dearest dear did call:
     "She's married, sir, she's a rich man's wife;
     She's married to one who is better for life."

5   "If the girl is married whom I adore,
     I'm sure I'll stay on land no more;
     I'll sail the seas till the day I die;
     I'll split through waves, rolling mountains high."

6   "O do not go on board again!
     O do not go to serve your king!
     There is many a fairer girl than I;
     O do not go where the bullets fly!

7   "If you have written to this town,
     I never have received one;
     It is my father's fault, you'll find;
     O do not blame this poor heart of mine!

8   "There is a river in this town,
     In which my body will be found;
     It shall be buried beneath yonders tree,
     And remember, love, that I died for thee."

9   "I'll curse all gold and silver too;
     I'll curse the girl that won't prove true,
     Who all her former vows did break
     And married another for riches' sake."

D

Communicated by Professor Walter Barnes, Fairmont, Marion County, December, 1916; obtained from Mr. George Gregg, Durbin, Pocahontas County, who got it from his grandfather. A confused version in seven stanzas, one of which is from "The Little Sparrow" and one from "The Butcher Boy."

CAROLINE OF EDINBURGH TOWN

THIS song is common in broadsides on both sides of the water and is included in many American songbooks. It has been noted as in oral circulation in Kentucky, Ohio, Nebraska, and Michigan. For references see *Journal*, XXXV, 362.

A

Communicated by Professor Walter Barnes, Fairmont, Marion County, January 10, 1916; obtained from Miss Lou F. Hart, Tunnelton, Preston County. A second copy (B) was communicated by Mr. George Paugh, Thomas, Tucker County, January 10, 1916; obtained from Mrs. Stella Thomas, Ben Bush. It does not differ materially from A, but is less correct.

1 Come all young men and maidens, and listen to my rhyme,
   'T is of a fair young damsel that 's scarcely in her prime;
   She beats the blushing roses, admired by all around,
   Comely young Caroline of Edinburgh Town.

2 Young Henry was a Highlandman, a-courting to her came;
   But when her parents came to know, they did not like the same;
   Young Henry was offended and unto her did say:
   "Arise, my dearest Caroline, and with me run away.

3 "We both will go to London, and there we 'll wed a-speed;
   And there my dearest Caroline will see happiness indeed."
   Then, being enticed by Henry, put on her other gown,
   And away went Caroline of Edinburgh Town.

4 Over hills and mountains together they did roam,
   Till they arrived at London, far from her happy home,
   She said, "My dearest Henry, you must ne'er on me frown,
   Or you 'll break the heart of Caroline of Edinburgh Town."

5 They had not lived in London more than half a year,
   Until hard-hearted Henry proved to her severe;
   Said Henry, "I 'll go to sea; your friends did on me frown;
   Go beg your way without delay to Edinburgh Town."

6 Then, pressed with grief without relief, this maiden she did go
   Into the wood to find food that on the bushes grow.
   Some strangers they did pity her, and some did on her frown,
   And some did say, "Why did you stray from Edinburgh Town?"

7 Beneath the spreading oak tree this maid sat down to cry,
  A-watching of the gallant ships, as they went passing by;
  She gave three shrieks for Henry, and plunged her body down,
  And away floated Caroline from Edinburgh Town.

8 A note, likewise her bonnet, she left upon the shore,
  And in this note a lock of hair, with words, "I am no more;
  I'm fast asleep, I'm in the deep, the fishes watching round,
  Comely young Caroline of Edinburgh Town."

9 Come all ye tender parents, ne'er try to part true love;
  You're to see in some degree the ruin it will prove.
  Likewise young men and maidens, ne'er on your true love frown,
  Think of the fate of Caroline of Edinburgh Town.

113

THE SAILOR AND HIS BRIDE

A

"The Sailor and his Bride." Communicated by Mrs. Elizabeth Tapp Peck, Morgantown, Monongalia County, March 29, 1916; obtained from her mother, who learned it from her mother, Mrs. Elizabeth Wade Mack.
This is "The Sailor Boy's Bride"; broadside, De Marsan, List 15, No. 90.

1   The moon had risen on the eastern hill,
The stars they shone in twilight still,
While the sailor boy and his lovely bride,
Were walking by the ocean side.

Refrain

Le lu, la lo, le lu, la lo,
Le lu, la lo, la lo, la le, la lo
While the sailor boy and his lovely bride,
Were walking by the ocean side.

2   "It was scarce three months since we were wed,
And O how quick the moments fled;
That we should part at the dawning of the day,
And the proud ship bear my love away."

Refrain

Le lu, la lo, le lu, la lo,
Le lu, la lo, la lo, la le, la lo
"That we should part at the dawning of the day,
And the proud ship bear my love away."

3   "Long months passed away and he came no more,
To his weeping bride on the distant shore;
The ship sank down at the howling of the storm,
And the sea closed over my lover's form."

Refrain

Le lu, la lo, le lu, la lo,
Le lu, la lo, la lo, la le, la lo
"And the ship sank down at the howling of the storm,
And the sea closed over my lover's form."

4 "I wish I was a-sleeping too,
   Beneath the ocean's blue,
   With my soul in heaven and my body in the sea,
   And the proud waves rolling over me."

Refrain

Le lu, la lo, le lu, la lo,
Le lu, la lo, la lo, la le, la lo,
"With my soul in heaven and my body in the sea,
And the proud waves rolling over me."

ℬ

"The Sailor Boy." Communicated by Miss Nellie Donley, Morgantown, Monongalia County, December, 1916; obtained for her by Miss Jessie Fox, for whom it was written down by Miss Sina McElroy.

1 "'T was early spring, the year was young,
   The flowers they bloomed, the birds they sung;
   There was not a bird that was happier than I,
   When my loved sailor boy was nigh."

2 The moon had risen on the eastern hills,
   The stars they shone, the twilight still;
   The sailor boy and his lovely bride
   Were walking by the ocean's side.

3 It's scarce three months since they were wed,
   And O how swift the moments fled!
   Long months passed away, and he came no more
   To his weeping bride on the lonely shore.

4 "The ship went down at the howling of the storm,
   And the sea closed over my lover's form."

   .   .   .   .
   .   .   .   .

5 "O that I were sleeping too,
   Beneath the waves of the ocean blue,
   My soul in heaven, my body in the sea,
   And the proud waves rolling over me!"

I I 4

PRETTY SALLY

THIS is the English song usually known as "Sally and her True-love Billy" or "Sally and Billy"; also as "The Bold Sailor" and "The (Young) Sailor from Dover" (see *Journal*, XXIX, 178, note 1; add De Vaynes, *The Kentish Garland*, No. 153, II, 678). For other American texts see Barry, *Journal*, XXVII, 73 (Kansas; reported from Iowa); Campbell and Sharp, No. 36 (North Carolina, Virginia, Georgia); Tolman, *Journal*, XXIX, 178 (Indiana); Belden's Missouri collection. The piece, as Barry has noted, is a variety of "The Brown Girl" (Child, No. 295), a ballad known in print in the latter half of the eighteenth century; or rather, as Kittredge suggests, it is mixed with a version of "The Brown Girl" similar to that taken down in Devonshire by Baring-Gould and printed by Child as Version B.

A

"Pretty Sally." Contributed by Mrs. E. A. Hunt, Belington, Barbour County, January, 1917.

1 There was a royal damsel, from London she came,
A royal fair damsel, called Sally by name;
Her beauty was so great, and her riches so high
That upon this poor man she would not cast an eye.

2 "O Sally, pretty Sally, O Sally, my love," said he,
"I fear that your love and mine won't agree;
I fear that your beauty to mine rue [1] untrue,
Unless your hatred is turned into love."

3 "No hatred to you, sir, nor no other man,
But to say that I love you is more than I can;
So you may drop your intentions, we'll end our discourse;
I'll never wed with you, sir, unless I am forced."

4 "No forcing, pretty Sally, no forcing, love," said he,
"No forcing, pretty Sally, for you to marry me;
But the time it will come when you will relent,
And for your past actions I hope will repent."

5 So the fourteen weeks were over, were over and past,
This royal fair damsel fell sick at the last;
. . . and she knew not for why,
She sent for this young man she once did deny.

[1] Unintelligible.

6 "O Sally, pretty Sally, O Sally, love," said he,
   "Am I the doctor, that you have sent for me?"
   "Yes, you are the doctor, both kill and can cure,
   And without your assistance I am lost, I am sure."

7 "O where does the pain lie?   Does it lie in your side?
   O where does the pain lie?   Does it lie in your head?"
   "Neither of them; the right you have not guessed:
   The pain that torments me lies sore in my breast."

8 "O Sally, pretty Sally, O Sally, my love," says he,
   "O don't you remember when I first courted thee,
   . . . you denied me with scorn?
   And I'll reward you for what's past and gone."

9 "O for what's past and gone, love, forget and forgive,
   And do grant me some longer on this earth to live."
   "I never will forgive you as long as you have breath,
   And I'll dance on your grave when you are buried in the dust."

10 Off of her fingers she pulled diamonds three,
   Saying, "Take these and wear them while dancing on me;
   And when you're done dancing, call Sally your queen,
   And fly from your country, never more to be seen."

11 Now Sally she is dead and in her low grave doth lie,
   And William he's dead and buried close by.

ℬ

"A Rich Irish Lady."   Communicated by Miss Lily Hagans, Morgantown,
Monongalia County, 1916; obtained from Miss Callie Nuzum, Harrison County,
who got it from an old gentleman of her neighborhood.

1 From London came a beautiful lady, called Sally by name;

   .   .   .   .

   A rich wealthy merchant, worth thousands a year,
   He came to court her, as you shall hear.

2 She being so handsome, her portion so high,
   That upon this young man she could scarce cast her eye;
   She was tangled in love, but knew not the reason why;
   But she sends for this young man that she once did deny.

3 "Am I the doctor, that you send for me here,
Or am I the young man that you once loved so dear?"
"O yes, you are the doctor, that can kill or can cure,
And without assistance I'm ruined, I'm sure."

4 "O where doth your pain lie, doth it lie in your side?
O where doth the pain lie, doth it lie in your head?"
"O no, loving sweetheart, the right you've not guessed;
For the pain that doth pierce me, doth lie in my breast."

5 "You've laughed at my courtship, denied me with scorn;
And now I reward you for what's past and gone."
"For what's past and gone, forget and forgive;
And grant me, O darling, some longer to live."

6 "O no, I won't, Sally, whilst e'er I draw breath;
But I'll dance o'er your grave when you're laid in the earth."
Off her finger diamond rings she pulled three
Saying, "Take care of these, love, while dancing o'er me."

C

"Pretty Sally." Communicated by Mr. J. Harrison Miller, Wardensville, Hardy County, 1916; obtained from Mrs. Sofia Funk, who secured it from Zachariah Wilson. He took it down and learned it while serving in the Civil War on the Confederate side.

1 There was a fair damsel, from London she came,
A beautiful damsel, called Sallie by name.
There was a young squire, hired at six hundred a year,
And he came to court Sallie, for he loved her very dear.

2 But Sallie being rich, her fortune very high,
Upon this young man she scarce cast an eye.
"Sallie, O Sallie!" said he,
"I am sorry your love and mine can't agree;

3 "We'll make no great out, but your love will improve,
Unless that your hatred will turn into love."
"No hatred for you, sir, nor for another man!
But to say that I love you, I am sure I never can.

4 "So drop your intention, and end your discourse,
For I never will have you unless I am forced."
When six weeks had come on, when six weeks had passed,
Pretty Sallie she had a misfortune at last.

5 She was pierced to the heart, and she knew not what for;
　So she sent for this young man whom she slighted before.
　"Good morning, pretty Sallie, good morning," said he;
　"It's where does your pain lie?　In your head or your knee?"

6 "The pain that I feel, sir, lies deep in my heart;
　The pain that I feel, sir, lies deep in your heart.
　It's you are my doctor, you can kill or can cure;
　Without your assistance I must die, I am sure."

7 "O Sallie, O Sallie, O Sallie!" said he,
　"It's don't you remember when I came to court thee?
　You laughed at my courtship and bade me begone;
　But now I reward you for what is past and gone."

8 "For things past and gone, love, forget and forgive;
　And grant me some longer, in this world to live."
　"I would freely forgive you, although you would n't me;
　And I'll dance on your grave while you lay in the earth."

9 She pulled from her fingers diamond rings, she said three,
　And gave them to William, to William for his fee:
　"I'm going to leave you; in my cold bed of clay
　My rosy red cheeks shall moulder away."

D

"A Rich Irish Lady." Communicated by Miss Lalah Lovett, Bulltown, Braxton County, May, 1917; obtained from Mr. John N. Wine, Napier, who learned it from his father.

1 There was a rich lady, from London she came;
　A beauty she was, and Sally by name;
　Her riches so great that no tongue could express them;
　And her beauty was more than her riches at best.

2 There was a young man came to see her;
　The squire's young son she then did deny;
　She then did deny him and shun him with scorn;
　I believe he'll reward her for what's past and gone.

3 There was six months came past, ere a little on a rise,
　Miss Sally was taken with tears in her eyes.
　Miss Sally was taken, they did not know why,
　For the sake of this young man she once did deny.

4 They sent for this young man, the squire's young man

. . . .

He says, "Am I the young man you sent for here?
Or am I the doctor, can kill or can cure?"

5 "I think you're the doctor, can kill or can cure;
Without your assistance I'm ruined, I'm sure."
"O Sally, O Sally, O Sally," said he,
"Don't you remember when I courted thee?

6 "You then did deny me and shun me with scorn;
And now I'll reward you for what's past and gone."
"For what's past and gone you must forget and forgive,
And grant me some longer life here to live."

7 "I'll never forget you, and that ain't the worst:
I'll dance on your grave when you're cold in the dust."
She pulled rings from her fingers, diamond rings three:
"Here, take these and wear them while dancing on me."

8 O Sally's now dead, as we all might suppose;
She has left to some lady all of her fine clothes.
She's taken up her lodging in the banks of cold clay,
While her rosy red cheeks lay mouldering away.

$\mathcal{E}$

"A Royal Fair Damsel." Contributed by Mr. T. J. Doolittle, Fairmont, Marion County. An abbreviated text in seven stanzas.

F

"The Rich Irish Lady." Communicated by Mrs. Hilary G. Richardson, Clarksburg, Harrison County, March, 1916; obtained from Mrs. Rachel Fogg, originally from Doddridge County, who learned it from her mother. A confused text in five stanzas.

115

A GAY SPANISH MAID

COMMUNICATED by Professor Walter Barnes, Fairmont, Marion County, February, 1917; obtained from Mr. George Gregg, Pocahontas County.

1 A gay Spanish maid, at the age of sixteen,
   O'er the meadows did roam far and wide;
Beneath a beech tree she sat down for to rest,
   With her gay gallant youth by her side.

2 "Our ship sails to-morrow, my darling," he said,
   "And together we'll ramble no more;
So to-night when your parents retire to their rest,
   Will you meet me, my love, by the shore?"

3 So that night when her parents retired to their rest,
   Lovely Nell she crept out the hall door,
With her hat in her hand she ran down the white sand,
   And she sat on a rock by the shore.

4 The moon was rising from far o'er the deep,
   And the sea and the sky seemed to meet,
When a wild rushing wave came from far o'er the deep,
   And it broke on a rock at her feet.

5 Her lily-white hand to her bosom she clasped,
   When she thought of her boy in the storm:
"God bless you," he'd said, "and your parents at rest!
   And from you I am far, far away.

6 "So that night we were tossed to and fro in the wind,
   And in vain many lives tried to save;
I jumped to a plank and escaped to the shore,
   While the rest they went down in the strand.

7 "No more I'll return to that girl on the shore,
   As she thought of her boy in the storm;
She died like a rose that was bitten by the frost,
   And has left me in sorrow to mourn."

116

THE PRETTY MOHEA

THIS song has been printed or reported from North Carolina, Kentucky, Missouri, Michigan, Iowa, and Montana. Kittredge remarks that it appears to be a chastened American remaking of a piece well known in English broadsides, "The Indian Lass." The latter occurs also in a New York broadside (De Marsan, List 14, No. 40). For references see *Journal*, XXXV, 408; add Bradley, *Harper's Monthly Magazine*, May, 1915, CXXX, 906; Minish MS., II, 53.

Three variants have been found in West Virginia, under the titles, "Pretty Maumee," "The Little Maumee," and "The Pretty Maumee."

A

"Pretty Maumee." Contributed by Mr. J. Harrison Miller, Wardensville, Hardy County.

1 As I went out rambling for pleasure one day,
  The scenes of creation were pleasant to see;
  As I was amusing myself on the grass,
  Who should I spy near me but a fair Indian lass.

2 She sat down beside me and took up my hand,
  Saying, "You are a stranger in a strange land."
  Saying, "If you are willing, you are welcome to come
  And live in a cottage that I call my home."

3 "Oh no, my fair maiden, that could never be,
  For I have a sweetheart far over the sea;
  I'll never forsake her, for I know she won't me,
  For her heart is as true as the little Maumee."

4 So one fair morning, one morning in May,
  To this fair maiden these words I did say:
  "I'm going to leave you; so farewell, my dear;
  My ship sails are spreading, and home I must steer."

5 The last time I saw her was down on the strand,
  And as my boat passed by her, she waved me her hand,
  Saying, "When you get home, dear, to the one that you love,
  Remember the maiden in the cocoanut grove."

6 And as my boat landed on my own native shore,
  With friends and relations around me once more,
  I stood and gazed round me but none could I see,
  That was fit to compare with the pretty Maumee.

7 For the girl I loved dear had proven untrue,

.   .   .   .

So I'll turn my course backward, from this land will I flee,
And go spend my days with the pretty Maumee.

B

"The Little Maumee." Communicated by Mr. Greenland Thompson
Federer, Morgantown, Monongalia County, January, 1917; found in an old
manuscript songbook owned by Lizzie Kelly, Independence. The name Ella
Roby written at the end of the song seems to indicate the person from whom it
was obtained.

1 As I was a-roving for pleasure one day,
In self-recollection as the time passed away,
As I was amusing myself on the grass,
Oh, who should I spy but a sweet Indian lass.

2 She stood there beside me and took up my hand,
Saying, "You look like a stranger, not one of this land."
Says she, "My pale-faced one, if you will agree,
I will teach you the language of the little Maumee."

3 She sat down beside me still holding my hand,
Saying, "You look like a stranger, not one of this land."
Says she, "My pale-faced one, if you will consent,
We'll live here together in peace and content."

4 "O no, my fair jewel, that never can be,
For I have a sweetheart in my own country;
O no, my fair jewel, that never can be;
I'll never forsake her, and I know she won't me."

5 The last time I saw her was down on the sand,
And as my boat passed she gave me her hand,
Saying, "Wherever you wander, wherever you go,
Remember the maiden where the cocoanuts grow."

6 Now I am back on my own native shore,
With friends and relatives around me once more;
Of all that's around me and all that I see,
There is none to compare with the little Maumee.

C

"The Pretty Maumee."   Contributed by Miss Alice Barnes, Bruceton Mills, Preston County, April 25, 1916.

1 As I was a-roaming for pleasure one day,
Who but an Indian maiden, came 'cross on my way.
She came and sat down by me, and took up my hand,
Saying, "You are a stranger, not one of this land.

2 "If you will agree, sir, to stay here with me,
I will teach you the language of the pretty Maumee,
And together we'll wander, and together we'll go,
Till we come to the river where the cocoanuts grow."

3 "Ah no! my fair-faced one, that never can be;
I've a sweetheart in London, across the wide sea.
And I cannot forsake her, for I know she won't me;
For her heart is as true as the pretty Maumee."

4 .   .   .   .
.   .   .   .
"And together we'll wander, and together we'll go,
Till we come to the river, where the cocoanuts grow."

117

THE SOLDIER'S WOOING

THE only version of this ballad found in West Virginia, though imperfect, retains the elements of the story. Barry, who prints a copy from New Jersey (*Journal*, XXIII, 447), points out that the ballad is somehow derived from the seventeenth-century broadside "The Master-piece of Love Songs" (see Ebsworth, *Roxburghe Ballads*, VI, 229; J. R. Smith's *Catalogue*, p. 75; Ashton, *A Century of Ballads*, p. 164), and he remarks upon the resemblance to "Erlinton" (Child, No. 8). There are recent English versions in the *Journal of the Folk-Song Society*, I, 108, and Alfred Williams' *Folk-Songs of the Upper Thames*, p. 115. American texts are published by Campbell and Sharp, No. 41 (North Carolina and Tennessee); Pound, No. 27 (Louisiana); and Tolman and Eddy, *Journal*, XXXV, 414 (Ohio: one stanza with tune), where Kittredge notes that the song was printed ca. 1800 in *The Echo; or, Columbian Songster*, 2d ed. (Brookfield, Massachusetts), p. 150. The song has been found also in Virginia (*Bulletin*, No. 4, p. 5), North Carolina (Minish MS.), Missouri (Belden, No. 84), and Canada (Tolman, *Journal*, XXIX, 188). Cf. N. I. White MS., II, 593 ("Yankee Soldier").

No local title. Communicated by Mrs. Hilary G. Richardson, Clarksburg, Harrison County, 1917; obtained from Mrs. Nancy McAtee.

1 . . . .
   . . . .
   These two couples rode to church, and, returning back again,
   There she met her cruel father and seven other men.

2 Said, "Daughter, O daughter, O daughter," said he,
   "You thought that you'd bring this great scandal on me;
   But if it's your intention to be a soldier's wife,
   Down in these lonesome valleys I'll end your sweet life."

3 The soldier overheard him, dismounted well armed,
   He swore he'd gain the day or die on the ground;
   He drew his sword and pistols and caused them to rattle;
   The lady held her breath, while the soldier fought the battle.

4 The first one he come to, he pierced him through amain;
   The next one he come to, he done just the same.
   "Let's run," said the rest, "for here we'll all be slain!
   To fight a free, bold soldier, I find it all in vain."

5 Up stepped her father, saying, "Don't let my blood run cold,
   And you shall have, my daughter, ten thousand pounds in gold."
   "Fight on!" said the lady, "that portion is too small."
   "Well, hold your hand, dear soldier, and you can have it all."

6 They mounted their horses and off they did ride,
  A fine weddin' supper for them they did pervide;
  He named them his sons and called them his heirs;
  It was n't out of free good will, but surely out of fear.

7 Come all of you ladies, wherever you may be,
  And never slight a soldier in any degree;
  For a soldier they are brave, and jolly, brisk and free,
  They will fight for their rights and their sweet libertee.

118

LADY LEROY

TOLMAN (*Journal*, XXIX, 180) prints a text from Illinois; Shoemaker (*North Pennsylvania Minstrelsy*, p. 60), one from Potter County, remarking that the song "was much sung in this part of the country in the early days."
Communicated by Mr. C. F. Lee, Davis, Tucker County; obtained from Miss Ruth Litz, who had it from her grandmother, a native of Ireland.

1 Bright Phœbus had risen and shines on the sea;
  The fields are all green, and all nature seems gay.
  I espied a fair couple on Erin's green shore,
  A-viewing the ocean where the wild billows roar.

2 Said he, "Noble Sally, you're the maid I adore;
  To go and to leave you, it grieves my heart sore.
  Your parents are rich, and they are angry with me;
  If I longer tarry here, they my ruin will be."

3 She dressed herself up in a suit of men's clothes,
  And away to her father Miss Sally she goes;
  She purchased a vessel, paid down the demand,
  Saying, "Hurry up, love!   There's nothing to lose."

4 .   .   .   .
  .   .   .   .
  They hoisted their topsails and hooted for joy,
  And over the wide ocean sailed the Lady Leroy.

5 When her cruel father, this news he did hear,
  He swore a revenge on his own daughter dear;
  He swore that his daughter should ne'er be his wife,
  And for her disobedience he would end her sweet life.

6 He bade his captain get ready, and fix for a fight;
  To bring them to justice was all his delight:
  "Go pursue them and catch, and their lives destroy;
  For he shall ne'er enjoy the fair Lady Leroy."

7 So proud of his message, this bold captain goes,
  In pursuit of these lovers like a bold daring foe;
  He espied a tall ship and his colors let fly,
  When he hailed her and found she was the Lady Leroy.

8 "O you must return to old Erin's shore,
Or a broadside of shot into you I will pour."
And Sally's true lover, made then this reply:
"We will never surrender until we conquer or die."

9 Then broadside after broadside upon them did pour,
And louder than thunder bright cannons did roar;
And Sally's true lover gained the victory;
And for these two lovers, they may ever go free.

10 They landed in Boston, that city of fame;
Captain and sailor will tell you the same.
Here's a health to you, Harry, and the Lady Leroy,
The source of his comfort, and her only joy!

119

THE BANKS OF THE SWEET DUNDEE

OF the English broadside song "The Banks of Sweet Dundee" (or "Undaunted Mary") a fragmentary Ohio text is printed by Tolman and Eddy (*Journal*, XXXV, 354). Barry records the piece (No. 50); it is known in Nova Scotia and New Brunswick. Belden has found it in Missouri. It has been published in various American songbooks and broadsides. For full references see Kittredge, *Journal*, XXXV, 355.

A

"On the Banks of Sweet Dundee." Communicated by Miss Mildred Joy Barker, Morgantown, Monongalia County, October 2, 1916; obtained from her mother.

1 'T is of a girl in London, most beautiful untold;
  Her parents died and left her five thousand pounds in gold;
  She lived with her uncle, the cause of all her woe,
  And you shall hear this maiden fair did prove her overthrow.

2 Her uncle had a plowboy, whom Mary loved full well,
  Down in her uncle's garden, those tales of love did tell;
  There was a wealthy squire, who often came to see,
  But Mary loved her plowboy best, on the banks of the sweet
      Dundee.

3 Her uncle rose one early morn, and, walking up straightway,
  He knocked upon her bedroom door and unto her did say:
  "Arise, arise, my pretty maid, a lady you shall be,
  For the squire is waiting for you on the banks of the sweet
      Dundee."

4 "A fig for all your squires, your lords and dukes likewise!
  For Willie's eyes appear to me like diamonds in the skies."
  "Begone, you unruly female! unhappy you shall be,
  For I mean to banish Willie from the banks of the sweet
      Dundee."

5 The press-gang came to William, when he was out alone;
  He boldly fought for liberty, although there were six to one;
  The blood did flow in torrents: "Pray kill me now," said he,
  "For I'd rather die for Mary on the banks of the sweet Dundee."

6 As Mary walked out one morning, lamenting for her love,
  She spied this wealthy squire, down in her uncle's grove;
  He laid his hand upon her: "Stand off, stand off!" said she,
  "For you've slain the only lad I love on the banks of the sweet
     Dundee."

7 He clasped his arms about her, he tried her voice to drown;
  Two pistols and a sword he spied beneath her morning gown;
  Young Mary drew those pistols, and the sword she used so free,
  She shot and fired and killed the squire on the banks of the sweet
     Dundee.

8 Her uncle overheard the noise without and hastened to the
     sound:
  "Since you have killed the squire, I'll give you your death
     wound."
  "Stand off, stand off!" said Mary, "undaunted I will be,"
  And the pistols drew and her uncle slew on the banks of the
     sweet Dundee.

9 A doctor soon was sent for, a man of noted skill,
  Who, likewise for a lawyer, for him to draw his will;
  He willed his gold to Mary, who fought so manfully,
  And he closed his eyes, no more to rise, on the banks of the sweet
     Dundee.

B

"Sweet William." Communicated by Mr. George Paugh, Thomas, Tucker
County, October, 1915; obtained from Mrs. Stella Thomas, Ben Bush, who
learned it about twenty years before from Mrs. Molly.

1 There was a farmer's daughter, a beauty to behold;
  Her parents died and left her ten thousand pounds of gold;
  She stayed with her uncle, the cause of her woe,
  And you may hear the interfere that caused and overthrough.

2 Her uncle had a plowboy that Mary loved full well,
  And in the garden walking, some tales of love they told;
  There was a wealthy squire, who often came to see,
  But still she loved her William, on the banks of a sweet Dandee.

3 Her uncle and the squire rode out one summer's day;
  Her uncle came to her and unto her did say:
  "Go dress yourself, my Mary; a lady you shall be,
  The wealthy squire is waiting on the banks of the sweet Dandee."

4 "A fig for all your squires, your lords, and dukes as well!
   Young William has already proved bright diamonds in my eyes;
   You're going to ruin a female that never can happy be,
   If you intend to banish William, on the banks of the sweet
     Dandee."

5 The brave ones they went to him, where he was all alone;
   He boldly fought for liberty, but there was ten to one;
   His blood it overflowed to ruin: "Pray, kill not!" said he,
   "For I'll freely die for Mary on the banks of the sweet Dandee."

6 As Mary was out a-walking one morning for her love,
   She spied the wealthy squire down in her uncle's grove;
   He threw his arms around her and bade her to sit down,
   Two swords and a pistol, beneath his morning gown.

7 . . . .
   . . . .
   She snatched the weapons from him, and drew somenthly,[1]
   And killed the wealthy squire, on the banks of the sweet Dandee.

8 Her uncle heard the noise, all hasten to the ground,
   Saying, "Now you've killed the squire, I'll give you your death
     wound."
   She rose up on her feet, and dandy she did be,
   Her dagger drew, her uncle slew, on the banks of the sweet
     Dandee.

9 A doctor soon was sent for, a man of noble's killed;[2]
   And likewise a lawyer, to sign a death will.
   He willed his gold to Mary, who had fought somanthye,[1]
   And he closed his eyes no more to rise, on the banks of the sweet
     Dandee.

---

[1] For *so manfully.*   [2] For *noble skill.*

120

WILLIAM TAYLOR

THIS is the famous English ballad of "William Taylor" or "Bold William Taylor": see broadside printed by H. Such, No. 344; Ashton, *Modern Street Ballads*, p. 259; Sharp, *Folk-Songs from Somerset*, V, 46, 48; *One Hundred English Folksongs*, No. 71; Sharp, *English Folk-Songs*, I, 114; *Journal of the Folk-Song Society*, I, 254; III, 214; V, 68, 161. For references see *Journal of the Folk-Song Society*, V, 163–164. Firth prints the song as "The Female Lieutenant; or, Faithless Love Rewarded" from a broadside without imprint (*Naval Songs and Ballads*, p. 326); he remarks (p. 363) that the Douce collection has "The Female Sailor's Garland" in three parts.

For American texts see *Journal*, XXII, 380 (Barry; Massachusetts, from Ireland; Pennsylvania); XXVIII, 162 (Perrow; North Carolina); Babcock, *Folk-Lore Journal*, VII, 30 (Virginia); Campbell and Sharp, No. 51 (North Carolina); Mackenzie, p. 137 (Nova Scotia); cf. Barry, *Journal*, XXII, 74 (tune only); Belden, *Journal*, XXV, 9; F. C. Brown, p. 10.

A comic version ("Billy Taylor"), differing but slightly from the standard text (which, indeed, is comic enough without any change) was popular on the English stage from the latter part of the eighteenth century until the middle of the nineteenth, and even later. It appears sometimes in Cockney lingo, sometimes in ordinary language: see *Journal of the Folk-Song Society*, V, 69, 163; engraved broadside, published September 24, 1804, by Laurie and Whittle, London; Firth, *Naval Songs and Ballads*, p. 327 (from *Fairburn's Naval Songster for 1805*, p. 16); *The Universal Songster, or, Museum of Mirth* (London, 1834), I, 65; *The Vauxhall Comic Song Book*, edited by J. W. Sharp, 1st Series, p. 27; *Sam Cowell's Budget from Yankee Land*, p. [10]; *The Dublin Comic Songster*, 1841, p. 13; Hodges broadside; *Notes and Queries*, 11th Series, I, 115. This text is found in American songbooks (both in Cockney dialect and in regular English): as, *The Vocal Annual or Singer's Own Book for 1832* (Boston), p. 28; *The Shamus O'Brien Songster* (cop. 1866), p. 37; *Billy Emerson's New Comic Songster* (New York, 1868), p. 41; *The "Brigham Young" Songster* (cop. 1871), p. 3; *Birch and Backus' Songs of the San Francisco Minstrels* (cop. 1881), p. 99. Naturally enough, it turns up now and then (somewhat modified) in oral circulation: see Greig, *Folk-Song of the North-East*, CI; Murison MS., fol. 53.

Communicated without title by Mrs. Hilary G. Richardson, Clarksburg, Harrison County, 1917; obtained from Mrs. Nancy McAtee.

1 William Taylor and his own true lovyer
   Went to church there married for to be,
And there he was seized by the British captain,
   And off to the wars he was forced away.

2 This kind-hearted lady she follered him after,
   And she enlisted on a man-of-war,
With her lily-white hands so neat and so tender,
   All besmeared with pitch and tar.

3 The very next morning there was a scrummage,

    .   .   .   .

   The lily-white buttons flew off her waistcoat,
      And there appeared her snowy-white breast.

4 "Lady," said the captain,
      "What misfortune brought you here?"
   "I am a-seeking for my William Taylor,
      That was forced away to the war."

5 "If you are seeking for your William Taylor,
      That was forced away to the war,
   He is married to another lady
      And is living on the island of Pain.

6 "If you will arise to-morrow morning
      And put on your clothes by day,
   There you will see your William Taylor,
      A-walking with his lady so gay."

7 The very next morning she arose early
      And put on her clothes by day,
   And there she spied her own true lover,
      A-walking with his lady so gay.

8 "William Taylor, you are my own true lovyer,
      And all for your sake I have ventured my life;
   This lady that got you shall never enjoy you,
      For this moment I'll end your life."

9 Then she called for a brace of pistols;
      The brace they was giving at her command,
   And down she shot her William Taylor,
      As he had hold of his lady's hand.

10 Then to the bars she was seized as a criminal,
      And her plea you all shall hear:
   "Take me from this world of sorrow,
      For I am lost for the shooting of my dear."

121

DOG AND GUN

In West Virginia this song goes by the titles, "The Squire" and "The Farmer's Bride." Five texts have been recovered in which the stories do not differ in any important particular.

"Dog and Gun" is the English song usually entitled "The Golden Glove" or "The Squire of Tamworth," which was printed as a broadside in this country early in the nineteenth century. For references see *Journal*, XXIX, 171; Campbell and Sharp, p. 330. American texts from recitation or singing are printed by Tolman, *Journal*, XXIX, 171 (Kansas from Pennsylvania); Wyman and Brockway, p. 49 (Kentucky); Campbell and Sharp, No. 52 (North Carolina; tunes from North Carolina and Virginia). Cf. Barry, No. 38; Belden, No. 45 (*Journal*, XXV, 12); Shearin and Combs, p. 11. The song occurs also in a Philadelphia chapbook of about 1830 (Harvard College, 25276.43.81) and in the *Singer's Journal*, I, 451.

A

No local title. Communicated by Mrs. W. M. Parker, New Haven, Mason County, July 29, 1916; obtained from Miss Alverda Everett, Romney, whose mother learned it many years before.

1 There was a rich merchant in London did dwell,
  He had but one daughter, whom none could excel;
  She courted a young farmer, and to prevent the day
  Of their marriage, they sent this young farmer away.

2 There was a rich squire who lived in the town,
  Who courted this fair damsel of fairest renown;
  He courted for to marry, was all his intent,
  For friends and relations had give their consent.

3 The day was appointed, the knot to be tied,
  The farmer was chosen to wait upon the bride;
  No sooner did this lady on the farmer cast an eye,
  "O my heart! O my heart!" and for sorrow she cried.

4 Instead of getting married she went to her bed,
  The thoughts of the farmer were rolling in her head;
  The thoughts of the farmer were rolling in her mind,
  And a way for to gain him she quickly did find.

5 So early the next morning this lady arose,
  And dressed up herself in a suit of man's clothes;
  Waistcoat, coat, and breeches this lady put on,
  And away she went hunting with her dog and her gun.

6 She hunted all round where the farmer did dwell,
  She felt in her heart that she loved him so well;
  Often did she fire, but nothing did she kill,
  Till at last the young farmer came into the field.

7 "Why ain't you at the wedding?" this lady replied,
  "To wait upon the squire and give to him his bride?"
  "O, kind sir, the truth to you I'll tell;
  I can't give her away, I love her too well."

8 It pleased this young lady to hear him so bold;
  She gave him a glove all flowered with gold,
  Saying, "This I did find as I came along,
  As I was out hunting with my dog and my gun."

9 She then returned home with her heart full of love,
  Relating the news that she had lost one of her gloves;
  "And if any man will find it and bring it to me,
  I vow and declare his sweet bride I will be."

10 No sooner than the farmer had heard of the news
   Than he ran to the bride without his hat or shoes,
   Saying, "Here, kind miss, I have brought you your glove;
   Now will you be so kind as to grant me your love?"

11 "My love's already granted," this lady she replied,
   "I love the sweet breath of a farmer," she cried;
   "I'll be the mistress of your dairy and the milker of your cow,
   While my jolly young farmer goes whistling after his plow."

12 The day they were married she related the fun,
   How she hunted her love with her dog and her gun;
   "And now I have got him so fast in a snare,
   I'll enjoy him forever — so, fare you well, squire."

ℬ

"The Squire." Contributed by Miss Sallie D. Jones, Hillsboro, Pocahontas County, January, 1917; learned forty-six years before from Miss M. E. Harper as "she walked back and forth spinning yarn from carded rolls on a big wheel." A good text in eleven stanzas.

C

No local title. Contributed by Mr. John B. Adkins, Branchland, Lincoln County, April 1, 1916; learned, he does not know how, but his father, who was then sixty years old, says he knew it when a boy. A good text in eleven stanzas.

D

"The Farmer's Bride." Communicated by Mrs. Don McClaugherty, Montcalm, Mercer County; learned from her mother, Mrs. Alice Burgess, who learned it from her mother, Mrs. Harriet Clemons, Randolph County. Ten stanzas, more or less confused.

E

"It's of a Squire." Communicated by Miss Lucinda Strother, Weston, Lewis County; obtained from her mother and Mrs. Mary Frazier. A somewhat confused copy, beginning: "It's of a young squier and his muckineer."

122

PRETTY POLLY

THIS is the favorite English song of "Polly Oliver" or "Polly Oliver's Rambles," common in broadsides (as Catnach; Such, No. 369; Bebbington, Manchester, No. 267; Pearson, Manchester). See Ebsworth, *Roxburghe Ballads*, VII, 739; Chappell, *Popular Music*, II, 676; Kidson, *Traditional Tunes*, p. 116; Baring-Gould, *English Minstrelsie*, VII, xxi; *Notes and Queries*, 3d Series, XII, 229; Buck, *The Oxford Song Book*, p. 152 (rewritten).

For American texts see *Journal*, XII, 248 (Newell; North Carolina); XXIV, 337 (Barry; Massachusetts, from Ireland); Campbell and Sharp, No. 44 (North Carolina); Belden's Missouri collection. Cf. Barry, No. 34 (tune in *Journal*, XXII, 75); Shearin and Combs, p. 27.

Communicated by Professor Walter Barnes, Fairmont, Marion County, July, 1915; obtained from Mr. G. W. Cunningham, Elkins, Randolph County, who learned it from Ellen Howell, Dry Fork.

1 Pretty Polly lay musing on her downy bed,
   Some folly, some fancy came into her head:
   "Neither father nor mother can make me false prove;
   I 'll dress like a soldier and follow my love."

2 So early next morning pretty Polly arose,
   She dressed herself in a suit of men's clothes;
   Her hair on her shoulders on links it did hang,
   And every degree she looked just like a man.

3 She went to the stables and viewed the stage round,
   Till at length she found one that could travel the ground;
   With a brace of brass pistols and a sword by her side,
   She her father's best gueldon [1] like a soldier did ride.

4 She rode till she came to the town of renown,
   And there she put up at the price of a crown;
   The first one that came to her was a brave English lord,
   And the next was Duke William, pretty Polly's true love.

5 Saying, "Here is a letter from Polly, your love;
   O, here is a letter from Polly, your dear;
   And under the sealing is a guinea to be found,
   That you and your sailors may drink her health round."

6 Miss Polly, being weary, she hung down her head,
   She called for a candle and likewise a bed.
   "A bed!" said the captain, "I 've one at my ease,
   And you may lie with me, young man, if you please."

---

[1] For *gelding.*

7 "O, to lie with the captain's a dangerous thing
For a new-listed soldier who fights for the king;
For to fight before Sepoy or to fight on the land,
I'm a new-listed soldier, just under command."

8 It was early next morning pretty Polly arose;
She dressed herself in her own wearing clothes;
Came stepping down stairs, saying, "How constant I prove!
O, here is pretty Polly, Duke William's true love."

9 Now Polly she's married and lives at her ease,
She goes when'er she will and returns when she please;
She has left her old parents in sorrow to mourn,
They'd give thousands of pounds for pretty Polly's return.

123

THE JACK OF TAR

THIS song, of which I have seen no other American version, is known in England as "The Saucy Sailor." See Sharp, *One Hundred English Folksongs*, No. 45 (references, p. xxxi); *Journal*, xxxv, 373. The situation is like that in the next piece (p. 390).

Communicated by Miss Mildred Joy Barker, Morgantown, Monongalia County; obtained from her mother, who learned it from her father, Martin Brookover.

1 "Come, my fairest, come, my dearest,
        And listen unto me;
    Will you marry a poor sailor boy,
        Who has just come home from the sea?"

2 "You are ragged, sir, you are dirty,
        And smell so strong of tar;
    Begone, you dirty sailor boy!
        Begone, you Jack of tar!"

3 "Though I'm ragged, miss, though I'm dirty,
        And smell so strong of tar,
    I have pockets filled with silver, love,
        And gold laid up in store."

4 Soon as these words were spoken,
        Down on her knees she fell,
    Saying, "Forgive me, noble sailor!
        I love the sailor well."

5 "I will cross o'er the briny ocean,
        Where the meadows grow so green;
    But since you refused my offer, miss,
        Another shall wear the ring."

6 "You may cross o'er the briny ocean,
        Where the meadows grow so green;
    But since I refused your offer, sir,
        Another may wear the ring."

124

YOUNG JOHNNY

THIS is the favorite song of "The Green Bed" (also known as "Jack Tar" and "The Liverpool Landlady"), common in English broadsides and orally current in England and Scotland (see references, *Journal*, XXXV, 373). For American texts see *Journal*, XXV, 7 (Belden; Missouri); XXVIII, 156 (Perrow; North Carolina); XXXV, 373 (Tolman and Eddy; Ohio); Belden, *Herrig's Archiv*, CXX, 68 (Missouri); Campbell and Sharp, No. 48 (North Carolina); Mackenzie, pp. 70, 190, 193 (Nova Scotia); cf. Shearin and Combs, p. 14 (Kentucky).

No local title. Communicated by Miss Mary Meek Atkeson, Morgantown, Monongalia County, January, 1917; obtained from Miss Berda Lynch.

1   Young Johnnie sailed from London,
     Young Johnnie sailed from sea,
   Young Johnnie sailed from London
     To where he used to be.

2   O what for luck had Johnnie,
     O what for luck had he,
   O what for luck had Johnnie,
     While sailing o'er the sea?

3   "My luck," said poor Johnnie,
     "Was misfortune and disgrace."
   .   .   .   .
   .   .   .   .

4   "Call down your daughter Mollie,
     And place her on my knee;
   We'll drown out all melancholy,
     And happy we will be."

5   "My beds they are all full, John,
     And have been for a week,
   And since you have no money,
     Your lodging is to seek."

6   His hand ran in his pocket,
     And, there to behold,
   .   .   .   .
     Both pockets full of gold.

7   "When I had no money,
        My lodging was to seek;
    Before I'd stay here now,
        I'd lie out in the street.

8   "Now I am single,
        And the dollars I can whirl;
    Give me a glass of brandy,
        And some better girl."

125

THE MILKMAID

For English references see Sharp, *One Hundred English Folksongs*, p. xxxi (No. 44). No song is better known in America. It has often been printed in songbooks: as, *The Universal Songster* (New York, 1829), p. 119; *The New York Songster for 1836*, p. 61; *The Souvenir Minstrel*, edited by C. Soule Cartee (Philadelphia, 1837), p. 87; *The American Minstrel* (Cincinnati, 1837), p. 221; *The Virginia Warbler* (Richmond, 1845), p. 99; *The Southern Warbler* (Charleston, 1845), p. 99; *Home Sentimental Songster* (New York, T. W. Strong), p. 239; *The Book of Popular Songs* (Philadelphia, 1861), p. 123; *The Vocalist's Favorite Songster* (New York, 1885). See Pound, No. 112.

The only American text, so far as I know, to show the English refrain of "dabbling in the dew" is West Virginia A.

A

Contributed by Mr. Wallie Barnett, Leon, Mason County, 1916; learned from his mother.

1   "Where are you going, my pretty little fair maid,
      Red rosy cheeks and curly black hair?"
    "I'm going a-milking," so kind-like she answered him.
      Sailing in the dew makes a milkmaid fair

2   "What is your father, my pretty little fair maid,
      Red rosy cheeks and curly black hair?"
    "My father's a farmer," so kind-like she answered him.
      Sailing in the dew makes a milkmaid fair

3   "What is your mother, my pretty little fair maid,
      Red rosy cheeks and curly black hair?"
    "My mother's a weaver," so kind-like she answered him.
      Sailing in the dew makes a milkmaid fair

4   "What is your fortune, my pretty little fair maid,
      Red rosy cheeks and curly black hair?"
    "My face is my fortune," so kind-like she answered him.
      Sailing in the dew makes a milkmaid fair

5   "Then I will not marry you, my pretty little fair maid,
      Red, rosy cheeks and curly black hair."
    "Nobody cares, sir," so kind-like she answered him.
      Sailing in the dew makes a milkmaid fair

B

Contributed by Miss Mabel A. Myers, Summersville, Nicholas County, July 20, 1916; learned from her mother.

1 "Where are you going, my pretty maid?"
   "I'm going a-milking, sir," she said.

2 "May I go with you, my pretty maid?"
   "Yes, if you please, kind sir," she said.

3 "What is your fortune, my pretty maid?"
   "My face is my fortune, sir," she said.

4 "Then I can't marry you, my pretty maid."
   "Nobody asked you, sir," she said.

126

MY PRETTY MAID

For this song, usually known as "Seventeen Come Sunday," see Johnson, *The Scots Musical Museum*, No. 397 (as altered by Burns); Cromek, *Select Scotish Songs*, 1810, II, 116; Lyle, *Ancient Ballads and Songs*, 1827, p. 155; Ford, *Vagabond Songs and Ballads of Scotland*, I, 102; broadside, "Soldier and the Fair Maid" (Forth, Pocklington, No. 66); Sharp and Marson, *Folk-Songs from Somerset*, II, 4; Sharp, *One Hundred English Folksongs*, No. 61; Sharp, *English Folk Songs*, I, 104; Butterworth, *Folk Songs from Sussex*, p. 16; *Journal of the Folk-Song Society*, I, 92; II, 9, 269; IV, 291; Baring-Gould, *Songs of the West*, No. 73, III, 42 (rewritten; cf. IV, xxxiv). Cf. Child, IV, 389.

Contributed by Miss Bessie Bock, Farmington, Marion County; learned from her grandmother, a lady of Scotch-Irish descent, who learned it when a little girl and who would be eighty years old if now living.

1 "O where are you going, my pretty maid?
 O where are you going, my honey?"
 She answered me so modestly,
  "An errand for my mommie."

2 "How old are you, my pretty maid?
 How old are you, my honey?"
 She answered me so modestly,
  "I'm seventeen come Sunday."

3 "O where do you live, my pretty maid?
 O where do you live, my honey?"
 She answered me so modestly,
  "In a wee, wee cot with my mommie."

4 "Will you marry me, my pretty maid?
 Will you marry me, my honey?"
 She answered me so modestly,
  "If it were n't for my mommie."

127

KITTY WELLS

THE proper title is "Kitty Wells," and the song regularly begins "You ask what makes this darkie weep." In a New York broadside, De Marsan (List 6, No. 32), it is ascribed to Thomas Sloan, Jr. See H. A. Franz, *American Popular Songs* (Berlin, 1867), p. 31; *The Captain Jinks, of the Horse Marines, Songster* (cop. 1868), p. 44; *Dan Bryant's "Shoo Fly" Songster* (cop. 1869), p. 41; *The "Blonde" of the Period Songster* (cop. 1869), p. 41; *Singer's Journal*, I, 28; Partridge broadside (Boston), No. 540; Partridge's *New National Songster*, I, 38; *Gus Williams' Old-Fashioned G. A. R. Camp-Fire Songster*, p. 7; Shoemaker, p. 119; Pound, p. 65, and No. 94; Shearin and Combs, p. 22.

"Katy Wells." Communicated by Miss Violet Noland, Davis, Tucker County, March 24, 1916; obtained from Mr. John Raese, who learned it when a boy and wrote it down in 1880.

1   You might ask what causes me to weep,
      While others 'round me are so gay;
    What makes the tears roll down my cheeks
      From early morn till close of day.

Chorus

While the birds are singing in the morning,
    And the myrtle and the ivy are in bloom,
And the sun over the hilltops a-dawning,
    It was then we laid her in the tomb.

2   My mournful story you shall hear,
      While in my memory fresh it dwells;
    It will cause you to drop a tear
      Over the grave of my sweet Kate Wells.

3   I never shall forget the day,
      While together 'round the dell,
    I kissed her cheek and named the day
      That I should marry Kate Wells.

4   But death came in my cabin door
      And stole from me my joy, my pride;
    But when I found she was no more,
      I laid my banjo down and cried.

5   The springtime has no charms for me,
      Though flowers are blooming in the dell;
    'T is that sweet form I can not see,
      The form of my dear Kate Wells.

128

THE YELLOW ROSE OF TEXAS

THIS song was once popular on the Minstrel stage. See *Christy's Plantation Melodies No. 2*, p. 52; *The Christy's Minstrels' Song Book* (London), II, 84 (with music); *Beadle's Dime Song Book No. 3* (cop. 1859), p. 8; *American Dime Song Book* (Philadelphia, cop. 1860), p. 38; *The Book of Popular Songs* (Philadelphia, 1861), p. 310; *"Ham-Town Students'" Songster* (cop. 1875), p. 85; *J. H. Haverly's Genuine Refined Minstrel Songster*, p. 12; *Sheffer & Blakely's New Coon Done Gone Songster*, p. 53; *Singer's Journal*, I, 64; De Marsan broadside, List 10, No. 108. Belden has found the song in Missouri.

Communicated by Mr. J. Harrison Miller, Wardensville, Hardy County.

1   There is a yellow rose in Texas
        That I am going to see;
     No other darkey only knew her,
        No darkey only me.
     She cried so when I left her,
        It like to broke my heart,
     And if I ever find her,
        We never more shall part.

Chorus

     She's the sweetest rose of color
        That this darkey ever knew;
     Her eyes are as bright as diamonds,
        And they sparkle like the dew.
     You may talk about your dearest May,
        And sing of Rosa Lee,
     But the yellow Rose of Texas
        Beats the belles of Tennessee.

2   The Rio Grande is flowing,
        And the starry skies are bright;
     She walks along the river,
        In the quiet summer night.
     She thinks if I remembers,
        When we parted long ago,
     I promised to come back again
        And not to leave her so.

3   O now I'm going to find her,
     For my heart is full of woe;
  And we'll sing the song together
     That we sang so long ago.
  I will play the banjo gaily,
     And we'll sing songs of yore,
  And the yellow Rose of Texas
     Shall be mine forevermore.

129

THE DRUNKARD'S DREAM

THIS is common in English broadsides under the title "The Husband's Dream" (Ryle & Co.; Such, No. 341; Bebbington, Manchester, No. 128; Gilbert, Newcastle, No. 135) and is found under that title in a New York broadside (De Marsan, List 11, No. 43). As "The Drunkard's Dream" it is printed in *The Singer's Journal*, II, 446. See also Shearin and Combs, p. 33; Belden's Missouri collection.

A

Communicated by Miss Violet Noland, Davis, Tucker County, March 24, 1916; obtained from Mr. John Raese, who learned it when a boy and wrote it down in 1880.

1 "O Demrid, you look so healthy now,
    You dress so neat and clean;
I never see you drinking now;
    Come tell me where you have been.

2 "Your wife and children, are they well?
    You once did use them strange;
O are you kinder to them getting?
    How came this happy change?"

3 "It was a dream, a happy dream,
    That heaven sent to me,
To snatch me from a drunkard's curse,
    Grim death and misery.

4 "I laughed and sung in drunkard's glee,
    While Mary's tears did stream;
Then like a beast I fell asleep
    And had this happy dream.

5 "I dreamed once more I staggered home;
    I found a solemn gloom;
I missed my wife; where could she be,
    And strangers in the room.

6 "'Poor thing, she's dead,' they say,
    'She has led a wretched life!
Grief and woe has broke her heart,
    Who'd be a drunkard's wife?'

7   "My little children oft awake,
      'O father, dear,' they say,
  'Poor mother has been weeping so,
      Because we had no bread.'

8   "' Speak to me! do speak to me!
      No more I 'll cause you pain;
  I 'll never grieve your broken heart;
      I never will drink again.' "

9   He pressed her to his throbbing heart,
      While Mary's tears did stream;
  Then ever since we have been blest
      For sending such a dream.

ℬ

Communicated by Professor C. E. Haworth, Huntington, Cabell County.
He obtained it from Mrs. J. A. Rollyson.

1   "O Ed, you look so happy now,
      And are so neat and clean;
  I have not seen you drunk about;
      Pray tell me what this means."

2   "I dreamed one night I staggered home;
      It was a dismal gloom;
  I missed my wife; where could she be?
      Strangers were in the room.

3   "I heard them say, 'Poor thing she 's dead!
      She 's led a wretched life;
  For grief and pain have broke her heart;
      Who 'd be a drunkard's wife!'

4   "My children they were crying round
      And scarcely drew their breath;
  They stooped and kissed her lifeless lips,
      So pale, so cold, like death.

5   "'Papa dear, come wake her up!
      Come wake her up!' they said;
  'And have her speak or smile once more,
      And we 'll ne'er cry for bread.'

6   "'O Mary dear, come speak to me!
    Come speak to me!' I cried;
 'I'll never break your loving heart,
    I'll ne'er get drunk again.'

7   "And then I woke, it was a dream
    That heaven had sent to me;
 And I found my Mary by my side,
    As well as she could be.

8   "I clasped her to my loving breast,
    While tears of joy did stream,
 And ever since I've heaven blest
    For sending me that dream.

9   "For I am happy now at home
    With wife and children dear,
 And I will ne'er a drunkard roam;
    Farewell to rum's career!"

130

FORWARD, BOYS, HURRAH!

COMMUNICATED by Mr. George W. Cunningham, Elkins, Randolph County, July 26, 1916; obtained from Mrs. Ida Harding Caplinger, who learned it from her mother while living in Baltimore.

Communicated, with scarcely any variations except in arrangement of stanzas, by Miss Sallie Evans, Elkins, Randolph County; obtained from Miss Katherine Hart, who received it from Mrs. Caplinger.

1 These temperance folks do crowd us awfully,
　　Crowd us awfully, crowd us awfully,
　These temperance folks do crowd us awfully,
　　You need not think I care.

Chorus

　Then forward, boys, hurrah!
　　We'll join this glorious fray;
　We'll hoist our flag and on to victory,
　　The right shall gain the day.

2 I'm not the man to lose my liberty,
　　Lose my liberty, lose my liberty,
　I'm not the man to lose my liberty,
　　I hain't a bit to spare.

3 I'd like to know what's all this fuss about,
　　All this fuss about, all this fuss about,
　I'd like to know what's all this fuss about,
　　There's something smashing through.

4 They stick the pledge, these blue teetotallers,
　　Blue teetotallers, blue teetotallers,
　They stick the pledge, these blue teetotallers,
　　Beneath each ruby nose.

5 They talk of woe and want and poverty,
　　Want and poverty, want and poverty,
　They talk of woe and want and poverty,
　　There's truth in that I s'pose.

6 My coat, I know, is rather seedy,
　　And my pants are tattered too;
　My right foot goes but poorly booted,
　　And the left one wears a shoe.

7 I wish these folks would cease to pity me,
      Cease to pity me, cease to pity me,
   I wish these folks would cease to pity me,
      I'm not yet quite bereft.

8 Though, come to search my once fat pocket-book,
      Once fat pocket-book, once fat pocket-book,
   Though, come to search my once fat pocket-book,
      There's not a sixpence left.

9 There's a wife down town would smile like Venus,
      If I'd sign the pledge this day;
   There's a bright-eyed child would dance and caper,
      You may pass the pledge this way.

131

TEMPERANCE SONG

CONTRIBUTED by Mr. F. A. Bradley, Grafton, Taylor County; learned from his grandmother when he was a child. Belden has found this piece in Missouri ("The Drunkard's Doom").

1 I saw a man at early dawn
   Stand at the grogshop door;
His eyes were sunk, his lips were parched;
   I viewed him o'er and o'er.

2 An infant child stood by his side
   And unto him it said:
"Dear father, mother lies sick at home,
   And sister cries for bread."

3 He staggered into the grogshop door
   And to the landlord said,
"Fill up my bowl once more."

   .   .   .   .

4 The landlord rose at his request,
   With liquor filled his bowl;
He drank while wife and children starved,
   And ruined his own soul.

5 One year ago I passed that way:
   A crowd stood round the door;
I asked the reason and one replied,
   "The drunkard is no more."

6 The hearse drove slowly, slowly on,
   No wife nor children there;
They'd gone before their murdered,[1]
   And left this world of care.

7 Young men, from this take warning;
   Touch not the glistening bowl,
For it hastens you into your tomb
   And ruins your own soul.

[1] Belden's text reads *the murderer*.

132

WHEN I WAS ONE–AND–TWENTY

Communicated by Mr. C. L. Underwood, Moundsville, Marshall County; obtained from his father, who learned it when a boy in Tyler County.

1 When I was one-and-twenty my daddy set me free,
He gave me money plenty to go out upon a spree;
O money being plenty, and whiskey being free,
When one glass was empty another was filled for me.

2 I gathered up the saddles and started for the barn,
I saddled up old Grayie, thinking of no harm;
I mounted on her back, and rode away so still,
Then I never drew a sober breath until I came to Sistersville.

3 There was some acquaintances I did recall;
They told me of a place where there was going to be a ball;
I was hard to persuade, but at last I did give way,
And they took me to the place where the fiddler was to play.

4 Now for some fun, boys, I will tell you in advance!
Four of us got the floor, to take a civil dance;
The fiddler being ready, his arms being strong,
Then we played "The Drowned Irish Boy" for four hours long.

5 "Daylight now, boys! you have danced long enough!
Let us spend a single moment getting cash for snuff."
You will run around and talk, you will make a dreadful flourish,
When you are guilty of the same crime, perhaps a great deal worse.

6 Now come on, good honest people, who carry news about,
And tell no lies on me, for I am mad without;
For I am down and out . . .
All caused by the use of whiskey and snuff.

133

JONAH

COMMUNICATED by Mr. John H. Toler, Sun Hill, Wyoming County, February 29, 1916; obtained from his brother, who got it from the Rev. F. M. Farley. For three comic stanzas on Jonah see Perrow, *Journal*, XXVI, 159 (Indiana).

1 In the Bible we are told
   Of a prophet that was called
      To a city that was steeped in awful sin;
   All the people in that place
   Were devoid of saving grace,
      And the prophet seemed afraid to enter in.

Chorus

Over there, over there, in that land so bright and fair,
On the halleluia stand, I'll take Jonah by the hand,
      And he'll tell me all about it over there.

2 So this prophet forth was sent,
   That old Niveth [1] might repent,
      But instead of that to Tarship [2] he set sail;
   O, the winds began to blow;
   Overboard did Jonah go,
      And he found a mercy seat inside the whale.

3 In the dark and stormy deep
   Tears of grief did Jonah weep,
      And the big fish spit him out upon the shore;
   Then old Jonah went his way,
   And he preached both night and day,
      And he did n't care to backslide any more.

4 There are some folks don't believe
   That a whale could him receive,
      But that does not make my song all untrue;
   There are whales on every side,
   With their big mouths open wide:
      Just take care, my friend, or one will swallow you!

---

[1] Error for *Nineveh.*   [2] For *Tarshish.*

5 Many souls are tossed about
   By the whales of fear and doubt,
      But the Saviour waits to take them by the hand;
   If you'll listen to his voice,
   And will take him for your choice,
      He will lead you to that Promised Land.

134

THE LITTLE FAMILY

FOR American texts of this ballad on the Raising of Lazarus see Tolman, *Journal*, XXIX, 182; XXXV, 388 (Ohio). Cf. Belden, No. 38 (*Journal*, XXV, 17).

A

"The Little Family." Communicated by Mrs. Hilary G. Richardson, Clarksburg, Harrison County, September, 1916 (see *Journal*, XXXII, 499).

1 There was a little familee that lived in Bethanee;
   Two sisters and a brother composed the familee.
   At evening and morning they riz their voices high
   With singing and with praying, like angels in the sky.

2 And while they lived together, so poor, so good, so kind,
   Their brother was afflicted and duly thrown in bed;
   Poor Martha and her sister stood weeping by his side;
   Yit he grew no better, and lingered on and died.

3 . . . .
   . . . .
   The news came to the sisters, put Lazarus in the tomb,
   So swiftly did he travel, to wipe away their gloom.

4 When Martha saw him coming, she met him on the way,
   And told him how her brother had died and passed away.
   He charged her and he blessed her, he told her not to weep,
   For in him was the power to wake him from the sleep.

5 When Mary saw him coming, she ran and met him too,
   And at his feet fell weeping; she wep' a tale of woe.
   When Jesus saw her weeping, he fell a-weeping too,
   And wep' until she showed him where Lazarus lay in tomb.

6 He rolled away the cover and looked upon the grave,
   And prayed unto his Father his loving friend to save.
   When Lazarus saw his power, come from the gloomy mound,
   With full strength and vigor he walked upon the ground.

7 Now if you do love Jesus and do his holy will,
   Like Martha and like Mary, do always use him well,
   From death he will redeem us and take us to the skies;
   He'll bid us live forever where pleasure never dies.

B

"The Death of Lazarus." Communicated by Mr. J. Harrison Miller, Wardensville, Hardy County, October, 1916; obtained from Mrs. Sofia Funk, who had learned it in childhood.

1 There was a little family that lived in Bethany;
Two sisters and a brother composed the family.
In prayer and in singing, like angels in the skies,
In morning and in evening they raised their voices high.

2 And while they lived so happy, so poor, so kind, so good,
Their brother was afflicted, and rudely thrown in bed.
The dues [1] went to the sisters, with Lazarus in the tomb,
To try their hearts to comfort and drive away the gloom.

3 But Jesus heard the tidings, while in a distant land,
And quickly did he travel, to seek the lonely band,
When Mary saw him coming, and Martha saw him too,
And at his feet stood mourning, rehearsed the tale of woe.

4 When Jesus saw her fretting, he went in sorrow too,
Until they went and showed him where Lazarus laid in tomb.
They rolled away the cover and looked in the grave,
And prayed unto his Father, his loving friend to save.

5 .   .   .   .
   .   .   .   .
By his almighty power, he raised him from the grave;
Within full life and vigor, he walked upon the ground.

6 So if we all love Jesus and do his holy will,
Like Mary and like Martha, do always use him well,
From death he will redeem us, and take us to the skies,
And bid us live forever where pleasure never dies.

[1] *Jews*(?).

135

THE TWELVE JOYS

ONE version has been found in West Virginia. A Connecticut text has been published by Newell, *Journal*, V, 535.

For Old Country texts see Sandys, *Christmas Carols*, 1833, p. 157; Sylvester, *A Garland of Christmas Carols*, p. 133; Husk, *Songs of the Nativity*, p. 87; Bramley and Stainer, *Christmas Carols*, p. 28; W. J. Phillips, *Carols*, p. 90; Bullen, *Carols and Poems*, p. 55; Sharp, *Folk-Songs from Somerset*, V, 65; Sharp, *English Folk Carols*, p. 33; Shaw and Dearmer, *The English Carol Book*, p. 56; Gillington, *Old Christmas Carols of the Southern Counties*, p. 2; *Journal of the Folk-Song Society*, V, 18, 319; *Journal of the Irish Folk-Song Society*, XII, 24. The number of Joys varies. Originally it was five, as in the numerous Middle English poems on this theme catalogued by Carleton Brown, *A Register of Middle English Religious and Didactic Verse* (see "Five Joys" in his Index of Subjects, II, 422).

Communicated by Mrs. Hilary G. Richardson, Clarksburg, Harrison County, 1916; obtained from Mrs. Rachel Fogg, formerly of Doddridge County, who learned it from her mother (printed in *Journal*, XXXII, 501).

1   The very first blessing that Mary had,
     It was the blessing of one,
  For to think that her son Jesus
     Was God's eternal son,
     Was God's eternal son.

2   And the very next blessing Mary had
     Was the blessing of two,
  For to think that her son Jesus
     Could read the Bible through.

3   The very next blessing Mary had
     Was the blessing of three,
  For to think that her son Jesus
     Could make the blind man see.

4   The very next blessing that Mary had
     Was the blessing of four,
  For to think that her son Jesus
     Could make the rich man poor.

5   The very next blessing that Mary had
     Was the blessing of five,
  For to think that her son Jesus
     Could make the dead man live.

6 The very next blessing Mary had
    Was the blessing of six,
For to think that her son Jesus
    Could make the sick man well.

7 The very next blessing Mary had,
    It was the blessing of seven,
For to think that her son Jesus
    Carried the keys of heaven.

8 The very next blessing that Mary had
    Was the blessing of eight,
For to think that her son Jesus
    Could open the gates of heaven.

9 The very next blessing Mary had
    Was the blessing of nine,
For to think that her son Jesus
    Could turn water to wine.

10 The very next blessing that Mary had,
    It was the blessing of ten,
For to think that her son Jesus
    Could write without a pen.

11 The very next blessing Mary had,
    It was the blessing of eleven,
For to think that her son Jesus
    Could make the way to heaven.

12 The very next blessing Mary had,
    It was the blessing of twelve,
For to think that her son Jesus
    Done all things well.

136

WICKED POLLY

Communicated by Mrs. Cora Hoffman McCay, Morgantown, Monongalia County, March 7, 1916; written down by Joseph Wesley Saer in the back part of an old ledger. Mr. Saer was born August 21, 1800.

For references to other American texts see *Journal*, XXIX, 192; XXXV, 430.

1 Young people, hear, and I will tell:
   A soul, I fear, is gone to hell,
   A lady who was young and fair,
   Who died in sin and black despair.

2 Her tender parents oft did pray
   For her poor soul from day to day,
   And gave her counsel, good advice;
   But she delighted still in vice.

3 She'd go to frolics, dance and play,
   In spite of all her friends could say;
   "I will turn to God when I get old,
   And then he will receive my soul."

4 At length I heard the spirit [say],
   "Thou sinful wretch, forsake thy way;
   Now turn to God, or you shall dwell
   Forever in the flames of hell."

5 "I am too young," she then replied;
   "My comrades all will me deride;
   I will turn to God when I get old,
   And then he will receive my soul."

6 It was not long till death did come
   And called the hapless sinner home;
   And when upon her dying bed,
   She called her friends and thus she said:

7 "My friends, I bid you all farewell;
   I die and now I sink to hell;
   There I must lie and scream and roar,
   I am lost and damned forevermore.

8   "My weeping mother, fare you well!
    The pains I feel, no tongue can tell;
    O mother, your poor child is lost;
    Your hopes are all forever crost."

9   Her hay [1] sister standing by,
    Saying, "Sister, you're about to die;
    Your race is run, your time is past;
    You must come to the grave at last."

10 O what an awful thing to see!
    She's now dropped into eternity,
    Wringing her hands and gnashing her teeth;
    There is no redemption to relief.

[1] *Only*(?).

137

THE TRUE LOVER'S FAREWELL

This is part of the song known as "Turtle Dove" or "The True Lover's Farewell." For texts without the "shoe" stanzas (which do not properly belong here: cf. p. 83) see Campbell and Sharp, No. 61 C; Sharp and Marson, *Folk-Songs from Somerset*, II, 26; Sharp, *One Hundred English Folksongs*, No. 55; Sharp, *English Folk Songs*, I, 92; Hammond, *Folk-Songs from Dorset*, p. 34; Butterworth, *Folk Songs from Sussex*, p. 20; *Journal of the Folk-Song Society*, II, 55; III, 86; IV, 286. The stanzas occur in Campbell and Sharp, No. 61 A. Belden has both forms. See p. 93 above. The song goes back to seventeenth-century broadsides of "The Unkind Parents; or, The Languishing Lamentation of Two Loyal Lovers" (Ebsworth, *Roxburghe Ballads*, VII, 552; cf. *Journal of the Folk-Song Society*, IV, 288). For the connection with Burns's "Red Red Rose," see *Centenary Burns*, III, 402; cf. Shearin, *Modern Language Review*, VI, 514.

On "The True Lover's Farewell" was founded the comic song "Fare you well, my own Mary Ann." This was published at Baltimore (cop. 1856) as "My Mary Ann, The Yankee Girl's Song as Sung by Mrs. Barney Williams, Words by Barney Williams, Music by M. Tyte"; and as "Our Mary Ann. Sung by Mrs. W. J. Florence, with immense applause, throughout the United States, Great Britain, and Ireland," in *Songs of the Florences* (New York, cop. 1860), p. 12. See also *Bryant's Programme and Songs* (New York, 1859), Vol. II, No. 4, p. 7; *The Shilling Song Book* (Boston, cop. 1860), p. 39; *Uncle Sam's Army Songster* (Indianapolis, cop. 1862), p. 61; *The General Lee Song Book*, p. 36; De Marsan broadside, List 3, No. 14; London broadside, Ryle & Co. One version, without local title, was contributed by Mr. Elmer K. Merinar, Sherrard, Marshall County, November 9, 1915; learned from the singing of other people.

1   "Farewell, farewell, my pretty maid,
         Fare-thee-well for a while;
     For I'm going away ten thousand miles,
         Ten thousand miles from here.

2   "Who will shoe your bonny feet,
         And who will glove your hand?
     Who will kiss your red, rosy lips,
         While I'm in some foreign land?"

3   "My father will shoe my bonny little feet,
         My mother will glove my hand;
     But my red, rosy lips shall go wanting,
         Till you return again."

4   "You know a crow is a coal, coal black,
  And turns to a purple blue;
 And if ever I prove false to you,
  I hope my body may melt like dew.

5   "I'll love you till the seas run dry,
  And rocks dissolve by the sun;
 I'll love you till the day I die,
  And then you know I'm done."

138

THE GREEN WILLOW TREE: OR,
ONCE I HAD PLENTY OF THYME

THIS is an excellent version of the favorite English folk-song "The Sprig of Thyme." See Child, v, 258 (from *Five Excellent New Songs*, Edinburgh, 1766); Baring-Gould and Sheppard, *Songs of the West*, No. 7, I, 14 (cf. IV, xv); Kidson, *Traditional Tunes*, p. 69; Sharp, *Folk-Songs from Somerset*, v, 16; Hammond, *Folk-Songs from Dorset*, p. 10; Merrick, *Folk-Songs from Sussex*, p. 34; Sharp, *One Hundred English Folksongs*, No. 34; Sharp, *English Folk Songs*, I, 45; *Journal of the Folk-Song Society*, II, 288; III, 77; A. Williams, *Folk-Songs of the Upper Thames*, pp. 84, 85; broadsides (A. T. Nappey, York; Bebbington, Manchester, No. 291); Kidson and Neal, *English Folk-Song and Dance*, p. 58; Barry, *Journal*, XXII, 79 (tune only); Belden, *Publications of the Modern Language Association*, XXXIII, 363.

"The Sprig of Thyme" is almost inextricably entangled in tradition with "The Seeds of Love." See Whitaker, *History of Whalley*, II (1801), p. 358; Chappell, *Popular Music*, p. 520; Bell, *Songs and Ballads of the Peasantry*, p. 220; Baring-Gould and Sheppard, *Songs of the West*, No. 107, IV, 50, cf. IV, xlii (see Child, v, 259); Sharp and Marson, *Folk-Songs from Somerset*, I, 2, cf. 57; Sharp, *One Hundred English Folksongs*, No. 33; Sharp, *English Folk Songs*, I, 42; Butterworth, *Folk Songs of Sussex*, p. 6; Merrick, *Folk-Songs of Sussex*, p. 34; Greig, *Folk-Song of the North-East*, LXVII; *Journal of the Folk-Song Society*, I, 86, 88, 209, 210; II, 23; V, 93; Alfred Williams, *Folk-Songs of the Upper Thames*, p. 86; broadsides (Pitts; Such, No. 94; A. T. Nappey, York; Cadman, Manchester, No. 90).

For the crossing of both songs with the ballad of "The Gardener" (Child, No. 219) see Child, v, 258, 259.

Communicated by Miss Mabel Richards, Fairmont, Marion County, January, 1916; obtained from Mrs. John Hood, Lowesville.

1 Once I had plenty of thyme,
    I could cherish the night and the day,
  Until a saucy soldier chanced to pass along,
    And he stole all my thyme away,
    And he stole all my thyme away,
    And he stole all my thyme away,
  Until a saucy soldier chanced to pass along,
    And he stole all my thyme away.

2 It's very good drinking of ale,
    It's very good drinking of wine,
  It's far better sitting by the saucy black-eyed boy,
    That stole away this tender heart of mine,
    That stole away this tender heart of mine,
  I never will be false to the one that I love best,
    That stole away this tender heart of mine.

3 The gardener he stood by and said he would choose for me,
    He chose for me the lily, the violet, and the pink,
    But I did refuse all three;
The lily I do not like; the violet it fades so soon;
As for the pink, I did it overlook and said I would tarry till June.
    June is the red rosebud and that is the flower for me:
I never will be false to the one that I love,
    That I met neath the green willow tree;
    The willow tree may twist and the willow tree may twine,
But I never will be false to the one that I love,
    That stole away this tender heart of mine.

4 Look to the birds in the bush,
    Likewise the robin and the thrush,
        For birds of one feather will always flock together,
Let parents say little or much,
Let parents say little or much,
Let parents say little or much,
        For birds of one feather will flock together,
Let parents say little or much.

139

THE GREEN LAURELS

THIS song, sometimes known as "The Orange and Blue," has been found in Missouri by Belden in forms that closely resemble the West Virginia texts. Barry prints a tune in *Journal*, XXII, 76.

The first stanza and the chorus appear in English tradition as a two-stanza song, "The Orange and Blue" (*Journal of the Folk-Song Society*, I, 246; V, 70). The first stanza begins a gypsy song in Gillington, *Songs of the Open Road*, p. 8. A form of this stanza also appears in the broadside entitled "The Irish Transport" (Ryle & Co.; Bebbington, Manchester, No. 185; Cadman, Manchester, No. 205; William Jackson & Son, Birmingham):

> I oftentimes wondered how women could love men,
> And I oftentimes wondered how men could love them,
> Since women was my ruin, my sad ruin and downfall,
> Which has caused me to lie betwixt lime and stone wall.

For stanza 2 see "The Wagoner's Lad," Pettit's version, stanza 3 (*Journal*, XX, 269); Campbell and Sharp, No. 64, B 6; "The New River Shore," stanzas 1, 2 (Mackenzie, p. 162); "Forsaken," lines 9, 10, 13, 14 (Perrow, *Journal*, XXVIII, 170); "The Rue and the Thyme," stanza 5 (Greig, LXXXVII).

For stanza 3 see "The Rue and the Thyme," stanzas 2, 3 (Greig, LXXXIV; LXXXII, stanza 4).

For stanza 4 see "The Green Mountain," stanzas 1, 3 (*Journal*, XXX, 348); Pettit's "Wagoner's Lad," stanza 6 (*Journal*, XX, 269); "Streams of Lovely Nancy" (references in *Journal*, XXX, 347).

A

"The Green Laurels." Communicated by Miss Mary Meek Atkeson, Morgantown, Monongalia County, 1917; obtained from Miss Ila Hall. "Origin blue" in the Chorus is a manifest error for "orange and blue."

1 I oftentimes have wondered how women loved men,
  But I ofttimes have wondered how men could love them;
  They will love you a little and give your heart ease,
  And when your back's on them, they'll love who they
    please.

Chorus

Then green grows the laurel, and so does the rue;
How sad's been the day I parted from you!
But at our next meeting our love we'll renew;
We'll change the green laurel for the origin blue.

2 Some will love a short love, and others love long,
  Some will love a weak love, and others love strong;
  Some will love a short love and others love long,
  And some will love an old love till the new love comes in.

3 I wrote my love a letter all bounded in pain;
  She wrote me another all bounded the same:
  Say, "You may keep your promise and I will keep mine;
  We'll change the green laurel for the origin blue."

4 On the top of yon mountain, where the green grass does grow,
  Way down in yon valley, where the still waters flow,
  I saw my old true love, and she had proved true;
  We changed the green laurel for the origin blue.

ℬ

"Green Grows the Wild Isle." Communicated by Mr. J. F. Marsh, Charleston, Kanawha County, September 20, 1916; obtained from Miss Zettie Provett, Wyoming County, who learned it from her mother.

1 I once had a sweetheart, but now I have none,
  He's gone and left me to live here alone,
  He's gone and left me contented to be,
  He's loving another girl better than me.

Chorus

Green grows the wild island and so does the rose,
It's sad to my heart when parting from you;
And I hope the next meeting we will prove true,
And change the green islands to the red, white and blue.

2 He passed by my window both early and late,
  The looks that he gave me it made my heart ache;
  The looks that he gave me ten thousand would kill,
  His loving another girl make him quite ill.

3 He wrote me a letter, one red rose a line,
  I wrote him another all tangled in twine,
  Saying, "Keep your love letters and I'll keep mine,
  Talk to your sweetheart and I'll talk to mine."

4 I often have wondered how women loved men,
  I often have wondered how they loved them;
  But I have some experience I'll have you to know,
  That men are deceitful wherever they go.

140

YOUNG LADIES (LITTLE SPARROW)

AMERICAN texts of this song (sometimes called "Little Sparrow") have been printed or recorded as follows: *Journal*, XXIX, 184 (Tolman; one stanza in an Indiana version of "There is a Tavern in the Town"), 200 (Rawn and Peabody; Georgia); Wyman and Brockway, p. 55 (Kentucky); Campbell and Sharp, No. 65 (North Carolina, Kentucky, Tennessee); McGill, p. 23 (Kentucky); Sharp, *American-English Folk-Songs*, 1st Series, p. 32 (the same as Campbell and Sharp, No. 65 A); Child MSS., I, 84 (North Carolina); Minish MS., III, 35 (North Carolina); Belden, No. 88 (Missouri); Shearin and Combs, p. 26 (Kentucky).

The piece is somehow related to the celebrated Scottish song "O Waly, Waly, gin Love be Bonny" (Child, IV, 92), printed in the early part of the eighteenth century, but even then regarded as old. Stanza 3 of the Scottish song corresponds to West Virginia A 8, B 3; stanza 9 (not in the West Virginia texts) to lines 17–20 of the Wyman text (McGill, stanza 5; Campbell and Sharp, B 5, and the sole stanza of E; Minish, stanza 5). "Waly, Waly" stands in close relation to "James Douglas" (Child, No. 204).

A

"Young Ladies." Communicated by Mr. J. H. Shaffer, Newburg, Preston County, who obtained it from Mrs. A. R. Fike, Terra Alta.

1 Come all ye fair and handsome ladies,
    Take warning how you court young men;
For they're like a bright star on a summer's morning,
    They first appear and then they're gone.

2 They'll tell to you some flattering story,
    And swear to God that they love you well,
And away they'll go and court some other,
    And leave you here in grief to dwell.

3 I wish to God I never had seen him,
    Or in his cradle he had died;
For to think so fair and handsome lady,
    Was one in love and be denied.

4 I wish I was in some tall mountain,
    Where the ivy rock is black as ink;
I would write a letter to my false lover,
    Whose cheeks are like the morning pink.

5   I wish I was some little sparrow,
        And one of them that could fly so high;
    I would fly away to my true love's dwelling,
        And when he would speak I would be close by.

6   O I would flutter in his bosom
        With my little [ex]tended wings;
    I would ask him, I would ask him,
        Whose tender heart he had tried to stain.

7   My troubles now are just beginning,
        My troubles like some mountain tall;
    O I'll sit down in grief and sorrow,
        And there I'll talk my troubles o'er.

8   Love is handsome, love is charming,
        Love is beauty while it's new;
    Love grows older, love grows colder,
        Fades away like morning dew.

ℬ

No local title.   Communicated by Mr. Guy Overholt, Erwin, Preston County,
who obtained it from Mr. Ralph Buckley, Buckeye, Pocahontas County.

1   Come all ye fair and handsome ladies,
        Be careful how you trust young men,
    For they are like a star upon a summer's morning,
        They disappear and then are gone.

2   They tell to you some tattling stories,
        And then declare they love you well;
    This is the way they go and love some other,
        And leave you in this world to mourn.

3   O love is handsome, love is charming,
        And love is pretty while it lasts;
    But love grows cold as love grows older,
        And fades away like morning dew.

4   I wish to God I never had seen him,
        Or in my cradle I had died,
    To think a fair and handsome lady,
        Was stricken with love and then denied.

5 I wish I were on some tall mountain,
     Where the marble stones are black as ink;
  I'd write a letter to my false lover,
     Whose cheeks are like the morning pink.

6 If I were just a little sparrow,
     Or some of those that fly so high,
  I'd fly away to my false lover,
     And when he'd speak I would deny.

7 But I am none of those little sparrows,
     Or none of those that fly so high,
  So I'll sit down in grief and sorrow,
     And pass all my troubles by.

141

YOUTH AND FOLLY

This song is a counterpart to "Little Sparrow," from which it has borrowed certain stanzas (see p. 419). In "Youth and Folly" the young man is the sufferer. Stanza 2 belongs to the famous Scottish song, "O Waly, Waly, gin Love be Bonny" (see Child, IV, 92, 93), but occurs also in some texts of "Little Sparrow." Cf. Sharp, *One Hundred English Folksongs*, No. 39; *Folk-Songs from Somerset*, III, 33; *Journal of the Irish Folk-Song Society*, VIII, 16. For stanza 5 cf. "Maggie Goddon" (p. 424). The first stanza corresponds to the last of "Young Riley" in modern English broadsides (Catnach; Such, No. 83; Fortey); see "George Reilly" (p. 323).

Communicated by Miss Lalah Lovett, Bulltown, Braxton County, 1916; obtained from John N. Wine, who learned it from his father.

1 Youth and folly make youngsters marry,
    And when they're married they must obey;
For many a bright and sunshiny morning
    Has turned to a dark and rainy day.

2 O love is warming, O love is charming,
    Love's quite handsome while it's new!
But as love grows older, love grows colder,
    And fades away like the morning dew.

3 It was all in the sweet month of April,
    While summer flowers were in their bloom,
Trees were budding, sweet birds were singing:
    Times ain't with me as they have been.

4 Great Jehovah, have mercy on me!
    My comrades, come to set me free;
I never courted but one fair lady;
    Her name was Polly, she told me.

5 Polly, O Polly, you are my darling!
    Come set yourself down awhile by me,
And tell to me the very reason
    Why I was slighted so by thee.

6 I am in love, I dare not own it,
    The very pain lies on my breast;
I am in love, and the whole world knows it,
    That a troubled mind can find no rest.

7   I wish to God I never had seen you,
        Or in my cradle I had died;
    To think as nice a young man as I am
        Should be in love and be denied.

8   I wish I was on some stormy ocean,
        As far from land as I could be;
    And sailing for some better country
        Where there no grief could trouble me.

142

MAGGIE GODDON

Contributed by Mr. W. E. Boggs, Matewan, Mingo County, 1918. Learned about forty years ago from his brother, who was killed shortly after at Ashland, Kansas, by cowboys. Compare "Youth and Folly" (p. 422).

1   I wish I was once a-sailing
    As far from land as far could be,
Far across the deep blue waters,
    Where I have no one to trouble me.

Chorus

Sweet Maggie Goddon, you are my bride;
    Come set you down upon my knee;
Tell to me the very reason
    Why I was slighted just by thee.

2   The sea is deep, I can't swim over,
    Neither have I the wings to fly;
There I hear some jolly sportsman,
    To carry over the love and I.

3   I wish I had a glass of brandy,
    I'll tell to you the reason why:
While drinking, I am thinking,
    Does my true love remember me?

143

A FORSAKEN LOVER

For full references, English and American, see Kittredge, *Journal*, XXX, 349–352. Add Campbell and Sharp, p. 215; *Singer's Journal*, I, 738; *Journal of the Irish Folk-Song Society*, IV, 33; Herd, *Ancient and Modern Scottish Songs*, 1776, II, 180.

Communicated by Miss Violet Noland, Davis, Tucker County, March 24, 1916; obtained from Mr. John Raese, who learned it when a boy and wrote it down in 1880.

1 O Johnny is on the water,
      Let him sink or swim!
    For if he can live without me,
      I can live without him.

2 Johnny is a young boy,
      But still younger am I;
    For how often has he told me
      How constant he would be!

3 I'll take off this black dress,
      And I'll flourish in green;
    For I don't care if I am forsaken,
      I am only nineteen.

4 O meeting is a pleasure,
      But to part with him was grief;
    But an unconstant true lover
      Is worse than a thief.

5 A thief can but rob you
      And take all you have;
    But an unconstant lover
      Will take you to your grave.

6 The grave it will rot you
      And turn you to dust;
    There is scarce one out of twenty
      That a young girl can trust.

7 They will court you and kiss you
      And get your heart warm;
    Then, as soon as your back's turned,
      They'll laugh you to scorn.

8   The cuckoo is a pretty bird,
      She sings as she flies;
    She brings us good tidings
      And tells us no lies.

9   Forsaken, forsaken,
      Forsaken am I!
    He will think himself mistaken,
      If he thinks that I'll cry.

144

LOVE HAS BROUGHT ME TO DESPAIR

THIS is a remarkably full version of the English song "A Brisk Young Sailor" — that song which, in an abbreviated form, is known as "There is an alehouse in yonder town" (or, in this country, as "There is a tavern in the town"). For English texts, longer or shorter, see Bebbington's broadside No. 193 (Manchester); Kidson, *Traditional Tunes*, pp. 44, 46; Leather, *The Folk-Lore of Herefordshire*, p. 205; Sharp, *One Hundred English Folksongs*, No. 94; Sharp, *English Folk Songs*, II, 40; R. Vaughan Williams, *Folk-Songs from the Eastern Counties*, p. 9; Butterworth, *Folk Songs from Sussex*, p. 14; Broadwood, *English Traditional Songs and Carols*, p. 92; Kidson and Neal, *English Folk-Song and Dance*, p. 57; *Journal of the Folk-Song Society*, I, 252; II, 155, 158, 168; III, 188; v, 181, 183, 184, 188.

The usual opening of the song (when it does not begin at once with the alehouse, stanza 4 of the present text) is as follows — to quote the Bebbington broadside:

> A brisk young sailor courted me,
> He stole away my liberty,
> He stole my heart with a free good will,
> I must confess I love him still.

Instead of this, the West Virginia version has three quite different stanzas. These seem to be adapted from some form of the old ballad entitled "The Famous Flower of Serving-Men" (Child, No. 106), in which we find:

> 2 I was by birth a lady fair,
> My father's chief and onely heir,
> But when my good old father dy'd,
> Then was I made a young knight's bride.
>
> . . . .
>
> 5 My servants all from me did flye,
> In the midst of my extremity,
> And left me by my self alone,
> With a heart more cold then any stone.
>
> . . . .
>
> 19 My father was as brave a lord
> As ever Europe did afford;
> My mother was a lady bright,
> My husband was a valient knight.

One English text (*Folk-Song Society*, II, 158) agrees in part with the West Virginia song at this point, having as stanza 1:

> Her father bin a noble knight:
> Her mother bin a lady bright:
> I bin an only child of her
> False lover brought me to despair.

Stanzas 8–10 of our West Virginia text recur in the English broadside ballad "Sheffield Park" (Catnach; Jackson & Son, Birmingham; Gillington, *Eight Hampshire Folk-Songs*, p. 14), which is the direct ancestor of "The Butcher Boy" (see p. 430, below). These stanzas, however, are all found in some other versions of "A Brisk Young Sailor." The opening stanza of "Sheffield Park" runs as follows:

> In Sheffield Park O there did dwell
> A brisk young lad, I loved him well,
> He courted me my love to gain,
> He's gone and left me full of pain.

The concluding stanza in the West Virginia text, though found in several of the English versions, probably does not belong to this piece. It is a ballad commonplace. In "The Forlorn Lover," for instance, a seventeenth-century broadside lament, which shows some elusive resemblance to our song, we find:

> O dig me a grave that is wide, large, and deep,
> With a turf at my head, and another at my feet!
> There will I lie, and take a lasting sleep,
> And so bid her Farewell for ever.[1]

A similar stanza, or stanzas, occurs also in several versions of "The Twa Brothers" (Child, No. 49) and of "Sir Hugh" (Child, No. 155).

"A Brisk Young Sailor" has significant points of contact with the seventeenth-century broadside (Pepys, V, 217) "An excellent New Song, call'd Nelly's Constancy; or, Her Unkind Lover" (Ebsworth, *Roxburghe Ballads*, VI, 791).

For references see *Journal*, XXIX, 170; Broadswood, *Journal of the Folk-Song Society*, V, 185.

Communicated by Mrs. Walter Parker, New Haven, Mason County, July 29, 1916. She writes: "I have copied this song from a quaint old manuscript dated February 20, 1859, and signed Robert B. Welch. He was a Civil War veteran and died several years ago. I have copied it exactly, except all the *s*'s were *z*'s in the manuscript and most of the words began with capitals."

1 My father he is a wealthy knight,
　My mother she is a lady bright,
　And I their child, their only heir,
　But love has brought me to despair.

2 I was courted by a wealthy knight,
　Who at my beauty took delight;
　He courted me both night and day,
　Until my heart he did betray.

3 But now he has left me all alone,
　A discontented life to mourn.
　I'll mourn for him — no other one —
　As long as I have life to mourn.

---

[1] Bagford collection (Ebsworth, *Roxburghe Ballads*, VI, 233, stanza 11); entered in the Stationers' Register, March 1, 1675 (Eyre, *Transcript*, II, 499; Rollins, *Index*, No. 907).

4   There is a tavern in the town,
    Where goes my love and there sits down;
    He takes strange girls upon his knee,
    And is not that a grief to me?

5   A grief to me, I'll tell you why,
    Because they have more gold than I;
    But gold will melt and silver fly,
    But constant love will never fly.

6   Down in the meadow, I've heard some say,
    There is a rose blooms night and day;
    Down in the meadow she quickly ran,
    Picking flowers as they sprang.

7   She picked of purple, she picked of green,
    She picked of every kind she seen,
    She picked of red, she picked of blue,
    But little thought what love could do.

8   Now these green flowers must be your bed,
    The heavens is your coverlet.
    Almighty, mourn, O mourn for me,
    O mourn unto eternity!

9   Now when they found that she was cold,
    They went to her first love and told:
    "I am glad she is dead, I wish her well,
    I hope her soul may land in hell."

10   O cruel man, what's that you say?
    She has wished you many a happy day,
    Whilst on your bosom she breathless lay,
    When your poor soul be tost away.

11   They dug her grave both wide and deep,
    A marble slab laid at her feet,
    A turtle dove sit on her breast,
    To let him know she has gone to rest.

145

THE BUTCHER BOY

THREE variants have been found in West Virginia, none of them perfect. Jersey City, New York City, and London City claim in turn this famous butcher boy.

"The Butcher Boy" is made up of modified extracts from (1) "Sheffield Park";[1] (2) "The Squire's Daughter"[2] (called also "The Cruel Father, or, Deceived Maid"[3]); (3) "A Brisk Young Sailor" (or its abbreviated version, "There is an alehouse in yonder town"[4]); and (4) "Sweet William" ("The Sailor Boy"[5]). To (1) it owes stanzas 1 and 4; to (2), stanzas 6 and 7;[1,2] to (3), stanzas 2, 3, and 8; to (4), stanza 5. For American texts and for references, British and American, see *Journal*, XXIX, 169; XXXI, 73; XXXV, 360; Pound, No. 24; Lomax, p. 397 ("Rambling Boy"); Minish MS., III, 49.

A

"The Butcher's Boy." Communicated by Miss Sallie Evans, Elkins, Randolph County, 1917; obtained from Miss Nellie Haddix, who got it from her mother, who learned it from her parents. The words in brackets I have inserted from the De Marsan broadside.

1   In Jersey City, where I did dwell,
    A butcher's boy I loved so well,
    He courted me my life away,
    And then with me he would not stay.

2   [There is an inn] in this same town,
    Where my love goes and sits him down,
    Takes a strange girl on his knee,
    And tells her what he would not me.

3   It's a grief to me, I'll tell you why,
    Because she has more gold than I;
    But her gold will melt and her silver fly,
    In time to come she will be poorer than I.

4   She goes upstairs to make her bed,
    Nothing to her mother said;
    Her mother comes up saying,
    "What is the matter, dear daughter dear?"
    "O mother, mother, you do not know,
    The grief and pain and sorrow and tear.

---

[1] Broadsides (Catnach; Jackson & Son, Birmingham); Gillington, *Eight Hampshire Folk-Songs*, p. 14.

[2] Broadside (W. Shelmerdine & Co., Manchester).

[3] Slip without imprint (eighteenth or early nineteenth century).

[4] See p. 427.   [5] See p. 353.

5   "So get a chair and sit me down,
    Pen and ink to write it down";
    On every line she drops a tear,
    Whilst calling home her Willa dear.

6   Father comes home, saying,[1]
    "Where is daughter dear?"
    He goes up stairs, the door he broke;
    There he found her hanging on a rope.

7   [He took his knife and cut her down,
    [And] in her breast these lines he found:
    ["O what a silly maid was I,
    To hang myself for a butcher's boy!"]

8   "Go dig my grave both broad and deep,
    Place a marble stone at my head and feet;
    Upon my breast a turtle dove,
    To show the world I died for love."

𝓑

"The Butcher Boy." Communicated by Professor C. E. Haworth, Huntington, Cabell County, 1917; obtained from Miss Virginia Ransom, who got it from a woman servant who had lived in Kentucky.

1   In New York City used to dwell
    A butcher boy I loved so well;
    He courted me my life away,
    And then with me he would not stay.

2   There was a strange girl in that town,
    My love he goes and sits him down,
    And takes that strange girl on his knee,
    And tells to her what he won't tell me.

3   O Grace, O Grace, I'll tell you why:
    Because she has more gold than I;
    Gold will rust and silver fly,
    And then she'll be poor as I.

4   She ran upstairs to fix her bed,
    And nothing to her ma she said.

    .   .   .   .
    .   .   .   .

    [1] "And when her father he came home" (De Marsan).

5 They went upstairs and went and looked,
They found her hanging by a rope;
They took and cut her down,
And in her bosom these words they found:

6 "Go dig my grave both long and deep,
And place marble stones at my head and feet,
And across my breast place a turtle dove,
To show this world I died for love."

C

"In London City." Communicated by Mr. C. R. Bishop, Green Bank, Pocahontas County, 1917; obtained from Miss Valera Ervine. A fragmentary text.

146

FAREWELL, SWEET MARY

CONTRIBUTED by Miss Sallie D. Jones, Hillsboro, Pocahontas County, January, 1917, who writes: "The words of 'Farewell, Sweet Mary' were learned from a youth who was enamored of a girl whose name was Mary, who lived in a farm house just over the hill from his home. She would have none of his advances, however, and he used to go to the top of the hill, and in a rich, mellow voice make the welkin ring with the words of this song. This was in Pendleton County, about forty-seven years ago."

Almost every word of this little lyric turns up elsewhere.

Stanza 1 coincides with stanza 3, lines 1, 2, of Wyman's text of "The Wagoner's Lad" ("Loving Nancy"), p. 64, and with stanza 4, lines 3, 4, of Campbell and Sharp's text B of the same (No. 64). Cf. also Perrow's "Old Smoky" (*Journal*, XXVIII, 159), stanza 10, line 1, and Campbell and Sharp's version A of "The Wagoner's Lad" (which runs almost word for word with "Old Smoky"), stanza 10, line 1. Stanza 1 occurs also in "Jack o' Diamonds," (Lomax, p. 292), which is a version of "The Rebel Soldier," and in "Sweet Lily" (Perrow, *Journal*, XXVIII, 177).

The chorus is adapted from the farewell words in "The Wagoner's Lad" (see Campbell and Sharp, A 8, B 3, 4; D 4); Perrow, stanza 8.

Stanza 2 belongs to "The Forsaken Girl," a version of "The Poor Stranger" (see p. 284): Pettit *Journal* (XX, 268), stanza 4, lines 1–2; McGill, p. 50, stanza 4, lines 1–2; it is found, accordingly, in "The Rebel Soldier" (p. 279), and "Jack o' Diamonds." But the lines have been taken up by "The Wagoner's Lad": see Pettit's version (XX, 268), stanza 5, lines 1–2; Campbell and Sharp, A 11; Perrow's "Old Smoky," stanza 11. The same phrases have been adapted in another little lyric collected by Belden in Missouri, "Down in the Valley," stanza 2 (*Journal*, XXX, 346).

For stanza 3 see "Jack o' Diamonds," stanza 4; and for the first half see "The Rue and the Thyme" in Greig, *Folk-Song of the North-East*, LXXXIV, LXXXVII (stanza 3); "The Rebel Soldier" (p. 279). Cf. Campbell and Sharp, No. 76 A, 4 (B 5).

1 Your parents don't like me,
       And well do I know,
    They say I'm not worthy,
       To knock at your door.

Chorus

Farewell, sweet Mary,
    I bid you adieu,
I am ruined forever,
    By the loving of you.

2   I'll build me a castle,
        On the mountain so high,
    Where the wild geese may see me,
        As they do pass by.

3   I'll eat when I'm hungry,
        And drink when I'm dry;
    I'll think of sweet Mary,
        And sit down and cry.

147

MARY O' THE DEE

THIS is the celebrated song of "Mary's Dream" by John Lowe (1750–ca. 1798). There is a version in the Scottish dialect, probably by Allan Cunningham, which has often been erroneously regarded as the original. See Johnson, *The Scots Musical Museum*, No. 37 (also the Additional Illustrations in the 1839 edition, I, 115); *The Vocal Magazine* (Edinburgh), II (1798), Song 29; Cromek's *Remains of Nithsdale and Galloway Song*, 1810, pp. 342–366; Buchan, *Gleanings*, 1825, p. 112; *Universal Songster* (London, 1834), III, 213; Davidson's *Universal Melodist*, II, 66, 126; Christie, *Traditional Ballad Airs*, II, 14, 298; Chambers, *The Songs of Scotland prior to Burns*, ed. 1890, p. 448; *Songs of Scotland*, 3d ed., p. 144; Helen M. Johnson, *Our Familiar Songs*, p. 309.

The song has often been printed in America: see, for example, *The American Musical Miscellany* (Northampton, Massachusetts, 1798?), p. 195; *The Temple of Harmony* (Baltimore, 1801), p. 69; *The Warbler* (Augusta, Maine, 1805), p. 80; *The Nightingale or Ladies' Vocal Companion* (Albany, 1807), p. 28; *The Merry Songster* (Boston, 1810), p. 9; *The Songster's Companion* (Brattleboro, Vermont, 1815), p. 256; *The New American Songster* (Philadelphia, 1817), p. 71; De Marsan broadside, List 2, No. 42; *Singer's Journal*, I, 220; Perrow, *Journal*, XXVIII, 157. Cf. Belden, No. 86.

Communicated by Miss Sallie Evans, Elkins, Randolph County; obtained from Orra G. Warkman, who got it from his great-grandmother, Mrs. Lucinda Waldo.

1   The moon had climbed the highest hill
     That rises o'er the source of Dee,
  And from its eastern summit shed
     A silver light o'er tower and tree.
  Mary had lain her down to sleep,
     Her thoughts on Sandy, far at sea,
  When soft and low a voice she heard,
     Saying, "Mary, weep no more for me."

2   She from her pillow gently raised her head
     To ask who there might be;
  When she saw young Sandy shivering stand
     With pallid cheek and hollow e'e:
  "O Mary dear, cold is my clay,
     It lies beneath the stormy sea;
  The storm is past and I'm at rest;
     Dear Mary, weep no more for me.

3   "Three stormy nights and stormy days
    We tossed the raging main;
We long had strove our bark to save,
    But all our striving was in vain.
Even then when horror filled my breast,
    My heart was filled with love for thee;
The storm is o'er and I'm at rest:
    Sweet Mary, weep no more for me.

4   "O Mary dear, thyself prepare
    To go with me unto that shore
Where love is free from grief and care,
    And I and thou shalt weep no more."
Loud crew the cock, the shadows flee,
    And no more of Sandy could she see;
But soft a pausing voice still said,
    "Dear Mary, weep no more for me."

148

MARY OF THE WILD MOOR

For references see *Journal*, XXIX, 185; XXXV, 389. Add Shoemaker, p. 96; Pound, No. 35; Partridge broadside (Boston), No. 145; Alfred Williams, *Folk-Songs of the Upper Thames*, p. 213.

A

"A Cold Winter's Night." Contributed by Mrs. William H. Bishop, Spencer, Roane County, January, 1917; obtained from Mrs. G. Shirkey in Charleston about 1880.

1 'T was all on a cold winter's night,
   When the winds blew across the wild moor,
That Mary came wandering along with her child,
   Till she came to her own father's door.

2 "O why did I leave this dear spot,
   Where once I was happy and free?
And now doomed to roam without friends or a home,
   And none to take pity on me?

3 "O father, dear father," she cried,
   "Do come downstairs and open the door!
For the child in my arms will perish and die
   From the winds that blow 'cross the wild moor."

4 But the old man was deaf to her cries,
   Not a sound of her voice did he hear,
But the watchdog did howl and the village bell toll
   And the winds blew across the wild moor.

5 O how must the old man have felt,
   When he came to the door the next morn
And found Mary dead, but the child was alive,
   Closely clasped in its dead mother's arms.

6 With anguish he tore his gray hair,
   While the tears down his cheeks they did roll,
Saying, "There Mary died, once the gay village bride,
   From the winds that blew 'cross the wild moor."

7 The old man with grief pined away,
   And the child to its mother went soon;
There's no one, they say, has lived there to this day,
   And the cottage to ruin has gone.

8 The villagers point out the spot,
        Where the willows droop over the door,
     Saying, "There Mary died, once the gay village bride,
        From the winds that blew 'cross the wild moor."

B

"Mary of the Wild Moor." Contributed by Miss Maude Grove, Deepwell, Nicholas County, August 3, 1915; learned from her mother, who in turn learned it from Miss Lena Cox about forty years before. Miss Cox was a daughter of Isaac Cox, one of the early public-school teachers of Nicholas County. Seven stanzas.

C

"Mary of the Wild Moor." Contributed by Mr. J. R. Waters, Morgantown, Monongalia County; obtained from Mrs. F. M. Brown, Belington, Barbour County, who learned it more than fifty years previously in Delaware County, Ohio. Seven stanzas.

D

"The Winds that Blow Across the Wild Moor." Communicated by Mr. C. R. Bishop, Green Bank, Pocahontas County, 1917; obtained from Miss Valera Ervine. Six stanzas.

149

THE GYPSY'S WARNING

AMERICAN texts are recorded by Belden, No. 35; Pound, p. 43; F. C. Brown, p. 12. The song was published "with music arranged by Henry A. Coard" at Brooklyn (cop. 1864). The author of the words is unknown. It is common in songbooks and broadsides: as, *The Gipsy's Warning Songster* (cop. 1867), p. 5; *The Pretty Little Sarah Songster* (cop. 1867), p. 7; *The Captain Jinks, of the Horse Marines, Songster* (cop. 1868), p. 33; *Dan Bryant's "Shoo Fly" Songster* (cop. 1869), p. 45; *The Daisy Deane Songster* (cop. 1869), p. 8; *The Vocalists' Favorite Songster* (cop. 1885), p. 183; *Singer's Journal*, I, 11; De Marsan broadside (New York), List 18, No. 26; Partridge broadside (Boston), No. 1022; Wehman broadside (New York), No. 95. There is an "Answer" to the song, beginning "Lady, do not heed the warning." It is recorded by Belden (No. 35), and printed by Shoemaker, p. 94.

Communicated by Mr. C. R. Bishop, Green Bank, Pocahontas County, 1918; obtained from Mrs. M. H. Moomau, who got it from her mother, who learned it while at school in Timberville, Virginia. A less complete text was contributed by Mr. Sam Turman, Buchanan, Boyd County, Kentucky, July, 1918.

1   Do not trust him, gentle lady,
     Though his voice be low and sweet;
  Heed him not who kneels before thee,
     Gently pleading at thy feet.
  Now thy life is in its morning,
     Cloud not this thy happy lot;
  Listen to the gypsy's warning:
     Gentle lady, heed him not.

2   Do not turn so coldly from me;
     I would only guard thy youth
  From his stern and withering power;
     I would only tell thee truth.
  I would shield thee from all danger,
     Save thee from the tempter's snare:
  Lady, shun that dark-eyed stranger;
     I have warned thee, now beware.

3   Lady, once there lived a maiden,
     Pure and bright and like thee fair,
  But he wooed, yes, wooed and won her,
     Filled her gentle heart with care;
  Then he heeded not her weeping,
     Nor cared for her life to save;
  Soon she perished, now she's sleeping
     In the cold and silent grave.

4   Keep your gold, I do not wish it!
        Lady, I have prayed for this,
    For the hour that I might foil him,
        Rob him of expected bliss.
    Gentle lady, do not wonder
        At my words so cold and wild;
    Lady, in that green grave yonder
        Sleeps the gypsy's only child.

150

FAIR FANNY MOORE

TAKEN from an old manuscript belonging to Mr. Sam Turman, Buchanan, Boyd County, Kentucky. The song is signed "B. P." This song has been printed by Lomax, p. 219; Shoemaker, p. 59 (Pennsylvania); Pound, No. 97 (Montana). Belden has found it in Missouri (No. 25, and *Journal*, XXV, 12).

1　Yonder stands a cottage, deserted and alone;
　　Its paths are neglected, by grain overthrown;
　　Go look, and you will find there some stains on the floor:
　　Alas! it is the blood of fair Fanny Moore.

2　As Fanny set blooming, two lovers came one day;
　　The first was young Ranold with a lovely degree;
　　He offered his love, his riches orle [1]
　　But his riches and his love failed to allure the heart of fair Fanny
　　　　Moore.

3　The next came young Edward of a highly degree;
　　He offered his love and his rapture did he;
　　And soon to the altar he went to secure
　　The hand and the heart of the fair Fanny Moore.

4　As Fanny set blooming in her cottage one day,
　　As business had called her fond husband away,
　　Young Ranold the haughty opened the door
　　And clasped to his bosom fair Fanny Moore.

5　"O Fanny, O Fanny, beware of your fate!
　　Except [1] of my offer before it is too late,
　　For I have come here to secure
　　The hand or the life of the fair Fanny Moore."

6　"O spare me! O spare me!" this fair Fanny cried.
　　. . . . .
　　"Go ye, go ye to the land of the rest!"
　　And he hurried a dagger in her snow-white breast.

7　As Fanny lay bleeding from bloodstain she died;
　　Young Ranold was arrested and taken and tried,
　　And hung to a tree just out the cottage door
　　For taking the life of fair Fanny Moore.

[1] So in MS.

151

ERIN'S GREEN SHORE

OTHER titles for this song in West Virginia are "The Irish Dream" and "The Irishman's Dream Song." A good text was found in Michigan in 1921 by Dr. Alma Blount. The piece is common in English broadsides (Such, No. 135; Walker, Durham, No. 6; George Walker, Jun., Durham, No. 213; Cadman, Manchester, No. 104; Livsey, Manchester, No. 331; Bebbington, Manchester, No. 180; Jackson & Son, Birmingham).

A

"Erin's Green Shore." Contributed by Mr. S. L. Moore, Burton, Wetzel County.

1　One evening so late as I rambled,
　　　On the banks of a clear purling stream,
　　I sat down on a bed of primroses,
　　　And so gently fell into a dream.
　　I dreamed that I saw a fair female,
　　　Her equal I ne'er saw before;
　　She sighed for the songs of her country,
　　　As she strayed along Erin's green shore.

2　I quickly addressed this fair female,
　　　Saying, "Please won't you tell me your name?"
　　She says, "I'm a daughter of David O'Conor,
　　　From England I've lately sailed o'er;
　　I've come to awaken my brethren,
　　　That slumber on Erin's green shore."

3　Her cheeks were like two blooming roses,
　　　And her teeth were like the ivory so white;
　　Her eyes were like two sparkling diamonds,
　　　That sparkled and dazzled at night.
　　She resembled the goddess of freedom,
　　　Liberty was the mantle she wore,
　　Bound round with the shamrock and roses,
　　　That grew along Erin's green shore.

4　In a transport of joy I awakened,
　　　And found it was all but a dream;
　　This beautiful damsel had vanished,
　　　And I longed for to slumber again.

May the heaven above be her guardian,
    For green was the mantle she wore;
May the sunbeams of glory shine o'er her,
    For I never shall see her no more.

B

"Erin's Green Shore." Contributed by Mr. John B. Adkins, Branchland, Lincoln County, May, 1916; Mr. Albert Adkins helped him "piece it out"; said by old people to have been a great favorite in days gone by.

1   One evening for pleasure I rambled,
        On the banks of a cool pearly stream,
    I sit down on a bed of primroses,
        And softly I fell in a dream;
    I dreamed that I saw a fair maiden,
        Her equals I had ne'er seen before;
    She sighed for the wrongs of her country,
        And she strayed along Erin's green shore.

2   Her eyes were like two sparkling diamonds,
        Or the stars of a cold frosty night;
    Her cheeks were like two blooming roses,
        Her teeth were like ivory so white.
    She resembled the goddess of freedom,
        And liberty was the mantle she wore;
    It was trimmed with the roses of Shamrock
        That grew along Erin's green shore.

3   So quick as I seen this fair maiden,
        I said, "Please come tell me your name.
    In this country you know I'm a stranger,
        Or I never would have asked you the same."
    "I'm the daughter of Daniel O'Connell,
        Quite lately from England came o'er;
    I came to awaken my brethren,
        Who slumbers on Erin's green shore."

4   In transport of joy I awakened,
        But alas! what I feared, was a dream,
    For that beautiful maiden had left me,
        And I longed for the slumbers again.
    May the heaven above be her guardian!
        Her face I shall never see more;
    May the sunbeams light her pathway brighter,
        As she strays on Erin's green shore!

C

"The Irish Dream." Communicated by Miss Mary Meek Atkeson, Morgantown, Monongalia County; obtained from Miss Anna Lynch.

1 One evening, as I rambled for pleasure
    On the banks of a clear pretty stream,
I sat down on a bank of wild roses,
    And so gently fell into a dream.
I dreamed I saw a fair female,
    Whose equal I had ne'er seen before,
As she stole from the wrongs of her country,
    And strolled along Erin's green shore.

2 So quickly I addressed this fair female,
    Saying, "Jewel, come tell me your name.
I know you're a stranger in this country,
    Else I would not have asked you your name."
"Yes, I came to this country a stranger,
    I know not my friends from my foes;
Since I find you're a true son of freedom,
    My story to you I'll disclose.
I'm a daughter of Aaron Goconlogue;
    From England I've lately sailed o'er;
Sailed over to awaken my true-love,
    That slumbers along Erin's green shore."

3 From the joys of the sunbeams I awakened,
    And found this had all been a dream;
This beautiful female had left me,
    And I long to be slumbering again.
Her cheeks were like two blooming roses,
    Her teeth like the ivory so white;
Her eyes were like two sparkling diamonds,
    Or the stars of a clear, frosty night.

. . . .

    Green was the mantle she wore,
Bound around with red locks and red roses,
    That grew along Erin's green shore.

D

"The Irishman's Dream Song." Communicated by Mrs. Hilary G. Richardson, Clarksburg, Harrison County. A confused and partly unintelligible variant in six stanzas.

152

POOR LITTLE JOE

CONTRIBUTED by Miss Maude Groves, Deepwell, Nicholas County, August 23, 1915; learned from James Rader, at Earle, West Virginia. Cf. Pound, p. 36. See *Partridge's New National Songster*, I, 47.

1 While strolling one night mid New York's gay throng,
  I met a poor boy, he was singing a song;
  Although he was singing, he wanted for bread,
  And although he was smiling, he wished himself dead.

Chorus

Cold blew the blast, down came the snow,
He had no place to shelter him, no place to go;
No mother to guide him, in the grave she was low,
Cast on the cold street, was poor little Joe.

2 I spoke to the poor boy, out in the cold,
  He had no place to shelter him, no place to go;
  No mother to guide him, in the grave she was low,
  Cast on the cold street, was poor little Joe.

3 A carriage passed by with a lady inside,
  I looked on poor Joe's face and saw that he cried;
  He followed the carriage, she not even smiled,
  But fondly caressing her own darling child.

4 I looked on this waif, and thought it was odd:
  Is this poor ragged urchin forgotten by God?
  I saw by the lamplight that fell on the snow,
  The pale, deadly features of poor little Joe.

5 The lights had gone out, the clock had struck one,
  Along came a policeman, his duty was done;
  You could tell by the sound of his dull heavy tread,
  You'd think he was sinking the grave of the dead.

6 "O what is this?" the policeman he said.
  It was poor little Joe; on the ground he lay dead,
  With his eyes turned to heaven, covered with snow;
  Died on the street did poor little Joe.

153

THE ORPHAN GIRL

CONTRIBUTED by Miss Maude Groves, Deepwell, Nicholas County, August 23, 1915; learned from Mrs. Rowena Smith. The same song, with little variations, was communicated by the following:

Mr. J. H. Shaffer, Newburg, Preston County, January 6, 1916; obtained from Mrs. A. R. Fike, Terra Alta.

Anna Copley, Shoals, Wayne County, January 28, 1916; obtained from Mr. Burwell Luther, who learned it about 1885 from English people by the name of Mustard, in Adams County, Ohio.

Mr. C. R. Bishop, Green Bank, Pocahontas County; obtained from Mrs. Dora Moomau, who learned it at school in Timberville, Virginia.

Cf. Perrow, *Journal*, XXVIII, 170 (North Carolina); Shearin and Combs, p. 32 (Kentucky); F. C. Brown, p. 10 (North Carolina).

1 "No home! no home!" plead a little girl,
    At the door of the rich man's hall,
  As she trembling stood on the polished steps
    And leaned on the marble wall.

2 Her clothes were thin and her feet were bare,
    And the snow had covered her head.
  "Who'll give me a home?" she feebly said,
    "A home and a crust of bread?"

3 "My father, alas! I never knew,"
    With tears in her eyes so bright;
  "My mother she sleeps in a new-made grave;
    'T is an orphan that begs to-night.

4 "I'll freeze," she said, as she sank on the steps
    And strove to cover her feet
  With her tattered dress, all covered with snow,
    All covered with snow and sleet.

5 The rich man sleeps on his walnut couch
    And dreams of his silver and gold,
  While the poor little girl, on her bed of snow,
    Whispers, "So cold! so cold!"

6 The hours pass by, and the midnight change
    Rang out like a funeral bell;
The earth was wrapped in a wintry sheet,
    And the drift of the snow still fell.

7 The morning dawned, but the poor little girl
    Still lay at the rich man's door;
But her soul had fled to a home in heaven,
    Where there's room and bread for the poor.

154

THE BLIND MAN'S REGRET

COMMUNICATED by Miss Evelyn Mathews, Glenville, Gilmer County, March, 1917; obtained from her father, who got it from Mr. F. M. Bush. The blind man was a native of Gilmer County, a shoemaker by trade. In the war between the States, he did not want to take sides; so he made shoes in a cave, the bad light of which caused him to lose his sight. So runs the story.

1 Young people attention give
    And hear what I do say;
I wish your souls with Christ to live
    In everlasting day.

2 Remember you are hastening down
    To death's dark, gloomy shade;
Your joys on earth will soon be done,
    Your flesh in dust be laid.

3 When I was young and in my prime,
    I used to go so gay;
For I did not think right of time,
    But idled time away.

4 But when too late, I thought of time,
    For time had passed and gone;
For now I'm old and am quite blind,
    I cannot see my home.

5 Lost time is never found again,
    What we call time enough;
For time and tide wait for no man,
    It proves quite small enough.

6 'T was in the year of eighty-four
    My eyes became quite dim,
For it has been twelve years or more
    Since I could see a hymn.

7 But now I'm getting old and gray,
    My way I cannot see,
For I can scarcely see a day,
    And that is hard for me.

8 The beasts and birds around me play,
    Their sports I cannot see;
For they rejoice in their own way
    Because of liberty.

9 The beauties of the earth are gone,
    That I can see no more,
For soon I'll reach my long-sought home
    Beyond the other shore.

10 And now, kind friends, one thing I ask:
    Do not let time pass by;
Although it may be a hard task,
    Please think while you are young.

11 And now, dear friends, farewell, farewell!
    We soon shall meet above,
With saints and angels there to dwell
    In joy and peace and love.

155

THE DISHONEST MILLER

THERE are several American texts of the famous English broadside ballad "The Miller's Advice to his Three Sons, On taking of Toll," which was known early in the eighteenth century. For references see *Journal*, XXXV, 390; add Alfred Williams, *Folk-Songs of the Upper Thames*, p. 192.

A

"The Dishonest Miller." Contributed by Miss Lily Hagans, Morgantown, Monongalia County, 1915. She learned it from her mother, who learned it from Elizabeth Ray Willey, *née* Ray, who was born in Wheeling. The Rays came to this country from the Isle of Wight about 1830.

1　There was an old man and he lived all alone,
　　And he had with him his three sons grown;
　　Now when he came to make his will,
　　He had nothing left but a little old mill.
　　　　Phi tra la, diddle dumpy dee

2　He called to him his eldest son:
　　"Son, my days are almost done.
　　Now, if to you the mill I make,
　　Pray tell to me the toll that you will take."
　　　　Phi tra la, diddle dumpy dee

3　"Father," said he, "my name is Rex,
　　And out of one bushel I'll take one peck;
　　And if to me the mill you make,
　　I've told you the toll that I will take."
　　　　Phi tra la, diddle dumpy dee

4　He called to him his second son:
　　"Son, my days are almost done.
　　Now, if the mill to you I make,
　　Pray tell me the toll that you will take."
　　　　Phi tra la, diddle dumpy dee

5　"Father," said he, "my name is Ralph,
　　And out of one bushel I'll take one half.
　　Now if to me the mill you make,
　　I've told you the toll that I will take."
　　　　Phi tra la, diddle dumpy dee

6   He called to him his youngest son:
    "Son, my days are almost gone.
    Now, if you to the mill I make,
    Pray tell me the toll that you will take."
        Phi tra la, diddle dumpy dee

7   "Father," said he, "my name is Lex,
    And out of one bushel I'll take three pecks;
    And if perchance the mill doth lack,
    I'll take the whole and swear to the sack."
        Phi tra la, diddle dumpy dee

    "The mill is yours," the old man said;
    He shut his eyes, and then he was dead.

ℬ

"The Old Miller." Communicated by Miss Lily Hagans, Morgantown, Monongalia County, July, 1916; obtained from Miss Callie Nuzum, Harrison County.

1   There was an old man lived on Dundee,
    He had three sons, you plainly see;
    The old man dying his mill must leave,

    .   .   .   .
        Tim o rie Father rie day

2   First he called to his eldest son;
    Says he, "My race is almost run,
    And if to you the mill I give,
    Pray tell to me what toll you'll have."
        Tim o rie Father rie day

3   "O father, you know my name is Jack,
    And every bushel I'll take the peck,
    And every bushel that I do grind,
    I'll show as good living as I can find."
        Tim o rie Father rie day

4   "O son, O son, it's that won't do;
    It's you won't do as I have done;
    The mill to you I will not give,
    For by such toll no man can live."
        Tim o rie Father rie day

5 Next he called his second son;
Said he, "My race is almost run,
And if to you the mill I give,
Pray tell to me what toll you'll have."
    Tim o rie Father rie day

6 "O father, you know my name is Alf,
And every bushel I'll take half,
And every bushel that I do grind,
I'll show as good living as I can find."
    Tim o rie Father rie day

7 "O son, O son, it's that won't do;
It's you won't do as I have done;
The mill to you I will not leave,
For by such toll no man can live."
    Tim o rie Father rie day

8 It's next he called his youngest son;
Says he, "My race is almost run,
And if to you the mill I give,
Pray tell to me the toll you'll have."
    Tim o rie Father rie day

9 "O father, you know your darling boy;
Steal all the corn is all the joy;
Steal all the corn and swear to the sack,
And slash the boys if they come back."
    Tim o rie Father rie day

10 "O son, O son, it's that will do;
It's you will do as I have done;
The mill is yours!" the old man cried,
And shut his old eyes and instantly died.
    Tim o rie Father rie day

C

"The Old Miller." Communicated by Professor Walter Barnes, Fairmont, Marion County, July, 1915; obtained from Mr. G. W. Cunningham, Elkins, Randolph County, who learned it from Solomon Rhodeman, Pendleton County.

1 He called up his eldest son:
"Son, O son, my life is run;
If to you this mill I make,
How much toll do you mean to take?"
    Whack fol la, fol la too-la-day

2 "Dad, O dad, my name is Dick;
   Out of a bushel I'll take a peck;
   And out of all the grain I'll grind
   A living I can surely find."
      Whack fol la, fol la too-la-day

3 He called up his second son:
   "Son, O son, my life is run;
   If to you this mill I make,
   How much toll do you mean to take?"
      Whack fol la, fol la too-la-day

4 "Dad, O dad, my name is Ralph;
   Out of a bushel I'll take a half;
   And out of all the grain I'll grind
   A living I can surely find."
      Whack fol la, fol la too-la-day

5 He called up his youngest son:
   "Son, O son, my life is run;
   If to you this mill I'll make,
   How much toll do you mean to take?"
      Whack fol la, fol la too-la-day

6 "O dad, I am your darling boy;
   Stealing corn is all my joy;
   I'll steal the corn and swear to the sack,
   And whip the boy when he comes back."
      Whack fol la, fol la too-la-day

7 The old man turned up his toes and died;
   The old woman sniffed up her nose and cried;
   The old man died and made no will,
   And hanged if the old woman did n't get the mill!
      Whack fol la, fol la too-la-day

D

"The Honest Miller." Contributed by Miss Mildred Joy Barker, Morgantown, Monongalia County, October 2, 1916; obtained from her mother, who says that it has been known in the family for many years. Both of Miss Barker's grandfathers, Martin Brookover and Zachwell Morgan, were millers and sang this song. Practically identical with B.

E

"The Dishonest Miller." Contributed by Mrs. Charles B. Cannaday, Morgantown, Monongalia County, July 10, 1916; obtained from her mother, Mrs. Louise Spencer Foster, who learned it about 1850, when she was a little girl, from her brother in Ohio. Practically identical with B.

F

"The Old Miller." Contributed by Miss Carrie H. Hess, Spencer, Roane County, August 8, 1916. A somewhat corrupt text in eight stanzas.

G

"The Old Miller." Contributed by the Rev. P. L. Glover, Morgantown, Monongalia County, January 17, 1916; learned from John M. Lowe, Pine Grove, Wetzel County, back in the seventies. One stanza.

H

"The Dishonest Miller." Contributed by the Rev. F. V. Arnett, Pullman, Ritchie County, August 24, 1923. Good text in eleven stanzas.

I

No local title. Contributed by Miss Florence Plymale, Shoals, Wayne County. Fragment of two stanzas. Refrain: "Jim-whack-to-folly-riley-I-oh."

156

FATHER GRUMBLE

SIX good variants have been found in West Virginia under the titles "Father Grumble" and "The Old Man Who Lived in The Woods."

For American texts and tunes see *Journal*, XXVI, 365 (Pound; Kansas; reprinted by Pound, Ballads, No. 36); XXIX, 173 (Tolman; Virginia and Indiana); XXV, 366 (Tolman and Eddy; Ohio); Campbell and Sharp, No. 112 (North Carolina); Belden's Missouri collections. For the Scottish "John Grumlie" (of which the American piece is a version) and its literary kin, see Child, *English and Scottish Ballads*, VIII (1858), 116; Kittredge, *Journal*, XXVI, 364. Add *Journal of the Irish Folk-Song Society*, I, 43.

A

"Father Grumble." Contributed by Mrs. Charles B. Cannaday, Morgantown, Monongalia County, July 10, 1916; learned in Ohio from an English servant, who came to this country about 1880.

1 There was an old man who lived in the woods,
        As you shall plainly see,
    Who thought he could do more work in a day
        Than his wife could do in three.

2 "With all my heart!" the good dame said,
        "And if you will allow,
    You shall stay at home to-day,
        And I'll go follow the plow.

3 "But you must milk the tiny cow,
        Lest she should go quite dry;
    And you must feed the little pigs
        That are within the sty.

4 "And you must watch the speckled hen,
        Lest she might go astray;
    And not forget the spool of yarn
        That I spin every day."

5 The old woman took the stick in her hand
        And went to follow the plow;
    And the old man took the pail on his head
        And went to milk the cow.

6 But Tiny she winked, and Tiny she blinked,
        And Tiny she tossed her nose;
    And Tiny she gave him a kick on the shins,
        Till the blood ran down to his toes.

7   And a "Ho, Tiny!" and a "So, Tiny!
    Pretty little cow, stand still!
If ever I milk you again," he said,
    "It will be against my will."

8   And then he went to feed the pigs
    That were within the sty;
And knocked his head against the shed
    And caused the blood to fly.

9   And then he watched the speckled hen,
    Lest she might lay astray;
But he quite forgot the spool of yarn
    That his wife spun every day.

10   And when the old woman came home at night,
    He said he could plainly see
That his wife could do more work in a day
    Than he could do in three;

11   And when he saw how well she plowed,
    And made the furrows even,
He said his wife could do more work in a day
    Than he could do in seven.

B

"The Old Man Who Lived in the Woods." Communicated by Miss Louise Wilt, Elkins, Randolph County; obtained from her grandmother, who learned it during the Civil War.

1   There was an old man who lived in the woods,
    As you shall plainly see;
He said he could do more work in a day,
    Than his wife could do in three.

2   The old woman said, "I will agree,
    But this you must allow,
That you will stay at home to-day
    While I go follow the plow.

3   "You must milk Tennie the cow,
    For fear she should go dry;
And you must feed the little pigs
    That live in yonder sty.

4   "And you must watch the speckled hen,
      For fear she lay astray;
  And you must wind the bobbin of yarn
      That I spun yesterday."

5   The old woman took the staff in her hand
      And went to follow the plow;
  The old man took the pail on his arm
      And went to milk the cow.

6   But Tennie she flinched, and Tennie she winced,
      And Tennie she curled up her nose;
  And Tennie she gave the old man such a kick,
      That the blood ran down to his toes.

7   Then, "Whoa, Tennie! soa, Tennie!
      I pray, my good cow, stand still!
  If ever I milk you again in my life,
      It will be sorely against my will."

8   He went to feed the little pigs
      That live in yonder sty;
  The old one ran against his legs,
      And knocked him down in the mire.

9   He went to watch the speckled hen,
      For fear she'd lay astray;
  And he forgot the bobbin of yarn
      His wife spun yesterday.

10   And when he saw how well she plowed,
      Said he, "I plainly see
  My wife can do more work in a day
      Than I can do in three.

11   "Yes, by the sun and moon and all stars
      That shine in yonder heaven!
  My wife can do more work in a day
      Than I can do in seven."

C

"Father Grumble." Contributed by Mr. Wiatt Smith, Huntington, Cabell County; learned from his mother, who learned it from her father's sister, Miss Eliza Wiatt.

1 There was an old man who lived in the woods,
   As I have heard them say,
Who swore he could do more work in an hour
   Than his wife could do in a day.

2 "Be it so," the old woman said,
   "For that I will allow:
You may stay at home to-day,
   And I'll go follow the plow.

3 "But you must milk Teenie, the cow,
   For fear she will go dry;
And you must give the pigs their hire,
   That are within the sty.

4 "And you must watch the speckled hen,
   For fear she'll lay astray;
And you must wind the bobbin of thread
   That I spun yesterday."

5 So the old woman took the staff in her hand
   And went to follow the plow;
And the old man took the pail on his head
   And went to milk the cow.

6 Teenie winced, and Teenie flinched,
   And Teenie she stuck up her nose;
And she dealt the old man such a deuce of a kick
   That the blood ran down to his toes.

7 "Saw, Teenie! whoa, Teenie!
   My good little cow stand still!
If ever I do milk you again,
   'T will be against my will!"

8 He went to give the pigs their hire
   That were within the sty;
And the old sow ran between his legs
   And threw him in the mire.

9   He went to watch the speckled hen,
      For fear she'd lay astray;
  Forgot to wind the bobbin of thread
      His wife spun yesterday.

10   And the old man swore by the light of the moon
      And all the stars in heaven,
  That his wife could do more work in a day
      Than he could do in seven.

D

"Father Grumble." Communicated by Mr. C. L. Broadwater, Mannington, Marion County; obtained from his father, who learned it from his mother.

1   Old Grumble swore by the light of the moon,
      And the green leaves on the tree,
  That he could do more work in a day
      Than his wife could do in three,
  That he could do more work in a day
      Than his wife could do in three.

2   "So be it! So be it!" the good wife said;
      "But this you must allow,
  That you will work in the house to-day,
      And I'll go follow the plow.

3   "O you must watch the speckled hen,
      Or she will lay astray;
  And you must wind the bobbin of thread
      That I spun yesterday.

4   "And you must milk the pretty brown cow,
      For fear she might go dry;
  And you must feed the little fat pig
      That lives in yonder sty."

5   The good wife took the staff in hand
      And went to follow the plow;
  Old Grumble took the shining pail
      And went to milk the cow.

6   "So, Teeny! so, Teeny! My pretty brown cow,
      Stand still! stand still!
  If ever I try to milk you again,
      It will be against my will."

7 But Teeny she hinched, and Teeny she flinched,
        And Teeny she turned up her nose;
    And gave the old man such a kick in the face
        That the blood ran down to his toes.

8 Old Grumble went to feed the pig
        That lived in yonder sty;
    He struck his head against a beam,
        Which caused his brain to fly.

9 The dinner to get, the table to set,
        The bed to make up smooth;
    The house to sweep, the bread to knead,
        Too much for him in truth.

10 So Grumble saw by the light of the moon,
        And the green leaves on the tree,
    That his wife could do more work in a day
        Than he could do in three.

$\mathcal{E}$

"Father Grumble." Contributed by Mr. C. B. Montgomery, West Liberty,
Ohio County, July, 1915; learned from his mother and his grandfather, who
originally came from Maryland.

1 Father Grumble said, as sure
        As the moss grew on the tree,
    That he could do more work in a day
        Than his wife could do in three.

2 Mother Grumble said,
        "That you may have it now;
    You may do the work in the house,
        And I will follow the plow.

3 "And don't forget the crock of cream
        That standeth in the frame;
    And don't forget to fatten the pot,
        Or it'll all go into flame.

4 "And don't forget the speckled hen,
        For fear she'll lay astray;
    And don't forget the bobbin of thread
        That I spin every day.

5 "And don't forget the muley cow,
  For fear she will go dry;
And don't forget the little pig
  That standeth in the sty."

6 He went to churn the crock of cream
  That standeth in the frame;
And he forgot to fatten the pot,
  And it all went into flame.

7 He went to look for the speckled hen,
  For fear she'd lay astray;
And he forgot the bobbin of thread
  That she spun every day.

8 He went to milk the muley cow,
  For fear she would go dry;
She kicked and hunched, and hunched and punched,
  And kicked him right over the eye.

9 He went to feed the little pig
  That stoodeth in the sty;
Piggy bit him on the arm
  And made the old man cry.

F

"Father Grumble." Communicated by Miss Lily Hagans, Morgantown, Monongalia County, December, 1915; obtained from Mrs. Carroll Frost, who learned it from her mother, a Baltimorian.

1 Old Grumble he did swear
  By all the stars in heaven,
That he could do more work in a day
  Than she could do in seven.

2 Mis' Grumble did agree
  And went to follow the plow;
Old Grumble took his pail in his hand
  And went to milk the cow, cow.

3 He went to turn the cheese
  That lay 'round in the frames;
And he forgot the fat in the pot,
  And all went up in flames.

4   He went to wind the yarn
      That his wife spun yesterday;
  And he forgot the speckled hen,
      And so she laid astray, astray.

5   He went to feed the pigs
      That lay 'round in the sty;
  He hit his head against a beam,
      And the hair begin to fly, fly.

6   He looked up to the sun,
      And saw 't was almost done;
  He thought it had been a very long day
      And his wife would never come, come.

7   Mis' Grumble came at last;
      He told her all his trouble, trouble;
  She turned herself quite 'round, she did,
      And wished it had been double, double.

G

"Old Grumble." Communicated by Hattie M. Wickwire, Albright, Preston County, June, 1923; obtained from Maurice Wilhelm, a traveling stave-maker.

1   Old Grumble he came in from work,
      As tired as he could be;
  He swore he could do more work in a day
      Than his wife could do in three,
      Than his wife could do in three,
      Than his wife could do in three;
  He swore he could do more work in a day
      Than his wife could do in three.

2   Mrs. Grumble had both brewed and baked;
      She was tired, too, I vow;
  She said, "You do the work in the house,
      And I'll go follow the plow.

3   "But be sure to watch the speckled hen,
      Or she will go astray;
  And don't forget to wind the yarn
      That I spun yesterday.

4 "Now don't forget to milk the cow,
   For she is kind and tame;
   And don't forget to watch the fat,
   Or it will turn to flame.

5 "Don't forget to churn the cream,
   Or it will turn to whey;
   Don't forget to feed the pig
   That in the sty does lay."

6 Old Mrs. Grumble put on her hat
   And went to follow the plow;
   Old man Grumble took the pail
   And went to milk the cow.

7 The cow she hooked, the cow she kicked,
   The cow she wrung her nose,
   And kicked old Grumble on the shin.
   Till the blood run to his toes.

8 He went to feed the little pig
   That lay within the sty;
   He bumped his head upon the door,
   Till the brains began to fly.

9 He forgot to feed the speckled hen,
   And she did go astray;
   And he forgot to wind the yarn
   That she spun yesterday.

10 He forgot to churn the cream,
   And it turned to whey, you know;
   He forgot to watch the fat,
   And it to flame did go.

11 Old Grumble then went off to bed,
   And sure, sure then was he
   That his wife could do more work in a day
   Than he could do in three.

157

AN OLD WOMAN'S STORY

THIS is the song known in Scotland as "The Wife of Kelso" or "The Wily Auld Carle." American texts may be found in *Journal*, XXIX, 179 (Tolman; Ohio); Campbell and Sharp, No. 45 (North Carolina); cf. Shearin and Combs, p. 10 (Kentucky); Belden's Missouri collection. The piece must be carefully distinguished from "Johnny Sands" (see references, *Journal*, XXIX, 178; XXXV, 385; cf. Pound, No. 48).

Communicated by Miss Laura Remke, Elm Grove, Ohio County, March, 1917; obtained from Mr. McCullock, West Liberty.

1 'T is an old woman's story I will tell;
   She loved her old man dearly, but another twice as well.

      Sing tetherancy I rea,
      Sing tetherancy I!

2 She went to the doctor's to see if she could find
   Something or other to put her old man blind.

3 She got some marrow bone and made him take it all;
   Says he, "My dear beloved wife, I cannot see you at all."

4 Says he, "I'd go and drown myself, if I could find the way."
   Says she, "I'll go and show you, lest you should go astray."

5 So they walked along together till they came unto the shore;
   Says he, "My dear and loving wife, you'll have to push me o'er."

6 Then she got back a step or two, to push her old man in,
   And he being nimble-footed, head foremost she went in.

7 Now he being tender-hearted, for fear that she might swim,
   He got a long, slim hickory pole, and pushed her farther in.

8 When he woke up next morning, his heart began to quell;
   So he gave the boy five shillings this story never to tell.

158

THE SPANISH LADY

THIS brief ditty, sometimes used as a game-song, is formed upon "O No, John," for which see Sharp, *Folk-Songs from Somerset*, IV, 46; Sharp, *One Hundred English Folksongs*, No. 68; Sharp, *English Folk Songs*, II, 116; Buck, *The Oxford Song Book*, p. 147; *Journal*, XXXV, 405; Pound, p. 43; Wyman MS., No. 49. It keeps, however, only the opening stanza of "O No, John" (see also Gomme, *Traditional Games*, I, 320; Kidson and Moffatt, *Eighty Singing Games*, p. 84). Fragments of that song are used as game-rhymes in Indiana (Wolford, *The Play-Party in Indiana*, p. 73) and Missouri (Belden's collection); cf. Pound, p. 77.

For texts similar to the West Virginia piece see Newell, *Games and Songs of American Children*, p. 55; Barry, *Journal*, XXIV, 341; Broadwood and Fuller Maitland, *English County Songs*, p. 90; Butterworth, *Folk Songs from Sussex*, p. 2; Gillington, *Songs of the Open Road*, No. 10, p. 22. Gardiner, *Folk-Songs from Hampshire*, p. 41; *Journal of the Folk-Song Society*, IV, 297; Ebsworth, *Roxburghe Ballads*, VIII, ii, 852; Alfred Williams, *Folk-Songs of the Upper Thames*, p. 196. Of these, all have stanza 3, and all but Newell have stanza 5. Neither of these two stanzas belongs to "O No, John." For stanza 5, in other contexts or alone by itself, see Ashton's *Real Sailor-Songs*, 72; *Journal of the Folk-Song Society*, I, 29, 45; *Journal of the Irish Folk-Song Society*, IX, 28. Stanza 3 has some resemblance to lines in "The Quaker's Wooing," which is also used as a game-song (Newell, p. 94; Rosa S. Allen, *Family Songs*, p. 14; Pound, No. 108; *Focus*, III, 276; *Journal*, XVIII, 56; XXIV, 342). Stanzas 2 and 3 occur in one West Virginia version of "A Pretty Fair Maid" (No. 92).

For references to similar songs see Kittredge, *Journal*, XXXV, 406.

Communicated by Miss Violet Noland, Davis, Tucker County, 1916; obtained from Mr. John Raese, who heard it sung when he was a boy.

1   Yonder stands a Spanish lady;
      Who she is I do not know;
    I'll go and court her for her beauty,
      Let her answer yes or no.

Refrain

  Rattle O ding, ding dom, ding dom,
  Rattle O ding, dom day

2   "Madame, I have gold and silver,
      Madame, I have house and land,
    Madame, I have a world of pleasure,
      And it shall be at your command."

3   "I care not for your gold and your silver,
      I care not for your house and land,
    I care not for your worldly pleasure:
      All I want is a handsome man."

4   Blue it is a handsome color,
        When it gets a second dip;
    The first time a young man starts out courtin',
        He is apt to get a slip.

5   The ripest apple soon gets rotten,
        The hottest love it soon gets cold;
    A young man's word is soon forgotten,
        Pray, young man, don't be so bold.

159

SOLDIER, SOLDIER, WON'T YOU MARRY ME?

AMERICAN texts have been printed as follows: Newell, *Games and Songs of American Children*, 1884 (1903), p. 93; Perrow, *Journal*, XXVIII, 158 (Virginia); Campbell and Sharp, No. 90 (North Carolina); Pound, No. 109 (Nebraska); Sharp, *Folk-Songs of English Origin Collected in the Appalachian Mountains*, 2d Series, p. 62 (Kentucky); Sharp, *Nursery Songs from the Appalachian Mountains*, No. 5. Cf. F. C. Brown, p. 10. The song is well known on Cape Cod. English texts may be found in Dearmer and Shaw, *Song Time*, p. 82; *Journal of the Folk-Song Society*, V, 156.

Communicated by Mr. Fred Smith, Glenville, Gilmer County; obtained from William Gainer.

1 "Soldier, soldier, won't you marry me,
    With your musket, fife, and drum?"
  "O no, pretty Miss, I can't marry you,
    I've not got any hat to put on."

2 Away she went to the hatter's shop,
    As fast as she could go;
  She got him a hat of the very best kind,
    And the soldier put it on.

The song continues, "Soldier, soldier," etc., as above, with each of the following articles of clothing: collar, tie, shirt, vest, coat, belt, trousers, socks, shoes. It concludes:

21 "Soldier, soldier, won't you marry me,
    With your musket, fife, and drum?"
  "O no, pretty maid, I can't marry you,
    I've got forty wives at home."

160

A BACHELOR'S LAMENT

BARRY, *Journal*, XXV, 281, prints a good version from Massachusetts, and cites two stanzas of a version from New Jersey. Belden has a good version from Missouri (No. 105).

Communicated by Miss Mary Meek Atkeson, Morgantown, Monongalia County, 1917; obtained from Miss Berda Lynch.

1   As I was walking all alone,
    I heard an old bachelor making his moans:
    "I wonder what the matter can be.
    Dog them pretty girls won't have me!

2   "I've courted the rich and I've courted the poor,
    And ofttimes been kicked out at the door;
    I've offered them silver, and offered them gold,
    And many a lie to them I've told.

3   "I've rode six horses plum to death,
    I've rode them as long as they had breath;
    Three new saddles down to the tree —
    Dog them pretty girls won't have me!"

161

LITTLE JOHNNY GREEN

This is the well-known song "My Grandma's (or Grandmother's) Advice," extremely popular in the fifties and sixties. Harvard College has "My Grandmother's Advice. Song Sung with great applause by the Tremaine Family Words & Music by M Arranged for the Piano by Edward Kanski" (cop. 1857), and "My Grandmother's Lesson Song Composed by A. N. Johnson" (cop. 1857). It is a modification of "The Old Maid" ("When I liv'd with my Grandam on yon little green") in *The Lover's Harmony*, No. 17, p. 134 (London, Pitts [1840]), which goes back to the eighteenth century and was printed, under the title "Die an Old Maid," in the *Virginia Centinel and Gazette* (Winchester), March 2, 1795. For references see *Journal*, XXXV, 402; add Alfred Williams, *Folk-Songs of the Upper Thames*, p. 74.

Communicated by Mr. Richard E. Hide, Martinsburg, Berkeley County, December, 1915; obtained from his mother, who learned it from an aunt. The song had been known in the family for about seventy-five years.

1   My grandmother lived on yonder little green,
Fine old lady as e'er was seen;
She often cautioned me with care
Of all false young men to beware.

2   "These false young men they flatter and deceive;
So, my love, you must not believe;
They'll flatter, they'll coax till you are in their snare,
Then away goes poor old grandma's care."

3   The first came a-courting was little Johnny Green,
Fine young man as e'er was seen;
But the words of my grandma rung in my head,
And I could not hear one word he said.

4   The next came a-courting was young Ellis Grove;
'T was then we met with a joyous love;
With a joyous love we could n't be afraid;
You'd better get married than die an old maid.

5   Thinks I to myself: "There's some mistake.
What a fuss these old folks make!
If the boys and the girls had all been afraid,
Then grandma herself would have died an old maid."

162

THE FROG AND THE MOUSE

For full information as to the history and ramifications of this song see Kittredge, *Journal*, XXXV, 394. Add Sharp, *Nursery Songs from the Appalachian Mountains* [1921], No. 1; Talley, *Negro Folk Rhymes*, pp. 167, 190.

A

"The Frog Went A-Courting." Communicated by Miss Nellie Donley, Morgantown, Monongalia County, December, 1916; obtained from Florence Noud, who learned it from some cousins to whom it had been taught by a nurse from the South.

1 Frog went a-courting, he did ride,
        Tappin
    Frog went a-courting, he did ride,
    With a sword and a pistol by his side,
        Tappin

2 He went to Miss Mousie's den;
    He said, "Miss Mousie, are you within?"

3 "Yes sir, yes sir, I am in;
    Lift the latch and walk right in."

4 He took Miss Mousie on his knee
    And he said, "Miss Mouse, will you marry me?"

5 "Not without Uncle Rat's consent,
    I would n't marry the President."

6 Mr. Rat went to town,
    To buy his niece a wedding gown.

7 Where shall the wedding supper be?
    Down in the hollow of an old oak tree.

8 What shall the wedding supper be?
    A slice of cake and a cup of tea.

9 First came in was a little brown bug;
    He drowned himself in the 'lasses jug.

10 Second came in was a wee little fly;
    He ate so much he almost died.

11   Last came in was a little brown snake;
     He coiled himself on the wedding cake.

12   They all went down to the lake for a spree;
     The little frog died of a tummy ache.

13   Sword and a pistol on the shelf —
     If you want any more, you'll sing it yourself.

𝓑

"The Marriage of the Frog and the Mouse." Contributed by Miss Emma
Boughner, Morgantown, Monongalia County. She was helped in recalling it
by Mrs. E. B. Hall and Mrs. S. J. Posten.

1   Frog went a-courting, he did ride,
            Mmn-huh, mmn-huh
     Frog went a-courting, he did ride,
     Frog went a-courting, he did ride,
            Mmn-huh, mmn-huh

2   He rode up to Miss Mousie's door,
     Just as he had done before.

3   He rode up to Miss Mousie's den
     And said, "Lady Mouse, are you within?"

4   "O yes, kind sir, I sit and spin;
     Just raise the latch and walk right in."

5   He took Lady Mouse upon his knee
     And he said, "Lady Mouse, will you marry me?"

6   At length Uncle Rattie he came home,
     And said, "Who's been here since I've been gone?"

7   "O a nice young gentleman dressed in blue,
     And asks consent to marry me."

8   Uncle Rat laughed till he shook his fat side,
     To think his niece might be a bride.

9   But where shall the wedding supper be?
     Way down yonder in a hollow tree.

10   The first that came was a bumble bee,
     Carrying a fiddle upon his knee.

11　The next that came was a big black bug,
　　On his back was a whiskey jug.

12　Bread and butter lie on the shelf,
　　If you want any more you can sing it yourself.

The following stanzas were supplied by Mrs. John Harrington Cox.

What shall the wedding supper be?
Two black beans and a cup of tea.

Frog went swimming across the lake,
And he was swallowed by a big black snake.

C

"Frog Went A-Courting." Contributed by Mrs. Tallman Dowdy, Wayne Court House, Wayne County, 1918; learned when she was a child, from her sister.

1　There was a frog lived in a well,
　　　Tid-e-ra-e-ral, tid-e-ra-e-ral
　　There was a frog lived in a well,
　　　Tid-e-ra-e-ral, tid-e-ra-e-ral
　　There was a frog lived in a well,
　　And in a mill a mouse did dwell.
　　　Ding-dong-de-day

2　Mr. Froggie wanted a wife
　　And he mounted his horse and he rode for his life.

3　He rode up to the mill door
　　And there he made a very roar.

4　Miss Mouse was sitting at spin
　　And she rose up and let him in.

5　He took Miss Mouse upon his knee
　　And he said, "Pretty Miss, will you marry me?"

6　"As for that I cannot say,
　　For Mr. Mouse has gone away."

7　Mr. Mouse came home next day
　　And said, "Who's been here since I went away?"

8　"The finest fellow that ever was seen,
　　And he has come for to marry me."

9　Mr. Mouse gave his consent,
　　And the weasel wrote the publishment.

10 O where shall the wedding supper be?
    Way down yonder in a hollow tree.

11 O what shall the wedding supper be?
    Dogwood bark and catnip tea.

12 The first came in was a hopping flea,
    And he danced a jig with a bumble bee.

13 The next came in was a cabinet bug,
    And on his back he swung his jug.

𝒟

"A Toad Went A-Courting." Communicated by Mr. Harper Mauzy, Franklin County, January, 1916; obtained from his mother. A short version in ten stanzas, with the following:

> The next came in was Mr. Tick,
> He ate so much till it made him sick.

> The next came in was Dr. Fly,
> And said that Tick would have to die.

𝓔

No local title. Communicated by Mrs. Hilary G. Richardson, Clarksburg, Harrison County, 1917. A fragmentary version in eight stanzas.

F

No local title. Contributed by Miss Julia Otto, Wheeling, Ohio County. A fragmentary version in eight stanzas, with the following:

> The first came in was an old brown cow,
> Tried to dance and did n't know how.

> The next came in was an old gray mare,
> Hip stuck out and shoulder bare.

> The next came in was a little black dog,
> Chased Lady Mousie in a hollow log.

𝒢

No local title. Contributed by C. Woofter, Glenville, Gilmer County, December 18, 1923; learned from an old negro woman, who lived in a negro settlement on Steer Creek, Calhoun County. A fragmentary version in four stanzas, in which Uncle Rat was the one who wanted a wife and rode down to the miller's house to get her. It has the following refrain:

> To tiddle de dum
> Rode till he came to the miller's house
> Off come in and take a chair
> To tiddle de dum

163

THE FOX

For other versions, English and American, see *Boston Transcript*, April 10, 1909 (nine stanzas); Neff (Missouri; Kittredge MSS., IV, 92); Belden's Missouri collection; F. C. Brown, p. 12 (North Carolina); Halliwell, *Nursery Rhymes*, 1842, p. 30; Logan, *A Pedlar's Pack*, p. 292; Graham, *Traditional Nursery Rhymes*, p. 37; Hewett, *Nummits and Crummits*, p. 196; Baring-Gould and Sharp, *English Folk-Songs for Schools*, p. 64; *Notes and Queries*, 1st Series X, 371; Alfred Williams, *Folk-Songs of the Upper Thames*, p. 247; cf. Brushfield, *The Broadside Ballads of Devonshire and Cornwall*, p. x. Harvard College has an eighteenth-century broadside ("Bold Reynard the Fox").

Communicated by Miss Sallie D. Jones, Hillsboro, Pocahontas County, January, 1917; obtained from Mr. Edward Fenwick, a very old man, who came years ago from England.

1 The fox peeped out one moonlight night so bright,
   When the stars and the moon they shone:
   "A-zocks!" says the fox, "I'll go through that town to-night,
   Before I do lay me down."

2 Then, fox he came up to the Castle wood,
   And upon his two hind legs he stood,
   Saying, "I think a little fresh meat would do me some good,
   If I could but get safe through that town."

3 Then, fox he came up to Rickaby's yard,
   Where the ducks and the geese were afraid;
   He took one by the long neck and slung him over his back,
   And he galloped so fast through that town.

4 Old Charles he got up with his night cap on,
   And, spying bold Reynard tripping off with one,
   He put spurs to Black Sloven, and swore he would have him
   Before he got safe through that town.

5 Old Charles went so fast through the streets of that town,
   And he thought, "I'll run the sly thief down!"
   But foxy had more wit, and he gave poor Charles the slip,
   As he galloped so fast through that town.

6 The fox he came to the Castle hill,
   Where the trumpets and the horns they sound so shrill:
   "A-zocks!" says the fox, "I'll have music to my will,
   Since I have got so safe through that town."

7 The fox, tripping off, now hied to his den,
   Where he'd got young ones, nine or ten,
   And the youngest of them all says, "O daddy, go again!
   Since you have brought such good meat from the town."

164

THE RANGER

"RANGER" is a corruption of "Reynard." Barry (*Journal*, XXVII, 71) prints a Massachusetts text (as well as two stanzas from Kansas), which begins:

> Come, all ye merry hunters who love to chase the fox,
> Who love to chase Bull [1] Reynard among the hills and rocks.

Baring-Gould (*A Book of Nursery Songs and Rhymes*, p. 7) prints a version beginning:

> There were three jovial Welshmen, they would go hunt a fox.
> They swore they saw sly Reynard run over yonder rocks.

See also Alfred Williams, *Folk-Songs of the Upper Thames*, p. 67.

Communicated by Miss Emma Boughner, Morgantown, Monongalia County, 1917; obtained from Miss Jane Carle, Parkersburg, Wood County, who said it was crooned to her by a Dutch nurse. Title supplied.

1 The first I saw was a maiden,
　　　A-combing out her locks;
　She said she saw a ranger
　　　Among the hills and rocks.

Refrain

With a root-toot-toot and a harlow,
　　　Along the narrow strand,
With a rat-tat-tat and a tippe-tippe tan,
　　　And away with a roaring boo-woo-woo,
Come a roodle-doodle-doodle and a jongo sound,
　　　Away unto the woods they ran, brave boys,
　　　Away to the woods they ran.

2 The next I saw was a teamster,
　　　A-coming with his team;
　He said he saw a ranger,
　　　A-crossing the narrow stream.

3 The next I saw was a black man,
　　　As black as he could be;
　He said he saw a ranger
　　　Climb up the black-jack tree.

4 The next I saw was a driver,
　　　A-coming with his flock;
　He said he saw a ranger
　　　Crawl in behind a rock.

[1] For *Bold.*

5 The next I saw was a white man,
    As white as he could be;
   He said he saw a ranger
    Climb up a white-oak tree.

6 The next I saw was a hunter,
    A-coming with his gun;
   He said he saw a ranger
    And shot him as he run.

165

THE THREE FARMERS

THE following stanza, sung by the mad Celania in Davenant's comedy "The Rivals" (licensed and printed in 1668), Act III (quarto, p. 34; *Dramatic Works*, 1874, V, 264) gives proof of the early existence of something like this piece:

> There were three Fools at Mid-summer run mad
> About an Howlet, a quarrel they had,
> The one said 't was an Owle, the other he said nay,
> The third said it was a Hawk but the Bells were cutt away.

For texts of the song (which exhibit much variety) see Halliwell, *The Nursery Rhymes of England*, 1842, No. 208, p. 118 ("There were three jovial Welshmen"); Lang, *The Nursery Rhyme Book*, p. 169; Baring-Gould and Sharp, *English Folk-Songs for Schools*, No. 24, p. 50 ("The Three Huntsmen"); *Journal of the Folk-Song Society*, I, 128 ("Three Jovial Welshmen"); Alfred Williams, *Folk-Songs of the Upper Thames*, p. 179. Edwin Waugh elaborated the song in the Lancashire dialect ("Three Jolly Hunters": John Graham, *Dialect Songs of the North*, 2d ed., p. 6).

For American texts see Whiting, *Journal*, III, 242 ("There were three jolly Welshmen," North Carolina); Rosa S. Allen, *Family Songs*, p. 8; Newell, *Games and Songs of American Children*, 1884 (1903), p. 97; Barry, *Journal*, XXVII, 72 (Alabama); Barry, No. 81; Belden's Missouri Collection. The Hutchinson Family sang a form of the song in their concerts in the forties and fifties of the last century. Their version ("Cape Ann") is given in Davidson's *Universal Melodist*, London, II (1848), 317. It closely resembles the West Virginia text.

Contributed by Miss Sallie D. Jones, Hillsboro, Pocahontas County, January, 1917; learned from her brother about forty years previously.

1 Three farmers went a-hunting,
      And the first thing they did find
Was a barn in a meadow,
      And that they left behind.
   Lookee there now!

2 One said it was a barn,
      But the others said nay;
They said it was a church,
      With the steeple cut away.
   Lookee there now!

3 So they hunted and they hallooed,
      And the next thing they did find
Was a girl in a cottage,
      And that they left behind them.
   Lookee there now!

4   One said it was a girl,
        But the others said nay;
    They said it was an angel,
        With her wings cut away.
        Lookee there now!

5   So they hunted and they hallooed,
        And the next thing they did find
    Was an owl in a hollow,
        And that they left behind them.
        Lookee there now!

6   One said it was an owl,
        But the others said nay;
    They said it was the Evil One,
        And they all ran away.
        Lookee there now!

166

THE THREE ROGUES

THE two variants of this song found in West Virginia are forms of "In Good Old Colony Times." For texts and references (including material on the related English glee of "King Arthur") see *Journal*, XXIX, 167; XXXV, 350; Pound, No. 116.

A

Communicated by Mrs. Charles B. Cannaday, Morgantown, Monongalia County, July 10, 1916; obtained from her mother, Mrs. Louise Spencer Foster, who learned it about 1850 in Cambridge, Ohio. Text B, almost identical, was communicated by Miss Francis Klein, Grafton, Taylor County; obtained from Marguerite Thayer, whose mother learned it in Ohio.

1   In the good Old Colony times,
  When we were under the king,
 Three roguish chaps fell into mishaps,
  Because they would not sing,
  Because they would not sing,
  Because they would not sing,
 Three roguish chaps fell into mishaps,
  Because they would not sing.

2   The first he was a miller,
  The second he was a weaver,
 The third he was a little tailor,
  Three roguish chaps together,
  Three roguish chaps together,
  Three roguish chaps together,
 The third he was a little tailor,
  Three roguish chaps together.

3   The miller he stole corn,
  The weaver he stole yarn,
 The little tailor he stole broadcloth,
  To keep these three rogues warm,
  To keep these three rogues warm,
  To keep these three rogues warm,
 The little tailor he stole broadcloth,
  To keep these three rogues warm.

4 The miller got drowned in the dam,
   The weaver got hung in his yarn,
The devil caught the little tailor,
     With the broadcloth under his arm,
     With the broadcloth under his arm,
     With the broadcloth under his arm,
The devil caught the little tailor,
     With the broadcloth under his arm.

167

THE SKIN–AND–BONE LADY

For American texts see Perrow, *Journal*, XXVI, 142 (Pennsylvania, Kentucky, reported from Tennessee); Lomax, *The North Carolina Booklet*, July, 1911, XI, 29 (North Carolina); Kittredge MSS., XIII, 57 (from Professor A. A. Kern; Virginia); cf. F. C. Brown, p. 10 (North Carolina). Belden has texts from Virginia and Missouri.

For England see *Gammer Gurton's Garland*, 1801, p. 29; Halliwell, *Nursery Rhymes*, 1842, pp. 64, 180; Rimbault, *A Collection of Old Nursery Rhymes*, p. 32; Christie, *Traditional Ballad Airs*, I, 240, note; *Notes and Queries*, 8th Series, II, 69; Granger, *Folk-Lore*, XXII, 274; Parker, *Folk-Lore*, XXIV, 81.

A

Communicated by Miss Lily Hagans, Morgantown, Monongalia County, 1916; obtained from Mrs. Estelle Wallace.

1   There was an old lady named Skin-and-bones.
    Hm, hm

2   She thought she would go to church one day,
    To hear the parson sing and pray.
    Hm, hm

3   When she got to the church stile,
    She thought she'd rest a little while.
    Hm, hm

4   When she got to the church door,
    She thought she'd rest a little more.
    Hm, hm

5   She looked up, she looked down;
    She saw a corpse lie on the ground.
    Hm, hm

6   The woman to the parson said,
    "Will I look so when I am dead?"
    Hm, hm

7   The parson to the woman said,
    "You will look so when you are dead."
    Hm, hm

B

Communicated by Miss Lily Hagans, Morgantown, Monongalia County, 1916; obtained from Mrs. Julia McGrew, who said the last note of the music was very high and followed by a shriek. The lady was supposed to have fainted.

1   There was a lady all skin and bone,
     And such a lady was never known.

2   This lady took a walk one day,
     This lady rested on the way.

3   This lady came to a church stile,
     And there she rested a little while.

4   This lady came to a church door,
     And there she rested a little more.

5   She looked up and she looked down,
     And spied a corpse upon the ground;

6   And from the crown and to the chin,
     The worms crept out and the worms crept in.

7   This lady to the parson said,
     "Will I look so when I am dead?"

8   The parson to the lady said,
     "You will look so when you are dead,
     You will look so when you are dead."

168

BILLY BOY

FOR American texts see Clifton Johnson, *What They Say in New England* (Boston, 1897), p. 230; Shoemaker, pp. 102, 131 (Pennsylvania); Wolford, *The Play-Party in Indiana*, p. 24; Campbell and Sharp, No. 89 (North Carolina); Pound, No. 113 (Nebraska; cf. *Journal*, XXVI, 356); Waugh, *Journal*, XXXI, 78 (Ontario); De Marsan broadside, List 18, No. 4; *Beadle's Dime Song Book No. 10* (cop. 1863), p. 62. Cf. Shearin and Combs, p. 30 (Kentucky); F. C. Brown, p. 10 (North Carolina); Jones, p. 3 (Michigan); Wyman MS., No. 25 (Kentucky); Minish MS. (North Carolina); Belden's Missouri collection.

A parody written in the days of the Civil War ("Bully Boy, Billy") may be read in Child's *War-Songs for Freemen* (Boston, cop. 1862), p. 41.

For British references see Kittredge, *Journal*, XXVI, 357, note 1. Sharp (*One Hundred English Folksongs*, p. xxxiv) suggests that "Billy Boy" is "a comic derivative, or burlesque," of "Lord Randal" (Child, No. 12).

Hector Macneill's "My Boy Tammie" or "Tammy's Courting," modelled on the English song (see *The Vocal Magazine*, Edinburgh, 1797, Song CV), is found in American songbooks: as, *The Minstrel* (Baltimore, 1812), p. 106; *The Singer's Magazine and Universal Vocalist* (Philadelphia, 1835), I, 176; *The Bijou Minstrel* (Philadelphia, 1840), p. 117; *The Bonnie Dundee Songster* (cop. 1868), p. 68; *Delaney's Scotch Song-Book No. 1*, p. 16.

In addition to the texts given below, this song was reported by others as follows: Miss Sallie Evans, Elkins, Randolph County; Mr. N. D. Barber, Charleston, Kanawha County; Miss Emma Boughner, Morgantown, Monongalia County; and a second text by Mrs. Hilary G. Richardson, Clarksburg, Harrison County.

A

Contributed by Mr. S. F. Hull, Frankfort, Greenbrier County, January 19, 1916.

1   "Where have you been, Billy Boy?
        Where have you been, charming Billy?"
    "I have been to see my wife,
    She is the joy of my life:
    She is a young thing, too young to leave her mother."

2   "Did she ask you in, Billy Boy?
        Did she ask you in, charming Billy?"
    "Yes, she asked me in,
    With the dimples in her chin:
    She is a young thing, too young to leave her mother."

3   "Did she ask you to take a chair, Billy Boy?
     Did she ask you to take a chair, charming Billy?"
  "Yes, she asked me to take a chair,
  With the wrinkles in her hair:
  She is a young thing, too young to leave her mother."

4   "Can she bake a sweetened pone, Billy Boy?
     Can she bake a sweetened pone, charming Billy?"
  "Yes, she can bake a sweetened pone,
  You can eat it or let it alone:
  She is a young thing, too young to leave her mother."

5   "Can she bake a cherry pie, Billy Boy?
     Can she bake a cherry pie, charming Billy?"
  "Yes, she can bake a cherry pie
  Quick as a cat can wink its eye:
  She is a young thing, too young to leave her mother."

6   "Can she make a pair of breeches, Billy Boy?
     Can she make pair of breeches, charming Billy?"
  "Yes, she can make a pair of breeches
  Fast as you can count the stitches:
  She is a young thing, too young to leave her mother."

7   "How tall is she, Billy Boy?
     How tall is she, charming Billy?"
  "She is as tall as a pine
  And straight as a pumpkin vine:
  She is a young thing, too young to leave her mother."

8   "How old is she, Billy Boy?
     How old is she, charming Billy?"
  "She is twice six, twice seven,
  Twice twenty and eleven:
  She is a young thing, too young to leave her mother."

B

Communicated by Mrs. Hilary G. Richardson, Clarksburg, Harrison County, 1916; obtained from Mrs. Nancy McAtee.

1   "Where are you going, Billy Boy, Billy Boy?
     Where are you going, charming Billy?"
  "I am going to seek me a wife,
  For the joy of my life:
  She's a young thing and can't leave her mammy."

2 "Can she make a feather bed, Billy Boy, Billy Boy?
    Can she make a feather bed, charming Billy?"
"Yes, she can make a feather bed
And put the pillows at the head:
She's a young thing and can't leave her mammy."

3 "Can she bake a cherry pie, Billy Boy, Billy Boy?
    Can she bake a cherry pie, charming Billy?"
"Yes, she can bake a cherry pie,
Quick as a cat can wink her eye:
She's a young thing and can't leave her mammy."

4 "Is she fitted for your wife, Billy Boy, Billy Boy?
    Is she fitted for your wife, charming Billy?"
"She's as fitted for my wife
As my pocket for my knife:
She's a young thing and can't leave her mammy."

5 "How old is she, Billy Boy, Billy Boy?
    How old is she, charming Billy?"
"She's twice six, twice seven,
Twice forty and eleven:
She's a young thing and can't leave her mammy."

C

Communicated by Miss Julia Otto, Wheeling, Ohio County.

1 "Where have you been, charming Willie?
    Where have you been, charming boy?"
"I've been to see my wife, she's the secret of my life:
    She's a young girl and can't leave her mother."

2 "Did she ask you in, charming Willie?
    Did she ask you in, charming boy?"
"She asked me in, with a dimple in her chin:
    She's a young girl and can't leave her mother."

3 "Did she give you a chair, charming Willie?
    Did she give you a chair, charming boy?"
"She gave me a chair, with a wrinkle in her hair:
    She's a young girl and can't leave her mother."

4   "Did she light you to bed, charming Willie?
        Did she light you to bed, charming boy?"
    "She lit me to bed, with a candle in her head:
        She's a young girl and can't leave her mother."

5   "Can she bake a cherry pie, charming Willie?
        Can she bake a cherry pie, charming boy?"
    "She can bake a cherry pie while a cat can wink her eye:
        She's a young girl and can't leave her mother."

6   "How old is she, charming Willie?
        How old is she, charming boy?"
    "Twice six, twice seven, twice twenty and eleven:
        She's a young girl and can't leave her mother."

7   "How tall is she, charming Willie?
        How tall is she, charming boy?"
    "She's as tall as any pine, and straight as any pumpkin vine:
        She's a young girl and can't leave her mother."

𝒟

Communicated by Professor C. E. Haworth, Huntington, Cabell County; obtained from Miss Gladys Broyles, Monroe County, who got it from her mother.

1   "Where are you going, Billie Boy, Billie Boy?
        Where are you going, Billie Boy?"
    "I am going down the lane for to see Sallie Jane:
        She is a young thing and cannot leave her mammy."

2   "Does she invite you in, Billie Boy?
        Does she invite you in, Billie Boy?"
    "Yes, she invites me in, with a dimple in her chin:
        She is a young thing and cannot leave her mammy."

3   "Does she sit close to you, Billie Boy, Billie Boy?
        Does she sit close to you, Billie Boy?"
    "Yes, she sits as close to me as the bark upon a tree:
        She is a young thing and cannot leave her mammy."

4   "Can she make a cherry pie, Billie Boy, Billie Boy?
        Can she make a cherry pie, Billie Boy?"
    "Yes, she can make a cherry pie quick as a cat can wink its
            eye:
        She is a young thing and cannot leave her mammy."

5   "Can she make up a bed, Billie Boy, Billie Boy?
        Can she make up a bed, Billie Boy?"
    "Yes, she can make up a bed, and comb her woolly head:
        She is a young thing and cannot leave her mammy."

6   "Can she milk a cow, Billie Boy, Billie Boy?
        Can she milk a cow, Billie Boy?"
    "Yes, she can milk a cow when her mammy shows her how:
        She is a young thing and cannot leave her mammy."

169

THE OLD MAN WHO CAME OVER THE MOOR

FOR other American texts see Perrow, *Journal*, XXVIII, 158 (Kentucky); Campbell and Sharp, No. 108 (North Carolina, Virginia); Sharp, *Folk-Songs of English Origin Collected in the Appalachian Mountains*, 2d Series, p. 66 (Virginia); *Boston Herald*, August 25, 1923. Belden has found the song in Missouri (from Virginia). Different, but related, is the Indiana song printed by Tolman, *Journal*, XXIX, 188.

English and Scottish versions may be found in Bell, *Ballads and Songs of the Peasantry*, p. 237; Kidson, *Traditional Tunes*, p. 92; Mason, *Nursery Rhymes and Country Songs*, p. 33; Graham, *Dialect Songs of the North of England*, 2d ed., p. 11; Greig, *Folk-Song of the North-East*, CXLIX; Alfred Williams, *Folk-Songs of the Upper Thames*, p. 73; cf. *Journal of the Folk-Song Society*, II, 273. Kittredge notes that the song is closely related to "The Brisk Young Lad" in Herd's *Ancient and Modern Scottish Songs*, 1776, II, 150.

Communicated by Miss Lily Hagans, Morgantown, Monongalia County, February 5, 1916; obtained from Mrs. Carroll Frost, who learned it when she was a girl in Baltimore.

1 There was an old man who came over the moor,
   Heigh-O, but I won't have him!
 My mother she told me to open the door,
   Heigh-O, but I won't have him!

2 I opened the door and he bowed to the floor,
   Heigh-O, but I won't have him!
 With his old gray beard so newly shaven;
   Heigh-O, but I won't have him!

3 My mother she told me to hand him a stool,
   Heigh-O, but I won't have him!
 I hand him a stool and he act like a fool,
   With his old gray beard so newly shaven.

4 My mother she told me to give him a pie,
   Heigh-O, but I won't have him!
 I hand him a pie and he laid the crust by,
   With his old gray beard so newly shaven.

5 My mother she told me to show him the church,
   Heigh-O, but I won't have him!
 I showed him the church and left him in the lurch,
   With his old gray beard so newly shaven.

170

OLD GRIMES

THE first stanza will be recognized as belonging to the well-known poem by Albert Gordon Greene. The rest is a comic perversion after the fashion of a nursery rhyme.

Communicated by Miss Lily Hagans, Morgantown, Monongalia County, January 2, 1916; obtained from an old lady, Mrs. Boyd.

1   Old Grimes is dead, that good old man,
        We ne'er shall see him more;
    He used to wear an old gray coat,
        All buttoned up before, my boys,
        All buttoned up before.

2   I wish I had a load of wood,
        To fence my garden round;
    For the neighbors' pigs they do get in
        And root up all my ground, my boys,
        And root up all my ground.

3   Our old cat has got so fat
        She'll neither sing nor pray;
    She chased a mouse all round the house
        And broke the Sabbath day, my boys,
        And broke the Sabbath day.

4   Somebody stole my banty hen,
        I wish they'd let her be;
    For Saturday she laid two eggs,
        And Sunday she laid three, my boys,
        And Sunday she laid three.

171

THE COBBLER'S BOY

THIS ditty is related to "The Shoemaker" (North Carolina and Kentucky): Campbell and Sharp, No. 100; Wyman MS., No. 30; cf. Shearin, p. 20 ("The Old Shoemaker").

Communicated by Miss Elsa McCausland, Elm Grove, Ohio County; obtained from Mr. J. R. McCullough, West Liberty.

1 I am a cobbler's boy,
  And just obtained my freedom;
 And I've placed my affections on
  A very handsome lady.

Chorus

 Raddle daddle dink te tink te dum,
 Raddle daddle dink te di do,
  O she is my deary O

2 She has ten pounds of gold
  And some old scraps of leather,
 And one old pair of shoes,
  We'll darn them all together.

3 My mother loves this girl,
  My father loves her better;
 I love this girl myself,
  If I can only get her.

4 But now I've lost my wax,
  And O I cannot find it!
 It's enough to grieve any man:
  O darn it, now I've got it!

172

THE YOUNG MAN WHO TRAVELLED
UP AND DOWN

This looks like an imitation of the old English broadside song "Joan's Ale is New," entered in the Stationers' Register on October 16, 1594, and March 25, 1656 (Arber, II, 662, 665; Eyre, II, 42; Rollins, *Index*, Nos. 1288, 1289, cf. 2793), and included in D'Urfey's *Pills to Purge Melancholy*, III (1712), 133 ("The Jovial Tinker"): see Chappell, *Popular Music of the Olden Time*, p. 187; cf. Ebsworth, *Roxburghe Ballads*, VII, 164. For a modernized version see broadsides (Catnach; Such, No. 391; Harkness, Preston, No. 391); Bell, *Ballads and Songs of the Peasantry*, p. 197; Ford, *Vagabond Songs and Ballads of Scotland*, II, 130; Baring-Gould and Sheppard, *A Garland of Country Song*, p. 12; *Journal of the Folk-Song Society*, II, 234; VI, 12; Alfred Williams, *Folk-Songs of the Upper Thames*, p. 276; Buck, *The Oxford Song Book*, p. 194; *The Scottish Students' Song Book*, p. 178 (as rewritten by Baring-Gould).

Communicated by Mr. Floyd Sayre, Ripley, Jackson County, December 13, 1915; obtained from Mr. Bert Stewart, who learned it in the lumber camps.

1   Once there was a young man who travelled up and down,
He travelled to a place called Seaport Town;
The drums they did beat and the cannons they did roar,
And they told me there that the wars were o'er.

2   Along came the barber, a-thinking any harm,
With a great long beard as long as me arm:
"I'll be hanged if I can't get a kiss from the ladies out of
       doors;
I'll be hanged if I shave till the wars are o'er."

3   Along came the shoemaker, the honest trade of all,
With hammer, tacks, and pincers, and his long peg-o-all:
"I was drunk last night and I was drunk the night before,
And I'll not get sober till the wars are o'er."

4   Along came the teacher, with his cunning looks,
He said he made his living by the teaching of his books;
He has got a list of scholars and he can't get no more,
And he can't get the school till the wars are o'er.

5 Along came the blacksmith, the lowest trade of all,
He sold his bed and blanket for his iron and his coal;
Now he has to lay on the cold frozen floor,
And there he has to lay till the wars are o'er.

6 Along came the devil with a budget on his back,
He picked up the blacksmith to make up his pack:
"You may ride behind and I'll ride before,
And we'll jog along till the wars are o'er."

173

THE YOUNG MAN WHO WOULD N'T HOE CORN

CONTRIBUTED by Miss Lalah Lovett, Bulltown, Braxton County, 1916; learned from Miss Ellen Stump, Capon, Hampshire County.

Not recorded from England; very probably an American product. See Tolman, *Journal*, XXIX, 181; Campbell and Sharp, No. 116; Pound, No. 46; Barry, No. 72; Belden, No. 106.

1 I will sing you a song that won't detain you long,
   About a young man who would n't hoe his corn.

2 He planted his corn in the month of May,
   And in July it was knee-high.

3 And in September there came a frost,
   And all this young man's corn was lost.

4 He went to the fence and peeped within,
   But the grass and weeds had grown to his chin.

5 He went to his nearest neighbor's door,
   Where ofttimes he had been before.

6 Miss Courtship came along,
   And asked him if he'd hoed his corn.

7 He hung his head and drew a sigh,
   Saying, "O pray, Miss, I'll tell you why.

8 "I've tried, and I've tried and I've tried in vain,
   But I don't believe I'll raise a grain."

9 "Single I am, and single I'll remain,
   For a lazy man I won't maintain."

174

OLD JOE CLOG

COMMUNICATED by Mrs. Hilary G. Richardson, Clarksburg, Harrison County, 1917. Something like stanza 2 occurs in "Old Joe Clark" (Payne, *Publications of the Folklore Society of Texas*, I, 33). See also Perrow, *Journal*, XXV, 152, and XXVIII, 176. With stanza 4 cf. Halliwell, *Nursery Rhymes*, 1842, p. 135.

1 I wish I were a-sitting in a chair,
   One arm around the whiskey jug, the other round my dear.

   > Sure around Old Joe Clog,
   > Sure around I'm gone,
   > Good-bye, Betsey Brown.

2 I never did like Betsey Brown; I'll tell you the reason why:
   Her neck's so long and stringy, I fear she'll never die.

3 I never did like old Joe Clog; I'll tell you the reason why:
   He rode all round my garden fence and broke down all my
   rye.

4 When I was a little boy I used to hunt the squirrels;
   Now I am a great big boy, I'd rather hunt the girls.

5 When I was a little girl I liked to play in sand;
   But now I am a great big girl, I'd rather have a man.

175

OLD SAM FANNY

THIS is the nursery rhyme usually known in England as "Betty (or Johnny) Pringle's Pig." See Halliwell, *Nursery Rhymes*, 1842, No. 27, p. 18; Rimbault, *A Collection of Old Nursery Rhymes*, No. 34, p. 42; Mason, *Nursery Rhymes and Country Songs*, p. 32; Sturgis and Hughes, *Songs from the Hills of Vermont*, p. 46; Sharp, *Nursery Songs from the Appalachian Mountains*, No. 3; Wyman MS., No. 13a (Kentucky).

A

"Old Sam Fanny." Communicated by Mr. C. W. Chancellor, Parkersburg, Wood County, June, 1916; obtained from his grandmother, Mrs. W. E. Arnett, Fairmont, Marion County.

1 Old Sam Fanny had a pig, uh, huh!
    Old Sam Fanny had a pig,
    And it was so little that it would n't grow big, uh, huh!

2 There came a windy night one day, uh, huh!
    There came a windy night one day,
    And blew Sam Fanny's pig away, uh, huh!

3 Sam Fanny cried himself to death, uh, huh!
    Sam Fanny cried himself to death,
    And his old woman died for want of breath, uh, huh!

4 So this was the end of one, two, three, uh, huh!
    This was the end of one, two, three,
    Old man, old woman, and little piggee, uh, huh!

5 The ancient book lays on the shelf, uh, huh!
    The ancient book lays on the shelf,
    If you want any more, you can sing it yourself, uh, huh!

B

No local title. Communicated by Miss Sallie Evans, Elkins, Randolph County, 1917; obtained from Miss Katherine Hart, who got it from her parents.

1 Old Joe Finley had a little pig, uh huh!
    Old Joe Finley had a little pig,
    It lived all its life and it never grew big, uh huh!

2 The old woman went out to give it some bread, uh huh!
The old woman went out to give it some bread,
When she got there the piggie was dead, uh huh!

3 The old man grieved himself to death, uh huh!
The old man grieved himself to death,
Because the piggie could n't get its breath, uh huh!

4 The old Indian book lies on the shelf, uh huh!
The old Indian book lies on the shelf,
If you want any more, you can sing it yourself, uh huh!

176

GROUND HOG SONG

COMMUNICATED by Professor C. E. Haworth, Huntington, Cabell County, 1917;
a familiar song around West Union in Doddridge County.

For other versions see Wyman and Brockway, p. 30 (Kentucky); Minish
MS., 1, 41 (North Carolina); Shearin and Combs, p. 38 (Kentucky).

1   I shouldered up my gun and whistled for my dog,
I shouldered up my gun and whistled for my dog,
Agwine down the road for to ketch a ground hog.
    Sing a too ri addle dinka day

2   I went down the road and took to the brush:
"Whoop! Sick 'em, Tige! A hog-sign fresh!"

3   I holed him in a rock, I treed him in a log,
Worked and tugged for to ketch a ground hog.

4   It's run here, boys, with a great long pole,
To punch this ground hog out of this hole.

5   I punched him out, I pulled him out, I laid him on a log:
"Whoop! By golly! What a fine ground hog!"

6   I took this ground hog all to the house,
It tickled old marm till she made a big mouth.

7   I skinned him, I washed him, I put him on to boil;
I thought, by golly, I could smell him half a moile.

8   It's old Adam, the father of us all,
Fed us on ground hog before we could crawl.

9   It's come here, gals, I like your fun;
The hog's in the pot and the hide's in the churn.

177

DAVY CROCKETT

THIS is a fragmentary and instructively corrupted version of "Pompey Smash," once popular on the Negro Minstrel stage: see *The Negro Singer's Own Book* (Philadelphia, Turner & Fisher), p. 327; *Lloyd's Ethiopian Song Book* (London, [1847]), p. 25; cf. *Elton's Illustrated Song Book* (also published as *Elton's Songs and Melodies for the Multitude*), p. 108; Belden, No. 59.

The first stanza should run as follows:

> As I sing to folk now dat I tink is disarnin,
> I'll tell you whar I cum from and whar I got my larnin:
> I'm hot from ole Wurjinny, whar you fine all de great men,
> An I'm Pompey Smash, one de principal statesmen,
> I'm sekun bess to none, on dis side ob der sun,
> And by de laud, I weigh widout my head half a ton."

Stanza 3 becomes intelligible in the light of the original:

> Now I'll tell you 'bout a fite I had wid Davy Crockett,
> Dat haff hoss, haff kune, an haff sky rocket:
> I met him one day as I go out a gunnin,
> I ax him whar he guine, an he say guine a kunein.

Communicated by Mrs. Hilary G. Richardson, Clarksburg, Harrison County, 1917; obtained from Mrs. Nancy McAtee. Reported by title in *Journal*, XXXII, 499.

1 Come all of you young men,
> Where you are zerning,
> I'll tell you where I come from,
> And where I got my learning.

2 My name is Pomy Smash,
> And my principle is a statement:
> Second best to none by the side of the sun,
> My life without my head would weigh half a ton.

3 He said he was going cooning,
> And said I'd go along;
> I asked him for his gun,
> And he said he had n't none.

4 Said I, "Uncle Davy,
> How do you do without a gun?"

> . . . .

> . . . .

5 "Never do you mind,
      Just follow after Davy,
   And he'll pretty quick show you
      How to grin a coon crazy."

6 He grinned away a while,
      And he never 'peared to mind it;
   Eatin' away at sheep sorrel,
      And never looked behind it.

7 And Uncle Davy said,
      "I think it must be dead;
   I saw the bark fly
      All around the thing's head."

8 We went to the tree,
      The matter to discover,
   Where the nations rose,
      Round Pomy Smash's liver.[1]

9 There we saw a pine knot,
      As big as any squirrel

   .   .   .   .

      A-eatin' sheep sorrel.

10 I laid down my gun
       And took off my am-minition;
    Said I, "Uncle Davy,
       I'll cool your am-i-bition."

11 Then we locked arms,
       I thought my breath was gone;
    I never was squz so,
       Since the hour that I was born.

12 And then we did agree
       To let each other be,
    For I was too hard for him,
       And so was he for me.

13 And when we came to look,
       Both of our heads was missin';
    He'd bit off my head,
       An' I'd swallered his'n.

---

[1] A corruption of *An may de debil roast old Pompey Smash's liber.*

178

CREATION SONG

THIS is a variety of the famous minstrel song popular in the forties and fifties under the title "Walk in de Parlor" or "History of the World." Several versions may be distinguished:

I. "History ob de World as sung by A. F. Winnemore And his Band of Serenaders Music arranged for the Piano Forte by Augustus Clapp" (Boston, cop. 1847); *Nigger Melodies* (New York, Nafis and Cornish), p. 170 ("Walk in de Parlour"); *Christy's Negro Serenaders* (New York, T. W. Strong), p. 136 ("Walk in de Parlour"); *Christy's Nigga Songster* (New York, T. W. Strong), p. 131 ("Walk in de Parlour"); *The Negro Singer's Own Book* (Philadelphia, Turner & Fisher), p. 73 ("Walk In. As sung by the Black Apolloneans").

II. "Walk in de Parlor, arranged by E. P. Christy and sung by Thos. Vaughn, of Christy's Minstrells" (New York, cop. 1847); *The Ethiopian Glee Book* (Boston, Elias Howe, 1848, 1849), p. 100; *Christy's Plantation Melodies No. 1* (Philadelphia, cop. 1851), p. 56.

III. "De History ob de World. Sung by Wm. Parker in the Popular Extravaganza of the Buffalo Gals at the Adelphi. Also at his concerts in England. Arranged for the Piano Forte by T. Contreso" (Boston, cop. 1847); *The Ethiopian Glee Book* (Boston, 1849), p. 126; *Minstrel Songs, Old and New* (Boston, cop. 1882), p. 70; text in *Gus Williams' Old-Fashioned G. A. R. Camp-Fire Songster* (New York), p. 27.

IV. "History of the World; or, New Version of 'Walk in de Parlour, Boys.' Composed and sung by Charles White, with tremendous applause": *The Negro Singer's Own Book*, p. 203. Also in *The People's Free and Easy Songster* (New York, William H. Murphy), p. 29; *Handy Andy's Budget of Songs*, p. 29; *The Rose of Alabama*, p. 29; *The Negro Forget-Me-Not Songster* (Philadelphia, Fisher & Brother), p. 215; *Old Dog Tray Songster*, p. 215. This version (as well as No. V) celebrates General Zachary Taylor's victory over the Mexican commander Ampudia (September, 1847).

V. "A Nigger's History of the World. A New Version. As sung only by Charles White, the popular Ethiopian Serenader, at the Melodeon Concert-Saloon, New York": in *White's New Book of Plantation Melodies* (New York, cop. 1848), p. 23 (a songbook included also in *White's Complete Ethiopian Melodies* and in *Christy's and White's Ethiopian Melodies*); *Singer's Journal*, I, 259. This version is a variety of No. IV.

VI. "A Nigger's History of the World. A New Version": *The Book of Popular Songs* (Philadelphia, 1861), p. 311. A variety of IV and V.

VII. "Walkey in de Parlor, Boys. As sung by Mr. D. W. Lull, the celebrated Banjo Player": *The Negro Melodist* (Cincinnati, 1857), p. 60; *The Negro Singer's Own Book*, p. 52.

VIII. "The Nigger's History of the World, A Discription of Past Events, or Any an' Eberyting. Sung by Dan Emmit, at Boston, United States": *The Vauxhall Comic Song-Book*, edited by J. W. Sharp (London, T. Allman), p. 67. This version includes most of I and III, with many new stanzas.

See also Perrow, *Journal*, XXVI, 159, 160; F. C. Brown, p. 13.

Communicated by Mr. E. C. Smith, Weston, Lewis County, December 18, 1915, who writes: "An old manuscript containing 'The Creation Song' was given to me by Mrs. J. S. Hennen, Burton, Wetzel County. She got the song from a country preacher named Ireland about ten years ago, when she was teaching school in Duffy, Lewis County.

1 I'm right from Old Virginia, with my head full of knowledge;
I never went to free school, or any other college;
I'll tell you what I know, and it is a solid fact:
The world was made in the twinkle of a whack.

Chorus

Walk in, walk in, walk in, I say,
Walk in and hear the banjo play;
Walk into the parlor and hear the banjo ring,
And see the darkey's fingers as he picks upon the strings.

2 First he made the moon and then the sky,
Hung it up above and left it there to dry;
Then he made the stars in the twinkle of an eye,
To give a little light when the moon went dry.

3 Then he made an elephant, made him big and stout;
Then he wasn't satisfied and had to have a snout.
Then he made the ocean and the whale;
Then he made a rat with a great long tail.

4 The world was made in six days and finished on the seventh;
According to the contract, it should have been the eleventh;
But the mason got drunk, and the carpenter wouldn't work,
And the quickest way to do it was to fill it up with dirt.

5 Then he made a nigger, made him after night,
Made him in a hurry, and forgot to make him white.
Then he made a monkey and set him on a rail;
You couldn't tell the difference, but the monkey had a tail.

6 Adam was the first man and Eve the first mother;
Cain was a wicked man, and Cain killed his brother.
Old mother Miller can't sleep without a pillow,
And the strongest man a-living is Jack the Giant-Killer.

179

THE ARKANSAW TRAVELLER

A MORE "refined" but less humorous version of this dialogue, with music, was published (apparently in the fifties) by Blodgett & Bradford, Buffalo, in sheet-music form, and reprinted in *The Arkansas Traveller's Songster* (New York, cop. 1864), p. 5. It was entitled "The Arkansas Traveller. By Mose Case." There was this explanatory introduction: "This piece is intended to represent an Eastern man's experience among the inhabitants of Arkansas, showing their hospitality and the mode of obtaining it." Old theatre-goers will remember the opening scene of the once famous play of *Kit the Arkansas Traveller*, with F. S. Chanfrau in the title rôle.

Contributed by Mr. A. C. Payne, Barclay, McDowell County, August, 1918.

The performance consisted of the Fiddler's playing a few bars of the tune and then stopping and carrying on an imaginary conversation with the Traveller.

Traveller (riding up to the house). Hello, stranger!

Fiddler. Hello yourself! If you want to go to hell, go by yourself.

T. Why don't you play the other part of that tune?

F. Well, to tell you the truth, I don't know no other part to that tune; don't think there is another part to that tune.

T. Let me stay all night, and I'll learn you the other part to that tune; it'll be worth fifty dollars to you.

F. [The reply could not be remembered.]

T. Stranger, why don't you cover the other side of your house?

F. It's rainin' too hard.

T. Why don't you cover it when it ain't rainin'?

F. Why, it's just as dry a house as yours or as any other man's house when it ain't rainin'.

T. What makes your corn look yeller and bad?

F. Why, fool, I planted yeller corn.

T. How does your taters turn out?

F. Turn out the devil! They don't turn out at all. I dug a part, and the old sow rooted out the rest.

T. How fur is it to the fork of the road?

F. Fork the devil! I've lived here a hundred and fifty years and never knowed the road to fork nothin' yit.

T. Can I ford the river?

F. It looks reasonable; the geese been fordin' it all mornin'.

T. How far is it to Little Rock?

F. Little Rock the devil! I never heard tell of no little rock. Right across that hill one hundred and fifty miles is a hell of a big one.

T. I wish you'd head that steer.

F. Head the devil! Looks like he's got a head on.

T. I did n't mean that; I meant, turn him.

F. Looks to me like the hairy side's out.

T. I did n't mean that; I meant, stop him.

F. I've got no stopper fur him.

T. Which way's your daughter?

F. She's out digging ginseng, or some other kind of root. Old woman, this man's hungry. He said he'd learn me the other part of this tune and it's worth fifty dollars to me. Old woman, fix him something to eat.

Wife. I ain't got nothin' fur him. I don't like him too well nohow.

F. There's a middle of bacon in the smokehouse and a pone of bread in the oven. Give him that.

W. That's all I've got, old man.

F. There's plenty more where that come from. Old woman, what's this man goin' to sleep on? It's awful cold to-night.

W. There's a sheepskin under the bed and a goatskin in the closet. If he can't sleep on that, let him freeze, and go to the devil!

F. Why, old woman, that old hound of ourn could n't sleep on that. There's a good feather bed in the room and plenty of covers. Put him in that.

W. Old man, that's all we've got.

F. No matter, there's plenty more where that come from. You know he told me that tune was worth fifty dollars in cash to me.

[By that time the traveller had come in and was playing the other part of the tune on the man's fiddle.]

T. Is this a single-line or a double-line fiddle?

F. Single-line the devil! You old fool, don't you see there's four strings on it? Old woman, pick up that chair and bust him wide open. Put him out of here.

T. Hold a minute. Let me tune your fiddle. [Tunes up and plays a little.]

F. My God Almighty! For a little I'd kill you. You talk about a four-line fiddle. You been used to an eight-line fiddle. Old woman, what I've heard already is worth fifty dollars. Old man, play me the other part of that tune. I would n't take five hundred dollars for what I've heard. [The traveller plays the whole tune.]

Stranger, kick that old woman out and take that three-legged stool. That takes the rag off the bush. Come in and make my house your home as long as you live. Old woman, don't that cap the stack?

W. Cap the stack? It takes the rag off the bush.

F. You old fool woman, you wanted to turn him off, and I would n't take five hundred dollars for what I've heard. You old stingy devil, from this time on I 'low I'll keep everything that passes the road. Look what this man's learnt me! Stranger, lead up your horse to that block and give him a few punkins and take a few yourself. So, good-bye!

180

THE NIGGER TUNE

A GOOD text of this comic *cante-fable* is found in *The American Star Songster* (New York, 1851), p. 140. It is an adaptation (apparently American) of the English "Push along, keep moving," which was also well known in this country: see *The Universal Songster, or, Museum of Mirth* (London, 1827, 1834), I, 399 (credited to "Moor"); broadside, J. Kendrew, York; slip, Pitts; Ford, *Massachusetts Broadsides*, No. 3313 (ca. 1813); *The Theatrical Budget*, New Series, No. 4 (New York, 1828), p. 110 ("Dialogue, between an Irish innkeeper and an English gentleman"); *Sloman's Drolleries* (New York, 1828), p. 8 ("as sung by Mr. Eberle"); *The New England Songster* (Portsmouth, New Hampshire, 1832), p. 114. The motto "Push on, keep moving" became a catchword from Thomas Morton's popular comedy *A Cure for the Heart-Ache* (1797), in which one or the other phrase is constantly repeated by Young Rapid.

Contributed by Mr. A. C. Payne, Barclay, McDowell County, August, 1918.

1   I am a man, a pretty man,
        The ladies call me pretty;
     I teach the school, the higher school,
        In our own native city.

"What kind of a school did you teach?"
"I took the little boy through the a-b abs, i-b ibs, and o-b obs."
"Then what did you do?"
"I stuck in the mud, fool, that's what I do."

2   I next put up a blacksmith shop,
        A blacksmith shop improvin';
     'T is my motto and always been,
        To push along, keep movin'.

"What about your blacksmith shop?"
"Well, there comes a little boy in my shop the other day, picked up a red hot horse shoe. I guess he laid it down without tellin'. He went up the road singing that good old song we sing sometimes, 'Push along, keep movin'.'"

3   I next put up a whiskey shop,
        A whiskey shop improvin';
     'T is my motto and always been,
        To push along, keep movin'.

"What about your whiskey shop?"
"Why, there come a man in my shop the other day, said he wanted a little whiskey. I went around to git him some and I met that old

fool wife of mine, a glass of whiskey in one hand and a bottle in the other, reelin' first one way and then the other. She squalled out, 'Don't let no more of that whiskey go, there ain't no more than 'll do me.' I hauled back and took her by the side of the head. She went out of doors, 'Push along, keep movin'.'"

4   I next put up a carpenter shop,
      A carpenter shop improvin';
   'T is my motto and always been,
      To push along, keep movin'.

"What about your carpenter shop?"

"I went into my shop the other day, and got a letter from that old gal of mine out in the country. I did not know anybody in a mile of me. Standin' thar readin' of it, throwed my head back, here's that old fool wife of mine readin' of it over my shoulder. She picks up a great big piece of plank, she lit in on my hind parts. I guess I went out o' doors, 'Push along, keep movin'.'"

181

OLD NOAH

CONTRIBUTED by Mr. Decker Toney, Queens Ridge, Wayne County, January 20, 1916; learned from his mother, who learned it from Sarah Vance, who learned it from her uncle, Riley Vance.

1 Go way, old fiddle,
    People is tired of your squawking!
  Come listen to your better;
    Don't you hear the banjo talking?

2 It's about the possum's tail,
    I'll let you ladies listen —
  Whilst the hair it is not there,
    And why it is so missing.

3 "It's going to come to an overflow,"
    Says old Noah, looking solemn;
  Then he took the Herald,
    And he read the river column.

4 Then he put his men to work
    Clearing timber patches;
  Swore he was going to make a boat,
    To beat the steamer Natchez.

5 Old Noah kept them hewing,
    Chopping and sawing;
  All the wicked neighbors around
    Kept sassing him and jawing.

6 Old Noah did not miss them,
    He knew what was going to happen;
  For forty days and forty nights
    The rain kept on dropping.

7 Old Noah got his ark done;
    He had to herd his beasts;
  And in his show travelling,
    He praised his highest beasts.

8 He herded them into the ark,
    Except one Jersey heifer; with her he had to battle;
  But he got her safe into the ark,
    When he heard the thunder rattle.

9   The rain it struck to pouring down
        So burdently and heavy,
    The river rose immediately
        And bursted through the levees.

10   The ark it just kept sailing,
        Sailing and sailing;
    The lion he got his dander up
        And bursted through the railing.

11   Then Sam, our only nigger
        Was sailing in the package,[1]
    Got lonesome in the barber shop
        And could n't stand the racket.

12   He thought that he would amuse himself,
        He steamed some wood and bent it;
    So soon he had a banjo made,
        But at first he did not mean it.

13   He wet the leather, stretched it on,
        Made bridges, screws, and aprons;
    He fit it to a proper neck,
        Which was very long and tapering.

14   Of course the possum he is here,
        Just as fine as I am singing;
    The hide on the possum's tail
        Will do for the banjo stringing.

15   He took the hide, he shaved it out,
        From little east[2] to graces;
    He tuned her up, he strung her up,
        From little *e* to basses.

16   He tuned her up and struck a jig,
        Saying, "Never mind the weather!"
    She sounded like eleven banjos,
        Playing all together.

17   Some got to patting, some got to dancing,
        Old Noah called the figure;
    But the happiest man in our crowd
        Was Sam, our only nigger.

[1] Error for *packet*.   [2] Probably for *e's*.

182

A GLORIOUS WEDDING

COMMUNICATED by Miss Sallie Evans, Elkins, Randolph County; obtained from Miss Eleanor Keim, who got it from Lawson Ketterman, who learned it from his father.

1 I will sing you a song of a comical style;
  If it don't make you laugh, it will surely make you smile;
  It's about a wedding, a glorious affair;
  As I was the bridegroom, I happened to be there.

Chorus

  Up on the mountains, underneath the ground,
  Where the sweet tobacco never can be found;
  As long as I remember I never shall forget
  The night that I was married to the cross-eyed pet.

2 All about the place I will tell you, if I can;
  I'll start at the commencement, and stop where I began:
  Cider and beer on the table were put,
  As much as you could see with both eyes shut.

3 Old John McGill got as full as an egg;
  He fell in the corner and broke his wooden leg;
  He shouted for a doctor: "Shut up," said Johnny Green,
  "You don't want a doctor; it's a jointer that you need."

4 One fellow there, called Bottle-nosed Dick,
  Said he would show them a conjuring trick,
  By picking up a glass of another man's beer,
  Before you could wink your eye, he'd make it disappear.

5 The owner of the beer was so pleased with the joke
  That he hoped Dick would die with a paralytic stroke;
  They habbered and they jabbered and from words came to
      blows;
  They kicked one another till the nails fell off their toes.

183

HARD TIMES

THIS piece consists of parts of two songs run together. The second portion, beginning with stanza 7, is a part of "Hard Times," for which see *Beadle's Dime Song Book No. 1* (cop. 1860), p. 24; De Marsan broadside, List 10, No. 30. There is a curious variant in Lomax, p. 103; another, extending the satire to various religious denominations, in Belden's Missouri collection (No. 108). For a long American text, coinciding with the West Virginia version in but a single stanza (that describing the tinker) see a Boston broadside ("Hard Times") of the early nineteenth century in the collection of the New York Historical Society (Ford, *Massachusetts Broadsides*, No. 3160). A text recently recovered in England also has one stanza in common with the West Virginia text — that which satirizes the butcher (Alfred Williams, *Folk-Songs of the Upper Thames*, p. 104). A similar satire — "Chapter of Cheats. Or, The Roguery of all Trades" — is well known in English broadsides (Pitts, Catnach, Spencer, Bradford).

Communicated by Mr. Fred Smith, Glenville, Gilmer County, 1917; obtained from Mr. Farwell A. Bell.

1   Last Saturday night I went by the house,
And through the dark window I crept like a mouse;
I knocked at the door, and my love let me in,
And through the dark window I soon entered in.
    And it's hard times.

2   Such laughing and chatting as we did make,
I waked the old folks out of their sleep;
First said he, and then said she:
"What impudent scoundrel is this before me?"
    And it's hard times.

3   "O here is my heart and here is my hand,
Hold your wild temper till you know who I am;
Jamieson Wilks, I go by that name,
And courting your daughter is the purpose I came."
    And it's hard times.

4   "O you are so old, and she is so young,
You will get suited, and she will get stung;
You are so old, and she is so young,"—
She up with the broomstick and at me she come.
    And it's hard times.

5 Out of the window in the ice and the snow,
I mounted my horse and away I did go;
The blood it run down my shins in great grooves,
For I had never been beaten with a broomstick before.
    And it's hard times.

6 Come all ye young men, take warning from me,
Be careful when girls you go for to see;
Unless like me you'll meet with your doom,
Get beat like the devil and flogged with the broom.
    And it's hard times.

7 O there is a young gent as all of you know,
A-courting the girls he is sure to go;
The old folks will simper and sniver and grieve,
Say, treat him well, gals, and he'll come back again.
    And it's hard times.

8 And there is the young miss, the nice little dear,
At the ball and the party how nice she will appear!
Whale-boned corset her ribs do they squeeze,
And she'll have to unlace before she can sneeze.
    And it's hard times.

9 O there is the tinner, who mends all our ware,
For something to drink, ale or beer;
But before he is through he is half drunk or more,
And while mending one hole, he'll punch twenty more.
    And it's hard times.

10 O there is the baker, who bakes what we eat,
And there is the butcher, who sells us our meat;
It's up with the scales and let them come down,
And swears it's good weight when it lacks half a pound.
    And it's hard times.

11 O there is the sheriff, who thinks himself nice;
He comes to your house with a pack of lies,
Takes all your property he can sell,
Gets drunk on the money when you are doing well.
    And it's hard times.

12 O there is the judge, who thinks himself true,
 He sits on the bench and stares at you;
 For twenty-five cents he would send you to jail,
 And for five dollars he would send you to hell.
  And it's hard times.

13 O there is the doctor I almost forgot;
 I really believe he's the worst of the lot;
 He says he will cure you for half you possess,
 And then he will kill you and take all the rest.
  And it's hard times.

184

PUTTING ON THE STYLE

Communicated by Mr. G. O. Hall, Parkersburg, Wood County, May, 1917; obtained from his mother, who learned it when she was a girl from Miss Laura Smith, Middlebourne, Tyler County.

1 Eighteen hundred seventy-one,
    January the first,
  Thought I'd write a poem,
    If I could or durst;
  Looking through the window,
    Something makes me smile,
  'T is a fellow going in,
    Putting on the style.

2 Young man in his carriage,
    Driving on like mad;
  A pair of spanky horses,
    Borrowed from his dad;
  Cracks his whip supremely,
    Makes his lady smile;
  Is n't he going in,
    Putting on the style?

3 Sweet sixteen at meeting
    Goes to see the boys;
  Turns her head and giggles
    At every little noise;
  Simpers on this side,
    Then on that awhile;
  Is n't she going in,
    Putting on the style?

4 Preacher in the pulpit,
    Shouting with all his might,
  "Glory Hallelujah!"
    The people's in a fright;
  Thinks Satan's coming
    Up and down the aisle;
  The preacher's only
    Putting on the style.

5   Country town coquettes,
     Impudence and paint,
 Finger rings and broaches,
     Enough to annoy a saint;
 Has for every fellow,
     A winning-looking smile;
 Is n't she a-going in,
     Putting on the style?

185

GET UP AND BAR THE DOOR

(CHILD, No. 275)

"OLD John Jones." This excellent text, agreeing well with Child B, was reported by Mr. Carey Woofter, Glenville, Gilmer County, September, 1924. It
was taken down from the recitation of Mrs. Sarah Clevenger of Briar Lick Run,
near Perkins, Gilmer County. She learned it from her grandmother, Mrs. Re-
becca Clevenger, who came from Loudoun County, Virginia, seventy-eight
years ago, as the date in the family Bible gives it. So far as I know, no complete
text of this ballad has hitherto been publicly reported, but I understand that
Dr. B. L. Jones has found it in Michigan. The Virginia Folk-Lore Society Bulletin, No. 9, reports six lines from Wise County, "learned in Scotland more than
50 years ago."

This ballad was received too late to record it in its proper place among the
Child ballads in the early part of the volume.

1 The wind it blew from east to west,
       And it blew all over the floor;
    Said old John Jones to Jane, his wife,
       "Get up and shut the door."

2 "My hands are in the sausage meat,
       So I cannot get them free;
    And if you do not shut the door yourself,
       It never will be shut by me."

3 Then they agreed between the two
       And gave their hands on it,
    That whoever spoke a word the first
       Was to rise and shut the door.

4 There were two travellers journeying late,
       A-journeying across the hill,
    And they came to old John Jones's
       By the light from the open door.

5 "Does this house to a rich man belong?
       Or does it belong to a poor?"
    But never a word would the stubborn two say
       On account of shutting the door.

6 The travellers said good-evening to them,
        And then they said good-day;
     But never a word would the stubborn two say
        On account of shutting the door.

7 And so they drank of the liquor strong,
        And so they drank of the ale:
     "For since we have got a house of our own,
        I'm sure we can take of our fill."

8 And then they ate of the sausage meat
        And sopped their bread in the fat;
     And at every bite old Jane she thought,
        "May the devil slip down with that."

9 Then says the one to the other,
        "Here, man, take out my knife,
     And while you shave the old man's chin,
        I will be kissing the wife."

10 "You have eat my meat and drinked my ale,
        And would you make of my old wife a whore?"
     "John Jones, you have spoken the first word,
        Now get up and shut the door."

FOLK TUNES

Edited by Miss Lydia I. Hinkel, Head of the Department of Public School Music in West Virginia University, Morgantown, West Virginia.

INTRODUCTION

Folk-music is the product of a people, portraying the thoughts, feelings, and tastes that are communal rather than personal. It is always in the process of solution, its creation is never complete, and, owing to the manner in which it is perpetuated, it is liable to all sorts of modifications in the course of time and the process of transmission from one locality to another.

Certain conditions are favorable to the production of folk music, such as sparse settlements, isolation, oppression, hardship, lack of education, and so forth. These conditions existed in West Virginia in the early days. People were huddled back in the hills, cut off from communication with others, living far apart, enduring hardship, and having little opportunity for education. Consequently they entertained themselves, and one of the ways was by relating the old stories and singing the old songs which their grandparents and relatives had handed down to them. It is mainly from the oldest residents of West Virginia that we have been able to obtain these tunes, either by writing them down as these folk sing them, or having them write them down as best they can. Many of the tunes were sent in without any indication of time, with queer and incorrect note values, and without any key signature. Most of them were sung in a very low pitch, and, in all cases where they have not been too low for the average singer, I have adhered to the original key.

LYDIA I. HINKEL.

WEST VIRGINIA UNIVERSITY.

No. 1 (*B*) SIX KINGS' DAUGHTERS

Communicated by Professor Walter Barnes; obtained from Mr. G. W. Cunningham

He followed me up, he followed me down, And he followed me in-to the

room. I had not the power to speak one word, Nor a

tongue to an-swer nay, nay, nay; Nor a tongue to an-swer nay.

No. 3 THE MILLER'S TWO DAUGHTERS

Contributed by Mr. A. C. Cowgill, Cold Stream, Hampshire Co.

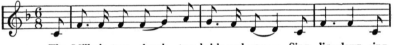

The Miller's two daugh - ters brisk and gay — Sing lie down, sing

lie down— The Mill-er's two daugh - ters brisk and gay— The

boys are bound for me— The Mill - er's two daugh-ters

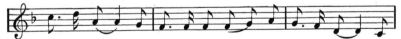

brisk and gay— The young one be - longed to Johnny Ray— And

I'll be kind to my true love, Be - cause he's kind to me.

No. 5 (*C*)   THE GREENWOOD SIDING

Communicated by Professor Walter Barnes; obtained from Mr. G. W. Cunningham

O ba - by, O ba - by, if   you were mine, All a -

long and a - lone - y;   I would dress you up   in

scar - let so fine, All a - long by the greenwood sid - ing.

No. 6 (*A*)   THE THREE CROWS

Contributed by the General Editor; noted by Miss Lydia I. Hinkel

There were three crows sat on . . a   tree, And they were

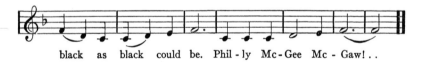

black as black could be. Phil - ly Mc - Gee Mc - Gaw! . .

No. 11   LADY MARGARET

Contributed by Mrs. Estelle Lowe, Harrison County; noted by Miss Lydia I. Hinkel

Sweet William rose one morning bright, And dressed himself in blue: Come

tell to me the long lost love, 'Tween La - dy Margaret and you.

No. 11 (*C*) SWEET WILLIAM AND LADY MARGARET

Communicated by Miss Sallie D. Jones; obtained from Miss R. Dice Smith

Sweet William a-rose one mist-y morning, And dressed himself in blue: Come

tell   unto me   the long long love, Be-tween Lady Magaret and you.

No. 16 (*F*)   BARBARA ALLEN

Communicated by Professor Walter Barnes; obtained from Mr. G. W. Cunningham

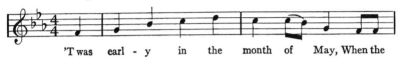

'Twas   earl - y   in   the   month of   May, When the

green   buds were   swell - ing, This young man on   his

death - bed   lay,   In .. love with   Barb-ary   Allen. . . .

No. 16 (*G*)   BARBARA ALLEN

Contributed by Mr. Josiah Keely

'Twas earl-y in the month of May, An' the ros-es all were blooming; Sweet

Wil-liam courted a fair young maid, An' her name was Barbra   Al - len.

No. 21 (*A*)   THE GYPSY DAVY

Contributed by the General Editor; noted by Miss Lydia I. Hinkel

The Gyp - sy Dav - y crossed the plain, He sang so loud and sweet - ly; He sang till he made the green woods ring, To charm the heart of a lad - y. Tum-a roe - eye ink - a - too-dle ink - a - too-dle - a Tum-a roe - eye ink - a - too-dle - a - dy.

No. 25 (*L*)   THE HOUSE CARPENTER

Contributed by Professor A. J. Hare; music noted by Professor F. C. Butterfield

"Well met, well met, my pret-ty fair maid, Well met, well met," said he; "I have just re - turned from the salt, salt sea, And 'tis all for the love of thee."

No. 37 (A) MCAFEE'S CONFESSION

Contributed by the General Editor; noted by Miss Lydia I. Hinkel

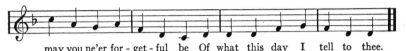

Draw nigh young men and learn from me, My sad and mournful histo - ry; And

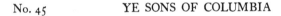

may you ne'er for - get - ful be Of what this day I tell to thee.

No. 45 YE SONS OF COLUMBIA

Ye he - roes of Co - lum - bia, at - ten - tion I do crave Of a

sor - rowful dit-ty I will tell, That happened here of late in the

In - di - an - a state Of a he - ro who man - y can't ex - cel.

No. 47 (D) THE WRECK ON THE C. & O.

Communicated by Professor Walter Barnes; obtained from Mr. G. W. Gragg

A - long came the F. F. V., the fast - est on the line, A-

run - ning on the C. & O. road, twenty minutes be - hind the time; A-

run-ning in - to Sew-ell yard, was quartered on the line, A-

wait-ing for strict or - ders and in the cab to ride, And

when she blew for Hin-ton, her . . eng - i - neer was there, George

Al - ley was his name, with bright and wavery hair; His

fire-man named Jack Dix - on, . . was standing by his side, A-

wait-ing for strict or - ders and in the cab to ride . . .

Many a man's been murdered by the railroad, railroad, railroad, Many a man's been

murdered by the rail-road, and laid in his lone-some grave.

No. 47   THE WRECK ON THE C. & O.

Contributed by Mr. John Toler; noted by Professor F. C. Butterfield

A - long came the F. F. V., the fastest on . . . the line,

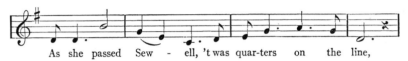

Running on the C. and O. road, a quarter be - hind time;

As she passed Sew - ell, 't was quar-ters on the line,

Wait - ing to get ord - ers, Hinton, late, be - hind time.

No. 50   JOE BOWERS

Contributed by the General Editor; noted by Miss Lydia I. Hinkel

My name it is Joe Bow - ers, I've got a broth-er Ike; I

came from old Mis - sou - ri, Just all the way from Pike; I'll

tell you how I came here, and how I came to roam And

leave my poor old ma - ma so far a - way from home.

No. 80 (*A*)   YOUNG CHARLOTTE

Communicated by Miss Sallie D. Jones

Young Charlotte lived on a mountain side In a wild and lone-ly spot; There

were no dwell-ings for three miles wide Ex - cept her fath - ers cot.

No. 89 (*C*)   YOUNG BEEHAM

Communicated by Professor Walter Barnes; obtained from Mr. G. W. Cunningham

He   stepped up   to her with a knife in his hand, Saying, "Come fairest

Pol - ly   no   time for   to stand," He pierced her   to the heart,   the

blood it did   flow,   He   cov-ered her   ov - er   and home he did   go.

No. 96 (*A*)   WILLIAM HALL

Communicated by Professor Walter Barnes; obtained from Mr. G. W. Cunningham

There was a   jol - ly brisk young farmer 'Round near Alex-andria's town, Who

courted a fair and handsome young lady Of great credit   and renown. Who

courted   a   fair and handsome young lady Of great cred-it   and   renown.

No. 102 (*A*)   MOLLIE VAUNDERS

Communicated by Miss Violet M. Hiett; obtained from Mrs. S. D. Stump

Come all ye young fel-lows, Who de-light in a gun, Be-

ware of late shoot-ing . . . Af - ter the sun's down; I 'll

tell you a story, Which hap - pened of late, Con -

cern - ing Mol - lie Vaunders, Whose beau - ty was great.

No. 103   CHARMING BEAUTY BRIGHT

For seven long years I . . . served my . . king; In

sev - en long years I . . . came home a-gain, With my

heart so full of woe and my eyes so full of tears, Oh how

hap - py would I be To get sight of my dear.

No. 121 (B)   THE SQUIRE

Communicated by Miss Sallie D. Jones; obtained from Miss R. Dice Smith

In - stead of get - ting mar - ried she went sick to bed; The

thoughts of the far - mer were roll - ing in her head; The

thoughts of the far - mer were roll - ing in her mind, And a

way for to gain him she quick - ly did find.

No. 140   YOUNG LADIES

Contributed by the General Editor; noted by Miss Lydia I. Hinkel

Come all ye fair and handsome ladies, Take warning how you court young men; They're

like a star on a summer's morning, They first ap-pear and then they're gone.

No. 145   THE BUTCHER BOY

Contributed by the General Editor; noted by Miss Lydia I. Hinkel

In Jer-sey ci - ty there did dwell, A butcher boy I loved him well, He

courted me my life a - way, And then with me he would not stay.

No. 155 (*A, B*) THE DISHONEST MILLER

Communicated by Miss Lily Hagans

There was an old man and he lived all alone, And he had with him his

three sons grown; Now when he came to make his will, He

had nothing left but a lit-tle old mill. Phi tra la la diddle dumpy dee.

No. 162 FROG WENT A-COURTIN'

Contributed by the General Editor; noted by Miss Lydia I. Hinkel

Frog went a-court-in', he did ride, mmm huh! Frog went a-court-in',

he did ride, mmm huh! Frog went a-court-in',

he did ride, With a sword and a pis-tol by his side, mmm huh!

No. 163 THE FOX

Communicated by Miss Sallie D. Jones; music noted down by Miss R. Dice Smith

The fox peeped out one moon-light night so bright,

When the stars and the moon they shone: "A-zoocks!" says the fox, I'll go

through that town to-night, Be-fore that I do lay me down.

No. 165   **THREE FARMERS**

Contributed by Miss Sallie D. Jones; music by Miss R. Dice Smith

Three farmers went a-hunt - ing, and the first thing they did find, Was a

barn in a mead-ow, and that they left be - hind. Lookee there now!

No. 165   **THE THREE FARMERS**

Contributed by the General Editor; noted by Miss Lydia I. Hinkel

Three farmers went a - hunting, and the first thing they did find, Was a

barn in a meadow, and that they left behind. Lookee there now!

No. 168   **BILLY BOY**

Contributed by the General Editor; noted by Miss Lydia I. Hinkel

Where have you been, Bil - ly boy, Bil - ly boy? Where

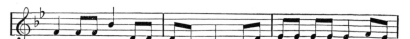

have you been, charming Billy? . . I have been to see my wife, she's the

joy of my life, She's a young thing, too young to leave her mother.

INDEXES

INDEX OF TITLES

INDEX OF FIRST LINES